Epic Recession

EPIC RECESSION

Prelude to Global Depression

Jack Rasmus

PlutoPress
www.plutobooks.com

First published 2010 by Pluto Press
345 Archway Road, London N6 5AA and
175 Fifth Avenue, New York, NY 10010

www.plutobooks.com

Distributed in the United States of America exclusively by
Palgrave Macmillan, a division of St. Martin's Press LLC,
175 Fifth Avenue, New York, NY 10010

British Library Cataloguing in Publication Data
A catalogue record for this book is available from the British Library

ISBN   978 0 7453 2999 4   Hardback
ISBN   978 0 7453 2998 7   Paperback

Library of Congress Cataloging in Publication Data applied for

This book is printed on paper suitable for recycling and made from fully managed
and sustained forest sources. Logging, pulping and manufacturing processes are
expected to conform to the environmental standards of the country of origin.

10   9   8   7   6   5   4   3   2   1

Designed and produced for Pluto Press by
Chase Publishing Services Ltd, 33 Livonia Road, Sidmouth, EX10 9JB, England
Typeset from disk by Stanford DTP Services, Northampton, England
Simultaneously printed digitally by CPI Antony Rowe in England, UK
and Edwards Bros. in the United States of America

To Ingrid, my wife,
best friend and lifelong companion

Contents

Introduction:
Epic Recession—Past, Present, and Prologue

Like a global economic pandemic, the financial crisis that initially erupted in the U.S. in August 2007 spread rapidly from housing markets to other credit markets at an unprecedented rapid rate. Leaping national boundaries in a matter of weeks, it infected economies worldwide just as swiftly and deeply. It thereafter quickly transmitted to the real (non-financial) economy in the U.S., driving the latter into recession by December 2007 in just three months. As the real, non-financial sectors of the economy progressively weakened throughout 2008, the financial fragility of the system deteriorated further as well, finally erupting in a second, even worse financial instability event by late summer 2008. The full-fledged banking panic that exploded in September 2008 resulted in a general credit crash affecting all businesses, precipitating mass layoffs unprecedented in scope and magnitude comparable to the early years of the Great Depression of the 1930s. Millions of home foreclosures followed. Consumption nearly collapsed and business investment ground to a halt while world trade, shipping, and exports shrunk at record rates. This was no typical post-1945 recession. Something quite new, and far more severe, was emerging.

By late 2008 the accelerating decline of the real, non-financial economy began now to overlap with the financial crisis that was clearly also entering a new, more severe phase. Driven by the faltering real economy, falling asset prices, then prices for products, and finally wages, in turn placed increasing strain on the already weakened financial system. Collapsing asset prices, bank losses and the inevitable write-downs opened gaping black holes in bank balance sheets. Financial institutions across the board followed with a virtual shutdown of entire credit markets. Unable to obtain credit for even continuing daily operations, non-financial businesses continued mass layoffs into 2009, intensified their cost-cutting, reduced prices of their products further, and began cutting wages and hours of work in various forms. Not only were the two crises—financial and real—thus increasingly overlapping, but both were now feeding back upon each other in a dangerous downward spiral.

With financial and real economic cycles thus exacerbating each other, the dual cycles that fundamentally differentiate Epic Recessions from other recessions soon began to intensify in a manner not seen since the late 1920s. Like a hurricane that gathers destructive force when wind and water reinforce each other, the convergence of financial and real cycles amplified the combined negative consequences of each.

But underlying and driving the dual economic storm are even more fundamental forces. Beside 'wind' and 'water,' which are only apparent causes of the storm, there are the deeper causal forces of 'heat' and 'barometric pressure': the former a decades-long development of fragility at the core of the system of banking and finance in the U.S.; the latter a similar decades-long developing consumption fragility within the core of the consumer base in the U.S.—i.e. the nearly two-thirds of the workforce in the U.S., the approximately 100 million working- and middle-class families. In short, consumption fragility simultaneously deepened within the real economy, just as a corresponding financial fragility progressed within the financial sector as well.

Financial and consumption fragility meant that once the break came, the financial instability and real economic downturn occurred at a faster pace, became more widespread, and progressed deeper than any prior post-World War II recession in the U.S. This occurred, in part, because both forms of fragility—financial and consumption—developed more or less in tandem, mutually reinforcing each other. That had never happened before, at least not since 1929.

Developing in parallel with the forces of fragility, however, lay a set of equally critical forces partly responsible for the growing financial and consumption fragility and, in turn, partly a product of that same fragility. These include processes of debt accumulation, deflation, and default. Together, debt, deflation, and default processes exacerbate both forms of fragility and are themselves impacted in turn by deepening financial and consumption fragility.

But debt, deflation, and default are still not the most fundamental causes and forces. They serve rather as enabling causes linking the still unidentified fundamental forces to financial-consumption fragility. The fundamental forces are those causal forces that in effect drive the debt accumulation, and subsequent debt unwinding, that leads to the collapsing of financial and consumption fragility that produce economic crises called Epic Recessions.

The fundamental causes are those that create the financial and consumption fragility in the first place, and that set in motion the debt accumulation and subsequent debt unwinding. On the financial side, these forces include the unprecedented explosion in global liquidity, the rise of a global network of speculator-investors that wield and manipulate that liquidity (the 'global money parade'), the new forms of 'shadow' (i.e. non-bank) financial institutions, new financial instruments (products), and the new financial markets that together serve as conduits for the money parade. Together, they represent as well a growing relative shift to speculative forms of investment at the expense of real (i.e. long-run income stream generating and job producing) physical asset investment. On the consumption fragility side, the fundamental forces are the decades-long compression of real earnings and income for the vast majority of the workforce, and, like the speculator-investor, their consequent turning as well to debt-financed consumption—a turn not to realize rapid and excessive profits but instead to maintain standards of living.

A central theme of this book is that these fundamental forces have been for at least the past three decades responsible for both the deepening fragility in the financial system and the growing fragility in the structure of consumption in the U.S. economy. It is these two forces that ultimately set in motion processes of debt, deflation, and default that eventually provoke a collapse of both financial and consumption fragility. And it is the collapse of fragility that exacerbates in turn the processes of debt, deflation, and default that drive the economic crisis faster, deeper, and more widely than normal recessions in the postwar period—in effect, they precipitate economic downturns that can only be described as Epic in their defining quantitative and qualitative characteristics.

What some have called a 'global savings glut,' the unprecedented three-decades-long accumulation of investor (individual and institutional) income and wealth, this book calls the 'global money parade'—a pool of perhaps $20–30 trillion sloshing around the global economy on short notice and at will, provoking financial and other speculative bubbles with increasing frequency and severity. This global money parade, i.e. global savings glut, does not seek long-term investment in real assets that actually produce things of some use, but rather creates short-term paper products and markets that produce no real income stream or jobs, save for financial traders and whiz-kid business school finance interns. What some identify as a growing problem of 'global imbalances,' we term the growing relative weight and mix of forms of excess speculative investment in relation to total investment.

To follow the trail back from the apparent, to the enabling, and ultimately to the essential and most fundamental, requires the recognition that the current recession did not begin in 2007 with the bursting of the housing bubble, any more than that it ended in late 2009 when gross domestic product (GDP) temporarily ceased to decline further. The crisis is a process reflecting both financial and non-financial forces and their mutual interaction. Those processes have been at work for at least three decades. And they continue to this day.

Representing a convergence of financial and real economic forces not witnessed for even longer, i.e. more than seven decades, the events set in motion in 2007 produced no normal economic downturn but rather a crisis-level event. But in what sense not normal? How so a crisis event?[1] And if the current crisis is not a normal economic contraction, what then is it? If not a recession in a normal sense, how then is the crisis different quantitatively and qualitatively from the nine prior 'normal' recessions in the U.S. between 1948 and 2001?[2] If worse than a normal recession, is it a depression? And if not a depression nor a normal recession, what then?

One would think such basic questions would be the subject of intense and widespread debate among economists, financial analysts, and government policymakers. But that has not been the case. With a few notable exceptions, nearly all have continued to focus on the appearances of the crisis, trying to fit the anomaly represented by this new kind of economic crisis into the 'square peg' of their outmoded theories and models; or, what is perhaps worse, are content to substitute labels or a patchwork of past conceptual apparatuses for a deeper analysis of fundamental processes and causes.

THE 'EXPERTS' DEBATE THE CRISIS

An example of just this kind of 'labeling in lieu of analysis' and conceptual-model shape shifting took place on April 30, 2009, in New York City with a panel of economists, historians, and financial business experts. The purpose was to discuss the deeper meaning of the current crisis. Among those present were economists Paul Krugman, Robin Wells, and Nouriel Roubini, financial investor George Soros, and historian Niall Ferguson. All had previously attempted to describe the crisis in a broader sense in prior publications, some choosing to call it either a 'Near Depression,' a 'Mini-Depression,' or a 'Great Recession.'

In the debate, Harvard historian Niall Ferguson chose to call the crisis a *'Great Recession.'* According to Ferguson, a bona fide depression typically lasts 43–65 months. Were the current economic crisis an average or normal postwar recession it would have bottomed out by April 2009 after 17 months.[3] According to Ferguson, the current crisis was a 'Great Recession' and therefore distinct from a normal recession. However, Ferguson described the current crisis as "comparable in scale with 1973–1975," which did not qualify as a 'Great Recession.'[4] So we are left with the argument that the current crisis is a Great Recession but at the same time is comparable with 1973–75 that was not a Great Recession.

Ferguson's view is a good example of the many failed efforts to 'fit' the current crisis into the mold of a normal post-1945 recession. It also reveals the limits of trying to identify crisis events simply by their duration. The recessions of 1973–75 and 1981–82 are the favorite choices for those who attempt to argue that the recent crisis is no different from these earlier normal recessions; or conversely to argue that the earlier recessions were also by definition Great Recessions. But as will be explained in some detail in subsequent chapters, the current crisis is quite different both quantitatively and qualitatively from 1973–75, as it is from 1981–82 and all other post-1945 recessions in the U.S.

Ferguson's view also illustrates the limitations of merely classifying, then comparing, recessions using a single quantitative indicator; in his case measured in terms of GDP, which is the value of total annual output of the economy. But GDP is itself not the best indicator of recession, and an even poorer indicator of an economic crisis event. A simple adding of quarterly GDP declines from July 2008 to April 2009 results in a cumulative 12.5 percent. That's six times the average GDP decline of 2 percent in normal postwar recessions and three times that of the previously most severe recession of 1973–75. Thus, were one even to limit one's analysis merely to comparing GDP data, the current crisis is far more severe than 1973–75.[5]

By focusing on GDP Ferguson completely ignores other important quantitative measures, as well as essentially all qualitative characteristics. Take job loss as just one example. The decline in jobs since 2007, and in particular since November 2008, has been far more severe than during 1973–75. In fact, job loss from October 2008 through mid 2009 has tracked job loss in 1929–30 almost exactly in terms of rate of decline. And this is so despite the fact that official government definitions and methods for estimating unemployment significantly understate actual job loss. Since the Reagan administration in the 1980s, definitions, sampling techniques, statistical assumptions, and statistical operations on collected data have been altered. Unemployment statistics have been significantly modulated. The result of the changes has been to under-report unemployment today compared to the 1970s. Today's jobless figures are therefore even worse than they appear officially.

Apart from Ferguson's labeling the current crisis as a Great Recession, others have termed the crisis a '*Mini Depression*.'[6] That's the term given by business economist Bill Gross, chief investment officer of the giant $132 billion bond trading company, Pacific Investment Management Company (PIMCO). Gross has predicted that government policymakers will eventually need to spend several trillions of dollars, not mere billions, to check the downturn. That kind of massive bailout has no counterpart in any other normal postwar recession, according to Gross. Unfortunately, like Ferguson, Gross provides no other quantitative, or qualitative, measure to justify calling the current crisis a 'Mini Depression.' The distinguishing feature of a 'Mini Depression' is simply that recovery requires trillions of dollars—not mere billions—in stimulus. The magnitude of spending is the sole differentiating feature of the current crisis.

One of the more accurate and consistent predictors of the current crisis has been New York University Professor and chairman of the consulting firm, RGE Monitor, Nouriel Roubini. Roubini has chosen to apply an alphabet approach to describing the downturn and differentiating it from other economic contractions—recessions and depressions alike. Roubini calls the crisis a '*Near Depression*.'[7] According to Roubini, the trajectory of a Near Depression is U-shaped, meaning a sharp downturn followed by a long stagnation period many months longer than a normal recession, followed by the upturn phase of the 'U'. In contrast to the U-Shape of a Near Depression, a normal recession would be V-Shaped, that is with a sharp but brief decline and a just as rapid sharp recovery phase. A V-shape normal recession typically lasts eight months, according to Roubini, while a U-shape has a duration three times as long, roughly 24 months. Roubini then describes a bona fide depression as a L-shape event. But how much longer than 24 months is necessary to qualify as L-shape, and thus a depression, is not explained. With Roubini at least there's more information than in the case of Ferguson or Gross. Roubini's 'Near Depression' is three times longer than a normal recession, or around 24 months. But in terms of what measure? Employment? Production? GDP?

Alphabet metaphors are useful initial conceptual devices. But more useful would be to explain why a given event is 'V' while others are 'U' and 'L'-shaped. Can a 'V' become a 'U'? Can a 'U' evolve into an 'L'? Can the evolution process reverse, from 'L' to 'U'? What are the transmission mechanisms? What qualitatively differentiates the three? What dynamic forces, similar and different, underlie the static characteristics of 'V', 'U', and 'L'? And do we get a 'W' if a 'V' fails on the upswing or if a subsequent second banking crisis emerged in the U.S. or elsewhere?

Roubini attempts to differentiate a 'U' and 'L' from a 'V-shaped' downturn by introducing the concept of stag-deflation. Both 'U' and 'L'—Near Depression and depression—are characterized by falling prices, deflation, and stagnation in the real economy. On the other hand, what was generally referred to throughout the 1920s and early 1930s as the 'Depression of 1920–21' was a 'V-shaped' event, with a sharp initial downturn followed by a sharp recovery but nonetheless with falling prices and stag-deflation. In short, alphabetical descriptors and literary metaphors don't get one very far in terms of understanding the key qualitative and quantitative characteristics associated with recessions, depressions, or even events such as 'Near Depressions.'

More to the point was economist and *New York Times* columnist Paul Krugman, also a participant in the New York debate. In early 2009 he described the crisis in 2009 in less ambiguous terms: "Let's not mince words: this looks an awful lot like the *beginning* of a second Great Depression."[8] The operative word here of course is 'beginning' of a Great Depression. But what does the beginning of a depression look like? How is it different from, say, the latter stage of a serious recession? Is it just a question of quantity and magnitudes once again—whether duration, rate, or depth of decline? Or is there also something qualitatively different in the beginning stage of depression that warrants a deeper analysis and explanation?

Like many other mainstream economists today, Krugman believes that the current crisis is ultimately the product of a global 'savings glut.' Krugman describes this term differently from us. For Krugman, it does not represent a global accumulation and concentration of income and wealth by investors and corporations—i.e. a massive pool of liquidity that is easily and relatively quickly moved around by investors to take advantage of speculative investment opportunities as they emerge, or to create the same opportunities by speculative shifting. For Krugman it is simply "a vast excess of desired savings over willing investment."

For locating the origins of the current crisis in the global 'savings glut,' Krugman was accused by Ferguson as being "in thrall to Keynes."[9] But Ferguson has it backwards. The idea that Savings determines Investment—i.e. that Savings calls forth or is the source of Investment—is a decidedly pre-Keynes notion. Keynes actually argues the reverse: it is Investment that determines Savings. For Keynes, Savings does not finance investment; finance accommodates itself to the level of Investment, providing credit where Savings itself is not sufficient. Investment thereafter leads to profits, income and wealth accumulation, in turn producing Savings. In other words, Investment is not primarily a function of Savings. Savings is a function of Investment and Investment is a direct consequence of profit, not Savings.[10]

For example, U.S. government data show that the S&P 500 largest corporations earned approximately $2.4 trillion from roughly 2002 to 2006. They paid out $1.7 trillion in stock buybacks and another $900 billion in dividends, or a total of $2.6 trillion.[11] That means all current profits, plus an additional $200 billion of previously retained earnings, were distributed by corporations in dividends and stock repurchase during 2002–06. The record corporate profits from 2002–06 simply flowed through to corporations, as through a conduit, to investors cashing in record capital gains stock sales and dividend payouts.

George W. Bush's tax cut policies from 2001 to 2004 ensured government tax collectors were kept at bay. Bush proposed and passed a major bill every year for four years. These laws focused primarily on ensuring investors would get to keep the lion's share of the record dividend and capital gains payouts. Some estimates indicate 80 percent of the $3.4 trillion in cumulative tax cuts enacted from 2001 to 2005—i.e. four-fifths of which targeted capital gains, dividends, inheritance, top margin personal income tax rates, various credits and exemptions, etc.—flowed primarily to investors.[12] That's coincidentally just about the $2.6 trillion.

The consequence of the record corporate profits and payouts to investors, preserved by favorable tax changes, was a rapid increase in liquidity in the hands of investors over the 2002–06 period. Or, as some might put it, a $2.6 trillion incremental addition to the total 'global savings glut.' Not all this liquidity could be reabsorbed by normal, real physical asset investment in the U.S. economy. Much of it was undoubtedly diverted to offshore investment opportunities in emerging markets, or else found its way into various financial instruments, securitized assets, and divers financial derivatives products purchased in the U.S. or globally.

This is not some arcane academic point. Government policies promoting and encouraging speculative forms of investment since the late 1970s have contributed significantly to the excessive concentration of income and wealth that has taken place over the past three decades—both in the U.S. and globally. Speculation has also been a major (though not sole) contributing factor to the rising 'global savings glut.' That glut in turn has fed speculative investment trends, in particular in financial securities and proliferating forms of financial derivatives securities—profits from which feed an even greater 'global savings glut.'

As speculative investment increasingly concentrates income and wealth further at the top, other government and corporate policies implemented over the past three decades—in particular, within the developed economies of Europe, North America, and Japan—have simultaneously contributed to a stagnation of real weekly earnings and compensation in general for the overwhelming majority of middle- and working-class consumers—i.e. those at the middle and bottom of the income spectrum. Thus there has been an income shift working from two opposite directions, from 'the bottom up' as well as from 'the top down'. Both contribute significantly to global income inequality trends.

Just as the speculative investment shift creates growing *financial fragility* and instability, the stagnation of real incomes for the vast majority of consumers leads to a corresponding *consumption fragility* in the system. Both financial fragility and consumption fragility are driven by excessive debt accumulation. Financial fragility worsens as investors take on debt to leverage speculative investments in increasing volumes of financial securities;

in particular, derivatives. Consumption fragility grows as worker-consumers take on increasing amounts of debt in order to finance consumption purchases that stagnating real earnings can no longer sustain. The two processes explain why a 'savings glut' enjoyed by U.S. investors is possible in the midst of a simultaneous decline in the savings rate of ordinary U.S. consumers.

Various evidence suggests global investors as the primary source of the global savings glut. In just the U.S., for example, extensive analyses of Internal Revenue Service (IRS) tax data in recent years show that the share of taxable income by the wealthiest 1 percent of households in the U.S. (roughly 1.1 million) has risen from 8 percent in 1978 to 22 percent in 2006.[13] This shift corroborates other evidence showing that income redirected to offshore tax havens has risen from roughly $250 billion in the 1980s to a range of $6–11 trillion depending on the estimate source.[14] Other studies identify changes in government and corporate policies since the early 1980s that are responsible for a relative income shift from the 'bottom 80 percent' to the wealthiest 20 percent and even 1 percent in the U.S. annually, approaching, if not exceeding today, more than $1 trillion annually.[15] How income has been redistributed in the U.S. in recent decades is therefore relevant to understanding the current economic crisis. It has contributed to rising debt levels for both investors and consumers, and therefore to both *financial fragility* and *consumption fragility*. Understanding both financial fragility and consumption fragility, and the mutually determining relationships between them, is essential to understanding the broader economic crisis.

What is the impact of financial and consumption fragility on the current crisis? The role of exploding global liquidity and, in turn, its relationship to growing global income inequality? The growing relative shift to speculative investing as a percentage of total investment? Is speculative investing 'crowding out' investment in real physical assets? Is the former dependent on the latter? Or increasingly independent? What's the role of debt, deflation and default trends in the current crisis? None of these central questions were addressed by those participating in the April 2009 New York economic debate. Not much serious thinking thus far has been given to understanding the unique characteristics of the current crisis in relation to either normal postwar recessions or to depressions such as occurred in the 1930s. The terms like 'Great,' 'Mini,' or 'Near' that are thrown about fail to provide a theoretical explanation, or even a definition, of the unique character of the current economic crisis, apart from simply asserting that the current crisis is somehow 'more severe than' a recession but 'less severe than' a depression. That clearly is not sufficient. It does not tell us how the current crisis is different from a typical recession. Nor will it tell us much about whether, when, or under what conditions an economic crisis may transition into a depression.

AN INITIAL DESCRIPTION OF EPIC RECESSION

This book attempts to explain that unique form of economic crisis called an Epic Recession. But Epic Recession is not just another label for classifying and comparing types of recessions. It is not interested in 'worse than but not as worse as' simple descriptions. Based on historical occurrences, Epic Recession is an unstable, hybrid condition associated with dual financial-real cycle convergence. As a hybrid, it shares characteristics with both normal recessions and classic depression events. This often leads to its being confused with a normal recession or even depression. Its hybrid quality and instability means that an Epic Recession must either reduce in intensity and transition to an extended period of stagnation or else transform into a classic depression. An Epic Recession therefore may evolve into a depression, but it is not inevitable. A key question is, under what conditions might it cross an economic threshold and transform into a depression? In its alternative trajectory, Epic Recession is only partially checked and contained by government policies. It consequently leads to a prolonged stagnation, neither falling deeper into depression nor reverting to a normal recession, until a much more massive fiscal stimulus occurs.

Epic Recessions do not evolve out of recessions. They are not the same animal as normal recessions. Normal recessions are typically the product of government policy missteps or temporary external demand or supply shocks; they are never precipitated by major financial instability events. Normal and Epic Recessions are therefore fundamentally different events. Normal recessions lack the internal dynamics necessary to evolve into Epic Recessions. And normal recessions never evolve into depressions. In contrast, Epic Recessions are always associated with financial instability events, are imminently capable of transforming into depressions and occasionally do. That does not mean, however, that Epic Recession is always and everywhere merely the initial phase of depression. Each type of contraction—recession, Epic Recession, and depression—has its own set of dynamic forces.

These are not abstract points of mere theoretical import. For if Epic Recession has different origins and a different dynamic from a typical recession, government policy approaches to dealing with it—whether monetary, fiscal or other—that may succeed in containing a normal recession may not prove successful in containing an Epic Recession. In fact, failure by policymakers to understand this may actually contribute toward the transformation of Epic Recession into bona fide depression as the wrong policy tools are applied, thus allowing the dynamic of Epic Recession to deepen. The wrong tools, applied inappropriately, may actually exacerbate the crisis, thereby increasing its instability and even accelerating it along a path to depression.

Epic Recession may be further considered as those events and conditions that bridge the first round of financial instability and a second, more serious financial crisis that follows. A consequence in large part of the first financial crisis, Epic Recession becomes in turn a cause of the subsequent, even more serious financial instability event.

What's inevitably missing in contemporary 'expert' debates, such as occurred in New York, are how and why the two dual cycles, financial and real, consequently tighten, become increasingly congruent, and thereafter mutually interdependent. This dual cycle convergence is what results in the emergence of Epic Recession. How an Epic Recession thereafter evolves is largely dependent upon the relative magnitudes and causal interactions between the forces of debt, deflation, and default on multiple levels. Those magnitudes and interactions are key to the transition of Epic Recession to depression.

Epic Recession represents a true turning point. But turning 'from what' and 'to what'? As a true crisis event, Epic Recession is by nature transitional and junctural. As an Epic Recession, the current economic crisis is a transitional, junctural event.

DEPRESSIONS AND NORMAL RECESSIONS

So what is a depression? Or, for that matter, even a normal recession? It is amazing that thousands of professional economists today are unable to agree on a definition, or even concise explanation, of what constitutes a classic depression. After eight decades, the great economic event of the twentieth century, the Great Depression of the 1930s, has still not produced an agreed-upon explanation of its causes or its resolution. What provoked the Great Depression of 1929–40 and what caused it to end are still hotly debated.[16] Despite the volumes of articles written on what happened in the 1930s, depression is simply defined as a matter of degree—i.e. worse than a normal recession but without a concise definition as to how much worse. A consensus on qualitative characteristics of depressions versus normal recessions is even less common.

But depressions are driven by a dynamic of conditions and events that are quite different from typical recessions. Depressions are a series of downturns strung together, punctured and fused by an intervening series of banking and financial system collapses—followed by a fall-off in world trade; currency volatility and instability; a collapse of economic institutions; significant collapse of prices, production, and employment; synchronization across economies, and relative neutralization of monetary and fiscal policy measures. Normal recessions involve none of the above. They are events singular in nature.

Some refer to the severity of 25 percent unemployment as the defining characteristic of the Great Depression of the 1930s. Others refer to the collapse of the banking system or the international gold standard. Others to the nearly 50 percent fall in GDP or industrial production. Still others to the collapse of prices and the nearly 90 percent decline in the stock market. But there is no unanimity as to what combination of indicators, or what magnitude for each, constitutes a depression. There is even less agreement as to what qualitative characteristics are uniquely associated with depressions.

At the other end of the definitional confusion there is almost equally surprising ambiguity as to what precisely constitutes a normal recession. The notion that a recession is defined by two consecutive quarters of decline in GDP may be the common rule of thumb, but not the official definition. The official definition of recession is provided by economists at the National Bureau of Economic Research (NBER). According to the NBER's Business Cycle Dating Committee, "A recession is a significant decline in economic activity spread across the economy, lasting more than a few months, normally visible in real GDP, real income, employment, industrial production, and wholesale-retail sales. A recession begins just after the economy reaches a peak of activity and ends as the economy reaches its trough."[17] As is clear by the above definition, a lot of wiggle-room exists in interpreting how much and what combination of decline in real GDP, real income, etc., constitutes a recession.

While not a bona fide depression, it is nonetheless clear that the recent economic downturn is no ordinary normal recession. The depth, duration, speed of decline, and the rate of spread of the crisis; its synchronization from economy to economy across the globe; the obvious transmissions and linkages between the financial and real sides of the crisis; and the apparent limited effectiveness of normal monetary and fiscal in checking and containing the crisis, are all features decidedly untypical of postwar recessions.

SOME PRELIMINARY HISTORICAL OBSERVATIONS

In terms of appropriate historical parallels, the current Epic Recession shares characteristics with conditions that occurred in the very early phase, 1929–31, of the last Great Depression. It shares other characteristics with a still earlier period, 1907–14. A review of the business press in the initial years of the depression reveals that those who lived during the 1929–31 period did not see themselves as in the midst of a Great Depression. They thought what was happening in 1929-31 was a serious economic slowdown, to be sure. But a similar sharp economic contraction had occurred less than a decade earlier in 1920–21, and that was followed by a quick recovery. There was thus little apparent reason to those living the events of 1929–31 to think it might be different, or to believe there would be no similar quick recovery. Of course, they were wrong. The origins of 1921 were fundamentally different from the origins and run-up to 1929. 1920–21 was definitely not a depression, despite sharing some characteristics with depressions, such as severe price deflation.

Looking back further, into the nineteenth century, there were at least three events that have been called bona fide depressions. The first occurred between 1837 and 1843. A second commenced in 1873 and lasted to around 1879. A third originated in early 1893 and did not conclude until well into 1897. It is interesting to note that all were immediately preceded by some kind of speculative financial boom that went bust, followed thereafter by the sharp and deep contraction of the real economy in the wake of the speculative bust. The 1837 event was built upon speculation associated with canal building. The 1870s with railroad bond speculation. The 1890s with railroads, industrial mergers, and stock market speculation. The close association of abrupt downturns of financial cycles with real economic contractions of major dimensions—such as occurred in the 1830s, 1870s, and 1890s—raises the point that depressions, like Epic Recessions, are generally associated with financial busts. The depressions of the nineteenth century raise another interesting point: is it possible to determine if Epic Recession events followed the financial crises of the 1830s, 1870s, and 1890s, ushering in the subsequent depressions? Are Epic Recessions in effect potential 'transition events' between financial implosions and subsequent depressions? Is it inevitable that, should an Epic Recession occur, it will necessarily lead to depression? Might an Epic event be contained and prevented from transitioning to a depression? If so, what would that containment look like: a sharp recovery, a stagnation, a slow but steady recovery? Unfortunately, nineteenth-century data and statistics are notoriously poor, especially for periods before the 1880s, for purposes of quantitative comparison.

The next historic event was the financial panic of 1907. It shares similarities with nineteenth-century depressions and with subsequent depressions in the twentieth century. But it also appears different from both. Like depressions, it was clearly the product of an intense speculative boom over the preceding decade that culminated in the 1907 financial collapse. It did not lead to a bona fide depression, however. Instead, it was followed by a prolonged stagnation period. Economists today would call it an 'L'-shaped event. It ended only with the onset of World War I and massive fiscal spending. It is thus of particular interest. 1907–14 raises the further question of whether speculative financial busts must necessarily always subsequently transform into depressions, or just prolonged stagnation. Does Epic Recession then come in two forms, one might ask? A *transitioning* to depression form, and a *stagnating* form? A U.S. in the 1930s? And perhaps a Japan in the 1990s? Or does the difference lie in the nature and magnitude of the government fiscal-monetary response? In reviewing briefly the 1907 event, that year a major financial panic broke in New York and quickly spread to the rest of the economy. It was barely checked and contained, requiring most of the capital of the big New York banks, supplemented by all but $5 million of the U.S. Treasury's total approximate $75 million reserves.[18] This appeared sufficient to stabilize the financial system but insufficient for stimulating the real economy thereafter.

While it is generally recognized that the financial events of 1907 did not result in a depression, the period from 1907 to the outbreak of World War I in 1914 was marked by a drawn-out economic stagnation. Industrial statistics show that the 1907 panic was followed by a quick real economy decline in 1908, a roughly 13-month downturn. That was followed by a brief 18-month recovery, and that brief recovery in turn was followed by another downturn starting in January 1910 that lasted two years. A brief one-year recovery occurred thereafter, followed by yet another two-year drop in 1913–14. The point is that production in 1914 on the eve of the World War I was, for a large variety of industrial products, no greater in mid 1914 than it had been in 1908 after the financial collapse of 1907.[19] In other words, the economy essentially stagnated for more than five years, punctuated by brief periods of recovery that quickly collapsed once again. Could this experience also be considered an Epic Recession?

The 1907 panic eventually led to the formation of the Federal Reserve system (the Fed) and the structuring of a standing government institution— the Fed—designed to bail out the banking system when it collapsed under speculative overload on a more systematic basis instead of the U.S. Treasury's ad hoc efforts of 1907. The Fed would later be tested in another event in the 1930s and fail to stem either the financial collapse or the economy's precipitous subsequent decline, raising the fundamental question of whether central banks and monetary policy can ever stem a deep financial crisis or subsequent Epic Recession by themselves.

Historically, then, some forms of Epic Recessions might result in drawn-out periods of economic stagnation, and not necessarily involve a quick transition to a depression stage. In some ways the events of 1907–14 share some similarities with events that occurred in Japan in the 1990s. Both exhibited an extended period of stagnation following a financial bust.

A subsequent event, briefly mentioned above, that shares some characteristics with Epic Recession is what was called in the 1920s and early 1930s the Depression of 1920–21. While a deep downturn, this event lacked a converged financial cycle collapse. Lacking that financial element was likely key to the 1920–21 economic collapse. Although sharp and deep, being relatively short in duration (only 18 months), the 'false depression' of 1920–21 was ultimately 'V'-shaped in terms of recovery. Unlike a normal recession, however, 1920–21 was accompanied by severe price deflation and a significant level of business defaults in certain sectors of the economy. 1920–21 raises some critical questions about the importance of qualitative factors, and the limits of just a quantitative assessment, in attempting to define economic events that are more severe than normal recessions—i.e. Epic Recessions. Normal recessions thereafter also occurred in 1923–24 and 1926–27. The earlier event of 1920–21 was different from normal recessions in important quantitative ways. But was it different enough to qualify as an Epic Recession? Was it, like 1907–14, an example of an Epic Recession that failed, but perhaps for a different set of reasons? Or was 1920–21 perhaps the last phase of the 1907–14 event, with World War I as an interruption (and a dampening force) in the longer 1907–14, 1919–22 cycle?

Whereas 1907–14 might marginally be considered an Epic Recession that stagnated, in contrast to 1920–21, which definitely was not an Epic Recession, 1929–1931 was a classic Epic Recession event. Furthermore, it was a case of Epic Recession that (unlike 1907–14) turned over into a bona fide depression. 1929–31 also had many similarities to the current economic crisis. It is thus a key benchmark event from which to evaluate the current crisis of 2007–10.

From another perspective, the Epic Recession of 1929–31 might be considered the initial phase or stage of the depression of the 1930s. The Great Depression of the 1930s thus includes the Epic stage, 1929–31, as well as the deeper collapse that lasted from early 1931 to March 1933 and perhaps into the largely stagnant year that followed, 1934. Stagnation and a moderate recovery occurred from late 1934 to 1937. How and why the Epic Recession of 1929–31 transformed into a depression thus becomes an important inquiry.

Another important question is how to clarify the nature of the period 1938–41. The historical record is clear that government fiscal and monetary policy shifted dramatically toward tightening in mid 1937, precipitating a return to depression from May 1937 through mid 1938, and serious stagnation thereafter until late 1940. The 're-depression' of 1937–38 was not as severe as 1929–33 but was clearly more severe in terms of magnitudes of decline of output, jobs, etc., compared to any normal recession. On the other hand, it appeared to be the result of government policy errors, as is typically the case with many 'normal' recessions. So what was 1937–41? An 'L'-shaped Epic Recession that ended only with massive fiscal spending in 1940–41? Or a normal recession within the experience of the Great Depression of the 1930s? Once again the question comes to the fore of whether there can be an Epic Recession without a financial cycle crisis—which was not the case in 1938. Alternatively, can economic contractions produced by government fiscal or monetary policy errors—of which 1937–38 was a good example—ever qualify as Epic Recessions?

In the post-1945 period in the U.S. nothing comparable to Epic Recession occurred in the case of any of the nine (or ten) identified normal recessions. Bouts of financial instability occurred, but they were brief, narrow in scope, and did not converge with a decline in the real economy, the latter caused ultimately by non-financial forces. Neither 1973–75 nor 1981–82, the worst of the normal recessions, experienced systemic financial instability either before or during these recessions. All appear as the consequence of severe external shocks combined with, or without, policy actions intended or unintended. These are clearly normal recessions, and both quantitatively and qualitatively different from Epic Recessions and/or depressions.

The first appearance of anything remotely resembling convergence of financial and real cycles occurred in 1987–90, with the stock market crash of 1987 and the Savings and Loan and junk bond crises occurring thereafter. The recession of 1990–91 followed soon after. All three financial instability events were relatively quickly contained, however, by means of traditional monetary and fiscal policy means. Which raises another key point: what is the role of traditional monetary-fiscal policies in checking and containing financial instability events and consequent economic contractions? Under what conditions might government policies succeed in containing a converged downturn? Under which might they fail to do so? And what are the consequences for subsequent future instability and financial crises down the road if they succeed? If they fail?

Does Epic Recession best explain the financial crises and economic collapse in Sweden–Finland in 1991? Or in Japan in 1992? Is the latter, Japan, in particular best explained as a depression, a normal recession, or an Epic Recession event of the 'L'-shaped stagnation form? Continuing on the international scene, where does the 'Asian Meltdown' of 1997–98 fit in all this, if at all? Or other sovereign debt crises in recent decades in Mexico, Chile, Argentina, Russia, and elsewhere?

CAUSES FUNDAMENTAL, ENABLING, AND CONTRIBUTING

To understand Epic Recession, it is also essential to distinguish between causes that are *fundamental*, *enabling*, and simply *contributing*. Fundamental causes are those without which an Epic Recession could not occur. Enabling causes are those that accelerate the evolution and development of the event as well as exacerbate the rate of spread and depth of it. Contributing causes are personal and institutional factors that influence the outcome without determining its inevitable course or pace of development.

Fundamental causes are the various forces and processes identified at the outset of this introduction. They include the massive accumulation of excess global liquidity and its determinants; the network of speculator-investors and the associated institutions, instruments and markets that constitute the conduit for the speculative investment shift; the mutually determining processes of debt, deflation, and default; and the conditions of financial and consumption fragility and their causes. Without the determining presence of these fundamental forces there can be no Epic Recession. And when they are absent, the economic downturn cannot exceed that of a normal recession.

Enabling causes of Epic Recession considered include those causes sometimes mistaken as fundamental causes of Epic Recessions. Typical among these is financial deregulation. It is often argued that financial deregulation since the late 1970s, and in particular the repeal of the Glass–Steagall Act in 1999, is the prime cause of the financial crisis that erupted in 2007. This is incorrect, however. This book will show that, while an important enabling force, financial deregulation is properly understood as an enabling factor.

The same can be said for loose U.S. Federal Reserve Bank monetary policy regimes of excessive low interest rates or excess money supply policies. These, too, are enabling, not fundamental. Other enabling causes include technologies that have made possible the globalization of finance capital. This is not to de-emphasize the importance of enabling causes. The magnitude and rate of the spread of financial instability may be influenced by enabling causes. But enabling causes are not fundamental to financial crises or Epic Recessions.

Thirdly, there are what one might call contributing causes, in addition to fundamental and enabling causes. These include the influences of personalities and the decisions they make, or don't make. What Alan Greenspan did (or didn't do), what Hank Paulson did poorly or negligently, the strategic errors of Ben Bernanke, the proposals introduced by Barack Obama and Tim Geithner for mitigating the banking crisis, are all influencing. They have an impact and effect. But they would not even exist or happen without the fundamental enabling developments noted above. The same pertains to actions of institutions, whether government or corporate. Certainly the failure of the Securities and Exchange Commission (SEC), the rating agencies (Moody's et al.), complicity with the banks, accounting practices like 'fair value' and 'mark to market,' have all played a role. CEO incentive pay practices, the shadow banking system, and the creation of structured investment vehicles (SIVs), all played a part in the recent crisis. As did Fed policies such as 'quantitative easing,' zero interest rates, the U.S. Treasury's TARP (Troubled Asset Relief Program), and so on.

Since the chapters that follow are primarily interested in understanding the fundamental causes and forces that differentiate Epic Recession from normal recession, it is perhaps useful for the reader to see a graphic representation of the various forces and their inter-relationships briefly described above (see Figure I.1). The reader is cautioned, however, that this is only a 'static' representation. The full and sometimes complex relationships and processes between the various fundamental forces depicted by the following visual statement are explained in more detail in the chapters that follow.

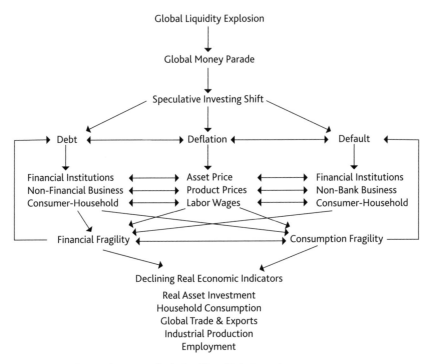

Figure I.1   Fundamental Forces and Relationships of Epic Recession

A NOTE ON THEORY

The explanation of Epic Recession presented in this book draws in part on the work of three economists: John Maynard Keynes, Irving Fisher, and Hyman Minsky. Each presented partial explanations of causes of financial instability and its impact on economic downturns more severe than normal recessions. But each only provided part of the total mosaic of explanation of the crises. This book attempts to build upon and extend beyond their contributions and fill in a few more of the pieces of that mosaic.

Keynes addressed indirectly the role of speculation in the investment process in his famous Chapter 12 of his classic 1936 book, *The General Theory of Employment, Interest and Money*. There he noted what appeared to be a growing trend toward excessive speculation in capitalist economies, and issued his classic warning to beware of enterprise (i.e. real asset) investment becoming but a 'bubble on a whirlpool' of speculation. Keynes provided some profound insights into the psychology of the speculator-investor. But to the extent that Keynes addressed speculation, it was the individual speculator and his/her behavior that he was concerned with. Elsewhere he offered another insight that is indirectly also of importance for understanding speculative investing. He maintained that there were two price systems—asset prices and product prices—and they functioned at times quite differently and independently from each other. Asset prices in particular do not always follow classic economic rules of supply and demand. That can have important implications for speculative investing and financial booms and busts. Elsewhere Keynes spent several chapters discussing in detail how interest rates and monetary policy might prove largely ineffective in generating sustained recovery from severe economic contractions like depressions. This was in contrast to more normal and mild economic downturns in which monetary policy and interest rates might more easily succeed in generating economic recovery. Keynes went on to discuss at length how fiscal policy measures—government spending in particular—were the key to stimulating demand and sustained recovery. But nowhere do we find in his work precisely how much demand was needed to engineer a recovery from a severe downturn of the dimensions at the time in 1936. Not least, at the end of his General Theory, Keynes noted that capitalism's great weakness was its apparent inability to provide full employment and its strong tendency toward income inequality favoring wealthier citizens.

Keynes leaves us with a basket of ideas that something endogenous goes wrong in the investment process in capitalism that causes extraordinarily severe contractions like depressions, that perhaps speculation plays a role some way in it all, that interest rates and monetary policies are largely ineffective in generating sustained recovery in such cases, that perhaps fiscal spending far more aggressive than the Roosevelt New Deal might be needed for sustained recovery, and that income inequality was related to all this. But a detailed analysis of the role of finance in relationship to investment is not provided. Notwithstanding his insightful commentaries on professional speculators and their danger to the system, there is even less on the role of institutional speculative behavior in relationship to investment.

Keynes focused more on what produces recovery from depression than on a specific, detailed explanation of how it all happened in the first place. In contrast, the famous American economist at the time, Irving Fisher, focused more on the process by which depressions originate and evolve. His main contribution was identifying the central role of debt and deflation as the key transmission mechanisms driving an economic downturn toward depression dimensions. Fisher described the growth of debt and the subsequent unwinding of that debt as the driver of deflation, which in turn then further exacerbates the debt problem. But he did not address the causes of that debt accumulation itself. Nor its relationship to investment, speculation, and asset price behavior in the debt run-up to a financial crisis. Unlike Keynes, Fisher also provided essentially no solution to the depression. There are only two choices: either let asset prices, production, and employment levels collapse—i.e. 'liquidate' the losses to unwind the bad debt accumulated in the run-up to crisis—or rely on the Federal Reserve to reflate the economy in some way. Keynes thus focused more on solutions to the crisis, saying relatively little about its origins; Fisher focused more on its origins and process of evolution via debt deflation, saying little of major import about its solutions.

Both Keynes and Fisher wrote in the 1920–30s. A later economist, Hyman Minsky, made his major contributions in the 1970s to early 1990s. Minsky attempted to fill in the gaps in Keynes–Fisher. Minsky took the analysis of the role of speculative investing further. Unlike Keynes, he focused more on the institutional bases for the speculative trend Keynes warned of. Minsky described how debt accumulation over the business cycle would eventually destabilize the entire financial system, provoking a financial crisis and subsequent real economic downturn. As the business cycle progressed over time, enterprise finance evolved from less to more unstable, thus making the enterprise and the financial system itself more 'fragile' over time and financial eruptions increasingly likely. Like Keynes, he attributed an important role to the asset price system. Like Fisher, he saw the process of excessive debt accumulation as key to growing financial instability and crisis. But Minsky focused primarily on business debt and deflation, and did not provide equivalent analyses of the role of consumer and public sector debt in the evolution toward financial crisis and subsequent real economic contraction. Yet it is total debt, and the relationship between its various forms (business, consumer, public), that is of importance. Addressing primarily financial fragility, Minsky further left out a treatment of equally important consumption fragility. And both he and Keynes focused on the dual price system, asset and product, but Minsky failed to include the third critical price system, wages. Finally, Minsky envisioned and proposed a program of fiscal stimulus to engineer sustained recovery. His program, however, is basically an extension of the Roosevelt New Deal set of programs, which may not prove any more successful than Roosevelt's in the 1930s.

This book undertakes the task of beginning to fill the gaps in theory and analysis left by Keynes, Fisher, and Minsky. These include a need to consider total debt—i.e. consumer and public—and not just business debt in an explanation of the crisis. The analysis of deflation must also consider all three prices systems: asset, product, *and* wage. Understanding the dynamic processes driving deep contractions requires not just understanding how debt and deflation interact but how debt–deflation interacts with defaults. Engineering a sustained recovery requires policies that moderate all three: debt, deflation, and default; addressing one, or even two, of the debt–deflation–default triad is not sufficient. Consumption, as well as financial, fragility is critical to any analysis. Both are dynamically related to the processes of debt–deflation–default. Moreover, it is essential to note that income concentration and inequality, not just debt levels and quality, drive both forms of fragility. The nature of speculation and speculative investing, and its host of supporting institutions and financial instruments, have changed significantly from even Minsky's time, let alone that of Keynes and Fisher. Speculative investing has risen in relative weight and mix to non-speculative forms of investing, and this is now having a growing negative impact on the real economy. Not just finance and consumption, but the entire system has become more fragile. Both financial and consumption fragility have rendered normal monetary and fiscal policies increasing 'inelastic,' as economists would say; i.e. following each financial crisis and real economic contraction, it takes ever-larger doses of monetary and fiscal stimulus to generate a recovery.

The preceding note on theory is, of course, all too brief to do full justice to the works of the three great economists in question—Keynes, Fisher, and Minsky. Moreover, it is just a partial overview of the main points of this book. More will be said of the relevant contributions of Keynes, Fisher, and Minsky in subsequent chapters. The reader is cautioned, however, not to expect a full theoretical analysis of their works or the profound issues they raise. That is the subject of this writer's subsequent effort in progress.

This book simply attempts to clarify the meaning of what's called an 'Epic Recession,' and its relative similarities and differences to normal recessions and depressions. The book is interested in the key determinants and processes by which Epic Recessions originate, evolve and transform into either classic depressions or periods of extended stagnation. It identifies and examines at some length two prior Epic Recessions in U.S. history in the twentieth century that resulted in either extended stagnation or depression. It then examines the current Epic Recession and considers which prior historical case the current Epic Recession might most resemble: the 'Type I' Epic Recession of 1907–14 or the 'Type II' of 1929–31. The book then provides an in-depth analysis of the recent downturn, a critique of government fiscal and monetary policies addressing the contraction, and concludes with a detailed 28-point program necessary for sustained long-run economic recovery.

HOW TO READ THIS BOOK

In speaking to audiences and providing radio and TV interviews over the past year, this writer encountered three basic questions asked invariably and repeatedly by audiences: 'How the hell did we get here?', 'Where is this thing going?', and 'What in the world should be done?' This book attempts to answer all three essential queries.

In so doing, the reader will find this book more than just a descriptive journalistic story of current events, heavy on clever style, metaphors and analogies, but light on content. What follows is not light literary commentary. Rather, it is an effort to understand the deep, historical, and fundamental forces that have determined the origin, trajectory, and future direction of the current crisis. It is an attempt to predict how we got here, and where it might all be going. But it is also an attempt to present solutions that are equally as fundamental as the problems confronted. The book is written with the conviction that it is necessary, but not sufficient, to explain how the crisis and Epic Recession originated, or even where it is going. It is necessary to critique and propose alternative solutions to it as well.

This book is divided into three parts. Part One consists of Chapters 1–3 and focuses more on theoretical description and explanation of the phenomenon of Epic Recession. It is more abstract than Part Two, which is historical, and Part Three, which addresses contemporary events. Part Two, Chapters 4–6, analyzes historical examples of Epic Recession prior to the current crisis of 2007–10. Part Three, Chapters 7–9, focuses on the origins and evolution of the current Epic Recession, 2007–10, the effectiveness of fiscal and monetary policies, a critique of the Bush and Obama administrations' efforts to contain the crisis, and this writer's own extensive, 28-point program for resolving the crisis.

There are three possible starting points for readers of this book: Chapter 1, Chapter 4, or Chapter 7.

For readers interested in more theoretical issues or in arguments and evidence differentiating Epic Recession from normal recessions and bona fide depressions, or for understanding the defining characteristics and dynamic processes of Epic Recessions, the reader should begin with Chapter 1 in Part One.

Part Two, Chapters 4–6, is for readers interested in an historical account of past depressions, recessions, and Epic Recessions as a comparative background and contrast to the current crisis. Part Two is also in a sense an empirical verification of the 'theory' topics addressed in Part One. Chapter 4 looks at financial crises and depressions in the nineteenth century. Chapter 5 considers what is called the 'Type I' Epic Recession of 1907–14. And Chapter 6 considers in some detail the origins of the depression of 1929–40, focusing specifically on the early period, 1929–31, which, it is argued, represents a 'Type II' Epic Recession. Start with Chapter 4.

Part Three consists of Chapters 7–9. If the reader is especially interested in the recent crisis, how it originated, how it evolved, where it might go, and solutions, start with Chapter 7, which provides a lengthy account of the origins of the current Epic Recession of 2007–10 as far back as the 1980s, and its evolution through to the third quarter 2009. It discusses possible directions in 2010 and beyond as well. An assessment is made that the current Epic Recession is more like a 'Type I' than a 'Type II' Epic Recession. Chapter 8 is a detailed critique of both the Bush and the Obama administrations' policies attempting to address and contain the crisis, focusing in particular on the policy evolution in the hands of administration economic strategists Alan Greenspan, Hank Paulson, Ben Bernanke, and Tim Geithner, as well as a description and critique of the Obama stimulus and bank bailout plans. The final chapter, Chapter 9, presents this author's 28-point program for recovery, focusing in particular on programs for housing, jobs, bank nationalization, and tax and general income restructuring.

Part One

Theory

1
Quantitative Characteristics
of Epic Recession

Chapter 1 and Chapter 2 that follows together provide a preliminary definition of 'Epic Recession.' These chapters identify and describe *static* characteristics that differentiate Epic Recessions from 'normal' recessions or a depression.[1] Chapter 3 will describe *dynamic* characteristics that further distinguish Epic Recessions from normal recessions or depression.

Static characteristics may be either quantitative or qualitative. If quantitative, the question arises, what is the magnitude of a characteristic necessary to qualify as 'Epic'—in contrast to a lesser magnitude in the case of a normal recession or greater magnitude in the case of a depression? And if qualitative, what are the characteristics that are unique to Epic Recessions that are not present in cases of normal recessions, or are absent in cases of Epic Recession but occur in depressions? Differences in both magnitude (quantitative) and/ or uniqueness (qualitative) therefore serve as essential starting points for distinguishing Epic Recessions from normal recessions and depressions.

THREEFOLD CHARACTERISTICS OF EPIC RECESSION

This chapter considers five important *quantitative* characteristics that differentiate Epic Recessions from normal recessions. They include the depth of the economic decline, its duration, and levels or degrees of debt, deflation, and default.

The *qualitative* characteristics addressed in Chapter 2 include financial instability and fragility, a large shadow banking system, consumption fragility, a shift to speculative investing relative to traditional forms of investing, and global synchronization of the crisis.

Dynamic characteristics of Epic Recession discussed in Chapter 3 include several sets of particular relationships that are complex and interdependent. These include relationships and interdependencies between speculative and non-speculative forms of investing; between speculative investing and debt; between debt, deflation, and default; between defaults and financial and consumption fragility; and, finally, between government fiscal and monetary policies and the key processes of debt–deflation–default and fragility. The dynamic characteristics thus focus heavily on the *processes* by which quantitative and qualitative characteristics mutually determine each other in various causal relationships, transmission mechanisms, and feedback processes.

Of the five quantitative characteristics addressed in this chapter, the first two—depth and duration—are primarily descriptive. They describe the degree to which Epic Recessions differ from normal recessions. That is, Epic

Recessions are more severe in terms of both their depth of decline and their duration than are normal recessions. More severe as well are the remaining three quantitative characteristics: debt, deflation, and default. However, these latter three are important to Epic Recession in more than just degree of severity. They are central, and distinguish Epic Recession for more fundamental reasons as well. Epic Recessions are set in motion by financial instability and crisis. As will be shown, this is quite unlike normal recessions, which are not precipitated by financial instability and crisis. It is the accumulation of debt and price inflation that create the financial fragility that leads to the financial crisis event. Moreover, once the financial crisis erupts and evolves, it is once again debt and price that play a key role. Specifically, it is now the reversal—i.e. the unwinding of debt and now price deflation—that results in the deepening and spread of default—bank, non-bank business, and consumer alike—that subsequently drives the real economy into Epic Recession. Thus, it is not simply that debt–deflation–default are more severe in terms of level or degree in the case of Epic Recession compared to normal recession. The three characteristics are also critical elements that, along with other key elements described shortly, drive a transition to Epic Recession. In a sense, therefore, it is debt, deflation and default that in turn produce the more severe depth and duration characteristics associated with Epic Recession.

Of course, even more fundamental are those forces that produce the excessive debt accumulation and price inflation in the first place, creating a condition of financial fragility that ultimately provokes the financial crisis. As will be discussed in more detail in the next two chapters, the key to the more fundamental forces is the major shift to speculative forms of investing and the growing weight and mix of those forms compared to non-speculative forms of investment in the economy. Understanding what underlies that speculative shift takes analysis even deeper. And once the financial crisis has erupted and the transition to Epic Recession has begun, on the 'downside' or the 'bust phase' of decline yet more forces begin to play a contributing role to the transition to Epic Recession as well. But more on all that subsequently. For the remainder of this chapter, it is necessary first to understand simply in a *static* sense how debt–deflation–default, and depth and duration, are characteristics of Epic Recession.

QUANTITATIVE CHARACTERISTICS OF EPIC RECESSION

The characteristics of *depth* are measurable in several possible ways. This chapter identifies five such ways or indicators by which to distinguish depth in an Epic Recession: gross domestic product (GDP), employment, industrial production, exports, and the stock market.

The *duration* characteristics are measured in terms of what is called the 'peak to trough' of an economic decline—i.e. how long in months or quarters that the decline continues from its immediate pre-recession high point to its recession lowest point, and thereafter how long it takes from the low point to return to the previous high point. The 'peak to trough' to recovery may describe a recession either as a 'V', an 'L', a 'U', or a 'W' in duration terms. 'V' represents a sharp decline and just as sharp a recovery; 'L' a long-term stagnation following the initial decline; 'U' a decline followed by a lengthy period before recovery; and 'W' a double-dip decline, followed by recovery, followed by another decline and recovery.

The *debt* characteristic is defined as total debt, which includes public debt (federal, state, and local government), consumer debt, and business debt—the latter of which can be segmented in turn into bank and non-bank business debt. Whether the debt is short term or long term in its payment structure is also a factor, as is the interest rate level and total cost of the debt repayment as well. *Deflation* is defined as a negative price change. Three kinds of price systems are included in the consideration of deflation: asset price deflation, product price deflation, and labor market or wage deflation. Wages are defined broadly, not simply as hourly wage rates. Wages include weekly earnings, and thus are inclusive of hours worked, as well as other forms of pay such as fringe benefits and paid time off (paid vacations, paid holidays, sick leave, etc.). Finally, *default* is considered in terms of several elements, including financial institution insolvency, non-bank business bankruptcy, consumer delinquencies (involving combined mortgage and installment debt), and public sector default that may include even government bond defaults by both state and federal governments.

What, then, it might be asked, are the respective levels of depth of decline, duration, debt, deflation and default that are necessary to characterize a recession as 'Epic' in contrast to a normal recession or a depression? Answering this question allows a discussion of the current crisis quantitatively, i.e. in something more than vague general terms like 'Near Depression' or 'Great Recession,' as many economists and commentators have been content to do to date.

DEPTH AS A CHARACTERISTIC

GDP as a depth indicator

If GDP is used as an indicator of depth, then Epic Recessions are associated with a decline in GDP for at least two quarters of between 5 percent and 15 percent.

This compares with normal recessions globally that on average experience GDP declines of 2 percent over the course of the recession and rarely for more than one quarter of more than 4 percent.[2] The 5–15 percent for Epic Recession also contrasts with depression GDP declines of 15–40 percent or more over a longer duration of decline. For example, the worst period of the U.S. Great Depression, from 1929 to 1933, witnessed a drop in GDP from $103.6 billion to $56.4 billion or, in percentage terms, 45.6 percent.[3]

A study in early 2008 of the 'big five' post-1945 recessions globally prior to 2007 (Finland, Sweden, Norway, Spain and Japan), predicted in early 2008 that the current U.S. crisis might be even worse than the worst recessions globally. The study predated by months the deep decline in U.S. GDP that occurred in the fourth quarter of 2008. The 'big five' economies in question had 'peak to trough' declines of less than 5 percent. The decline of the U.S. economy from October 2008 through June 2009 witnessed GDP declines of 6.1 percent, 5.7 percent, and 1.5 percent, respectively—thus making the recent U.S. decline decidedly worse than even the prior 'big five' global recessions to date.

In the U.S. since 1945, the National Bureau of Economic Research (NBER), the organization that dates and analyzes recessions in the U.S., identified ten normal recessions from the late 1940s to 2007.[4] The Federal Reserve Board of Minneapolis website has mapped these recessions. Its mapping shows, in all nine cases, recovery beginning, or the decline stabilizing, after only six months from the start of each recession. Eight of the nine recessions, moreover, were clearly rapid 'V'-shaped recoveries, the 1973–75 recession being the sole exception. This 'V'-shape trajectory of prior 'normal' recessions in the U.S. is not shared by the current Epic Recession.[5]

What the above comparison of prior normal recessions in the U.S. and the current Epic Recession reveals is that the current Epic Recession of 2007–10 clearly eclipses all prior recessions in the U.S. in terms of the depth of decline, when measured in terms of GDP. But alternative measures of depth are also possible. They may include total jobs lost, the unemployment rate, industrial production, global exports, stock market indices, etc. These alternative measures record even more severe depth of decline for the current economic downturn when compared to prior normal recessions in the U.S.

Unemployment as a depth indicator

In terms of unemployment levels, in an economy the size of the U.S., an Epic Recession occurs when 15 million or more lose their jobs and the unemployment rate exceeds 10 percent.

Given an economy and work force the size of the U.S. (approximately 153 million), a normal recession would result in job losses of less than 15 million and an unemployment rate below 10 percent. Were there a Depression today in the U.S. similar to that of the 1930s, it would mean a job loss today of 38 million or more and an unemployment rate of 25 percent. In the Great Depression of the 1930s in the U.S. the total workforce was about 40 million. Around 10 million officially went jobless and the unemployment rate officially reached 25 percent by 1933. (These numbers may have been an underestimation since they do not include farm labor unemployment. The jobless levels may have been as high as 13 million and the true unemployment rate therefore well over 30 percent, in fact.)

An Epic Recession in today's U.S. economy means job losses of more than 15 million but less than 30–38 million, and an unemployment rate between 10 percent and 25–30 percent. The unemployment rate for the purposes of our definition here is measured by what is today called the 'U-6' unemployment rate, which includes involuntary part-time workers, discouraged workers, and others without jobs but willing to work if offered a job. After 20 months from its start the official government unemployment rate had risen from 4.9 percent to 9.8 percent, but the U.S. Labor Department's more accurate U-6 unemployment rate rose to 17.0 percent.[6] That 17 percent is still a long way from depression levels of 25–30 percent, but well above unemployment rates in prior 'normal' recessions in the U.S. which typically ranged from 6 percent to 10 percent at the worst stage of the recession.

Those who argue that the current Epic Recession is no different from the worst of the prior recessions in the U.S. tend to compare the current downturn with the two worst prior recessions of 1973–75 and 1981–82. Those who compare it with 1973–75 argue that the GDP decline during 2008–10 was no worse than in 1973–75. Others focus instead on comparisons of unemployment rates today with the recession of 1981–82. But the comparison of 2008–10 with 1981–82 in terms of even 'official' unemployment rates is grossly misleading. The most recent official unemployment rate of 9.8 percent for 2007–10 is actually far worse than for 1981–82. This again is partly due to changes in the way unemployment data are now gathered and manipulated. But it is also true because of major structural changes in the labor markets in the U.S. since 1973 that make the three periods non-comparable. First, there was no U-6 unemployment rate in the 1970s and 1980s. The numbers of involuntary part-time, discouraged, and marginally attached but willing to work were far fewer then compared to today. The growth in involuntary part time, discouraged, and temporary workers—sometimes called 'contingent labor'—is largely a phenomenon that has grown since the 1980s and at an accelerating pace. Today's U-6 unemployment rate of 17 percent is almost certainly much higher than anything that might have been comparable in 1981–82 and 1973–75.

Epic Recession can also be compared to normal recessions in terms of cumulative total job loss after 18 months into the downturn. In normal recessions in the U.S., the cumulative job loss after 18 months of recession was on average 2 percent of total employment. What are generally identified as the 'worst' of the normal recessions—1973–75 and 1981–82—in the U.S. had a cumulative job loss after 18 months of 1.7 percent and 2.9 percent, respectively. In contrast, the current Epic Recession had a cumulative job loss after 18 months of 4.5 percent of the total workforce—in other words, twice as severe compared to the previous nine normal recessions in the U.S.[7] Furthermore, after 18 months the current Epic Recession has continued to lose jobs well past the 18-month point at which other normal recessions had clearly begun to reverse the process and recover jobs.

Still another illustration of how the 2007–10 recession is not really comparable with 1981–82 is the especially rapid rise in joblessness in just the past year, 2008–09. When properly calculated in U-6 terms, approximately a million jobs a month were lost from November 2008 to May 2009, and about a half million a month thereafter. Much publicity has been made of the apparent slowdown of job losses during the summer of 2009. Officially (i.e.

not measured in terms of U-6) 200,000 to 300,000 jobs were lost each month in August–September 2009. However, not mentioned is that a million jobs also disappeared in those two months as a result of workers simply leaving the workforce. Those million jobs are not included in the official calculations of the unemployment rate. Even when adjusted for the smaller size of the labor force in 1981–82 and 1973–75, nothing similar in terms of the massive collapse of jobs in the year October 2008 to October 2009 has ever occurred on such a scale in any prior recession in the U.S. Nor have so many simply left the labor force itself in such a short period.

In an earlier publication this author had predicted in February 2008 that there would be mass layoffs coming at the end of 2008; and subsequently, in December 2008, predicted that unemployment would reach 20 million by the end of 2009.[8] In retrospect, those numbers now appear overly-conservative. Unemployed levels by the end of 2009 may now quite possibly range between 22 million and 24 million. In terms of various employment measures, in other words, the recent recession has been clearly Epic in character.[9]

Apart from the obvious measuring of depth in terms of GDP or employment, it is also possible to measure depth of decline in terms of industrial production, global exports, or stock market decline. And here, once again, a similar picture emerges, clearly distinguishing Epic Recession from earlier normal recessions.

Industrial production, exports, and the stock market as depth indicators

Epic Recession occurs when industrial production declines between 10 percent and 20 percent over a twelve-month period. Normal recessions record declines of less than 10 percent while depressions register annual declines in industrial production of 20 percent or more.

Industrial production in the U.S. peaked in January 2008 at about a 2–2.5 percent annual growth rate and began to slow thereafter. It declined around midsummer 2008 and fell precipitously after October 2008 to around 13.5 percent by May 2009, for an annual drop of around 15 percent.[10] Globally, industrial production fell about as fast in the euro-area and in Japan even faster, collapsing by about 40 percent. In contrast, during the depression of the 1930s it dropped about 50 percent, while in normal recessions in the postwar period it fell on average well below 10 percent.

A study by economists Barry Eichengreen and Kevin O'Rourke, updated in June 2009, concluded that "World industrial production continues to track closely the 1930s fall, with no clear signs of 'green shoots.'" The U.S. and Canada as late as mid 2009 were still experiencing a fall in industrial output "approximately in line with what happened in the 1929 crisis," with German and British industrial output tracking their rate of fall in the 1930s, Italy and France "doing much worse," while "Japan's industrial output in February [2009] was 25 percentage points lower than at the equivalent stage in the Great Depression."[11]

Eichengreen and O'Rourke's study shows, in addition, that the collapse of world trade occurred over 2008–09 even faster than during the first year of the Great Depression. After twelve months the volume of world trade had declined nearly 20 percent.[12] As another business press observer put it, "the decline in world trade in the first year is equal to that in the first two years of the Great Depression. This is not because of protection, but because of collapsing demand for manufactures."[13]

Countries like Germany, Japan, and even China, all more dependent on exports than the U.S., experienced declines in trade far worse than the global average, while U.S. export volumes have fallen approximately 21 percent. Thus, it may be argued that, similar to industrial production,

Epic Recession is characterized by a drop in exports within a twelve-month period of more than 10 percent, whereas the drop in the case of normal recessions is less than 10 percent and depressions more than 20 percent.

Eichengreen and O'Rourke also note that depression-like falls in world stock markets occurred in 2008–09. Their global index of aggregate stock markets shows a drop after twelve months of more than 40 percent on average. If one compares just S&P 500 stock average in the U.S. in 1929–31 with the current Epic Recession, then at twelve months into the downturn the drop in the S&P 500 in the 1929–30 period was almost exactly the same as 2007–08, or approximately 45 percent. The U.S. market eventually fell from a high of 14,400 in October 2007 to a low of about 6,700 in early 2009, or just under 60 percent. As of late 2009, the acclaimed stock market recovery of 2009 had only recovered about half of its decline.

Epic Recessions are associated with sustained declines in markets of 40–60 percent. Normal recessions experience briefer declines in stock market aggregates and generally less than 40 percent. In contrast, depressions experience stock declines sustained over multi-year periods of more than 60 percent.

The stock market collapse of the 1930s experienced at least five recoveries on its way to a bottom of –89.2 percent from its 1929 highs.[14] A bottoming-out thus did not happen until 45 months after 1929. A sustained clear recovery did not commence until 1935, and that, too, relapsed in late 1937.

Depth characteristic indicators defining Epic Recession in relation to normal recessions and depression are summarized in Table 1.1.

Table 1.1 Comparative Summary: Depth

Indicator	Epic Recession	Depression	Normal Recession
GDP	–5% to –15%	–20% to –40%	–2% to –5%
Unemployment Rate	+10% to +20%	> +20%	< +10%
Industrial Production	–10% to –20%	> –20%	< –10%
Exports	–10% to –20%	> –20%	< –10%
Stock Market Index	–40% to –60%	> –60%	< –40%

DURATION AS A CHARACTERISTIC

Yet another way to differentiate Epic Recession is by the characteristic of duration, or how long a decline in one or more of the depth indicators continues. This is typically done by measuring an economic downturn from its 'peak' to its 'trough'—i.e. its low point of the decline—after which recovery begins once again. The average 'peak to trough' for normal recessions since 1945 is approximately 10.5 months.[15] The two post-1945 normal recessions of longest duration were 1973–75 and 1981–82, both of which lasted 16 months. In terms of GDP only, thus far the current contraction has lasted 20 months.

When measured in terms of GDP, therefore, an Epic Recession lasts roughly 18–24 months. The duration of normal recessions in the U.S. has been on average less than a year. Depressions measured in GDP last a minimum of 36 months and some much longer. When duration is measured in terms of industrial production, exports, or stock declines, Epic Recessions last 12–24 months.

The depression of the 1930s experienced a 43-month downturn in gross national product (GNP), from around mid 1929 through the first quarter of 1933. A brief recovery followed, that was followed in turn by a second relapse and downturn in 1937–38 and a sluggish recovery until 1940.

In the nineteenth century, during the 1870s decade the depression endured 65 months, from October 1873 to March 1879. In the 1880s, another depression period went on for 38 months, from March 1882 to May 1885, followed by a brief aborted recovery and a second economic relapse of 13 months from March 1887 to April 1888. This experience of a deep and long downturn, followed by relative brief recovery, and in turn another decline, is thus not untypical of depressions, having occurred both in the 1880s and 1930s.[16]

A decline–recovery–decline, or 'W'-Shape, trajectory is sometimes associated with Epic Recessions as well. Something similar also occurred in the case of Epic Recession in Japan in the 1990s. And in the case of the major financial crisis known as the 'panic' of 1907, a recession of about one year followed the financial panic, followed in turn by a brief one-year recovery, another recession for two years from January 1910 to January 1912, another eleven-month brief recovery, and a third recession of two years from January 1913 to December 1914.[17] The stock market at the time rose and fell several times as the economic recovery repeatedly stalled after 1907.[18]

This extended period of stalled recovery, 1907–14, has been interpreted as a series of discrete, unrelated short cycles. But an argument can be made that the short cycles together represent a kind of Epic Recession—the kind that never developed the internal forces or momentum to make the transition to depression; or what, in Chapter 5, will be called a 'Type I' Epic Recession.

Not all Epic Recessions therefore transform into a depression. Those that do are called a 'Type II' Epic Recession. An example of 'Type II' is the 1929–31 period, which is addressed in Chapter 6. Thus Epic Recessions may settle into a period of protracted stagnation, marked by brief temporary re that soon falter and return the economy to a stagnation condition, o transform into a more virulent depression.

In the case of Japan in the 1990s, a financial crisis in the early 199. provoked a long-term stagnation of the real economy, punctuated by brief, unsustainable recoveries, that eventually settled back into stagnation. In both cases of 'Type I' Epic Recessions—1907–14 and Japan in the 1990s—the economy was clearly not able to generate a sustained recovery on its own. Normal government fiscal or monetary policies proved insufficient. Only extraordinary fiscal stimulus measures by government can succeed in checking the downward momentum, as well as generate sustained recovery in the case of Epic Recession. However, those extraordinary measures may be blocked politically since the Epic Recession may be incorrectly perceived as not serious enough to require extraordinary fiscal measures. Or government policymakers may misinterpret a slowing or temporary leveling off of the decline as a nascent recovery. (More on this in subsequent chapters.)

For now it is important to note that Epic Recessions may look more like 'W'-shape extended stagnation events that remain in a state of a relative low, moderately negative, or no growth, or Epic Recessions may make the transition to a bona fide depression event. In contrast, normal recessions lack the internal dynamics that prevent self-generating sustained recovery. Normal recessions are thus different from Epic Recessions not simply quantitatively but qualitatively as well. Normal recessions never make the transition to depression. They are cyclically responsive to traditional fiscal-monetary measures aimed at containment and generating recovery, whereas Epic Recessions are not, and require extraordinary stimulus—especially on the fiscal side.

Whether measuring duration in terms of GDP, industrial production, exports, or stock markets, the current Epic Recession has been far more severe than either of the two prior worst-case normal recessions of 1973–75 and 1981–82.

In terms of duration and employment, in 1973–75 employment levels recovered their pre-recession levels after just 18 months. In the 1981–82 recession it took 24 months to complete a full employment recovery cycle. In contrast, after 20 months the current Epic Recession has continued to experience job loss at an exceptionally high rate. Most accounts are that job loss will continue well into 2010 and perhaps beyond. That means a record time for employment levels to fully recover. Total employment in the U.S. at the start of the current Epic Recession in December 2007 was 146.6 million. By September 2009 it was down to 138.8 million and still falling. Thus the first half of the employment duration cycle has not even concluded. If the economy started tomorrow, adding net new jobs of 100,000 each month, it would take more than seven years, to 2016, to get back to the employment level of December 2007.

…neral experience job loss durations (peak to trough) of,
…onths. Normal recessions, in worst cases, range from
…sions may last more than 48 months.

…indicators defining Epic Recession in relation to
…depression are summarized in Table 1.2.

Comparative Summary: Duration*

Indicator	Epic Recession	Depression	Normal Recession
GDP	12–24 months	> 36 months	< 12 months
Industrial Production	12–24 months	> 24 months	< 12 months
Exports	12–24 months	> 24 months	< 12 months
Employment Level Declines	24–48 months	> 48 months	12–24 months

*Measured from peak to trough. Possible short-term recoveries with subsequent declines to trough.

DEBT AS A CHARACTERISTIC

Epic Recessions are always the consequence of a preceding financial crisis. Financial crises are in turn the result of excessive debt accumulation. Normal recessions are not associated with excessive debt accumulation or financial crises. Isolated financial events may occur before or during a normal recession. An individual bank may collapse or a particular credit market may experience severe stress. But the financial instability is never generalized across financial markets in normal recessions, as is the case with Epic Recession. Depressions are associated with a sequence of financial instability events. Both Epic Recessions and depressions are therefore the consequence, at least in part, of generalized financial crises. In contrast, normal recessions are not provoked by financial crises. That accounts in part for their shorter duration, less severe depth, and more elastic response to traditional fiscal-monetary policies.

Debt is a characteristic of Epic Recession in two ways. Excessive debt run-up is a characteristic, but debt unwinding is as well. Debt 'wind-up,' or excess accumulation, takes place during the boom period prior to the eruption of financial crisis and subsequent decline of the real economy. The period of financial crisis and downturn that follows is accompanied by the unwinding of that debt. How much debt needs to be 'unwound' determines in large part how deep the financial crisis is, how protracted, and how unresponsive it may be to policy actions by government.

Over the last three decades the U.S. economy has experienced an extraordinary accumulation of excess debt. Debt as used here refers to total debt, i.e. all forms of domestic debt, including consumer debt, business debt, and government debt. Government debt includes federal, and state and local government. Business debt is both non-financial and financial business debt. Consumer debt is divided into mortgage and consumer installment debt. Table 1.3, from the U.S. Federal Reserve's 'Flow of Funds' data, shows a three-decade run-up in total debt in the U.S., segmented by government, consumer, and business sources of that debt.

Table 1.3   Total Debt, U.S. 1978–2008 ($ billions, seasonally adjusted)

Year	Total Domestic	Total Households	Mortgage	Consumer	Non-Financial Business	Financial Business	Government (Fed/state/local)
1978	3,623	1,105	708	311	1,188	412	1,079
1988	11,596	3,043	2,054	745	3,410	2,145	2,997
1998	22,554	5,920	4,057	1,441	5,410	6,328	4,895
2008	50,666	11,434*	8,063*	2,595	11,153	19,486*	8,593

*$2.4 trillion of mortgage debt is adjusted from the Federal Reserve's data, reducing household mortgage debt by that amount and adding the same to financial business debt, based on Moody Inc.'s prediction of 8 million foreclosures in the current recession cycles. That debt must, upon foreclosure, revert back to the financial institution or else be written off as a loss. The $2.4 trillion is estimated based on 8 million foreclosures on mortgage loans averaging $300,000 that were incurred by homeowners during the residential mortgage boom of 2002–07. Total household debt includes elements other than mortgage and consumer debt not indicated by an additional column.

Source: U.S. Federal Reserve, *Flow of Funds Accounts of the United States*, First Quarter 2009, Washington D.C., June 11, 2009, Table D.3, "Debt Outstanding by Sector," p. 8.

The data show an unprecedented rise in total debt levels in the U.S., with the largest part of that debt rise associated with business and financial business in particular. Since the mid 1980s, financial sector debt tripled and then tripled again. This extraordinary debt accumulation cannot be attributed to normal business borrowing to invest in real physical structures, equipment, and other real assets. This financial sector-driven debt has been largely the result of bank and finance lending to finance speculative investment activity—i.e. borrowing to fund investment in financial assets, securities, and various financial instruments. The critical differences between non-speculative investment versus speculative forms of investment, and the linkages between speculative investing and debt, will be explained in more detail in Chapter 3. For now, it is important simply to note that business-corporate debt—and financial debt in particular—is the main cause behind the total debt run-up; more important than either consumer or government debt accumulation.

Notwithstanding this fact, the public press has tended to focus on consumer debt or government debt as the problem. They blame the consumer, living beyond his/her means and taking on credit and debt to finance unaffordable consumer spending. The problem is the greedy consumer, buying more than he/she can afford or taking on a mortgage beyond his/her means. Or it is the government, intent on spending on social programs and 'entitlements' like social security and Medicare, that is the prime culprit in the 'debt problem.' However, the data show clearly that the largest contributor to the excess debt accumulation in the U.S. economy has been neither the consumer nor the government; it has been the business sector, in particular the financial business segment of the economy.

Whereas the business-finance sector borrowing and debt accumulation is attributable largely to speculative investing, the rise in consumer and government debt since 1978 has been driven by a totally different set of factors.

In terms of federal government, debt accumulation has been the consequence of chronic government budget deficits. Those deficits in turn are the result of three developments: first, a three-decades-long restructuring of the tax system in which repeated tax cuts reduced wealthy investors' and corporations' tax contributions; second, by chronic war spending; and, third, increasingly in recent decades by the growing cost of the bailout of banks, financial institutions, and other businesses that has followed the financial crises that have occurred since the 1980s.

Since 1978 the overwhelming majority of tax cuts have accrued to the wealthiest 10 percent of households and corporations, beginning with $752 billion in tax cuts in the early 1980s, continuing to the massive tax cuts of more than $4 trillion that occurred under George W. Bush during his first term alone. In both cases, Reagan and George W. Bush, more than 80 percent of the tax cuts benefited investors and corporations. In between there have been dozens of additional tax bills, and tax reductions targeting select industries in other legislation, that have provided further largesse to the same investor-corporation target group. No doubt several trillions of this multi-trillion tax cut windfall for investors and corporations have flowed offshore in recent decades, into the dozens of island and small nation tax shelters or to fund investment in foreign emerging economies—either of which has meant the loss of hundreds of billions of dollars annually in tax revenues that might have been collected by the Internal Revenue Service (IRS).

In terms of war spending, it is widely recognized that the doubling and tripling of annual defense spending in the 1980s under Reagan resulted in the emergence of chronic budget deficits of hundreds of billions of dollars every year during that decade. While the first Gulf War in 1990 was paid for by U.S. allies in part, Japan and Saudi Arabia in particular, the same cannot be said for the costs of U.S. war spending since 2001. As Nobel Prize-winning economist Joseph Stiglitz estimated in a recent book, the cost of the second Gulf War since 2003 has been in excess of $3 trillion and still rising—with additional costs for the escalated conflict in Afghanistan adding significantly to the total.[19]

On the government social programs spending side, much is made of the contribution of what is called 'entitlements' spending to the U.S. to chronic annual budget deficits over the past two decades. By entitlements are meant primarily social security benefits and Medicare. But the claim that excessive spending on entitlements has been a major cause of chronic budget deficits (and thus the rising public debt level) has little validity. Social security has not only *not* contributed to government deficit spending and government debt, but has reduced what would otherwise be even larger annual budget deficits and therefore even greater public debt.

In 1984 the U.S. Congress passed an historic revision of how social security was financed, in anticipation of the coming retirement of more than 75 million 'baby boomers' after 2010. The payroll tax for social security was amended to increase the tax rate and the level of taxable income, and the latter was indexed to inflation. That meant the payroll tax would rise every year thereafter, which it has. The social security system is what is called a 'pay as you go' system. That means those paying the payroll tax provide the funds for those currently in retirement. The payroll tax was amended, however, to more than cover for those in retirement and to build up a major reserve in anticipation of the future baby-boomer retirees surge. As a result of the over-taxation, the Social Security Trust fund accumulated massive surpluses of hundreds of billions in some years over the next nearly quarter of a century, 1986–2009. Those surpluses have been used by the federal government to 'offset' the annual U.S. budget deficits. The accumulated amount has been, by some estimates, nearly $2.5 trillion. That transfer of funds from the Social Security Trust has, in short, reduced the amount of government debt accumulation—not increased government debt levels! That transfer from the 'entitlements' to the U.S. general budget to offset deficits and debt will continue until such time as more baby boomers retire and the annual surplus in the Social Security Trust is exhausted. That is expected to occur around 2017, give or take a year. Entitlement spending thus has not been responsible for excessive federal spending, deficits, and debt run-up, but just the opposite: it has served to reduce the annual deficits and debt.

In addition to tax restructuring and avoidance trends, and government war spending, a third and increasing element in growing government deficits and debt has been successive government bailouts of banks and other financial institutions in the wake of successive financial crises that have been occurring since the 1980s. For example, the Savings and Loan housing crisis that erupted in the 1980s required bailout funding of between $250 billion and $500 billion, depending on estimates. The latest banking crisis, that emerged in 2007 and is still continuing, has cost anywhere from $2.5 trillion to $5 trillion and will undoubtedly cost much more before it is over. In between, there have been additional unknown bailout costs associated with the Federal Reserve 'assisting' U.S. banks and hedge funds to bail out foreign banks, investors, and foreign government borrowers during the 1990s and the early 2000s.

One might argue that by providing excessive credit for speculative investing purposes in recent decades, banks have not only contributed to repeated financial crises and bailouts, but have in turn caused government debt to rise as a result of bailouts. Bailouts occur in two forms: directly via the U.S. Treasury and institutions such as the Federal Deposit Insurance Corporation (FDIC), as well as indirectly via the U.S. Federal Reserve Bank. Part of the federal government debt totals should therefore be added to the business-financial debt total. Financial business sector debt is actually higher than the federal 'Flow of Funds' data in Table 1.3 reflect. The total $46 trillion in total debt run-up since 1980, and especially the $28 trillion of that $46 trillion added since 2000, is therefore underestimated in Table 1.3 for the business-financial category and overestimated for the government.

Business pundits who choose to focus on government debt as the main problem tend alternatively to blame the consumer for the excessive rise in total debt levels in the U.S. economy. The oft-heard phrase is that 'consumers have been living beyond their means.' But a closer look at the composition of consumer debt does not support that claim.

Consumer debt is divided into mortgage debt and consumer debt. Mortgage debt is residential home loans, and consumer debt is auto loans, student loans, credit card debt, revolving installment loans, personal loans, and the like. Consumer debt has risen barely by $1 trillion since 2000, from $1.4 trillion to $2.5 trillion. In contrast, business-financial debt has accelerated by $11 trillion, from $6 trillion in 1998 to more than $17 trillion by 2008. Normal population growth accounts for part of the $1 trillion added consumer debt. Another contributing factor is the banks pushing credit cards on everyone over the age of 16 during the last decade. Another factor is consumers—especially those among the roughly 91 million households earning less than $80,000 annually—who have had to resort to credit usage to maintain their standard of living. It is a fact, for example, that since 1982 the real average weekly earnings of the approximately 110 million non-supervisory production and service employees in the U.S. is less today in real spendable dollars than it was in 1982.[20] Whether measured in terms of the 91 million households—the 'bottom' 80 percent of the income distribution—or in terms of the 110 million non-supervisory employees category—the fact is that their wages and weekly earnings (i.e. wages times hours worked) has stagnated now for more than a quarter of a century. Their turning to credit to maintain a standard of living was inevitable—and decidedly not an example of 'living beyond their means.'

The other element of debt accrued by households in recent decades is residential mortgage debt. But, as in the case of consumer debt, mortgage debt has not increased any more rapidly than other areas of debt accumulation when the subprime-driven home mortgage boom of 2002–07 is factored out. As pointed out in the footnote to Table 1.3, approximately $2.4 trillion of household mortgage debt will be either written off or transferred as lower-value bad-asset debt back to the banks and financial institutions that pushed these mortgages onto consumers during the housing boom of 2002–06 when clearly they could not afford them. More than $4 trillion in residential mortgage debt was incurred between 2002 and 2006. More than half of that has been estimated as subprime mortgages, Alt-A prime mortgages, or equally risky interest-only mortgages, option adjustable rate mortgages (ARMs), equity loans, lines of credit, 'jumbo' loans over $417,000, and the like. Some of that mortgage debt represents first-time homebuyers enticed into loans by banks by less than ethical means. Or it represents pre-existing homeowners refinancing homes in order to pay for soaring health care costs, usurious student loans to pay for escalating education costs for their children, or other 'big ticket' items they could no longer afford due to stagnating real earnings.

When the amount is shifted from household mortgage to financial institutions, the rise in household mortgage debt is no greater than the rise in household consumer debt in percentage terms. Total household debt thus roughly doubled from 1998 to 2008, just as it had from 1988 to 1998. That doubling is, of course, not an indication that 'all is well' on the consumer front over the past three decades. The doubling of consumer debt in fact is an indicator of growing 'consumption fragility,' which will be discussed in more detail in a later chapter. But the doubling in comparison to other categories of debt accumulation is no greater for consumers than for government.

The big contrast is between consumer and government debt, on the one hand, and business debt—financial sector business in particular. The tripling of business-financial institution debt every decade since 1978 is the real story behind the excessive run-up of debt in the U.S. economy over the last 30 years. And that story, as this book will try to explain, is a tale about the shift to speculative investing as the primary cause of runaway debt accumulation.

DEFLATION AS A CHARACTERISTIC

Deflation can be defined in several ways. It generally means a fall in price level that is negative; not just a decline in the rate of increase in inflation (which is called 'disinflation'). But the question immediately arises, which price level? Consumer prices? Wholesale prices? Prices companies charge each other? Prices used to calculate GDP? For our purposes, 'deflation' will refer to negative level change in both consumer prices and wholesale prices, as measured in terms of the Consumer Price Index (CPI) and the Producer Price Index (PPI).

But we are still only talking about product or commodity prices. Deflation (and inflation) also occurs in the case of asset prices. Inflation-deflation may also take place in terms of labor market prices, or what is more commonly called wages. These three sets of prices—asset prices, product (consumer and producer), and wages—are critical to the processes by which Epic Recessions emerge and evolve, and sometimes even make the transition to classic depressions. How deflation in the three price systems transmits to, and feeds back upon, each of the other price systems is also important. Finally, deflation plays a major role in how debt-unwinding after a financial crisis translates into defaults. Together the processes by which debt–deflation–default interact explain much of why and how Epic Recessions emerge and evolve.

Some further clarifying definitions are necessary at this point. Asset prices may refer to physical assets, such as industrial structures, office buildings, factories, shopping malls, hotels, multi-family housing, single-family residential housing, and countless other structures produced and used by business or government. Physical assets include equipment of all kinds, from transport vehicles to personal computers, as well as software and other similar 'soft' equipment. But asset prices can and do refer to financial assets or instruments. These may include common and preferred stock, bonds of many kinds and grades of quality, commercial paper, and what are called securitized assets of various kinds in which bonds and other financial instruments are combined into a new or 'derived' instrument, sometimes called a 'derivative,' of which many forms have proliferated in the past decade.

It is necessary to broadly define wages also, referring not only to hourly pay but to weekly earnings (i.e. hourly rate of pay times hours worked), and to include even broader indicators of pay like fringe benefits and other compensation.

We are interested in all three price systems in our analysis: asset prices, product prices, and wages. Consequently, asset prices will include both physical and financial assets. Product prices will include both consumer and producer prices. Wages are hereafter broadly defined as weekly earnings, plus benefit compensation, paid leave, and all forms of supplemental pay covering the roughly 110 million non-supervisory production and service employees in the U.S. Salaries, bonuses, and other forms of compensation for senior managers, and even mid-level management, are excluded.

Having thus defined the three price systems that are all subject to various degrees of deflation in Epic Recession, deflation in Epic Recessions is distinguished from normal recessions and depressions as follows:

In Epic Recessions, asset price deflation ranges 10 percent and 40 percent over a six- to twelve-month period. Product prices fall 2–7 percent, while wage cuts and wage deflation begin. In instances of depression, in contrast, asset and product prices fall deeper and longer and wage-cutting becomes generalized. In normal recessions, asset prices (in particular stocks) may deflate, but the declines are short and shallow; product price deflation rarely occurs and typically no more than 1 percent annually; and wage deflation is not at first an issue.

A full account of the three forms of deflation for the current Epic Recession will be given in later chapters directly addressing the Epic Recession of 2007–10. For present purposes, it is sufficient to note that the current Epic Recession has qualified in terms of asset, product, and wage deflation, as described immediately above. Briefly, both residential and commercial property asset prices fell from peaks to lows in late 2009 by 30 percent and 25 percent, respectively (with commercial property prices still in freefall as of late 2009); stock asset prices fell by 55 percent, and other forms of asset prices by well over 10 percent. Consumer product prices plunged by about 3 percent in the fourth quarter of 2008 alone and just under 2 percent year to year. Wholesale or producer prices fell by more than 5 percent. And wage deflation has clearly begun to spread throughout the economy in various forms and growing sectors.[21]

In addition to describing deflation quantitatively, it is no less important to address the question of how, in the case of Epic Recession, the three price systems are related and mutually interdependent. More on this in the following two chapters. But for now, as a preview, one can briefly explain the general relationship as follows: as Epic Recession evolves, asset price deflation begins to 'spill over' and provoke product price declines, which lead, after a lag in turn, to wage-cutting as well. Whether asset price deflation is moderate or significant and how quickly it occurs is a major determinant of the severity of product price deflation. Both asset and product price deflation severity in turn strongly influence how quickly and deeply wage deflation occurs in turn. The magnitude and quality of debt incurred during the boom period has a major influence on the subsequent asset price deflation, and thus through asset deflation, on product and wage deflation. Asset deflation exacerbates what in the next chapters are described as financial fragility. Wage deflation exacerbates what will be described as consumption fragility. Prior to and early in Epic Recessions, feedback effects between the three price systems begin but are not yet significantly widespread.

In depressions, asset price collapse is broad-based across multiple forms of assets, typically ranges from –40 percent to –90 percent, and is multi-year in duration. Consumer price deflation is –10 percent or more annually, producer price declines vary from –10 percent to –40 percent, and wage deflation is double-digit. Both consumer and producer price deflation also occur over multiple years. Asset price deflation spills over to the other price systems in a major way. Deflation is generalized across all three price systems. Asset price deflation is often well beyond –50 percent, product deflation approaches or exceeds –50 percent, and consumer price deflation is also well above double-digit levels. Meanwhile, feedback effects between the three price systems intensify. In terms of comparisons, normal recessions experience slight to moderate asset price deflation, typically limited to common stock prices.

Depressions are also characterized by the development and spread of what's called 'deflationary expectations,' which do not exist in normal recessions and which just begin to emerge in Epic Recessions. This is a condition in which, because prices are expected to continue to fall, consumers and businesses wait for prices to actually fall further and, in the process, create additional downward price pressures that in fact drive the price deflation deeper and wider. Deflationary expectations may infect all three price systems at some point. Of the three price systems, asset prices are the most volatile and financial asset prices even more volatile than physical assets. Deflation is a major cause of default, business and consumers alike. Default in turn results in further significant downward pressure on asset deflation and through it to product and wage deflation.

One of the major hallmarks of an Epic Recession's transformation to a bona fide depression is when both asset and product price deflation continue unabated and when wage-cutting and wage reduction is generalized. To contain an Epic Recession and prevent its transition to depression it is thus necessary, among other things, to prevent significant spillover of asset price deflation to product prices and, in turn, from product prices to wages. Containment also necessarily requires the prevention of deflationary expectations taking hold, which takes place and spreads in later stages of Epic Recession.

In terms of product price deflation, in normal recessions select categories of goods or services may decline, but the general price level measured as CPI or PPI does not (or if so, only slightly and very temporarily). In Epic Recession, product price deflation occurs but annual declines do not reach double-digit levels, which may be the case in depressions. In normal recessions, product prices 'disinflate'—i.e. the rate of inflation subsides—but actual declines in CPI or PPI rarely occur. Product prices rarely actually turn negative in normal recessions. If they do, the declines are relatively shallow and/or of duration of less than six months. Product prices slow down in their rate of increase or, at very worse, fall between 0 percent and −1.5 percent for a short period. Wage deflation pressure is even weaker. Feedback effects between the three price systems are largely non-existent.

When consumer product price deflation reaches and consistently exceeds annual declines of more than −5 percent it is typically an indicator that the momentum of forces in the real economy is such that an Epic Recession event may be approaching a transition to depression. For example, in the case of the 1929–31 period—which represents in our analysis an example of a 'Type II' Epic Recession—consumer prices fell roughly −6 percent in 1930 and another −8 percent in 1931 before breaking into the −10 percent annual range in 1932.

Defining wages as weekly earnings plus benefits, paid leave, and supplemental pay forms received by the 110 million non-supervisory production and service employees means wages are considered as a pool of multi-form earnings received by those in the labor force whose total annual income derives overwhelmingly from the work they directly perform (and therefore is not commingled with other forms of capital or transfer income).

This revised approach to measuring wage deflation is necessary because the U.S. government defines wages differently in its various databases, creating different, often conflicting meanings of what constitutes 'wage' and often including what is clearly non-wage incomes under a definition of wages. For example, the Bureau of Economic Affairs (BEA), an agency of the U.S. Department of Commerce that calculates GDP statistics, defines wages in a wholly inappropriate way. Redefining the meaning of what is a wage, the BEA considers 65 percent of the income of business proprietors as 'wages,' when that 65 percent should properly be defined as business profits. The transfer of 65 percent of the profits of 7 million proprietors serves to reduce the total profits share of national income while artificially raising the 'wages' share of national income. With proprietors' profits rising significantly since 1998, the inclusion seriously distorts the change in wages. Other U.S. government databases and surveys include wages and salaries, where salaries include upper- and senior-level executive management where a record escalation of total compensation has been the norm in the U.S. for several decades.

Nor is simply focusing on reductions in the hourly wage rate a sufficient way to consider wage deflation. Hourly wages may not be cut, but hours of work reduced greatly. 'Wage' deflation over-broadly defined, as it is by the government, may hardly register if the tens of millions of managers, supervisors, proprietors, and others are able to maintain or increase their salaries (i.e. 'wages') during an Epic Recession.

'Wage' deflation as defined in our approach picks up several important structural changes in labor markets and the workforce in the U.S. that are lost in official definitions and data on wages. Changing labor markets in the

U.S. and the dramatic weakening of collective bargaining and the unions has resulted in the creation of perhaps more than 40 million 'contingent' workers. These are those who are employed but who do not have a full time or permanent job. Their wage compensation is roughly 70 percent that of permanent employees. Moreover, the benefits composition of their total weekly earnings is typically 10–20 percent. There appears to be a cyclical and even longer-term structural trend toward creating more involuntary part-time workers, not just in the U.S. but globally. In the current U.S. recession alone, perhaps 10 million have been added to the ranks of the involuntary part-time employed. This means hours of work and weekly income deflation for tens of millions. That is properly a form of 'wage deflation' in the broader sense.

Hours of work are also significantly reduced in the course of Epic Recession and constitute yet another form of wage deflation. Average hours worked at mid year 2009 in the U.S., for example, were at an historic all-time low of 33 hours per week. A fast-developing trend across all industries in 2009 was 'involuntary furloughs,' or employer-mandated days off without pay, typically one to four days a month. Whether due to part-time conversions, full-time permanent workers' reduction of hours, furloughs, or elimination of overtime work, these are all properly forms of wage-cutting, the result of which is de facto 'wage deflation' when properly defined.

Wage deflation occurs as well indirectly when state and local governments pay local employers a subsidy to help retain jobs. Another trend is for workers to agree to give up part of their wages, to take an absolute hourly or weekly earnings cut, in order to save the jobs of others in their workforce that the company had planned to permanently lay off. The total 'wage pool' at the company is thus reduced—a collective wage cut. In addition, wage deflation may assume the form of a greater relative shift of costs of health care, pension, and other benefits by employers to their workers. Shifting health care costs, eliminating employer contributions to 401k personal pension plans, and reducing paid holidays/vacations—all are bona fide forms of wage reduction.

In Epic Recessions new forms of wage deflation multiply, spread and deepen. In normal recessions they are seldom resorted to by business, at least in the magnitude in which they occur in Epic Recessions. In depressions, direct reductions of hourly wages are the more dominant form of wage-cutting. In the current Epic Recession, the 10 million additional part-time employees, the general reduction of hours worked, the spreading furloughs trend, the reduction in employer contributions to health care, the elimination of paid holidays/vacations, and the suspension of employer payments to 401k pensions, are significant indications of wage deflation pressures occurring. These new forms of wage deflation are occurring, moreover, on base hourly wage rates and weekly earnings that have effectively stagnated in the U.S. since at least the early 1980s.

As will be argued subsequently, a nearly three-decades-long income stagnation, impacting literally many tens of millions in the workforce, has created a condition in the U.S. economy called, for lack of a better term, 'consumption fragility.' Both massive job layoffs and new forms of wage-cutting together cause a further deterioration in consumption fragility as the Epic Recession emerges and evolves.

DEFAULT AS A CHARACTERISTIC

Default as a characteristic has several dimensions. First, there is business-corporate default. This may include either financial or non-financial corporations. Financial corporations include banks in a traditional sense, or what is referred to as the (quasi-) regulated commercial banking system, and what are sometimes called financial intermediaries or the 'shadow' banking system. The latter is composed largely of virtually unregulated (until 2008) institutions like hedge funds, broker-dealers, mutual funds, and various additional forms. Outright failures or bankruptcies are a form of default, where the company (financial or non-financial) is liquidated, i.e. sold off in whole or part, as a result of filing bankruptcy. Or bankruptcy may be temporary, as the institution is reorganized and subsequently returns to operation. In the case of banks, they are often 'suspended,' then reorganized and return to operations. As used in this book, corporate default means either suspension of a corporation or when it is sold off in whole or part, i.e. 'failure' in the broad sense. But both failure and suspension are defaults, as are restructuring and reorganization.

Consumer default may be defined narrowly as the filing of personal bankruptcy, or more broadly as becoming 'delinquent' in the repayment of bills due for a given period of time. Consumer bankruptcy filing is certainly an indicator of default but is actually an end consequence of a prior delinquency or default. Whether personal or corporate, the final act of bankruptcy and dissolution of assets left does not pick up the true extent of the economic stress. Prior conditions of delinquency, suspension, and the initial act of filing of bankruptcy in one of the latter's various forms constitute the broader concept of default as used here. This broader concept is a more useful measure of serious business and consumer stress.

Default is defined as when the holder of a debt fails to make timely and full payments due on that debt. Payments typically include both principal and interest. Thus a homeowner with a mortgage payment may be delinquent when making a payment beyond 60 days' overdue, a time period after which default is considered as having occurred. In the case of corporate default, default is typically defined legally by each form of debt, and time periods vary in which it is required to 'service the debt,' or make payments of principal and/or interest.

In 2009 Moody's Investor Services estimated the corporate default rate for high yield (i.e. junk) bond debt to rise in 2010 in the U.S. between 12.2 percent and 14.6 percent.[22] That's an increase from 4.5 percent at the end of 2008 and from a mere 1 percent at the end of 2007. The European default rate was predicted to rise even higher, to 21 percent from 2.0 percent the year earlier. This particular corporate default rate is for the 'bottom tier' 15 percent of corporations in terms of their debt stress. 15 percent represents a huge number of the thousands of companies in this category. Moody's listed

283 large companies as especially likely to default, of which 45 percent are predicted to do so in 2009–10, representing $260 billion in assets.[23] The other major corporate rating agencies, Standard & Poor's and Fitch Ratings, reported similar trends. Standard & Poor's estimated 200 very large junk-bond dependent companies would default in 2009, representing an even larger total of $350 billion. An even more extreme assessment by Deutsche Bank analyst Jim Reid predicted that 53 percent of corporations that have issued junk bonds will default over the next five years.[24]

In the two prior recessions, 1990–91 and 2000–01, default rates peaked at levels of 11.1 percent and 12.1 percent, respectively. In the case of the depression of the 1930s a peak rate of 15.4 percent was reached in 1933, according to Standard & Poor's. The current Epic Recession is thus predicting levels of non-financial default closer to the 1930s than recent normal recessions.

In addition to corporate borrowing in the junk bond markets, there's the more than $700 billion commercial property market composed of office buildings, industrial structures, hotels, malls, resorts, etc. The third ratings company, Fitch, predicted a fivefold increase in defaults and delinquencies in the commercial property market.[25] As many as 41 percent of delinquent loans are expected to default, according to the FDIC.[26] Much more will be said in later chapters about this critical market, and the building and management companies in it, which at year-end 2009 appear to be approaching a 'subprime' mortgage-like implosion.

In the area of general loans to small-medium business, the crisis is no less acute. The lender to thousands of such businesses, CIT Group Inc., is projected to default as of late October 2009. Should it do so, it would become the fifth largest company in U.S. history to go bankrupt, with losses in excess of $70 billion, with $52 billion in outstanding credit default swaps. CIT's stress is a reflection of the hundreds, perhaps thousands, of its smaller corporate borrowers who are likely approaching default as well. In 2007 CIT provided $85 billion in loans and financing; in the first half of 2009 it has provided only $4.4 billion.[27] This means tens of billions of loans, at minimum, not flowing into smaller businesses from this one company alone—businesses that are too small or otherwise unable to access even the junk bond market.

The projected much higher corporate default rate for 2009–10 is in part due to the widespread practice of what is called securitization, as well as what appears to be a greater willingness of banks in recent years to roll over, or refinance, junk bond debt in the initial years, 2007–09, of the recent recession. Banks have also been delaying and postponing default proceedings on companies failing to make debt payments as a result of the widespread bank issuance since 2000 of what are called 'covenant lites' (allowing businesses to roll over debt in lieu of default), payments in kind (PIKs), debt exchanges (equity for loans), unused open lines of credit, and the like. This has created a "new breed of zombie companies—those which survive simply to repay their debts but cannot move forward because their debts remain so large."[28] 'Zombie' companies may be either banks, financial intermediaries/'shadow banks', or non-financial companies. To the extent these grow in number reflects continued and increasing financial fragility in the system. It may mean that defaults are being prevented or 'bottlenecked,' in the short run, only to surge in even greater numbers at some later point.

A survey by the research arm of the French group, Allianz, for example, in May 2009 predicted that bankruptcies globally would rise 35 percent, which follows a prior year, 2008, rise of 27 percent. The study noted that rarely do bankruptcy rates rise more than 10 percent in a given year, and never two years in a row at double-digit. For the U.S. the projected two-year rates of increase were even higher, at 54 percent and 45 percent.[29] Thus, it may be argued,

Non-financial corporate default rates in normal recessions barely attain double-digit levels, while in Epic Recessions they typically range from 10 percent to 20 percent or more.

It is somewhat more difficult to compare financial institution default in Epic Recession to normal recession and depression. Bank suspensions and failures don't appear as much of a problem in terms of number of failures prior to the recessions of 1990–91 and 2001, since financial crises were generally not associated with normal recessions prior to the 1980s.

Conversely, the number of 'shadow' banks and financial institutions have exploded after 1990. Shadow banks need to be included in any tally of default in the current Epic Recession. As others have estimated, the shadow banking segment by 2007 held roughly the same total assets as the traditional banking system, around $10 trillion each.[30] It appears, for example, that as many as 2,000 hedge fund shadow financial institutions disappeared after 2007. In just the six months from October 2008 through March 2009, more than 1,150 hedge funds shut down. Comparison is made difficult, however, since many hedge funds simply shut their doors due to mass withdrawals rather than having formally defaulted or gone bankrupt in a traditional sense. The hedge fund industry's total assets are predicted to shrink another $450 billion in 2009 after having fallen $600 billion in 2008 and $200 billion in 2007.[31] Then there's another shadow financial institution called the private equity firm. A creation of the last decade or so, the default rate for private equity firms is projected to rise to 20–40 percent, according to a study by Boston Consulting Inc..

The recent collapse of the shadow banking system—large segments of which are the creations of the last decade and a half—is a unique occurrence among post-1945 economic recessions in the U.S. It makes the current Epic Recession different, i.e. much worse and, in terms of financial defaults, relatively difficult to compare. Despite the difficulties, however, the various estimations of financial institutions' default rates show the current Epic Recession is, and will continue to be, more severe than prior normal recessions.

Apart from shadow bank defaults, comparing traditional bank defaults in the current Epic Recession with prior normal recessions is still difficult, given that even traditional bank suspensions and defaults typically lag a crisis by several years, and the process of bank defaults in today's Epic Recession may therefore only just have begun. Thus far, about 100 FDIC-insured smaller, regional, and community banks have 'failed,' with another 100 projected for the final months of 2009 as failures accelerate. Banks on the FDIC's 'troubled' list number about 900. A thousand or more banks may thus default in the most serious sense of 'failure' or even suspension before the current Epic Recession runs its course.

Comparing Epic Recession financial default is made even more problematic, given government policy and practice in the current Epic Recession of ensuring that the so-called 'big 19' banks do not default publicly and formally, even when technically they are insolvent and in earlier crises would have formally defaulted. It was likely in mid 2009 that perhaps as many as half of the 'too big to fail' big 19 banks in the U.S. remained insolvent, and therefore technically bankrupt, held up only by trillions of dollars of injection in the form of government-provided loans and liquidity. Bailing out banks, financial intermediaries, shadow banks, and even non-bank companies today thus means providing government-taxpayer funding to prevent default from technically occurring.

Other difficulties in comparing financial institution default occur when looking back to the most recent depression of the 1930s. Many thousands of banks failed between 1929 and 1933, were suspended and reorganized, or else went bankrupt in the formal sense. In 1933–34 alone, as many as 4,000 banks officially 'failed.' But once the FDIC law was passed, the failures virtually stopped. Thus comparing pre-FDIC with post-FDIC eras poses significant difficulty.

Notwithstanding these various difficulties in comparing default in Epic Recessions with normal recession and depressions, it is probably safe to say:

Financial institution defaults in normal recession occur in the tens or at most several hundreds, in depressions in the multiple thousands, and during Epic Recession in the low thousands, when shadow banks and other financial intermediaries as well as more traditional banks and financial institutions are considered.

Consumers are the final category for consideration in terms of the default characteristic. There are several ways to consider consumer default. One, of course, is personal bankruptcies. However, major changes in bankruptcy laws since 2000 make cross-time comparisons between the recent Epic Recession and prior normal recessions and depressions difficult. The filing of personal bankruptcy before 2000 was relatively more easy than after 2003 and subsequent changes in bankruptcy laws that made it more difficult for individuals (and easier for businesses). Personal bankruptcy filing may be caused by non-economic personal factors, moreover, making it a less reliable indicator of economic conditions. Personal bankruptcy filing is therefore not a good indicator of consumer default.

On the other hand, residential foreclosures, homeowners in formal foreclosure proceedings but not yet foreclosed, and mortgage delinquency rates involving failure of 60 days or more, are reasonable indicators of consumer default. Also relatively easy to quantify are consumer defaults on credit cards, auto loans, student loans, and personal and installment loans. Consumer credit card defaults occur when the bank or other issuers of the cards discontinue the cards and assume liability for the card balances. Similarly for auto loans, which default when the financial company holding the loan repossesses the vehicle; student loans, when the agency responsible declares the loan delinquent after failure to make payments for a defined period; or personal installment credit loans, when failure to pay is referred to a collections agency.

In the U.S. in mid 2009, foreclosures on residential mortgages reached nearly 6 million out of a total of roughly 55 million mortgages outstanding. Another 1.5 million are in 'foreclosure proceedings,' for a total of 7.5 million either foreclosed or about to become foreclosed. In addition to the 7.5 million there are pre-foreclosure delinquencies. According to the Mortgage Bankers' Association in the U.S., the delinquency rate on residential properties at mid year 2009 had risen to 9.24 percent from 6.4 percent a year earlier. That's another 5 million or so.[32] That amounts to about one in four of the 55 million mortgages in some stage of default, ranging from serious delinquency to concluded foreclosure.

In terms of credit cards, the delinquency rate by mid 2009 had reached roughly 7 percent, the highest on record since tracking in 1991, and was still rising. It compares to the less than 5 percent rate at the peak of the 2001 recession and a roughly 5 percent rate in 1991. Not only were the rates highest on record, but the amounts written off by bank card issuers reached record levels in percentage and absolute terms as well, running at about $150 billion a year on an annual basis with a 69 percent increase in 2009 over 2008.[33]

The absence of credit card data for the 1930s does not allow accurate Epic Recession versus depression comparison. But auto loans did exist, having first been created in the 1920s. Auto loan delinquencies at the start of the financial crisis in August 2007 were at 2.9 percent. At the end of 2008 they were running at 9.9 percent.[34] The national average for defaults on automobile contracts during the depression, based on data from the National Association of Sales Finance Companies, showed an overall default rate (i.e. percentage of cars repossessed) in 1929 of 4.2 percent—and that after nearly "one quarter of all American households purchased a car" in 1929. In 1930 the rate had risen to 5.4 percent, but escalated thereafter to 10.4 percent in 1932 and 15.1 percent in 1938.[35]

Given the recent history of availability of private market-provided student loans, data do not exist for a comparison with depression in the 1930s. During normal recessions prior to 1990, non-payment did not necessarily result in consumer default, as has been the case with bank-originated student loans in the past decade or so. Nonetheless, student loan default rates have risen by 50 percent from 2007 to 2009, or default rates from 4.6 percent to 6.9 percent of outstanding loans.[36] And this does not account for loans in 'forbearance,' where lenders allow borrowers to suspend payments temporarily. The 6.9 percent is thus likely higher.

In normal recessions, home foreclosures and delinquencies rates range typically well below 5 percent and those of commercial property defaults even much lower. Corporate bond and loan default rates remain below 5 percent, while credit card and consumer loan default rates (autos, student, personal) are also less than 5 percent. In contrast, in Epic Recessions, home mortgage foreclosures and residential-commercial property delinquency rates typically exceed 10 percent, as do credit card defaults and auto and student loan default rates. In depressions, default rates in all the above categories tend to exceed 15 percent.

The preceding presentation of data on quantitative characteristics of Epic Recession has been provided, in part, in order to clarify the nature of the recent economic crisis more concretely—in contrast to those who merely proclaim it has been 'worse than' other post-1945 recessions but 'not yet as bad as' the depression of the 1930s. As discussed in the introductory chapter, economists by and large have been content to describe the recession with vague generalities and phrases such as 'Great Recession' or a 'Near Depression. But to understand the nature and dynamics of the recent Epic Recession—and thus its possible evolution and potential solution—it is necessary to understand the crisis beyond mere generalities. That starts with understanding in what ways and how Epic Recession is differentiated from normal recessions and depressions, both in quantitative as well as qualitative terms. In this chapter, a first step was taken toward that first task of quantitative differentiation.

A second, more important objective of this chapter has been to identify and describe some essential forces unique to Epic Recession. This chapter has therefore introduced the idea that three of the quantitative characteristics—debt, deflation, and default—are central to understanding the nature of the current Epic Recession, as well as how and why it has evolved differently from normal recessions, as well as how and why it also contains the potential to transform to a bona fide depression under certain conditions. This idea of a debt–deflation–default nexus will be considered further in subsequent chapters; in particular, its critical relationship to the additional deeper factors of financial and consumption fragility, which will also be considered in more depth in various of the chapters that follow. How these five elements—debt, deflation, default, and financial and consumption fragility—impact and mutually determine each other is central to the analysis that follows. So is the even deeper relationship between these elements and the fundamental shift toward speculative forms of investment in the U.S. in recent decades and the various forces—institutional, policy, and other—that have enabled and driven that speculative shift.

The next chapter, Chapter 2, undertakes a further description of that shift and its enabling, contributing, and precipitating causes—institutional and non-institutional alike—and its relationship to financial and consumption fragility. Chapter 3 then considers the ways in which the quantitative and qualitative factors transmit and feed back upon each other, mutually determine each other, and in the process drive the evolution of Epic Recession—either to a condition of extended economic stagnation or to descent into depression.

2
Qualitative Characteristics of Epic Recession

This chapter focuses on qualitative characteristics of Epic Recession. These include financial fragility, financial instability, the growing influence of the 'shadow banking' system, consumption fragility, the growing weight and mix of speculative forms of investment in the economy, and the tendency toward synchronization across global economies. None of these characteristics exist, or their presence is minimal, in normal recessions.

FINANCIAL FRAGILITY

Financial fragility is a condition in which banks and non-financial companies are unable to cover their payments that come due on prior debt. Inability to make payments, sometimes called 'servicing of the debt,' may occur because a company experienced a fall in its cash or liquid assets on hand. It may also occur because the company previously took on excessive levels of additional debt. That additional debt may also be of poorer quality—i.e. debt of a higher interest payment or of shorter term. Debt servicing may therefore deteriorate due either to cash-liquid asset decline, debt level rise, debt quality deterioration—or all three.

Companies that experience rising debt payments typically have engaged in over-aggressive acquisitions and expansions during the boom phase of the business cycle, taking on excess debt to finance that expansion and/or assuming the debt load of the company acquired as well. The accumulated and more costly debt must still be 'serviced,' but now there is less cash or liquid assets on hand with which to make the payments. What this all describes is an increase in the company's 'financial fragility'—i.e. a growing difficulty in making debt payments as the income for making payments declines, the total debt rises, and the cost of the rising debt grows.

Both quantity and quality of debt are therefore important determinants of financial fragility. But so is a decline in cash flow and liquid assets that might be quickly converted to cash needed to cover debt payments. Refinancing of past debt by issuing new debt—i.e. 'rolling over the debt,' as it is called—may raise the payments required to service the new debt. Having 'rolled over' or refinanced the debt, a company may appear as if its financial fragility has been reduced when, in fact, the refinancing may actually exacerbate financial fragility. The new debt is larger, may carry a higher rate of interest and a shorter term. The total debt cost to the company may in fact have risen. And if the company's cash flow does not rise, then the ratio of cash flow to debt deteriorates.

The simple definition of financial fragility is therefore the ratio of business debt to cash flow. It may be estimated using corporate profits (i.e. the originating source of cash flow) as a substitute for cash flow. Using banking and finance industry profits, Table 2.1 shows a declining profits-to-debt ratio and thus growing financial fragility for the banking and finance industry between 1980 and 2008—i.e. a faster growth of debt than growth of industry profits.

Table 2.1 Estimating Financial Fragility: Bank and Financial Institutions, Domestic U.S.

Year	Finance Industry Profits ($ billions)	Finance Industry Debt ($ billions)	Profits-to-Debt Ratio
1980	34	578	1 to 17.0
1990	92	2,613	1 to 28.4
2000	189	8,157	1 to 43.1
2008	278	17,083	1 to 61.4

Sources: Data for domestic financial institution debt are from *Flow of Funds Accounts of the United States*, Federal Reserve Board statistical release, Second Quarter 2009, September 17, 2009, Table D.3. Data for domestic financial sector profits are from Bureau of Economic Analysis, *National Income Accounts*, revised August 20, 2009, Table 6.16 b-d.

From Table 2.1 it is clear that financial fragility in banking and finance has been growing in the system for decades. More ominous still, that fragility appears to have continued to grow following the eruption of the current financial crisis in 2007.

But financial fragility is not simply the ratio of profits to the level of debt; a closer approximation of financial fragility is estimated by comparing cash flow to debt. In this case, cash flow for all corporations to total corporate debt. This is represented in Table 2.2.

Table 2.2 Estimating Financial Fragility: Total Corporate Cash Flow and Debt, Domestic U.S.

Year	Corporate Cash Flow ($ billions)	Corporate Debt ($ billions)	Cash Flow-to-Debt Ratio
1980	271	1,488	1 to 5.5
1990	505	5,155	1 to 10.2
2000	877	12,790	1 to 14.5
2008	1,452	23,004	1 to 15.8

Sources: Federal Reserve *Flow of Funds*, Table D.3 and Bureau of Economic Analysis, *Undistributed Profits*, Tables 6.21 b-d, and *Capital Consumption Allowances*, Tables 6.22 b-d.

As in the example of financial fragility in banking and finance, total corporate financial fragility inclusive of all corporations (financial and non-financial) has grown steadily worse. The worsening of financial fragility for all corporations together is not as dramatic as for financial institutions, as might be presumed. But the trend is similar, nonetheless. The growth in the debt load for non-financial corporations, while significant, has not nearly equaled the increased levels of debt for financial corporations. Non-financial corporate debt since 1980 grew, for example, by $6.26 trillion, and by $15.61 trillion for banks and financial institutions.

The most accurate estimate of financial fragility is represented by the ratio of cash flow to the payments required to cover debt. Unfortunately, given the great variability in debt service payment terms and conditions, it is not possible to 'aggregate' the terms of payment across industries, let alone the entire economy. But the magnitudes and undeniable trends of both profits to debt and cash flow to debt indicate that financial fragility has been growing significantly since 1980 in the economy and, moreover, that fragility is accelerating and continuing to grow even after the commencement of the current financial crisis in 2007.

It appears that the more an industry is deregulated, the more likely financial fragility will rise. Recent history since 1980 shows that, once banks were deregulated, they attempted to expand by acquiring competitors. They acquired often weaker companies in the industry with serious problems of debt servicing of their own prior to acquisition. Increasing financial fragility as a result of acquisition of financially troubled competitors is exactly what happened to many of today's 'too big to fail' banks. A good example is the mega-bank, Citigroup, which had been expanding by multiple acquisitions globally for more than a decade before its de facto collapse in 2008. Its massive debt load played a major role in its de facto insolvency, which has only been prevented by a $400 billion-plus bailout by the Federal Reserve and the Treasury. A similar case is Bank of America. Its binge buying of mortgage lenders at the peak of the housing bubble all but ensured its extreme financial fragility and multi-billion-dollar bailout. Then there's Lehman Brothers and Bear Stearns, both of which made major acquisitions of housing lenders on the eve of the subprime bust. All expanded by acquisition late in the recent housing boom, taking on excess debt in order to buy up mortgage lenders. Not only did they take on debt to acquire the competitors, but that debt was also of rapidly deteriorating quality loaded with bad subprime and other residential mortgages.

Debt servicing problems due to mergers and acquisitions (M&As) applies not only to banking and finance corporations. The deregulation of other industrial sectors such as telecommunications, airlines and trucking in the 1980s and 1990s had a similar effect on leading companies in those industries as well. Deregulation means more intense competition, resulting eventually in lower product prices, and in turn revenue and cash flow problems which make it more difficult to service debt for companies taking on increased levels of debt. Deregulation thus leads to both higher debt loads and lower cash flow. Globalization has a similar effect on industries and companies as deregulation. In fact, the two often occur in tandem. Companies borrow even more as they attempt to expand abroad, adding further levels of debt, while facing more intense global competition that often translates, once again, into lower prices, revenues and cash flow. Debt servicing payments rise, as revenues and cash flow decline over time. It is possible therefore to generalize that deregulation of industries, in a context of globalizing markets and policies promoting free trade, eventually contributes to financial fragility.

A similar process occurs with 'consumption fragility' (more on which later in this chapter). Briefly, for now, consumers and households today face a decline in their disposable income (cash flow) as they are forced or enticed to take on more consumer debt in order to maintain consumption and living standards as their income stagnates or falls. Debt levels and servicing payments rise while real income stagnates or falls. Consumption fragility consequently rises. This is especially the case for the roughly 90 million of the total 114 million households in the U.S. for whom weekly earnings (hourly pay times hours worked per week) constitute overly 90 percent of their short-term income flow.

Should a company find itself unable to cover debt payments as its cash falls and its debt servicing rises, it must borrow further, preferably rolling over (i.e. refinancing) debt. If it can't roll over its existing, then it must borrow additional amounts—often on even more disadvantageous terms from the lender—and thus add to its debt level on even worse terms. Financial fragility deteriorates further.

If it can't borrow further to roll over or add debt to cover debt servicing payments, it must inevitably cut operational costs—typically its labor force and/or planned investments—in order to meet its debt payments. Jobs are cut and wages and other benefits are reduced. To raise more cash, prices of the company's products may also be reduced. If it finds that it can't cut costs or reduce prices further, then the remaining alternative is to sell off physical assets to raise cash to service debt. Buyers of assets are generally aware of the company's distressed debt situation and demand a deep asset price discount and buy only the most valued assets first. Thus, asset price deflation occurs in order to achieve quick cash, product prices are reduced in order to raise cash, and wage-labor costs are cut in order to preserve cash. The deflation across the three price systems may occur consecutively—i.e. from asset prices to product prices to wages—although in cases of severe financial fragility it may take place almost simultaneously in all three price systems.

In actual situations all three options are simultaneously undertaken. There may be other short-term options for the company as well. The company may choose to pay only the interest due on the debt and not the debt principal. But that is possible only if the terms on its original loan provides for that option, or if the lender voluntarily allows it. Other terms and conditions of the debt may also play a role. The lender may have special rights to intervene in the company's financial management, take other assets of the company and resell them, and a host of other possibilities called 'covenants.' Sometimes the company may have rights to make payments with other assets, called 'payments in kind' (PIKs). The company and lender may agree to a 'debt for equity' swap, in which the company exchanges stock for some portion of the loan's value.

If none of these short-term options are possible, the company's financial fragility reaches breaking point, at which it typically defaults on its debt payments—meaning it fails to make the payment on time. This is usually the last step toward bankruptcy filing, which itself may take several forms. The company may enter a liquidation bankruptcy where its assets are sold off to the highest bidder and the funds raised are paid to the lenders, or it may enter a restructuring bankruptcy in which the worst cash performing operations are sold off or liquidated and the lenders take control of the company in a now altered form. In either case, major reductions in employment, wages, and other labor costs are the outcome.

To sum up the process of how financial fragility typically deepens, when debt accumulation can no longer be financed out of rising asset prices or rising product prices—i.e. when inflation slows and peaks—then the debt accumulation must be serviced by other means: either by adding more debt, rolling over existing debt, cutting product prices to raise more cash, reducing wages and labor costs to preserve cash, or selling off the company's best assets to raise cash. But as a company attempts to deal with its growing financial fragility by raising more debt and engaging in deflation (asset, product, or wage) to raise cash to service debt, in effect it simultaneously increases its financial fragility. It raises cash in the short run at the expense of cash flow in the long run. Deflation is thus but a temporary solution to the worsening debt servicing problem. The same temporary limitations apply to taking on additional debt to financing existing debt servicing payments. Rolling over or adding more debt is a short-term palliative that does not resolve the growing financial fragility but actually exacerbates it in the longer term.

Debt is the means by which capital is able to expand beyond a normal historical rate. Normal rate is capital expansion financed by internal funds (profits or retained earnings) or by equity issuance—i.e. stock offerings. But internal financing implies the company is successful and has available excess retained earnings out of which to finance expansion. And even equity financing implies somewhat that the company has proven successful enough that stockholders want to buy its stock if additional shares are offered. In contrast to internal (retained earnings) or equity (stock) financing, debt financing (borrowing) requires no prior successful company economic performance. Debt financing is the means particularly suitable to finance unproven, high-risk ventures; to finance investments for companies with poor performance, or to finance investments where performance is not even an issue—i.e. where the objective is to realize short-term capital gains. Debt also has a unique advantage over other forms of financing. Unlike internal and equity financing, it has the quality of being 'leveraged'—i.e. an investor puts up a small fraction of his/her own money and borrows multiples of the remainder required for the investment. The small portion of funds committed is thus 'leveraged' into a much larger total. Because the nature of debt is to employ a third party's money, debt is more apt to be employed in far more risky investments. It is therefore a preferred form for financing speculative investments. Being so, it is not surprising that debt has exploded in recent decades as speculative forms of investing have accelerated as well. Leveraged debt and speculative investing go hand in hand. And rising asset price inflation is the glue that binds them together.

Recall Table 1.3 in the preceding chapter showing total debt accumulated in the U.S. since 1978. Of a rise in total debt, from $3.6 trillion in 1978 to $50.6 trillion in 2008, total business debt (financial and non-financial) accounted for no less than $30.6 trillion of that $50.6 trillion. That unprecedented, historic ramp-up in business debt translates into a significant increase in financial fragility—for the financial sector in general, as well as for various industries in the non-financial sector of the economy. Clearly, debt levels have been rising faster than income available to service that debt.

It is also apparent that the 'quality' of that rising debt level has continued to deteriorate as well, further intensifying financial fragility. The quality deterioration is evident in the growing volume and percentage share of non-financial debt shifting into what is called 'low speculative grade' (junk bond) corporate debt over the past decade, and especially so in the last 12–18 months as debt-stressed companies, unable to secure bank loans, have turned to junk bonds to cover operating costs. Bond issuance in 2009 was greater in volume than in 2007, while bank lending was down 69 percent compared to 2007.[1] Junk bond debt typically carries double-digit interest charges, at times in excess of 20 percent. In December 2008 junk bond borrowing rates rose to 21.8 percent. More than $100 billion in new junk bonds will have been issued in the U.S. in 2009 alone. Similar additional volumes have been issued globally in 2009 in euro, yen, and pound denominations. While junk bond issues hit record levels from late 2008 through 2009, the default rates have more than tripled over the same period, from about 3 percent to more than 10 percent.[2] Junk bond issuance allows debt-stressed companies to roll over or replace existing debt; sometimes at lower rates, but more often at the expense of adding an even larger volume of total debt and higher total cost in the longer term, thus increasing financial fragility and eventual defaults over the long run.

In the case of banks, Moody's Inc., the rating agency, has estimated that banks globally face the need to refinance $7 trillion in short-term debt over just the next two years, by 2012, plus another $3 trillion by 2015.[3] That's an historically unprecedented $10 trillion. Moreover, the average maturity for such debt is at its shortest in three decades, having fallen in just the last five years from 7.2 to 4.7 years. Such debt levels and debt quality are a clear sign of major problems with financial fragility remaining deep within the banking system. Over the long run this fragility means that bank profits will remain under significant pressure. In turn, bank lending, which has declined every month from October 2008 in the U.S., will continue to contract or remain at historically low levels. Furthermore, once the Federal Reserve and other central banks cease providing below-zero real interest loans to banks, as is currently the case, bank loan rates will no doubt rise. Non-bank companies will thereafter find credit even more difficult to obtain in 2010–12 than they do now.

In addition to debt levels and quality, defaults and bankruptcy are another clear indicator of continuing financial fragility. Both represent that the 'tipping point' in terms of financial fragility has been reached, where fragility no longer simply continues to build and intensify, but finally fractures. If increasing financial fragility and difficulty servicing debt results in default and bankruptcy, why, then, one might ask, has there not been thus far even more defaults and bankruptcies to date? There are several answers to this question.

First, defaults and bankruptcies occur with a lag and only after financial fragility has reached its limits. Bank defaults in particular may lag a financial crisis by several years. In other words, the worst in terms of defaults and bankruptcies may be yet to come—bank, non-bank, and consumer alike—is one possible answer.

Second, most of the large banks have de facto defaulted—technically, at least. Many of the big 19 'too big to fail' banks were effectively bankrupt as of late 2008 in the U.S. Only the Federal Reserve and U.S. Treasury have kept them afloat to date with several trillions of dollars of direct liquidity injections and bailouts. The Fed and the Treasury then engineered a partial artificial financial recovery in the spring of 2009, enabling bank stock prices to rise. This helped to shore-up bank balance sheets. But this 'recapitalization' via stock price recovery was, and can only be, partly and temporarily successful. Banks simply cannot fully recover losses via stock price appreciation. They cannot recapitalize themselves out of their massive debt load on hand, plus the trillions of dollars more still required to refinance in the next two years. Furthermore, stock price gains can reverse as easily as they rose. Much of the artificial stock recapitalization can evaporate as fast as it appeared. Many of the big 19 are therefore still very much on government 'financial life support' and will remain so for some time. A massive debt overhang still remains on their balance sheets and banks will have to continue to service that massive debt overhang. The bad debts are still there and haven't gone away. The government bailouts have not removed those debts, but have only offset them with more debt from the government. In short, temporary debt (Fed loans and Treasury injections) has offset permanent debt. Debt-based financial fragility thus remains at the big 19 banks, even if they will not be allowed to default and go bankrupt by the Fed and the Treasury.

Not so for the 8,400 small- and medium-sized community and regional banks in the U.S. They will be allowed to default and, in fact, are increasingly doing so. The lag in their case is just concluding and defaults and small bank failures are beginning to accelerate. Two hundred have 'failed' thus far in 2009, 100 of which in just the final three months. Another 400–500 in 2010 are predicted. The rapidly rising number of smaller bank failures reflects continuing financial fragility in this segment of the financial sector.

Then there are defaults and bankruptcies by non-bank companies. These, too, have been rising. Defaults by companies on speculative grade debt in particular has been rising progressively every quarter over the past year, and is expected to rise to more than 13 percent in the fourth quarter of 2009 in the U.S., and 15 percent in Europe in early 2010. Some sources have argued the default rate will soon peak and decline. Others, such as the largest bond firm, PIMCO, in the U.S. maintain that "corporate defaults will likely stay elevated in an environment of weak nominal economic growth."[4] Then there is default by consumers; in particular, residential homeowners. Defaults defined as foreclosures have exceeded 6 million so far, are predicted to rise to 8 million and could easily top 10 million by the end of 2010—i.e. nearly one in five of all mortgages outstanding. Delinquencies in payments are another reflection of fragility. Credit card defaults have escalated threefold in just one year, from 3 percent to more than 10 percent of all accounts. In short, defaults as a reflection of financial fragility in the system are, in fact, continuing to grow.

A rising ratio of debt to cash and liquid assets, and rising defaults and bankruptcies, are overt representations of financial fragility. But fragility is continuing to worsen beyond what overt data indicate. That is because companies have turned to short-term 'fixes' to stave off the defaults and bankruptcies temporarily, or they have exercised other temporary short-term solutions, in order to make their debt servicing payments.

For example, thousands of non-bank companies have recently staved off default and bankruptcy by rolling over or raising additional debt through the junk bond markets over the past year. There has been a virtual bubble in the junk bond market since 2008. Moreover, like the $7 trillion short-term bank debt requiring refinancing noted above, between 2011 and 2014, $250–500 billion in junk debt will also require refinancing. That will likely mean the further issuing of junk debt to finance existing junk debt. Speculative grade, or junk bond, debt thus only temporarily postpones the defaults and bankruptcies that would have occurred otherwise at record levels. But adding more junk debt serves only to delay defaults. And it provides no long-term solution to a company's debt servicing problems; in fact, it exacerbates them.

Defaults and bankruptcies have been postponed in other ways as well. Companies with aforementioned loan terms providing for covenants and PIKs, or debt swap arrangements, or other fortunate terms, may invoke those terms and buy time to avoid default. In addition, with the banks in trouble themselves and dealing with their own record levels of write-downs and write-offs, banks thus far have been reluctant to 'call in' many defaulted loans and have instead often postponed bankruptcy proceedings action for their borrowers. That is, at least for now. Thus many non-bank businesses have temporarily been given a reprieve. Another way in which default may be postponed is when companies turn to selling assets at below-market prices to raise cash. This rarely gets publicity in the mainstream business press, unless it's a notable large company. But asset price deflation is happening and is widespread. Deflation has also been taking place in product prices, especially at the wholesale or producer price level, while wage deflation is increasing in multiple forms as well. By reducing asset, product, and wage prices, businesses are in effect servicing debt loads by means of creating deflation. This process can continue for some time, but does have its limits. And when the limits are reached, default becomes the primary remaining option. The point, however, is that all these forms of postponements and temporary fixes nonetheless represent financial fragility in the system that may not be reflected in more overt indications of financial fragility.

Whether businesses playing the deflation card, banks' reluctance to call in debt when servicing defaults occur, medium- and larger-sized companies resorting to costly junk bond debt financing, non-financial corporations exercising covenants and PIKs to prevent or delay default proceedings—all represent a de facto greater degree of default in the system than actually occurring defaults suggest. Defaults are a mirror of a growing problem in debt servicing, and therefore of continuing financial fragility in the system. But behind the actual defaults and bankruptcies are also other indicators of intensifying financial fragility in the system.

A temporary rescue of the big banks, the accelerating failure rates of small- to medium-sized banks, the resort to junk financing and rising junk default rates, the imminent defaults soon to occur in the commercial property markets, the $10 trillion in short-term debt coming due for refinancing in two short years, the continuing consumer defaults in residential mortgages, credit cards, etc.—all are representations of financial fragility that is still very much present as of now; fragility that could easily continue to deteriorate even further in 2010. The main problem is that debt levels, debt quality, and debt servicing loans have hardly been removed from the system—whether for banks, businesses, or consumers. And until they are, financial fragility will not decline, but may actually deteriorate further.

FINANCIAL INSTABILITY

Financial instability occurs when financial fragility has reached, and passed, breaking point. Financial instability represents the fracturing of prior financial fragility. Financial instability may occur in the form of a financial institution bankruptcy and liquidation or in temporary failures called bank suspensions, after which the institution is reorganized and sold to new investors. Bank failure may be actual or de facto. In de facto failure, bankruptcy is artificially delayed as a result of central bank liquidity injections that prevent bankruptcy from legally occurring for an institution that is otherwise technically insolvent.[5] De facto failure occurs as well when technically failed institutions are consolidated or merged in order to avoid formal collapse. In other words, a bank 'failure' may take place as a formal bankruptcy and liquidation of assets, a temporary bank suspension, a merging of the institution with another more solvent bank, or a de facto insolvency where liquidity injections by the government prevents the former three from happening. While the number of formal bankruptcies and temporary suspensions is quantifiable, an even greater number of 'de facto' failures may in effect have occurred. Insolvency is not always publicly announced. In fact, both banks and the government try to avoid formal failures if possible. The U.S. government 'stress tests' of the big 19 banks in early 2009 are a good example of allowing de facto insolvency in order to avoid de jure bankruptcies that would further destabilize the entire financial system.

Formal bank failures are a clear indication of financial instability. However, a second indicator of financial instability is a deep contraction of a bank's capital and reserves. That contraction of capital and reserves might be due to several factors: massive withdrawals by investors, falling equity stock prices, or large asset write-downs or write-offs by the institution.

Another indicator of financial instability may be 'runs' on banks. Runs may be retail, as in the case of the general public as depositors in commercial banks withdrawing large amounts of deposits in a short period. The experience of the 1930s is a good example of retail runs, at least prior to 1934, during which average depositors withdrew their savings en masse from thousands of commercial banks. However, bank runs may be of a 'wholesale' character, and occur in non-depository financial institutions as well as commercial depository banks. Thus, professional investors—individual, fund-based, or other institutions—may engage in withdrawals from financial institutions in which they have invested funds. Runs may also take the form of rapid or large withdrawals of capital.

A fourth and final indicator of financial instability would be a deep and widespread contraction of credit availability. This may include a 'credit crunch' of significant dimension, or a more severe 'credit crash.' A credit crunch is something which occurred from August 2007 to the summer of 2008 in the U.S.; a virtual credit crash is what took place in the months immediately following October 2008 and the classic banking panic that occurred at that time.

Formal bank failures, temporary bank suspensions, forced mergers and consolidations, major loss of bank capital and reserves, runs on banks, credit crashes, and de facto insolvencies are all examples of conditions of financial instability in the banking system.

Normal recessions may experience some element of financial instability. But the financial instability is relatively moderate in terms of magnitude and/ or scope. A single large bank may need bailing out or consolidation. Or perhaps financial institutions in the region of the national economy fail and are consolidated. But financial instability is not generalized across multiple financial markets or geographically throughout the financial system of a given economy, as in the case of an Epic Recession. There is no sense of systemic crisis for the entire system in a normal recession, unlike an Epic Recession. Bank runs are not widespread or frequent. There may be a credit reduction but not a credit crash where, for a period, credit is unavailable in general. In normal recessions there may be scores or even low hundreds of failures, but not thousands, as in Epic Recessions. Bank capital may decline but not collapse by half or more. Insolvencies are not widespread or covered up. Furthermore, financial instability does not 'spill out' globally across multiple economies, as is also the tendency with Epic Recession. In normal recessions financial instability is more limited in scope, less severe, and is more easily and quickly contained from spreading across markets or geographically by monetary and fiscal policies. In Epic Recession, monetary and fiscal policies required to contain the financial instability are far greater in magnitude, generally have less of an impact, and must be sustained for longer periods in order to ensure economic recovery.

Financial institution failures

For two decades after the end of World War II there were essentially no financial instability events in the U.S.; neither limited events in terms of scope and magnitude impacting a particular institution, singular market, or region, nor certainly as a consequence of anything that might qualify as Epic Recession-related. By the mid 1960s, however, this began to change and financial instability began to grow but not yet in scope or magnitude associated with Epic Recession. Excessive speculation with the new 'negotiable CD'[6] market in 1966 precipitated a mild instability event that was quickly contained by the Federal Reserve as it injected additional liquidity into the banking system via its traditional discount window policy tool. In 1970 another event occurred with the new Real Estate Investment Trusts (REITs) speculating in the residential housing and commercial real estate markets. That, too, was contained. It was soon followed by the somewhat more serious financial instability of 1974 involving the commercial paper market and the rescue of several large banks, like the Franklin National Bank and Security National Bank of New York. The 1974 event was contained as well, including a bailout of the offshore branches of the failed banks. But compared to 1970 and 1966, the costs of bailouts had clearly risen, to around $7-$10 billion. The rescue efforts by the Fed were thus growing in magnitude as the scope of the financial crises were widening. While not yet events of Epic Recession dimensions, it was nonetheless clear that financial instability was progressively worsening, even in the early period of 1966–74.

During the crises of 1966–74, financial instability was the consequence of the effects of a normal recession—not the precipitating cause of those recessions. The financial instability did not provoke the recessions during that period, which were more the result of bad policy choices by the government or 'external' shocks. As noted previously, the differing relationships of financial instability to Epic Recession and normal recessions is one of reasons why most economists, 'monetarists' in particular, are unable to distinguish between normal recessions and Epic Recessions. Epic Recessions are in part set in motion by a major financial instability event, whereas in normal recessions financial instability is not only much more moderate an affair but follows the onset of recession. Moreover, in the case of Epic Recessions, financial crisis not only precipitates a real economic downturn, but continues to feed the momentum of the downturn. By means of various transmission mechanisms, in Epic Recession financial instability also tends to generalize beyond singular financial institutions or select credit markets; it synchronizes geographically both on- and offshore; it impacts main money center financial institutions; destabilizes international currency values and induces currency volatility; and it is not easily contained by traditional monetary or moderate fiscal policies. These are fundamental and major differences between financial instability associated with normal recessions and financial instability associated with

Epic Recessions. None of these conditions characterized any of the normal recessions and bouts of financial instability between 1966 and 1974.

The normal recession of 1981–82 was similar to 1966–74, in that the 1981–82 recession was not precipitated by financial instability. 1981–82 was 'normal' in the sense that it was provoked by a combination of bad policy by the Carter and Reagan administrations, as well as by external shocks in the form of excessive oil price hikes between 1979 and 1980. The recession of 1981–82 set in motion, once again, financial instability as key banks like the Penn Square Bank and Continental Illinois and numerous Savings and Loans (S&Ls) defaulted and failed between 1982 and 1984.[7] 1981–82 differed from the 1960s and 1970s recessions, however, in that the subsequent financial instability set in motion was quantitatively and qualitatively more serious. Far more financial institutions failed, and at a greater cost to the public than in the 1970s.

The financial institution failures of Reagan's first term were largely the result of Fed policy actions that raised interest rates to 18 percent. Not so for the second round of financial failures that defined Reagan's second term after 1984. Whereas the first-term failures involving savings and loan institutions were localized, after 1985 S&Ls failures become industry-wide. Now it was not Fed policies but new speculative investing bubbles to which the Reagan administration and Congress turned a blind eye. At mid decade, the corporate junk bond market was unleashed to finance a boom in corporate M&As. The junk bond boom also artificially drove up stock prices of the companies involved in the M&A movement, setting off a parallel common stock speculative boom. By 1987 the S&Ls debt load peaked and the industry began to implode. The junk bond frenzy also peaked. The stock market responded with the then record 508-point one-day drop in 1987. Commercial banks began to fail at a rate of 200 a year by 1988–89. S&L failures peaked as well in 1989 and continued at high levels through 1991, as did bank failures through 1992.

The events of the late 1980s to early 1990s—compared to earlier in the decade and the 1970s—showed that financial instability was worsening over time. The instability was affecting more than individual institutions or narrow geographic locales. Now it was entire markets (S&L and junk bonds) and a greater geographical impact.[8] The cost of bailing out the failed institutions was also rising significantly by the 1990s. Estimated costs of the S&L bailouts alone ranged from $250 billion to $500 billion.[9] But the financial instability and financial institution failures were not yet systemic or system-wide, nor yet geographically widespread or synchronized across economies. That, too, was destined to change. The instability and financial institution failures were, however, a dress rehearsal and warning of a much greater financial instability to follow in 2007.

In the meantime the focus of financial instability and financial institution failures shifted offshore of the U.S. The U.K. and Scandinavian banks had a crisis in the early 1990s. Japan imploded financially early in the decade as a consequence of excessive real estate speculation. It quickly descended into a long period of decline and stagnation which our analysis would characterize as a 'Type I' Epic Recession. By the mid 1990s the financial speculation manifested in a series of global 'sovereign debt crises,' as U.S. financial institutions provided liquidity in excess amounts to feed both real investment and accompanying speculative plays in emerging markets in Latin America, Asia, and elsewhere. U.S. banks pumped money into the new rapidly expanding hedge fund institutions that speculated extensively in foreign currency volatility and foreign stock markets. Sovereign debt crises involving Mexico, Argentina, Thailand, Indonesia, Korea, Philippines became norm, and these countries became the new location of the financial crisis. To prevent U.S. financial institution failures in the fallout, the Fed provided additional liquidity to the U.S. banking system and, for the first time, bailed out a non-commercial bank financial institution, the hedge fund Long Term Capital Management. While speculation in foreign currency and emerging markets was erupting in offshore financial instability, onshore in the U.S. two new speculative investment booms were beginning: the U.S. residential housing market and the 'dot.com' boom in technology stocks on the NASDAQ market in the U.S., both of which have their origins in 1997–98. Financial institution losses from these events would not materialize until well into the first decade of the new century, however.

In considering financial institution failures across periods it is necessary to include failures associated with both the traditional banking sector— which includes primarily commercial banks, S&Ls, and other long-standing institutions—and what is called the 'shadow banking system.' The shadow banking sector is the deep and widespread network of so-called 'financial intermediaries' that has expanded exceptionally rapidly since the late 1990s. The more notable among them are the hedge funds, private equity firms, mutual funds, money market funds, private banks, brokerages, structured investment vehicles (SIVs), conduits, insurance company 'banks,' credit card company 'banks,' and the like. This shadow banking sector as of 2007 had assets at least equivalent to the traditional banking sector.

The traditional banking system's total assets were estimated at around $10 trillion in 2007 before the onset of the financial crisis, with the six largest banks having $6 trillion of that total. In comparison, the shadow banking system in 2007 was estimated to have assets of around $10.5 trillion.[10]

The U.S. hedge fund segment of the shadow banking sector alone at its peak numbered in the thousands of institutions and held assets of approximately $2 trillion. In the last six months of 2008 alone, a record 1,122 hedge funds 'failed,' having lost between $600 billion and $800 billion. Through the first quarter of 2009 another 376 funds closed. Hedge fund losses for 2009, according to investment bank Morgan Stanley, were projected at mid 2009 at another $450 billion.[11]

Counting just Federal Deposit Insurance Corporation (FDIC)-insured commercial banks, savings institutions, and hedge funds—i.e. ignoring the thousands of other kinds of shadow bank financial institutions that failed in 2007–08—more than 1,500 financial institutions failed in just 2007–08 alone.

Table 2.3 compares financial instability in terms of bank and S&L institution failure, from the 1970s to mid 2009, plus just the hedge fund segment of the shadow banking sector from January 2007 through 2008.

Table 2.3 Financial Institution Failures, 1970–2008

Year	Total Institutions	Banks	Other
1970	7	7	0
1973	6	6	0
1974	4	4	0
1975	12	12	0
1976	17	17	0
1981	38	10	28
1982	117	41	76
1983	98	47	51
1984	103	79	24
1985	180	120	60
1986	203	144	59
1987	262	203	59
1988	470	280	190
1989	534	207	327
1990	381	169	212
1991	271	127	144
1992	180	121	59
1993	50	41	9
2001	4	4	0
2002	11	11	0
2003	3	3	0
2007	460	3	457
2008	1,553	30	1,523

Source: FDIC, *Failures and Assistance Transactions*, and *Wall Street Journal*, June 18, 2009, p. C1, for hedge fund totals.

Notwithstanding the highly visible problems of major banks that occurred from March 2008 through the first quarter of 2009, it has been the shadow banking sector—the same approximate size of $10 trillion in terms of assets as the traditional bank sector—that has imploded far worse.

Capital loss and insolvency

Financial instability is measurable not only in terms of failures or bankruptcies; it may also be measured in terms of conditions that may deteriorate prior to actual failure, suspension, or outright default-bankruptcy. Not all financial institutions in deep trouble actually experience failure or officially go bankrupt. That does not mean that their financial fragility has not deteriorated or that they are not financially unstable. Prior to 'failure' the institution may merge or consolidate with another to stave off financial collapse. Financial failure may also be avoided by arranging emergency financing or by restructuring. Institutions may swap debt for other assets, make PIKs and activate covenants (i.e. delays of payments) that were previously negotiated with creditors. The institutions may, in fact, effectively be insolvent—i.e. technically in default and in effect bankrupt. Technical default, simply put, is when an institution's assets are worth less than its debts on which payments must be made. Asset collapse may therefore serve as an indicator of growing financial instability.

Asset losses and write-downs are not the only indicator of financial instability. Instability may take the form of a virtual collapse of a financial institution's common stock price. By collapse is meant a decline of 70–80 percent or more. As banks register asset write-downs or losses, buyers of its stock then sell it off, thus causing a stock price decline. But the real intense downward pressure on a bank's stock prices, and thus capital reserves, typically grows as speculators enter the market and short-sell the institution's stock at first sign of potential losses and write-downs. That is precisely what happened in mid 2008 with the stock of investment banks Bear Stearns and Lehman Brothers, with quasi-government corporate-agencies like Fannie Mae and Freddie Mac, and with various financial institutions like AIG and others in September 2008. In Epic Recessions, stock prices for multiple institutions may be thus driven down to levels of 10 percent, or even 5 percent or less, of their prior value—i.e. levels far below those in normal recessions. Original losses and write-downs on a bank's investment portfolio are thus severely exacerbated at times by even greater losses in capital and reserves. When the two combine, technical insolvency is often the outcome.

Runs on the bank

Yet another factor driving insolvency in Epic Recession are massive withdrawals of deposits. Both institutional and individual investors may withdraw deposits. Following the credit crash of October 2008, for example, hedge funds and money market funds were especially impacted by mass withdrawals. Hedge fund assets were reduced from $1.9 trillion in June 2008 to $1.1 trillion at year-end of 2008. About one-fifth of that was due to losses, and the remaining $600 billion due to depositor withdrawals.[12]

Mass withdrawals of deposits from banks by the general public are called 'retail bank runs' on the banks. Retail withdrawals and runs were quite common and a major factor in depressions prior to 1934. The government agency responsible for insuring depositors, the FDIC, has insured deposits since 1934. With the introduction of depositor insurance in 1934, retail bank runs virtually ceased overnight. Since 1934, general depositor retail bank runs have not been a problem. But the FDIC insures only depositors at commercial banks and institutions (savings banks, for example). It does not insure investments at non-commercial banks and financial institutions. Thus, institutional bank runs may and do still occur. For example, today's $10 trillion-plus 'shadow banking' system is not insured by the FDIC. Non-depositor institutions like hedge funds, investment banks, private banks, and the like, that constitute the shadow banking system don't take deposits from the general public. They accept investments from individual investors and other institutions. Investors may and do make massive withdrawals from the banking system, but these are better described as 'wholesale' bank runs.

Unavailability of credit

Yet another obvious indicator of financial instability is a contraction of credit issued by banks and financial institutions—not only to other non-financial businesses and consumers, but also among and between financial institutions. Small- and medium-sized businesses are particularly dependent on bank credit availability. So are consumers. In a normal recession, a credit tightening occurs. Credit may become more expensive and in some cases unavailable to companies that are particularly poor credit risks. But in an Epic Recession a more severe credit contraction is the norm. Not only does the availability of bank loans become more limited, but other sources of credit dry up as well or become exorbitantly expensive. The terms of credit lending become far more restrictive. It is not just a question of high interest rates and the cost of credit. There may not be any credit at any price for a period. Other terms and conditions of credit become more severely restrictive as well.

In Epic Recessions banks and other financial institutions may even refuse to lend to each other. A good example is the excessive and extraordinary rise in bank-to-bank lending rates. One such rate is what is called the Libor (London Interbank Lending Rate). In 2007–08 it rose sharply and bank-to-bank lending essentially disappeared for a period. Another inter-financial institution lending market is called the Repo (Repurchase Agreements) market. It is an overnight interbank lending market in which short term securities are offered as collateral for cash. For a period in 2007–08, that, too, virtually dried up, despite rates falling almost to zero. No such general collapse of interbank lending occurs in the case of normal recessions, as it may in Epic Recessions.

Large corporations are generally less severely impacted by an intense credit contraction or credit crash in instances of Epic Recessions. They are more able to issue stock or to finance operations out of their large, retained internal funds. It is the smaller- and medium-sized businesses that are most impacted— in particular, construction firms, retail industry companies, and services of various kinds. During the depression of the 1930s it was similar. Those hardest hit by unavailable credit were small businesses, consumers, and farmers. Big companies weathered the storm fairly well.

In the current Epic Recession lending terms for small businesses continued to tighten even after 18 months into the recession. A Fed survey of loan officers showed that from January to April 2009 about 70 percent of financial institutions continued to raise rates on credit lines for small businesses and 40 percent continued to tighten standards for commercial and industrial loans, a main source of credit for small- to medium-sized businesses.[13] As of June 2009, no less than 59 percent of small business were relying on credit cards to finance day-to-day operations.[14] As a further indication of the extraordinary degree of the credit crunch in the recent Epic Recession, the CIT Group Inc., a lender to more than 1 million small- to medium-sized businesses in the U.S, was forced to file for bankruptcy, itself unable to obtain credit from larger banks and credit markets from which it obtained funds in order to lend in turn to smaller businesses.[15]

A similar picture was emerging in the euro-zone economies at mid 2009. After loans to the private sector grew annually at a rate of 10–12 percent from 2006 to 2008, lending rates had fallen to only 1.8 percent by mid year—the lowest since records were initially kept in 1992.[16]

On the consumer side, mortgage lending may become unavailable at any rate. Auto loans from car manufacturers or dealers may dry up. For both small businesses and consumers, credit cards are called in by card issuers, card terms and conditions are raised to onerous levels, credit limits are lowered, minimum monthly payments are doubled and tripled, and fees and penalties are hiked. In the first quarter of 2009 alone, according to the FDIC, credit card lines of credit were reduced by banks and other card issuers by more than $406 billion.[17]

The degree and duration of credit contraction in Epic Recession has no parallel in normal recessions. Qualitatively, in Epic Recessions multiple types of credit markets are simultaneously affected: bank to bank, bank to small business, or bank to consumers. In Epic Recession the credit contraction takes forms beyond simply rising interest rates. What is called 'intermediation,' the process by which lending actually works its way from institution to the borrower, plays a relatively greater role obstructing and preventing lending.[18] The contraction is deeper, more widespread, and of longer duration.

As financial fragility erupts and fractures, precipitating an Epic Recession event, the financial instability that follows is more severe, both quantitatively and qualitatively, than in the case of normal recessions. Total bank failures—whether measured in terms of bankruptcies, suspensions, reorganizations, etc.—are greater in number, as are the more difficult to quantify de facto insolvencies. Financial instability in the form of capital loss, stock price collapse, wholesale-institutional bank runs and withdrawals, and general unavailability of credit, are more intense and widespread. In contrast, in normal recessions financial fragility does not drive financial instability. The latter is thus less severe in scope or magnitude. Financial instability in its various forms and manifestations is more a consequence, not a cause, of the real economy's contraction. Because financial instability and financial crisis is not a driver of the real economy, the contraction does not occur as quickly, as deep, or for as long as during an Epic Recession. Because it is not a question of debt unwinding, the impact on deflation and default is not as serious in normal recessions. Because it is shallower and shorter, and there is no problem of financial fragility involved, the contraction is less likely to precipitate a corresponding collapse of consumption fragility that serves to exacerbate already developing processes of debt, deflation, and default.

THE SHADOW BANKING SYSTEM

A further important qualitative characteristic of Epic Recession is the proliferation and growing relative weight of financial intermediaries in the total financial institution mix. These are in effect non-bank banks and financial institutions. They are not formally part of the traditional banking system, but do integrate with that latter system in a number of critical ways. Shadow banks arise and evolve to exploit economic extra profits outside what may be a more regulated traditional banking system. They are particularly important for enabling the shift toward speculative forms of investment. Shadow banks grew within the last decade in the U.S. to where their total asset base was roughly equivalent to that of traditional banks—around $10 trillion each by 2007. Their growth was significant as well in the U.K. economy, and somewhat less so elsewhere in the euro-zone and Asian economies.

Shadow banks are financial institutions on the periphery of the traditional bank system and thus outside the regulatory institutions. They have always been a part of the U.S. financial system. They have simply changed in form and name over time, all the while continuing to innovate in terms of financial instruments and processes that allowed them to exploit speculative investment opportunities that traditional banks were restricted (though not totally prevented) from engaging in. The relative size, weight, and, in turn, their influence, has ebbed and flowed over time. There has been, however, an underlying long-term secular growth in their relative weight and influence.

The various forms of shadow banks over the last century are represented in Tables 2.4–6, as is their share of total assets compared to the traditional (or commercial) banking system.

Table 2.4 Shadow versus Traditional Banking System, 1900

Financial Institution Type	Share of Total Assets (%)
Commercial Banks	62.9
Mutual Savings Banks	15.1
Life Insurance Companies	10.7
Brokers and Dealers	3.8
Savings and Loans (S&Ls)	3.1
Other Insurance Companies	3.1
Other	1.3

Source: Eugene White, "Banking and Finance in the Twentieth Century," *Cambridge Economic History of the United States, Vol. III*, Cambridge University Press, 2000, p. 747.

Prior to 1914 the major form of shadow bank that competed directly with the traditional commercial bank sector was the state-chartered trust company. Trust companies exploded in number and share of assets after the depression of 1893–98, growing from 390 in 1897 to 1,504 by 1909, with assets equal to 27 percent of the commercial banks. The trusts were "a way around the restrictions placed on the investments of commercial and savings banks."[19] The trusts were the hedge funds of their day. Unregulated, they were critical to the financial instability and near collapse of the banking system known as the financial 'panic' of 1907. The trusts' sails were clipped after the 1907 panic and they were brought into the regulatory realm on the eve of World War I. The Federal Reserve Act of 1914 gave the regulated, commercial banks the right to set up trusts and to compete directly with the unregulated trusts. Many were simply absorbed by the traditional banks. This practice of eventually opening up the shadow banking sector to the commercial banks would have serious future consequences for financial instability.

Allowing commercial and shadow banks to integrate was a pattern repeated several times over the next century. Shadow banks operating in the unregulated, more speculative and more profitable financial markets, largely off-limits to the commercial banks, eventually gave way politically to allowing commercial banks to participate as well in the more highly speculative financial markets. As financial crises occurred, both shadow banks and their commercial bank partners were dragged down together. The solution proposed to prevent future crises was to bring shadow banks under the same regulatory umbrella as the commercial banks. However, thereafter new forms of shadow banks were created to get around the new regulatory limits and allow them once again to pursue more lucrative speculative opportunities on behalf of their investor clients. Excess speculative activity then led once again to integration of the two banking sectors, to financial instability and crisis, and to the process again repeating itself.

With the 'trust' shadow banks integrated, new shadow institutions came to the fore after the World War I. These were 'brokers and dealers,' the modern investment banks, finance companies, and the like. By 1929, on the eve of the depression of the 1930s in the U.S., the relative share and weight of the shadow banking system had grown from roughly 37 percent to a 50 percent share of total financial assets.

Table 2.5   Shadow versus Traditional Banking System, 1929

Financial Institution Type	*Share of Total Assets (%)*
Commercial Banks	50.4
Life Insurance Companies	13.3
Brokers and Dealers	7.6
Mutual Savings Banks	7.5
Savings and Loans (S&Ls)	5.6
Investment Companies	5.6
Other Insurance Companies	4.2
Finance Companies	1.9
Federally Sponsored Lending	1.7
Pensions	1.5
Other	0.7

Source: White, "Banking and Finance in the Twentieth Century," p. 748.

The changing structure of the shadow banking sector from 1900 to 1929 reflects the rise of bond speculation during World War I and after, as well as the boom in securities and common stock market speculation in the 1920s. The new speculative focus doubled the share of brokers and dealers by 1929. Investment banks exploiting the merger and 'holding company' movements of the 1920s grew, as did the rise of life insurance intermediaries as well.

The growth of life insurance and investment banks was closely linked. The half a dozen largest life insurance companies supplied the new investment banks with much of their capital to finance the new electric and power utility holding company trend and stock boom. The insurance sector also became a central player in funding farm and urban commercial property mortgage booms in the 1920s.

The consequence of all this was, according to one postwar study, that "In the 1920s non-bank intermediaries gained on banks at an especially rapid rate. The ratio of their assets to assets of banks rose from .77 in 1922 to 1.14 in 1929."[20] In other words, according to the alternate study, the shadow banking sector was now not simply as large as, but in fact larger than, the traditional banking sector.

Following the depression and World War II this relative weight and mix of shadow banks to traditional (regulated) banks eased. According to the then definitive study of the growth of shadow banks covering the period 1900–49, by Raymond Goldsmith of the National Bureau of Economic Research (NBER), commercial banks' share of financial assets to that of intermediaries' assets fell by more than 30 percent between 1900 and 1929, but then rose between 1929 and 1949 by 17 percent.[21] Investment banks and brokers in particular declined in relative assets, from $10 billion to only $2.7 billion.[22]

In other words, shadow banks declined relative to traditional banking following the collapse of speculative opportunities in the depression of the 1930s and the World War II period. It is perhaps not coincidental, given the depression–world war shift from shadow banks and speculation, that the frequency, magnitude, and scope of financial instability also eased from the 1930s through the 1950s. It would not be until at least the late 1960s to early 1970s when the shift began to reverse once again and shadow bank institutions and their markets began to grow once more in relative weight and mix. By 2007 the shadow banking sector was, once again, at least as large as the traditional banking sector.

Table 2.6, based upon data provided by the *RGE Monitor*, shows the shadow banking sector, with approximately $10.5 trillion in assets, approximately as large once again as the traditional banking sector with $10 trillion. The *Monitor*'s estimate was in part derived from a speech in early 2007 given by then New York Fed director and later U.S. Treasury Secretary, Tim Geithner. The estimate is expressed in terms of the asset types held by both the traditional commercial banking and the shadow banking sectors.

An alternative institution-type estimate of two sectors' respective relative size is reflected in the U.S. Federal Reserve's *Flow of Funds* data. It shows the traditional banking sector, commercial banks and savings institutions, with net lending of $856 billion in 2005. In contrast, the shadow banking system today—composed of insurance companies, private pension funds, money market funds, mutual and other funds, asset-backed securities (ABS) issuers, finance companies, REITs, investment banks, brokers and dealers, private banks of various kinds—together lent $1.35 trillion. The shadow banking sector figure would be even higher if it included quasi-government institutions such as government pension funds and the housing agencies like Fannie Mae and Freddie Mac. If the latter are included, the shadow sector in 2005 had net lending of roughly $1.66 trillion, or nearly twice that of the traditional banking sector.[23]

Table 2.6 Shadow versus Traditional Banking System, 2007

Banking Sector	Assets ($ trillions)
Traditional Banking	10.0
Top 5 Bank Holding Companies	6.0
Other Banks and Savings Institutions	4.5
Shadow Banking	10.5
Asset Backed Commercial Paper Conduits	
Structured Investment Vehicles	
Auction Rate Preferred Securities	2.2
Variable Rate Notes	
Triparty Repos	2.5
Hedge Funds	1.8
Top 5 Investment Banks	4.0

Source: *RGE Monitor*, May 26, 2009.

Shadow banking financial institutions differ in a number of significant ways from traditional banking institutions. First, as previously noted, they are virtually unregulated. They raise no funds from retail depositors. They raise funds outside the depositor market, which makes their borrowing potentially more volatile. They are required to keep no reserves, and thus maintain low liquidity. They often borrow short term from traditional commercial banks, thus extending their risk to the latter. Until early 2008, they had no recourse to the Federal Reserve's emergency discount window. Particularly important, shadow institutions are typically highly leveraged, meaning they borrow most of their funds to invest. Some shadow institutions by 2007 were leveraged to a ratio of up to 20 or 30 to 1 with borrowed money. And as their relative weight and mix grew, so did the fragility of the entire financial system, traditional and shadow. Leverage ratios of 20 or 30 to 1 mean that the institutions are massively top-heavy with debt. And when that debt unwinds, so do many of the shadow institutions.

What the history of shadow banking from 1900 to 2007 suggests is that there is, at minimum, a growing weight and mix of shadow banks' assets to total assets. At times this mix ebbs, and other times it flows. In both 1929 and in 2007 it had clearly flowed, bringing with it a growing problem of financial fragility. The consequence of this growing weight and influence of speculative investing is significant for its contribution to growing financial fragility and financial instability. It is also significant perhaps for its effects on real physical asset investment, job creation, and real income flows to non-investors—i.e. for the more than 150 million wage and salary earners in the

U.S. and, in particular, the 100 million or so non-supervisory production and service workers. Or, to put it succinctly, there is a possible relationship not only between speculative finance and growing financial fragility and instability, but also between speculative finance and a corresponding deterioration of consumption fragility.

CONSUMPTION FRAGILITY

Consumption fragility, like financial fragility, is also defined in terms of levels of debt, deteriorating debt quality, and faltering income flows necessary to service debt payments. Just as financial fragility grows as businesses encounter increasing difficulty in making payments on debt as the cost of debt rises and/or income for servicing that debt declines, so too does consumption fragility similarly increase when households encounter growing stress in making payments on debt as the cost of that debt rises as available household disposable real income stagnates or falls.

Household debt is composed of consumer credit, auto debt, student loan debt, personal loans, installment and revolving credit, single-family residential mortgages, credit cards, and other forms of personal debt. Household disposable income may derive from various sources. There are approximately 115 million total household units in the U.S. For the 90–93 million households that comprise all non-supervisory production and service workers (roughly 80 percent of the total labor force in the U.S.), household income is almost totally defined as weekly real earnings or take-home pay—i.e. hourly wages times total hours worked, minus all taxes and other deductions. (For those 115 million paid in terms of weekly salary, hours worked are not relevant.) For this 115 million and 80 percent, very little income is derived from sources other than take-home pay.

As a household moves 'up' in terms of income levels, non-wage income provides a growing share of total income. For example, for the 1 million or so wealthiest 1 percent of the estimated 115 million households in the U.S., weekly earnings and wages are negligible in total income. As a household moves up the income levels, income is derived increasingly from capital incomes: dividends, capital gains, interest, rent, and other forms of deferred compensation and 'perks' (if employed as senior managers).

It is the bottom 80 percent of households for whom consumption fragility has been a growing problem over the last several decades. And, as a general rule, the 'lower' the household ranks in the bottom 80 percent distribution, the greater the consumption fragility. Consumption fragility has been increasing for the bottom 80 percent due to consumers' rising total debt, deteriorating debt quality (i.e. rising interest costs, shortening lengths of term, and other restrictive conditions of payment), or slowing disposable income—or a combination of all three.

It is important to note the relationship between all three contributing elements to consumption fragility—i.e. disposable income, debt levels, and debt quality. As real disposable income from wages and earnings declines, the more households of necessity turn to adding debt in order to sustain consumption levels, and the more the quality of that debt deteriorates as the level of debt grows.

The stagnating-declining of real incomes plays an important role in driving consumer debt and eventual consumption fragility. This is in contrast to investor income, financial institution debt, and financial fragility. Whereas there is an indirect relationship between declining consumer disposable income and rising consumption fragility, there is a direct relationship between rising investor income and financial fragility. Rising investors' income increases excess investor liquidity that contributes to the shift to debt-driven speculative investment, which in turn exacerbates financial fragility. In contrast, stagnating or falling consumer disposable income (for the bottom 80 percent) leads to more debt-driven consumption that in turn exacerbates consumption fragility. Income inequality thus plays a role in each form of fragility, albeit in opposite ways.

Table 2.7 provides an approximation of rising consumption fragility, showing the rise of total household debt as a percentage of total disposable income in the period 1980–2008.

Table 2.7   Estimating Consumption Fragility: Household Debt and Disposable Income

Year	Disposable Income ($ billions)	Household Debt ($ billions)	Debt–Income Ratio (%)	Ratio Middle Three Quintiles (%)
1980	2,110	1,396	66	n.a.
1990	4,321	3,580	82	83 (1989)
2000	7,452	6,988	93	100 (2001)
2008	10,799	13,794	127	141 (2004)

Sources: Data for disposable income are from Bureau of Economic Analysis, Table 2.1, *Personal Income and Its Distribution*, updated November 11, 2009; for household debt from Federal Reserve, *Flow of Funds*, Table D.3, released September 17, 2009.

Columns 2, 3 and 4 of Table 2.7 include data from all households, which includes those of the wealthiest 20 percent. The fifth column gives the debt–income ratio of the 'middle 60 percent' of households, excluding the wealthiest 20 percent and the poorest 20 percent.[24] Both the fourth and fifth columns show an acceleration in debt–income ratios, especially over the last decade, and in particular for the middle-income groups which comprise the vast majority of the 110 million non-supervisory production and service employees today in the U.S.

The simple disposable income-to-debt ratio percentage does not tell the full story of growing consumption fragility in recent decades. Consumption fragility is indicated not simply by the ratio of disposable income to debt, but in terms of the cost of debt servicing given the level of disposable income. To estimate this, another set of sources is necessary. Table 2.8 provides a more accurate view of household debt service payments as a percentage of disposable income. It does so for all households, which includes the wealthiest 20 percent, for whom debt service payment stress has eased. Table 2.8 thus does not provide a figure for the bottom 80 percent, for whom debt servicing to income is undoubtedly worse than for the average that includes data for the wealthiest 20 percent. Nonetheless, despite this limitation, it reveals growing consumer fragility when measured as a percentage of debt service payments relative to disposable income.

Table 2.8 shows both a rising debt servicing ratio (DSR) which measures household debt service payments as a percentage of disposable income, seasonally adjusted, as well as a rising financial obligations ratio (FOR), which is a broader measure that includes mortgage debt, insurance, property taxes, auto leases, and consumer debt in general.

Table 2.8 Household DSR and FOR (%)

Year	DSR	FOR (Homeowners) (Incl. Renters)	
1980	10.61	13.40	15.41
1990	12.03	15.57	17.46
2000	12.59	15.13	17.65
2008	13.56	17.18	18.54

Source: Federal Reserve Board, *Household Debt Service and Financial Obligations Ratios*, Survey of Consumer Finances, 2007, updated through second quarter 2009, for data from 1980 to the present. Website: www. federalreserve.gov/releases/housedebt/default.htm. Data points are for end of fourth quarter in each year noted.

Whether the rise in consumption fragility as measured in either Table 2.7 or 2.8 is due to income stagnation, debt level rise, debt quality- or cost-deterioration—or a combination of all three—is unfortunately not indicated by either table. Rising consumption fragility may be caused by income stagnating or debt rising, or both in some combination. Stagnating real income has been a problem for the 110 million non-supervisory workers in the U.S. in particular (roughly the bottom 80 percent of households). But debt levels and debt servicing stress appears to have been rising for all households. As others have recently noted, "U.S. households by 2007 were paying over a fifth of their after-tax disposable income to the financial sector in debt servicing and financial fees."[25]

Epic Recessions have a greater potential to arise when consumption fragility has had a longer period in which to gestate and deteriorate: real disposable income stagnates or declines over a longer term and consequently debt levels and terms have time to grow worse as well. In fact, income deterioration acts as a catalyst in part for the rise in debt and debt servicing stress.

Over the multiple boom phases between normal recessions in the U.S. since the 1970s, consumers have taken on additional excess debt. At the same time the series of normal recessions occurring between recovery phases resulted in slower disposable income gains. Since the 1970s, consumer inflation has also clearly undermined real disposable income. The recurrent normal recessions have slowed or reversed disposable income growth, especially for the bottom 60 percent of households. In addition to these cyclical effects depressing disposable income, structural changes since the 1980s have also slowed or reduced real disposable income. The more notable of the structural changes include rising health care outlays not adequately accounted for by government inflation estimates; de-unionization and consequent falling wage differentials for tens of millions in the bottom 60 percent; the shift to fewer hours of work per week represented by the rising proportion of part-time workers in the workforce; the shifting of permanent jobs to temporary employment, averaging 30 percent lower pay levels; by a falling real minimum wage impacting another 10–20 million of the U.S. workforce; by the offshoring of higher-paid manufacturing jobs and their replacement with lower-paid service jobs; by the continued rise in the payroll tax as a percentage of total tax payments for those earning less than $100,000 annually. This is a short list of factors involved in the fundamental structural revolution in labor markets that has been occurring since the 1980s, causing a stagnation or reduction in take home pay and thus real disposable income for tens of millions in the bottom 80 percent, and the bottom 60 percent of households in particular. Consumers, like financial institutions, have thus become progressively fragile over the past several decades as well, and the last ten years in particular.

The advent of mass layoffs such as occurred beginning in the last quarter of 2008 is the kind of major event that can precipitate a fracturing of consumption fragility—just as the collapse of asset prices in 2007–08 played a similar role in precipitating the rupture of financial fragility. The developing consumption fragility over decades means that consumers have little in the way of income reserves with which to slow the sharp decline in consumption spending that is caused by mass layoffs. Consumption thus breaks and reduces to a lower equilibrium level in the economy. Financial fragility, instability, and financial crisis set the economy on the road to Epic Recession by causing a deep and long credit contraction. But Epic Recessions are precipitated ultimately by the extraordinary collapse of household consumption that may occur in the aftermath of a financial crisis.

The collapse of household consumption (sometimes referred to as collapse of household balance sheets) is a characteristic shared by the period 1929–31 as well as the period of late 2008 and after. As will be explored in Chapter 6 on the Depression of the 1930s, households took on extraordinary levels of debt in the 1920s in the form of mortgages, auto, and other personal loans. Simultaneously, real incomes for working-class households stagnated, while the share of relative income by wealthy households, investors and corporations rose dramatically. In other words, income inequality in favor of investors dramatically rose over the course of the 1920s, providing excess liquidity that fed the speculative surge of that decade. At the same time, real wages and income for tens of millions of wage-earners stagnated during the decade leading up to the depression, thus adding to consumption fragility. Consumption fragility rose as a result of both increasing consumer household debt accumulation and stagnating wages and consumer income. Both financial and consumption fragility increased over the decade. Rising debt levels were driving both, with growing income inequality stimulating the one (financial fragility) and exacerbating the other (consumption fragility).

The role of growth of income concentration among investors in the 1920s has been revealed recently in in-depth studies by economists Emmanuel Saez, Thomas Picketty, and others. Using Internal Revenue Service (IRS) databases, Saez and Picketty show a growth in the share of income of the wealthiest 1 percent of households in the 1920s from a low of 15 percent to nearly 24 percent by the end of the 1920s.[26] An argument can be made that this concentration of income among the wealthiest investors in the 1920s was both a cause of the debt-driven speculative investment boom of the decade and simultaneously a consequence of that boom. The income acceleration provided an important source of liquidity for purposes of speculation; the profits from that speculation in turn provided yet further liquidity. At the same time a parallel relative income decline by working, small farming, and many middle-class households contributed to the consumer debt-driven excesses of the decade as well.[27] The stagnation of income fueled the turn to debt as a means of financing consumption; the increase in debt levels and debt servicing in turn reduced the available amount of real income for consumption.

SPECULATIVE INVESTMENT SHIFT

Another important qualitative characteristic of Epic Recession is a growing relative shift, an increasing weight and mix, of forms of speculative investment in relation to non-speculative investment. The question therefore arises, what exactly is meant by 'speculative' investment? What follows is a brief digression on this fundamental question. The following is a brief explanation of what a speculative investment shift is.

Simply put, all investment is, in a sense, 'speculative' in that capital is committed in the present with the expectation of a return in the future. There is no guarantee that the return expected will be realized. One can only 'speculate' that there will be such a return in the future. All investing has the characteristic of 'expectation' of a future outcome. But the question is, expectation of what? That is where speculative and non-speculative investing differ.

For most real physical investment (i.e. in physical assets like plant, equipment, facilities, etc.) there is at least some form of physical collateral that might be sold to recover some of the original investment. In forms of investment involving pure financial securities, however, this is less so the case. Investing in common stock, for example, results in no recovery, in a total loss, should the company default, go bankrupt, or otherwise fail.

On the other hand, common stock investing may return many times the rate of the bond investment—*providing the stock price appreciates*! This latter point is important for the purposes of our definition. Common stock investing represents a basic form of speculative investing. It is investing in expectation of a *short term* and *significant return*, based on *price escalation*. While that is an initial working definition of speculative investment, it is not yet a full explanation by any means. In financial speculation the investor is not investing in a physical product, a discrete good or service. He/she is investing in a piece of paper, a financial instrument, that in effect is merely a representation of an originating good or service; a copy, a replication, not the original itself. 'Speculation' as used here refers to investment that is not concerned with a long-run income stream emanating from the investment, but is concerned with a short-run, price-driven, capital gain based on a representative bet that the price of the financial instrument will rise.

New financial intermediaries—i.e. shadow banks—have arisen historically time and again to bypass more established, and often regulated, financial institutions in order to exploit emerging new speculative investment opportunities. In the process the new institutions create new financial instruments to realize excess profits from the new speculative opportunities. The older financial institutions eventually follow suit, and the new and old institutions merge or integrate in various ways. An example of the latter development was the emergence and eventual integration of the 'trusts' and commercial banks of the late nineteenth and early twentieth centuries, and the similar emergence and integration of hedge funds and banks at the end of the twentieth century and the beginning of the twenty-first.

Corresponding roughly with the rise of the trusts in the late nineteenth century was the introduction and growth of common stock and stock speculation. Common stock speculation emerged as a major form of speculative investing at the turn of the twentieth century in the U.S. Stock investing is a consequence of the corporate form of business becoming widespread in the late nineteenth century. Stock issuance (and over-issuance, which was called 'stock watering' in the late nineteenth century) became an increasing practice, extending to smaller individual investors in the early decades of the twentieth century. Vast amounts of capital went into speculation in the price movements of stock, instead of real investment projects.

Initially that stock speculation required the formation of real assets—i.e. real companies with real products. However, while stock speculation may be based upon real physical asset creation in the short run, it becomes divorced from the original real assets in the longer run. What drives it increasingly over the longer term is ultimately the price of the stock itself, not the initial real assets. For example, waves of technology innovation created new industries, actual companies and products in the 1920s. Stock was issued as these industries and companies were formed. Eventually, however, speculation on the price movements of such stock became relatively more important. Holding companies were formed on which yet further stock was issued. Stock issued on the holding companies represented no real assets or real products. Those assets were already represented by the initial stock issued on the assets of the companies upon which the subsequent holding companies were based. Holding company stock issuance was thus pure 'speculative play.' Virtually all 'secondary' financial instruments—i.e. instruments based on initial, original instruments and assets—are thus, in the foregoing sense, speculative in nature. Speculation is investing that is divorced from (i.e. that is 'derived' from) the original asset and physical investment. That separation plays a major part in speculative investment's strong tendency to focus on price changes and capital gains derived from price escalation and not from product creation and sales.

This raises a further important point about speculative investing, which is its relationship to institutional forms. Investing in expectation of pure price movements, in contrast to investing in expectation of receiving a revenue stream from products produced by real assets, is inherently volatile. Investing based on price movements of financial instruments, whether stock or other, shares many characteristics with pure 'betting' or gambling. Volatility that is the essence of price movements may produce super-profits, or super-losses. But not all investors are initially willing to assume such risks. Financial institutions that serve traditional investors are at first typically reluctant to speculate with the average, traditional investor's deposits. The minority of investors seeking super-profits therefore seek out new institutional forms willing to accommodate their willingness to risk. They either create those institutions themselves, or others create the new institutions to accommodate their willingness to undertake excessive risk to obtain excess speculative profits. This is why shadow banks are perpetually created. It is also why prior traditional banking institutions eventually seek to acquire or emulate the newer shadow banks as well.

An early analysis of the role of institutional forms to speculative investing was provided by economist Hyman Minsky, who wrote from the 1960s to the early 1990s. Minsky's thesis, in brief, is that the increasing debt accumulation over long asset price-boom periods results in a growing debt load that must be serviced (repaid) regardless of eventual changes in economic conditions. Over the business cycle, investment shifts from what Minsky calls 'hedge financing' (not be confused with hedge funds) to 'speculative financing' in which borrowing occurs to cover interest payments, thus adding to debt servicing stress. An even more severe phase of debt financing is called 'Ponzi finance.'[28] The process continues until debt loads are such that a process of debt-driven asset deflation eventually occurs, as the company sells assets and inventory at firesale prices in order to meet debt payments that are no longer refinanced. Default and bankruptcy may eventually follow.[29]

Minsky's contribution to understanding the role of speculation in finance and investment is in identifying types of financing regimes that distinguish non-speculative finance from speculative finance. But Minsky did not focus on asset price speculation per se.[30] Nor did he explore the more complex relationship between consumer debt and consumption fragility. His focus was primarily on business debt and financial fragility. Minsky's focus helps explain how financial instability develops and precipitates a financial crisis. The key idea that financing institutions and financing regimes evolve over the course of the business cycle, becoming increasingly fragile and thus prone to instability, is one of several of Minsky's original contributions. But he does not explain the transmission of financial instability into the real economy, and the latter's collapse creating a recession of epic dimensions. A more detailed analysis of the 'real side' of the economy in relation to financial fragility is missing. So is the idea of consumption fragility, its relationship to financial fragility, and how both together are central to the emergence of a quantitative and qualitative more severe Epic Recession.

Minsky's ideas are partly based on the work of an earlier economist, John Maynard Keynes, in the 1930s. One of Keynes' great contributions was to explain in original and great detail how the process of investing drives real economic contractions; in particular, severe downturns like depressions. If Keynes represents a theory of how investment determines economic crisis, then Minsky represents a theory of how finance determines that investment. Prior to Minsky, economic theory post-1945 either ignored the role of finance in investment altogether, or was content to explore the relationship only in terms of how finance is related to investment and economic growth. There was little interest in how finance might contribute to the opposite—i.e. to economic instability and a collapse of economic growth.[31]

Keynes was not the first to explore the nature of speculative investing, as distinguished from other non-speculative forms of investment. A classic work by Phillip Carret in 1930 noted that "Speculation may be defined as the purchase or sale of securities of commodities in expectation of profiting by fluctuations in their prices," and that a pure speculator was someone who bought and sold in the same market "without rendering any service in the way of distribution, storage or transportation."[32] A speculator was a margin trader, "if not a gambler," someone who focused on the "psychology of the market" and was more "concerned with the trend of the general level of security price" than with contributions to real value represented by production, distribution, transportation or the like. As Carret noted, speculation had a close affinity to "the deep seated gambling instinct."[33]

The idea of speculative investing as gambling based on market psychology, betting on short-term price swings, seeking quick capital gains rather than a long-term income stream, was later explored by Keynes himself in a famous chapter of his book, *The General Theory of Employment, Interest and Money*, published in 1936. There he describes the psychology of the speculator, a professional divorced from the ownership of the company and its day-to-day management and thus little concerned about long-term returns and income streams from investments. Professional speculators attempt to estimate what the future price of the asset might be. But that estimation is based not only on what they themselves think the future price might be, but on what they think the average opinion of the uneducated mass of investors think the average opinion of the price in the future might be. The latter are the 'noise' traders. But as asset prices escalate, 'noise' trading becomes more important than information and a determining force in price inflation. Professional speculators find themselves dragged along into the speculative investment frenzy and maelstrom. The result is a 'bubble' in which asset price inflation becomes self-propelled and self-sustaining, driven by "average opinion thinking the average opinion thinks the price will continue to rise." A psychological 'herd instinct' takes over and tends to play a greater role as asset prices escalate. It is thus a process in which guessing, gambling, and betting become the investment behavioral norm. Keynes called it a casino, and he noted that Americans, particularly New York investors, were especially prone to this kind of financial gambling.[34]

The bubble, herd instinct, frenzy, gambling, and betting that characterize true speculative investing have a greater tendency to occur with financial asset prices than with physical assets or product prices. This is because, as noted, demand for financial assets becomes the primary driver of its price; and with price driving demand, a self-servicing cycle tends to set in between asset demand and asset price, with each driving the other. In contrast, prices for non-financial asset products and services simply don't behave that way. In other words, as Keynes and Minsky presciently noted, there is a kind of two-price system at work—one for financial assets and another for products.

Investment in financial assets, so long as prices of those assets continue to rise, is typically more profitable than investment in physical assets like plant, equipment, and facilities. Financial securities are essentially paper. They have no cost of goods or cost of sales to speak of. Nor costs of distribution. Their market demand is also immediately global. Their profit margins are therefore double or triple to begin with, and consequently so are potential profits as well. Their advantage is not only on the cost side. There are no supply limitations to financial securities production. They are only paper, and increasingly not even that—just electronic entries in most cases. Demand is therefore the primary determinant of price and profitability—just as price and profitability in turn become the primary determinant of demand. Prices are largely determined by their prices. This dominance of demand, and virtually costless supply creation, means that prices of financial security assets behave quite unlike prices of physical goods and services. Financial asset securities are truly a different animal in terms of product and price. The nature of both their demand and their supply are fundamentally different from products created from real physical assets. Most economists miss this fundamental distinction and view asset prices as determined in a similar fashion as prices of products—i.e. by supply and demand.

Another key aspect of speculative investing is its tendency toward ever greater use of what is called leveraging. Simply put, leveraging is borrowing a given amount of money capital in order to purchase a multiple amount of the given financial asset. Borrowing and leveraging may, of course, occur with non-speculative investing. In the case of speculative investing, however, the borrowing and leveraging serve to drive asset price inflation which in turn leads to still further borrowing and leveraging. The latter drive asset demand and price and in turn are driven by it. There is thus an upward spiraling tendency that is not present in borrowing for purposes of physical asset investing. For example, during the 1920s, leveraging in the form of so-called 'margin buying' of stocks became widespread, allowing both 'herd' and professional investors to purchase ever greater amounts of common stock. Only when stock prices peaked and then plummeted did the margin, or leveraging, cease. Whether in the form of margin buying or other forms, leveraging drives the upward spiral of financial asset prices—just as deleveraging in turn similarly drives a subsequent downward spiral. Leveraging for purposes of asset price speculation is thus another particular characteristic of speculative investing.

By 2007 leveraging had developed to new extremes. Over the most recent decade, leveraging had become even more pervasive and destabilizing than in the 1920s. A form of 'super-leveraging' was the norm. It was called 'securitization.' Securitization is multi-level leveraging. It is borrowing to purchase financial assets not only created from original physical assets (first derivative), but for purchase of financial assets based upon financial assets (second derivative). Or even third and fourth derivative assets based upon prior derivative assets. For example, a bond may be created from residential or commercial mortgages—a financial asset created from the original physical asset and instrument (the mortgage) of the home or office building. The bond represents a collection of mortgages (called a residential mortgage-based security (RMBS) for home mortgages, or a commercial mortgage-based security (CMBS) for a commercial property). The second derivative financial asset is thereafter composed of the RMBS and other financial assets, bundled into a derived asset called a collateralized debt obligation (CDO), marked up and sold for a further financial profit. That CDO may be bundled with other CDOs to create a purely 'synthetic' CDO—also marked up and resold for still further profit. That's a third derivative. A fourth derivative product might be a credit default swap (CDS), insuring against a failure of the prior financial asset (or betting that it will fail). Thus, speculative financing reached even greater heights by the twenty-first century. Securitization and the significant further expansion of forms of leveraging represent an essential characteristic of speculative investing.

Having provided an initial working description of speculative investment forms, how might one test the proposition that there has been an increasing shift toward speculative investing over the past several decades? There are unfortunately no data sources that provide a precise estimate of just speculative forms of investment as a breakout from total investment. There are data, however, that provide precise dollar values of non-speculative forms of domestic U.S. investment. The latter are to be found in the U.S. Bureau of Economic Affairs' database under the category of 'Private Non-Residential Fixed Investment.' Fixed investment includes U.S.-based investment in non-residential structures and equipment: commercial structures, office buildings, malls, hotels, industrial, manufacturing equipment, machinery, software, transport equipment, and the like. These totals are depicted in Table 2.9 for the period 1980–2009. For the purpose of comparison with speculative forms of investment, a proxy for the latter is corporate cash flow. Cash flow is what remains after taxes, dividends, real investment, and all other costs are paid. It is primarily composed of undistributed corporate profits and allowances for capital depreciation. Cash flow is not held by corporations as 'currency on hand,' as the term implies, but is actually invested in various near-liquid short-term financial securities. These might in part include government securities as a 'safe' short-term deposit of part of the total undistributed profits. But for the most part, cash flow is committed to short-term speculative plays, which the corporation can quickly cash out but may let ride so long as price appreciation of the financial asset in question continues. Rising cash flow is thus a proxy of sorts for estimating the shift toward speculative investing. Of course, not all speculative investing is financed out of corporate cash flow. It may also occur 'above the line,' as they say, on corporate income statements. And even that does not include such investing flows from individuals. The data in Table 2.9 therefore serve as a direction or trend toward speculative investing forms, not as a precise volume of speculative investment. Therefore, as a conservative estimate of the shift to speculative investing, the ratio of corporate cash flow to private fixed investment depicted in the table shows a definite growth of speculative investment in ratio to non-speculative forms of investment.

Table 2.9 Speculative Investment Shift: Corporate Cash Flow to Private Non-Residential Fixed Investment

Year	Corporate Cash Flow ($ billions)	Private Fixed Investment ($ billions)	Ratio Cash Flow to Investment (%)
1980	271	362	74
2000	877	1,268	81
2008	1,452	1,693	86
2009: II	n/a	n/a	> 95 (est.)

Sources: Bureau of Economic Analysis, *Private Non-Residential Fixed Investment*; *Corporate Undistributed Profits*, Tables 5.3.5 and Tables 6.21 b-d; and *Corporate Capital Consumption Allowances*, Tables 6.22 b-d, revised August 20, 2009.

Further supporting the idea of a shift toward greater speculative investment is a comparison of business debt and private non-residential fixed investment. Real asset investment as a percent of business debt has declined steadily. Since 2000 business debt has risen 69 percent, while real fixed investment was only 7.6 percent higher in mid-2009 compared to 2000. This means while business borrowing escalated over the period, the borrowing did not flow into real asset investment in the U.S. What did the increased levels of borrowing and debt then finance, if not real investment? The logical conclusion is that the lion's share of business borrowing went to finance financial instruments, securitized assets, derivatives of various sorts, and other forms of speculative investment. Alternatively, one might also argue the record borrowing and debt went to finance real investment outside the U.S. economy in China, emerging markets, and elsewhere. Or perhaps both—i.e. offshore real investment as well as financial instruments and derivatives globally. What is certain is that the historic escalation in business debt didn't produce a corresponding growth in real investment in the U.S., which has been lagging badly in the U.S. especially since 2000. It is thus a reasonable inference that the debt went largely to finance speculative forms of investing. The following Table 2.10

illustrates the escalation of total business debt growth and real investment between 2000-2008.

Table 2.10   Speculative Investment Shift: Business Debt and Private Non-Residential Fixed Investment

Year	Business Debt ($ billions)	Private Fixed Investment ($ billions)	Investment as % of Debt
1980	1,478	362	24.5
2000	6,595	1,268	19.2
2008	11,200	1,693	15.1
2009: II	11,153	1,365	12.2

Sources: Federal Reserve Board, *Flow of Funds*, Table D.3, September 17, 2009, and Bureau of Economic Analysis, *Private Fixed Investment by Type*, Table 5.3.5, revised October 29, 2009.

What Tables 2.9 and 2.10 together show is that, whether financing out of internal funds (cash flow) or out of borrowing (debt), an increasing share of liquidity is not leading to a corresponding increase in real investment in the U.S. That means either the investing is going offshore, or it is being redirected to speculative forms of investment, especially over the most recent decade.

The above tables and data represent but one of several possible ways of indicating the growing shift to speculative forms of investment. Analysis thus far has focused on levels of debt (i.e. an accumulated 'stock'). Focusing on annual lending 'flows' rather than total debt level, other observers have recently noted:

In the 1990s and 2000s, loan volumes rose to unprecedented levels, supporting global assets booms in property, derivatives and the carry trade. The share of lending by US banks to the US financial sector [read: from commercial banks to shadow banks like hedge funds, private equity firms, etc. Author's note]—instead of to the real economy—went from 60 percent of the outstanding loan stock in 1980 (up from 50 percent in the 1950s) to more than 80 percent in 2007.[35]

In other words, the shift toward speculative investing is not just a long-term trend dating from at least the 1980s, but a shift that has clearly begun to accelerate in the last decade in particular. The acceleration of this trend is most evident in the residential mortgage markets after 2000. If one considers the originating mortgage on a residential property a form of 'real asset investment,' then the growing share of subprime mortgages and the subsequent further securitization of those subprime mortgages together clearly represent evidence of a growing shift toward speculative investing in the housing markets. Table 2.11 illustrates the shift toward speculative financing in the residential mortgage markets, as subprimes and their securitized further resales as mortgage-backed securities (MBSs), rose sharply as a percentage of total mortgage originations.

Table 2.11 Speculative Shift of Residential Mortgages, 2002–06

Year	Total Mortgage Originations ($ billions)	Subprimes Origination ($ billions)	Subprime Share Total Mortgages (%)	Subprime MBSs ($ billions)	Securitized Subprimes (%)
2002	2,885	231	8.0	121	52.7
2003	3,945	335	8.5	202	60.5
2004	2,920	540	18.5	401	74.3
2005	3,120	625	20.0	507	81.2
2006	2,980	600	20.1	483	80.5

Source: Inside Mortgage Finance, 2007, as reported in Jan Kregel, "Changes in the U.S. Financial System and the Subprime Crisis," Levy Economics Institute, Working Paper no. 530, April 2008.

Tables 2.9 and 2.10 illustrated the speculative shift by comparing debt and cash flow to non-residential fixed investment—i.e. real investment in physical assets like structures, equipment, etc., but minus the particularly volatile residential housing sector. In Table 2.11 a view of just that housing sector is provided, showing within it a definitive shift toward speculative forms as well.

Table 2.12 shows housing and all other real asset investment combined in what is called total fixed private investment. The relative growth of that larger sector is then compared to a broader composite of three types of speculative financial assets and securities. Once again, with these even broader measures the picture is a clear shift toward more speculative forms of investment. The data further suggest that as the speculative forms have grown, the real investment forms have slowed in terms of growth—providing further evidence of the speculative shift.

Table 2.12 Combined Speculative Investing Shift: Composite of Three Securities versus Real Investment, 2002–06 ($ billions)

Year	Subprimes + ABS Issues + U.S. 10% Share of CDS	Real Private Fixed Investment
2002	559.4	1,570.2
2003	726.1	1,649.8
2004	1,306.0	1,830.0
2005	2,035.8	2,042.8
2006	2,775.2	2,171.1

Sources: Data from *Inside Mortgage Finance, 2007*; Federal Reserve, *Flow of Funds*, Table F.1, March 30, 2003 and June 11, 2009; *International Swaps and Derivatives Association*, as reported by Insurance Information Institute, New York, January 2009; and Bureau of Economic Analysis, *National Income Accounts*, Table 5.3.2 for 2001–06.

ABS (asset-backed securities) are a form of derivative instrument which, as in the case of all derivatives investing, constitutes a speculative form. Between 2002 and 2006, ABS issuers' annual net lending rose from $241.4 billion in 2002 to $799.2 billion—for a total five-year net lending of $2.437 trillion.[36] Comparing the two flows, speculative and real, shows a much faster rate of growth and an increase in the ratio of speculative investing to real asset investing. Considering just three categories of speculative investment (subprimes, ABS, CDS), speculative investing flows grew by nearly 396 percent over the course of the five-year period, while non-speculative physical asset investment grew by only 38 percent.

And the composite three securities (subprimes, ABS, 10 percent CDS) are only part of the picture. Still unaccounted for is investing by hedge funds, private equity firms, and the rest of the shadow banking sector in other speculative derivatives markets, like the collateralized loan obligation (CLO) market ($480 billion in 2006) and the leveraged buyout (LBO) loan market ($200 billion in 2006).

Also worth noting is that our 10 percent estimate of CDS volume is intentionally very conservative. CDS bets or trades over the same period, 2002–06, escalated from $2.1 trillion to $62 trillion by 2007.[37] These are, of course, global figures. The U.S. 10 percent share is estimated as follows: approximately 40 percent, or $24 trillion, of the $62 trillion is assumed to represent U.S. share of CDS trades. It is then assumed that only 10 percent of the $24 trillion might represent actual lending to purchase the CDS contracts. That's $2.4 trillion committed to speculative investing (i.e. betting', in the case of CDS), perhaps 80–90 percent of which was borrowed to leverage the CDS purchases, and the remainder actual purchases by investors. That's liquidity which might otherwise have been invested in real assets to produce, in turn, jobs, income, and government tax revenue in the U.S. As former Federal Reserve Chairman Paul Volcker remarked on the matter of CDS on the late-night Charlie Rose TV show: "You know, $60 trillion dollars worth of nominal insurance against credits, and they only had $10 trillion in credits! I mean what's going on here, why did we need $60 trillion worth of protection, because people are trading with each other, speculating in effect…it's a kind of dead use of credit, dead use of liquidity…."[38]

Key conclusions from the foregoing evidence—whether debt or lending flows—is that a shift toward speculative forms of investing has been building for decades, and that that shift began to accelerate in the most recent decade. That shift is heavily responsible for the corresponding growth of financial fragility over time. And it may very well be playing a role in the relative decline in real asset investment concurrently. Speculative forms of investment, in other words, may be 'crowding out' real physical asset investment that is the source of job creation and real disposable income growth for the bottom 80 percent of U.S. households. Thus, the speculative shift may act as a cause not only of growing financial fragility but also of deteriorating consumption fragility. One of the greatest problems confronting the U.S. economy in the first decade of the twenty-first century is that both forms of fragility—financial and consumption—are becoming worse. Recent fiscal and banking measures by the Obama administration in 2009 have not changed these trends significantly; nor solved the problem of dual fragility, financial and consumption. Although consumption fragility has its own independent causes, the shift to speculative forms of investment has been, and will continue to be, a major factor driving consumption fragility as well as financial fragility.

GLOBAL SYNCHRONIZATION

A final qualitative characteristic of Epic Recessions is the tendency of Epic Recessions to become synchronized globally.

Economic historians who have analyzed the several great depressions in the nineteenth century and in the 1920s and 1930s generally point to the gold standard and trade protectionism as key causes of the globalization of the depressions (or even as the primary root causes). They subsequently argue that, since today the world is no longer on a gold standard, and if it can prevent trade protectionism, then a synchronized global downturn and depression is avoidable. To argue to the contrary, however, synchronization does not require a gold standard. Other transmission mechanisms may apply. And while trade protectionism may exacerbate the economic decline it is not a prerequisite for a depression. In fact, if one simply looks at conditions in mid 2009, international trade had never been 'freer,' but exports and trade volumes continued to collapse around the globe in dramatic fashion during 2008–09. Clearly something else was at work propagating and spreading the crisis geographically, and doing so at an accelerating rate for a period.

The key to synchronization lies in the fact that Epic Recessions are always precipitated by severe financial fragility and financial crises. Since normal recessions are not accompanied by precipitating financial fragility and financial crises, they consequently do not synchronize. Given the interconnections between the banking and finance systems globally (which has always been the case, to a major extent), financial instability itself not only spreads rapidly in instances of Epic Recession, but the credit contraction that follows in the wake of financial instability spreads nearly equally as rapidly, causing real economies subsequently to contract more or less in tandem as well. What appears as synchronization, in other words, is at least in part a rapid rate of propagation and spread of the financial crisis and more or less simultaneous credit contraction across economies.

The important question is whether synchronization continues after the initial propagation and spread of the financial crisis and credit contraction. Continued synchronization depends, in part, upon the magnitude and swiftness of the fiscal and monetary responses of the respective national economies, as well as the relative severity of financial and consumption fragility at the outset of the crisis in each of the respective economies. In other words, synchroniza-tion is not constant and necessarily continuing. For example, in the current financial crisis and Epic Recession, China initially experienced a degree of both financial and real economic contraction. But it quickly moved to inject a massive fiscal spending program that was far larger in terms of its GDP than was the U.S. fiscal stimulus. It subsequently began recovering much quicker than the U.S. Nor was the degree of financial fragility as severe in China or Asia at the outset, compared to the U.S., the U.K., and other countries on the periphery of the European Union, like Iceland, Ireland, Spain, Greece and elsewhere. The transmission mechanisms and thus the synchronization that is a characteristic of Epic Recession therefore start with financial instability and financial crisis. Other factors thereafter may contribute to the continuation of synchronization after its initial occurrence. A collapse of consumption in one or more of the major global consumer centers of the economy, like the U.S., can have a major effect on other export-dependent economies. Currency instability and competitive currency depreciations may also play a role.

There are, of course, historical examples of Epic Recessions happening that do not necessarily result in a global synchronized economic contraction. Although not the subject of this book, Japan in 1990–2005 may well qualify as such an example. The U.S. in 1907–13 may be another. Several Latin American economies in the 1980s and 1990s may represent still another. Furthermore, not all characteristics of Epic Recession—quantitative, qualitative, dynamic— need necessarily occur in order to constitute an Epic Recession. It may be that Epic Recessions that do not synchronize globally are those that lack potential to make the transition to a bona fide depression. Synchronization may thus represent a necessary characteristic for the evolution of an Epic Recession into a depression. Examples of the latter may be the U.S. and European economies in the late 1920s to the 1930s.

3
The Dynamics of Epic Recession

The two preceding chapters addressed static quantitative and qualitative characteristics of Epic Recession. This chapter is concerned with the dynamic characteristics of Epic Recessions—i.e. those characteristics that explain the processes by which Epic Recessions evolve over time.

We begin by referring back to the graphic representation in the introductory chapter of the fundamental forces and relationships of Epic Recessions. That graphic, reproduced as Figure 3.1, indicates the various relationships and possible directions of mutual causation between the forces fundamental to the origins and evolution of Epic Recessions.

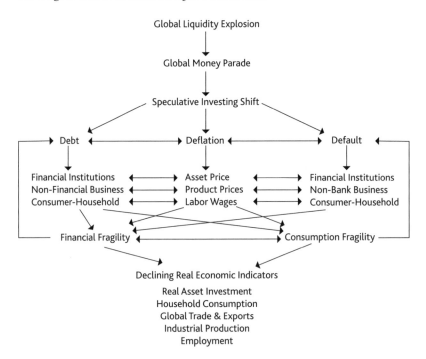

Figure 3.1   Fundamental Forces and Relationships of Epic Recession

GLOBAL LIQUIDITY EXPLOSION

At the top of the pyramid is the explosion in global liquidity. Liquidity is cash and near-cash forms of liquid assets that can be relatively easily and quickly converted to investment. That investment may take the form of real physical assets, like structures, equipment, inventories of products, etc.; or the form of financial assets, like bonds, commercial paper, stocks, derivatives financial instruments, and so forth. Whichever the form, the point is liquidity is the basis for investment. It is the source for issuing credit and thus debt. The extension of credit becomes the debt of the borrower of that credit. Liquidity enables banks to issue loans, corporations to issue bonds, speculators to purchase derivatives, etc.

There are several major sources responsible for the exploding liquidity in the U.S. and global economy over the last several decades. All have contributed to the growing volume of liquidity, such that today there is now a flood of liquidity awash in the global economy. The unprecedented surge in liquidity is the source of credit and corresponding debt accumulation. And it is that credit and debt acceleration that has fueled and enabled the run-up in speculative investing to historic, record levels in turn.

One source of the global liquidity explosion has been the U.S. central bank, the Federal Reserve (Fed). Since the dollar became the de facto global currency in 1944 (and the virtual de jure global currency since 1971, when the last fiction of a gold standard was abandoned), U.S. monetary policies for more than half a century have been injecting trillions of dollars into the U.S. and global economies. That's trillions of dollars of excess liquidity that has accumulated globally in the hands of investors public and private, corporate and sovereign, individual and institutional.

It represents a record volume between $20 and $40 trillion of investible money capital that cannot lie idle and must find an outlet.

The Fed enables the expansion of credit in the commercial banking system by means of buying government bonds back from the banks, changing their minimum reserve requirements of those banks, or loaning money to individual banks directly through the Fed's 'discount window.'[1] Since December 2007 it has added a fourth new 'tool' for injecting liquidity into the economy called targeted 'auctions,' designed to provide massive bailout funding for banks, shadow banks, and even non-financial corporations. By means of these special auctions over the last two years, the Fed has injected or committed to provide between $2 trillion and $11 trillion, depending on which accounting approach one chooses. But Fed actions since December 2007 constitute only the latest of a long string of liquidity pumping actions by the Fed.

When there's a recession, the Fed injects liquidity. That occurred in response to the normal recessions that happened in 1966, 1970, 1973–75, 1980, 1982, 1990, and 2001. In addition, every time there's a financial instability event, the Fed injects still more liquidity to offset banks' anticipated losses to keep them from insolvency and lending. That occurred in 1987–88 in response to the stock market crash of 1987; in 1989–92 to bail out the savings and loan and junk bond markets; in 1997–98 to rescue the Long Term Capital Management hedge fund and Asian banks and financial institutions with ties to U.S. banks; in 1999 to counter fears about computers coming to a stop with the change in the millennia (a phony mini-panic called the Y2K or 'year 2000'); 2000–01 to counter the tech-driven stock market bust, and 2002–04 to keep the housing market going as the rest of the economy faltered. On occasion the Fed has even injected liquidity to assist Presidents in their election bids or war policies, such as in 1971–72 in the case of Nixon and 2003–04 for George W. Bush.

In contrast to its long-term policy of pumping liquidity into the economy, the Fed has done little in the way of successfully retracting that same liquidity after recessions, major financial instability events, or following the accommodation of Presidents' political demands. The roughly 20 years of Fed 'net' liquidity injections into the U.S. economy, from 1986 to 2006 under the chairmanship of Alan Greenspan, has become known as the Greenspan 'Put.' Since 2007, an even greater net liquidity injection has occurred under its current chairman, Ben Bernanke. It will no doubt eventually become known as the 'Bernanke Put'—i.e. a far greater amount in a much shorter period of time.

The Fed's decades-long, pro-liquidity policies not only contributed to a build-up of liquidity within the U.S. economy, but did so throughout the global economy as well. To the extent easier credit from the Fed was accessible to U.S. banks with operations and dealings abroad—which has become the case increasingly since the early 1990s—some of that Fed-provided liquidity to those U.S. banks was undoubtedly diverted offshore. Similarly, loans to non-bank U.S. companies with foreign subsidiaries no doubt resulted in liquidity flowing offshore to those subsidiaries, as well as for those multinational companies' growing acquisitions of additional offshore assets since 1990. The latter is called foreign direct investment (FDI), and that, too, has been fueled by Fed monetary policies creating excess liquidity in the system.

Other U.S. government policies have also contributed to the growth of dollar liquidity globally. U.S. government policies providing foreign aid to sovereign countries for decades increased the flow of dollars and liquidity from the U.S. into the global system. So did funding of U.S. military bases and operations around the world. And policies of free trade, that resulted in chronic and rising U.S. trade deficits since the 1980s. Trade deficits have meant net annual outflows of hundreds of billions of dollars every year from the U.S. economy since the 1980s, culminating in more than $700 billion in trade deficits for four years running during the mid 2000s alone. A further consequence of U.S. free trade policies has been the expansion of U.S. companies' FDI which, as previously noted, has transferred additional billions of dollars offshore. Then there's the major structural changes that have occurred in the U.S. tax system since 1980 that have permitted wealthy U.S. investors, individual and institutional, to shift decades of money capital from capital gains, dividends, and interest income into offshore tax havens to avoid tax payments to the U.S.—in dozens of small or island nations from the Cayman Islands to the Seychelles to Vanuatu to Switzerland and beyond. All the above developments have combined to enable a flow of trillions of dollars into offshore venues—going into foreign central banks, private banks, and financial institutions, offshore hedge and investment funds, personal and corporate accounts in tax havens, etc. Thus, while the Fed has obviously been a major contributor to the steady growth of liquidity in the U.S. and the global economy, it hasn't been the only source. U.S. government military, trade, and tax policies have contributed as well.

In addition to the Fed, and U.S. military spending, trade and tax policies, at least two other major forces have additionally contributed to the historic expansion of liquidity worldwide in recent decades. One is what is sometimes called the 'global savings glut.'

There are different interpretations of the meaning of the global savings glut. For former Federal Reserve chairman Alan Greenspan, the global savings glut represents the accumulated reserves held by foreign central banks, private banks, and investors.

It is the global savings glut, as Greenspan defines it, that caused the flood of liquidity into the U.S. between 2002–05 that drove down mortgage interest rates, which in turn caused the subprime market boom. It wasn't the Fed lowering short-term rates to 1 percent and keeping them there for nearly two years that caused the speculative boom in residential housing.[2] The housing bubble occurred worldwide, not just in the U.S. It was the excess global liquidity that flooded into the U.S. housing market that was the culprit. The cause, therefore, was the glut—sometimes referred to as another sanitized term, 'global imbalances'—that was responsible. The bubble was thus beyond the Fed's or any central bank's control. But even if it is true, as Greenspan maintains, that the post-2002 boom occurred simultaneously in many global markets and not just the U.S. and the Fed therefore could not have been responsible; even if one were to agree with him that the global savings glut washing back onto U.S. economic shores circa 2002 was the sole cause of the U.S. subprime housing bubble—what, then, explains the origins of that global savings glut itself?[3]

First, data is irrefutably clear that the U.S. housing price bubble began in 1997, not in 2002. The speculation in residential housing markets preceded the Fed's 2002 lowering of rates as well as the alleged 2002–05 foreign investment inflows by at least five years.[4] Both the Fed's low 1 percent rates and the simultaneous global liquidity inflows contributed to the subprime housing bubble. But neither was the originating cause. The subprime boom of 2002–05 was just the culminating phase of the housing bubble.[5] What set off the start of housing speculation and the beginning of the run-up in housing prices around 1997–98 is the fundamental question Greenspan must answer, but doesn't. In addition, Greenspan must explain further why the dot. com technology stocks bubble originated around 1997 as well, and why the speculative bubble in Asian currencies that led to the Asian financial meltdown in 1997–98 (that in turn spread to Russia and Latin American economies, and required the bailout of the big hedge fund, Long Term Capital Management, in 1998) occurred as well, circa 1997–98? What was beginning to happen circa 1997–98 that precipitated all three bubbles? Was it just coincidental that all three speculative bubbles commenced around the same time? Or is there a common thread and origin to all three?

The global savings glut began with the river of dollars with which the U.S. flooded the world for decades as a direct consequence of its monetary, fiscal, and military policies. But that flow of dollars was only the start—a kind of priming of the global liquidity pump. The global savings glut has been an equally important factor contributing to the global liquidity explosion. The glut is the product of the past three decades of unprecedented profits, income, and wealth accumulation. But it is not faceless 'savings' or 'reserves,' as Greenspan and others call it. Those are misleading terms that function for the purpose of obfuscating a deeper meaning. The 'glut' is in fact the accumulation and concentration of income and wealth among certain strata of investors worldwide, taking the form of excess money and credit capital, that is now increasingly seeking out and flowing into speculative investment opportunities globally at an increasing rate. The glut therefore has a face: the rising global 'investor elite' of individuals, funds, investing institutions, corporations, banks, shadow banks, and central banks.

The income-wealth accumulated by that elite over more than three decades now has derived from both real asset and speculative asset investment, but increasingly in recent years from the latter and decreasingly from the former. The real asset investment has concentrated in manufacturing and infrastructure investment in the so-called BRIC countries—i.e. Brazil, Russia, India, and especially China—and to a more limited extent in certain industries like energy extraction and commercial building the petro-economies. The rising share of accumulation of income and wealth from speculative investing has come from commodities, oil, gold, metals, currency and stock speculation, futures and options trading, land and commercial properties, funding of mergers and acquisitions, infrastructure bonds, buying and selling in secondary markets, securitized financial assets, credit insurance, and a host of other derivative-based financial instruments.

Once again, the glut is therefore not really about 'savings' or foreign investors' reserves. That is a misnomer for what is in essence a concentration of income and wealth among a global strata of investors with a unique control of new, as well as old, forms of money capital. The glut represents global income inequality—not between nations, but between the investor classes within most nations and their non-investor countrymen. This investor elite of course includes members in the advanced economies of North America, Europe and Japan, just as it does those in Singapore, Hong Kong, Dubai, Seoul, Shanghai, Rio, Bangalore and elsewhere. It is not about Third World or 'emerging markets' investors. It reflects a global transformation of capital, as well as a restructuring of the various constituent elements of the class in control of that capital.

In addition to the Fed and U.S. military spending, trade and tax policies, and the global savings glut, there is yet a fourth major source of the global liquidity explosion. The policies of the Fed and the U.S. government since 1945 that have flooded the world economy with dollars, and the policies since 1980 that have set in motion the concentration of income on a global scale, do not, by themselves, fully account for the explosion of liquidity of recent decades. That record liquidity was also the consequence of the revolution in credit creation that has been unleashed in large part by the shadow banking system.

Normally liquidity is created in the banking system when the central bank of a country injects money into its banking system. That money injection increases the reserves on hand in the banks with which to extend credit to borrowers. As the banks lend the money to customers the money supply increases in the economy. The actual process of credit creation occurs when the private banks actually extend loans—i.e. credit—to borrowers who subsequently make investments. This describes a traditional process by which a central bank (the Fed) determines the amount and timing of liquidity injection and credit. But that liquidity creation process has been giving way progressively over recent decades to a different kind of credit creation system that is growing relatively more independent of the central bank and whatever action it may take. Central banks' injection of money into the banking system may lead to an increase in credit as banks loan out the money to borrowers. But banks' credit extension is not limited to this process. Banks and shadow banks provide credit, but have been doing so increasingly independently of the money supply and central banks (for example, the Fed) money supply management processes. In other words, credit is becoming unhinged from money.

In the new system of credit, financial instruments themselves are used as the basis of credit extension and thus borrowing and debt. For example, when a financial instrument, like a collateralized debt obligation derivative, is created based on a subprime mortgage, and the market value of that derivative rises, that increased market value is then used as the basis for issuing further credit to purchase yet more financial instruments. Investments are not made based on the central bank increasing or decreasing the reserves banks may have on hand. Loans and credit extensions now have little or nothing to do with banks' existing levels of loanable excess reserves. Because these financial instruments are tradable immediately on secondary markets short term, they are more or less 'liquid'; i.e. they can be used like money to purchase other financial assets. And as such financial instruments grow in volume and value, they are in effect increasing the overall liquidity within the system. Such credit financing is especially appropriate for investing in financial instruments. As the value of financial instruments rises (which presumes a continued rise in their price), it enables investing in still more similar financial instruments. The process would not be possible without the development of 'securitization' and highly liquid secondary markets for speculative financial instruments. In a sense, therefore, securitization and secondary markets create liquidity for financing still additional speculative investing.

A couple of additional concrete examples: credit default swaps (CDS) derivatives and 'naked short selling.' With CDSs an investor may speculate that a company will default, so he/she 'buys' an insurance contract (a CDS) to protect against that failure. But the speculator does not actually 'buy' in the sense of putting real dollars up to purchase the CDS contract. At most, he/she may put up a very small share of the actual cost of the CDS and leverage the rest—i.e. owe it as debt. All derivatives financial securities are in a similar way 'leveraged'; i.e. credit (and debt) far beyond what is invested in real money is extended to the borrower. Credit, and corresponding debt, is created independently of bank reserves and Fed efforts to manage levels of bank reserves.

The case of what is called naked short selling of stocks by speculators is even more blatant. Short selling has been around for some time. It is associated with stock selling. Professional stock traders borrow to buy stock at its current price with the expectation of selling it later once the price declines and pocketing the difference as pure speculative profits. The borrowing incurs a short-term debt for which an interest charge or fee must be paid. The borrowing also creates downward pressure on the stock price in question.

Naked short selling takes the speculative practice one step further. 'Naked' means traders don't even borrow the funds in order to buy. Naked short selling amounts to buying stock without putting a penny down—i.e. 100 percent leveraging. Naked short sales amount to selling something you never owned. In other words, it's another extreme form of speculation, more like pure betting when purchasing CDSs than buying and selling of a stock per se. Naked short selling results in even greater downward pressure on a stock's price. Naked short sellers played a major role in the collapse of Bear Stearns, Fannie Mae, and Lehman brothers in the intensifying financial crisis during 2008, as speculators turned increasingly toward naked short selling.[6]

Naked short selling has the eventual result of causing a rise in corporate debt for those companies targeted by the short sellers. To the extent that short selling drives down stock prices, it makes it increasingly difficult for corporations to raise capital by means of stock issuance. That forces them to borrow and increase their debt, or to forego real investment activity altogether, which often means a reduction in real investment and jobs. As the recent financial crisis spread globally, the practice of short selling was banned or severely restricted in many places in Asia, Australia, Europe—but not in the U.S. Naked short selling might also be considered a form of 'financial cannibalism,' in that investors in shadow banks prey upon investors in real asset institutions like non-financial companies.

Shadow banks, hedge funds, and their investors have been particular active in naked short selling during the recent financial crisis. According to the premier market research source tracking the hedge fund industry, Hedge Fund Research, hedge funds involved in short selling (including the increasing practice of naked selling) accounted for about 40 percent of the $3 trillion in global hedge fund assets in 2007–08.[7]

Investing in CDSs and naked short selling represent 'investment as betting' and thus an extreme form of speculative investing. But they would not be possible without the new forms of liquidity creation with which they are financed. These new forms of speculative investing typically often also result in an increase in debt levels for companies with real assets and therefore negatively affect levels of real asset investment in those companies. On the other hand, profits and returns to speculators are often significant. Driven by asset price inflation, speculative profits are often several magnitudes greater than profits from investment in real assets, so long as prices continue to rise. Speculative profits also have the added enticement that they can be realized in a much shorter time period. That capital-profit turnover time makes such investments further attractive. And so long as the price of the asset continues to rise, the expectation of profitability is more certain compared, say, to investing in real assets and real products for which demand may or may not materialize at all. Despite the frequency of financial crises in the past 20 years, it appears that profits from speculative investing have grown significantly faster than from real asset investing. For every speculator who waits too long to exit a bubble, and thus loses capital, in net terms more gain from the run-up and price bubble. That net growth in profits and wealth in turn adds to the global savings glut and the global pool of liquidity available for subsequent investing.

Financial deregulation increased the rate and geographic spread of speculative investing. It opened up and accelerated global capital flows. It permitted and stimulated the growth of shadow banking-financial intermediaries as the prime distribution channels for speculative investing and allowed the regulated banking system to play in those same channels and markets. But it did not create the fundamental requirement for speculative investing. That fundamental requirement was the explosion of liquidity. Without that liquidity, and the new forms of leveraging that accompanied it, there would be nothing to speculate with. The new forms of leveraging that expanded it, the new financial instruments that productized it, the new forms of institutions that distributed it, and the new markets in which those financial instruments were sold—are all predicated on the creation of a massive global pool of excess liquidity.

To sum up, there exists today a massive global pool of liquid and near-liquid money capital that must find an investment outlet. Estimated roughly in the range of $20–40 trillion worldwide, it is thus so excessively large that it cannot find sufficient real, fixed investment opportunities to absorb all of it. There is far more liquidity than real physical asset investment opportunities—notwithstanding the infrastructure growth in China, India, Brazil and the like. More critically, real asset investment may not be as profitable as speculative investing in any event. Meanwhile, that liquidity pool cannot and will not remain idle. It is therefore prone to seek out new price-driven speculative opportunities, which are more easily and quickly exploited, with faster turnover and often with greater returns, than physical asset investment in structures, equipment, inventories and such.

THE GLOBAL MONEY PARADE

The flooding of both the U.S. and global economy with U.S. dollars, the global savings glut, plus new forms of credit creation have produced a historic growth in available liquidity in the global economy. The volume of liquidity is only part of the story, however. Where that liquidity resides and to what uses it is being put are equally important. In what institutions is that liquidity 'deposited'? In what asset types is it invested? Who are the investors—institutional, corporate, and wealthy individual?

How much of the estimated $20–40 trillion in outstanding liquidity today resides in the global network of commercial banks, like J.P. Morgan Chase and Bank of America? How much of it in those institutions referred to as shadow banks or financial intermediaries—i.e. the investment banks like Goldman Sachs and Morgan Stanley? Giant hedge funds, like Citadel, and the hedge fund sector, which grew from just several hundred in the 1990s to more than 10,000 by 2008 with nearly $2 trillion in assets?[8] Private equity firms like Carlyle or Blackstone that controlled several trillions more at their peak? Finance companies like GMAC and GE Credit? Government-sponsored enterprises (GSEs; quasi-private financial institutions created by Congress) like Fannie Mae and Freddie Mac? Or in the allegedly more conservative investing institutions like the $4 trillion money market funds, the multi-trillion-dollar pension funds, emerging market funds, sovereign wealth funds of the oil-rich economies, etc.?

As noted in a previous chapter, for the U.S. alone it is estimated that the network of shadow banking institutions by 2007 accounted for more than $10 trillion, about equal to the assets of the commercial banking sector. And the U.S. share of the global shadow banking network is probably no more than 40 percent at most. Moreover, the commercial banks have over the last decade merged with shadow banks in various ways—at least the largest of the commercial banks. So it makes less and less sense over time to even refer to the distinction of the two banking sectors. Commercial banks have turned increasingly to the higher profitable speculative forms of investing. And they have long funded the shadow banks to a significant extent, have set up their own hedge funds and private equity firms, established private bank operations for their wealthiest clients, and acted in part like shadow banks in fact, if not in name. So part of the big commercial banks must be considered a segment of the shadow banking sector as well, and a significant amount of their lending activity has no doubt been increasingly speculative.

A testimony to that latter point is the huge amount of lending by commercial banks that has occurred since May 2009 to speculators in foreign currency and emerging markets. The banks borrow from the Fed at 0.25 percent and loan at substantially higher rates to clients speculating in Asian, Latin American, and Russian currencies. Less involved in highly speculative ventures as a general rule are the 8,200 or so smaller regional and community banks and thrift institutions in the U.S., although to the extent that this group has participated in financing subprime mortgages and highly leveraged commercial property deals, they, too, have forayed into speculative investment in major ways. All these represent a shortlist of institutional loci in which much of the world liquidity resides. Add to these institutions investing on behalf of clients (as well as on behalf of themselves as institutions), very wealthy individuals who invest directly themselves rather than via institutions, and the thousands of corporations that, to some degree, also invest directly with their companies' retained earnings.

These investors—individual, corporate, and institutional alike—have been shifting their liquidity increasingly in recent decades into speculative investments; i.e. investment opportunities of a short term, price-driven asset nature rather than in longer-term enterprise, equipment, and structures that payout with a longer, amortized stream of income. That is, investments in financial asset securities. The profits are greater due to the price volatility. The costs are lower since most speculative investing is in financial securities with no costs of production and low cost of sales. There are no potential supplier bottlenecks. Distribution is instantaneous and the market size is global. The turnover in profitability is as short as the investor chooses, and the short-term risk is less because the assets can be quickly resold in secondary markets most of the time.

These immense relative advantages in costs of speculative investing in financial securities, compared to investing in real physical assets, combined with the possible quick returns and the potential for excess price-driven profits, together result in a kind of 'global money parade' that sloshes around markets internationally seeking speculative opportunities—a financial tornado that causes speculative bubbles wherever it touches down.

That parade consists fundamentally of those investors globally that have become greater in number than ever before, controlling a share of total global liquidity that is at historic record levels, and that exhibit a growing preference for speculative investing. And where has most of the liquidity they control been going? Into foreign exchange trading, over-the-counter derivatives trading, buying and selling of securitized asset-backed securities (ABSs), collateralized debt obligations (CDOs), collateralized loan obligations (CLOs), residential and commercial mortgage-backed securities (RMBSs; CMBSs), credit default swaps (CDSs), interest rate and currency swaps, futures and options trades of all kinds, leveraged buyouts (LBOs), emerging market funds, high-yield corporate junk bonds and funds, into stock market speculation worldwide, into short selling of stocks, landed property speculation, and global commodities of all kinds, from food and metals to gold and oil. A global money parade marching to and fro across global financial markets, from one short-term speculative opportunity to another, at times exacerbating asset price volatility, at other times precipitating it, and sometimes even pushing asset inflation to the level of financial bust.

An important dynamic characteristic of Epic Recession is that it is typically preceded by a proliferation of multiple asset bubbles fueled by the global money parade that more or less mature in tandem. When one or more of the bubbles overextends and then collapses, it quickly precipitates similar collapses in other bubbles. The magnitude of the financial bust thereafter evokes a credit contraction well beyond that which may occur in a normal recession. How deep and widespread the contraction depends in part on the degree of financial fragility that has developed at the time of the financial bust; and in part on the degree of consumption fragility as well. Both forms of fragility are a function of debt, debt servicing capability, and income. As debt levels unwind in Epic Recession, the subsequent trajectory of the Epic Recession depends thereafter on the rate of deflation and defaults, and in turn on the ability or failure of government policies to check and contain the deflation–defaults and/or to reduce debt levels that exacerbate the deflation–default levels and rates.

The extent and composition of speculative investing is directly related to the degree of financial fragility. Data suggests the greater the speculative investing, the greater the financial fragility. The relationship between speculative investing and real asset investing, and the impact of the former on the latter, is also of importance to consumption fragility as follows: the failure to provide sufficient real asset investment over the long run seriously impairs and weakens consumption fragility, inasmuch as speculative investment indirectly contributes to consumption fragility through job loss and reduced wage income. That loss of jobs and reduced wage income takes place when real asset investment weakens over the longer term due to diversion of liquidity into increasing amounts of speculative forms of investing.

The characteristic of the speculative shift thus becomes of some importance. We have seen how and why the global money parade has become predisposed increasingly toward speculative forms of investing. How, in turn, the speculative shift is related to debt, deflation, and default is a related dynamic characteristic of Epic Recession requiring further consideration.

THREE ECONOMISTS ON SPECULATION AND INSTABILITY

A vast amount of total global liquidity is thus being redirected, and reallocated from market to market with increasing frequency, by the global money parade of institutions and their investors into speculative forms of investment. Chapter 2's initial definition of speculative investing provided a first approximation working definition. Data in various combinations were provided to show the trend toward speculative forms at the apparent expense of forms of real investment. Speculative investment, it was argued, was distinguishable from non-speculative forms by its focus on the short term, its lower cost of production and lack of supply-driven price constraints, its greater dependency on demand and consequent focus on price driven returns, its focus on short-term capital gains and disinclination toward investing in real assets with longer-term income streams, and its tendency toward investing as an act of 'betting' in its extreme forms like CDSs and short selling.

Having considered some dynamic relationships between global liquidity and the money parade on speculative investing, it is now necessary to explore the influence of speculative investing on the key processes of debt, deflation, and default that are central to the origin and evolution of Epic Recessions and, through the medium of debt–deflation–default, of speculative investing on financial and consumption fragility.

As a starting point, it is useful to return again to the three great economists, Keynes, Irving Fisher, and Hyman Minsky, for their respective further insights on the subject. Each provides a contribution from differing perspectives: Keynes on speculative investing and its long-term possible consequences for real investment; Fisher on the impact of debt on deflation and its financially and real destabilizing effects; and Minsky on the institutional aspects of speculation and its role in contributing to financial fragility and instability.

A decade before he wrote his *The General Theory of Employment, Interest and Money* in 1936, the famous economist, John Maynard Keynes, began to explore some of the relationships between speculation and asset price booms and busts. In his earlier work, *A Treatise on Money*, Keynes identified various stages of a business cycle in which speculative investment in financial securities tended to surge and overwhelm other forms of investment—a kind of first identification of the speculative shift and its consequences. Price inflation drove speculative investment to extremes as a result of the excess availability of credit (debt), which continued to grow so long as prices continued to rise. Eventually a point was reached, however, during which the psychological sentiment of investors shifted and price deflation drove the process in the opposite direction. As Keynes put it, "If everyone agrees securities are worth more...there is no limit to the rise in price of securities and no effective check arises from a shortage of money."[9] Speculation thus developed its own demand forces internally. That demand was an irrational general opinion on the part of investors as to the continued direction (and rate) of price increases. Rising prices drove speculation and, in turn, speculation drove up prices still further. It was not a question of supply *and* demand forces determining price inflation, as economists before him (and still today) like to argue—i.e. that both supply and demand together determine price. Indeed, the inference from Keynes is that supply was at times not at all a factor in the case of speculation in financial securities, while demand was potentially unlimited. Prices and markets for financial assets did not behave like prices and markets for products or real assets, that is for consumer or producer goods and services.

There was therefore a dual 'two price system' at work in the economy. The two systems may interact but behaved quite differently and were in many ways autonomous. Moreover, the system of prices for speculative assets could at times and under certain conditions overwhelm the normal product price system. More succinctly, the inference was that speculative investment might thwart or negatively impact non-speculative real asset investment in the course of a business cycle. Keynes' conclusion was that the entire process leads to financial instability and a collapse of the banking system as "the tendency of the financial circulation to increase, on top of the increase in the industrial circulation...breaks the back of the banking system."[10]

A decade later Keynes in his *General Theory* took up once again the question of the psychology of speculative investing, its growing influence, and the rise of enabling institutions (i.e. an early reference to forms of shadow banking?), and new markets for speculative investing, and possible negative consequences of these new 'speculative' focused institutions and markets for overall systemic economic stability. He spoke about the growing numbers of professional speculators, proliferation of institutions and markets feeding the growing speculative activity, and how speculative investing—unlike more traditional forms of investing—was a kind of 'third degree' investing removed from normal investing (a premonition of 'derivatives' perhaps?). Speculation is about "anticipating what average opinion expects the average opinion to be," trying "to guess better than the crowd how the crowd will behave," and a "gambling instinct." Keynes then linked speculation to the system of credit, noting in particular that speculation was dependent on "the state of credit" or borrowed funds (i.e. debt), and credit was dependent on the availability of liquidity.

Keynes further distinguished between speculative investing and what he called 'enterprise investing,' the latter a more traditional form of investing (i.e. first degree?) not focused short term or on exploiting price inflation for purposes of a quick capital gain. Once again implying the possibility of a speculative shift and its potential destabilizing effects, he raised the specter that speculative investing, growing in the long run—especially in America—might overwhelm non-speculative investment. As he put it, "Speculators may do no harm as bubbles on a steady stream of enterprise [investing]. But the position is serious when enterprise becomes the bubble on a whirlpool of speculation," and may eventually result in a situation in which "the capital development of a country becomes a by-product of the activities of a casino."[11]

After thus laying the groundwork for a deeper analysis of the relationship between credit, debt, forms of speculative investment, autonomy of asset prices, and the stability of the real, non-financial economy, Keynes moved on in subsequent chapters of his *General Theory* to other topics. We are left, however, with the clear suggestion that speculative investing may be broadly destabilizing to an economy and lead to serious economic crises.

What Keynes contributed to the analysis of speculative investing and its consequences was the idea of the trend toward professionalization, i.e. the growth of a professional class of investors and their institutions that were concerned only with short-term price escalation, quick returns from capital gains, and who were disinterested in investing in real assets and 'enterprise investing.' What he specifically called 'speculative investing' was herd- or mass psychology-driven investing. Second, the idea of a two price system—asset prices and non-asset prices—which behaved differently and somewhat autonomously and where the former might determine the latter. Finally, there was his pregnant notion that credit creation fueling speculative investing might prove nearly unlimited and might neutralize money supply operations by government monetary agencies like central banks.

What is missing in Keynes' analysis, however, is an explanation of the dynamic processes by which this may actually occur. Does speculation 'crowd out' real investing in real assets, to employ a term popularized by economists in recent years? Or does the extreme profitability of speculative investment in financial securities divert or 'suck in' investment capital from the non-speculative sector? What are the institutions of the professional investors and how do they create the 'whirlpool'? How does the 'speculative whirlpool' overwhelm normal enterprise (real asset) investing? How do asset prices, credit–debt, and product prices interact to destabilize the system? As others have ably pointed out, the structure employed by Keynes in his *General Theory* "implicitly precluded the notion of an asset price bubble" and did "not lend itself as easily to analyzing the macroeconomic effects of asset price misalignments."[12]

What was missing in Keynes was provided—but only in part—by the two other economists, Fisher and Minsky. Fisher focused on the relationship between debt and deflation;[13] Minsky on the institutional aspects and how investment over time shifted toward more speculative forms, causing the financial system to become progressively more 'fragile' and thus prone to financial crisis.[14]

To Fisher it was 'easy money' (i.e. excess liquidity and credit) that was central to the run-up of debt in the boom cycle. Easy credit also led to debt-driven asset inflation that eventually peaked, reversed, and resulted in asset deflation and debt unwinding during the decline phase. But Fisher focused less on the processes of debt–inflation as causes of financial crisis that leads to a collapse of the real economy, and more on how the process of real decline could transform into a depression as a result of debt–deflation. Without the debt–deflation process, the downturn would be mild, Fisher argues, presumably some kind of normal recession. But with unchecked debt–deflation, the process transforms into depression. Companies attempt to make debt service payments but their real debt burden rises as deflation accelerates. To meet rising real debt servicing payments, companies are forced to sell assets, stop new investment, cut production and employment, and reduce product prices. These actions aimed at servicing rising debt result in deflation—asset, product, and wage. Further deflation means still further rising real debt and debt service. Thus a downward spiral sets in involving debt, deflation, and more debt. It was, for Fisher, the 'great paradox' and "the chief secret of most if not all great depressions: the more the debtors pay, the more they owe."[15]

What Fisher provides is a description of a process by which financial instability and crisis propagates by means of debt–deflation throughout the real economy, accelerating the economic decline, and by implication how that decline feeds back to cause more financial stress. But the process is focused primarily on non-financial institutions. There is no distinction of how debt–deflation in the financial system transmits to the non-financial system. Nor is there any distinction between business debt–deflation and a possible similar process affecting consumer debt. Third, Fisher does not consider the further impact of the debt–deflation spiral on defaults. The latter, in fact, serve to accelerate the debt–deflation process—thus a factor playing a particularly important role in the general process. Fisher's solution to the general downward debt–deflation spiral leading to depression is twofold. Either the central bank (i.e. the Fed) can reflate the economy via massive monetary injection and provoke inflation (which reduces the debt service load), or business balance sheets can be allowed to cleanse themselves without government intervention. Fisher chose the former option, thus implying that central bank monetary policies can successfully chart a course out of deflation and depressions. Fisher did not consider, however, the implications and consequences of a massive monetary reflation.

In contrast to Fisher, Minsky focused primarily on the emergence of financial fragility and instability over the business cycle. Financial fragility is defined and measured in terms of growing difficulty in covering debt servicing payments. Over the boom phase this difficulty rose, as companies paying for debt costs out of income streams migrate to add more debt to cover principle or interest but not both, to companies that borrowed still more debt since they were unable to cover either interest or principle. Debt costs thus led to more debt and ultimately more debt and costs. Over time more businesses migrated to the second and third debt servicing levels. And when credit dried up, as in a financial crisis, the third category of businesses went bankrupt, unable to service their debt; as other firms added more debt to service costs, and as businesses that previously serviced debt costs out of income were driven to borrow in order to pay for debt.

Unlike Fisher, Minsky describes how financial instability spreads within the financial sector itself. The build-up of financial fragility is inherent within the financial and economic system, and not precipitated by any external event or 'shock.' Minsky provides for the first time an initial description of an institutional framework that leads to financial instability. Minsky also resurrects Keynes' two price system (asset versus product prices) distinction. Unlike Fisher, Minsky is less confident that central bank monetary solutions alone can contain the financial crisis or its real economic consequences. Both traditional fiscal and monetary policy may prove insufficient. There must therefore be industrial policy solutions added to the policy mix. 'Big Government–Big Bank' (i.e. Congress and the Fed) solutions may only serve to temporarily contain the crisis, and in so doing may create the preconditions for a subsequent more serious version of that crisis.[16] A deeper, more structural change is consequently necessary, beyond normal monetary or fiscal policy means.

What's missing in both Minsky and Fisher is a general explanation of consumer debt, consumer debt servicing, and therefore the role of consumption fragility in the general crisis. Or how both forms of fragility are related, or how both in turn are related to processes of debt–deflation–default that drive Epic Recessions. While some consideration is given to the strategic role of asset prices, how deflation transmits from asset prices to product prices is not explained. Also lacking is any consideration of an important third price system—the price for labor, or wage system—and its relationship to product and asset prices; i.e. how wage deflation is related to both product and asset deflation, and how all three interact to exacerbate both financial and consumption fragility and cause a more virulent form of economic contraction that this book calls Epic Recession. Finally, neither Fisher nor Minsky consider the further important connections between default (consumer, business, government), on the one hand, and the processes of debt–deflation, on the other.

All three—Keynes, Fisher, Minsky—make important contributions and provide insights into speculation and its consequences for financial instability, as well as its role in precipitating economic contractions that are not 'normal' but are fundamentally more severe and potentially protracted. All three provide important parts of the crisis mosaic. But none provide the full analysis of how a non-normal, i.e. Epic, contraction is related to the growth of both financial-consumption fragility and to the critical processes of debt–deflation–default that determine fragility and are, in turn, determined by it.

Understanding the origins and evolution of Epic Recession means understanding the dynamic and causal interrelationships between the six key variables: the shift toward speculative investing, financial fragility, consumption fragility, debt, deflation, and default. Together they constitute the defining characteristics of the increasingly unstable U.S. and global economy in the first decade of the twenty-first century.

SPECULATIVE INVESTING EFFECTS ON REAL ASSET INVESTMENT

In Chapter 2 and in prior commentary in this chapter, possible relationships between speculative investing and real asset investment were raised hypothetically. The speculative investment shift was corroborated by various evidence—i.e. cash flow and debt to non-residential fixed investment ratios, subprime to total mortgages, and securitized assets to total fixed investment. But the nature of the relationship between the two, speculative and non-speculative investment, is not explained by the data per se. The data show real asset investment slowing relative to speculative forms over the business cycle while speculative asset investing rises. But what accounts for that? Possible explanations were suggested. Speculative forms with their high returns over a shorter period might simply be 'crowding out' real investment, as liquidity and credit flows increasingly toward the former at the relative expense of the latter. Or the relatively higher return and shorter turnover of speculative investing could be diverting and 'pulling in' available liquidity and credit. Or perhaps it is neither. Perhaps the correct explanation is that real investment is not slowing any more than normally historically over the business cycle. Speculative investing is just growing at a much faster relative rate compared to real investment, and thus not necessarily at the expense of it.

These represent possible relationships between speculative and non-speculative forms of investing, with the former, speculative investing, as the dynamic factor determining the outcome of real asset investment. Speculative investing is the dominant force in the relationship between the two. But there is a second dynamic relationship that is the obverse of that just described—a relationship with real asset investment as the dominant force determining the volume and change of speculative investing, not vice versa.

REAL INVESTMENT AS THE BASIS FOR SPECULATIVE INVESTING

Speculative investment begins on a base of real asset investment. For example, a property, i.e. a real asset, must be built before a mortgage, or financial asset based upon that real asset, is in turn issued. Thereafter, additional financial assets may be issued based upon the initial financial asset. A mortgage forms the basis for the issuance of a mortgage bond composed of various individual mortgages or parts of mortgages. The growth in real assets thus initially provides the basis for subsequent expansion and growth of financial assets. But the process of financial asset creation soon diverges from its real asset base. And the more they diverge, the more asset price inflation is driven by forces independent of original real asset investment. And as asset inflation becomes more independent it also becomes more volatile.

Concerning the real investment side: in the early phase of a business cycle, opportunities for profitability from real asset investment are greater than in late stages of the cycle. Prices for materials and intermediate goods, and therefore costs, are relatively low. There are few pressures in labor markets to raise wages. Costs are therefore minimal and possibilities for rapid gains in productivity are higher. All things being equal, lower costs mean higher expected profits and therefore plans for increasing real asset investment. Expectations that prices will increase as the business cycle develops means additional expected profits and plans for investment. Product development preparation during the recession, in anticipation of recovery, provides an additional potential boost to investment. In short, expectations of profitability are higher than average in the beginning of a boom phase, and therefore plans for, and actual, investment are higher than average. But over the course of the business cycle, the above positive elements weaken, profitability ebbs, and with it plans for, and actual levels of, real asset investment. But that does not necessarily inhibit financial asset price inflation from accelerating.

As investment in real assets initially rises, the foundation for financial speculation also rises. In the beginning, speculative investing is based on prior real asset investing. For example, residential and commercial property real assets must be created first, before subsequent speculation on those assets is possible. Similarly, a supply of commodities—whether food, oil, metals, or in other forms—must be created before speculation on those commodities can occur. Issuing new stock with which to finance real investment results in stock price volatility, upon which speculators may then enter the market. Similarly for bonds created from bundling of mortgages. Whereas the initial mortgage represents a first-tier financial instrument, the stock price appreciation and bond yields represent second-tier financial instruments.

To summarize, real asset investment initially provides a basis for speculative financial asset investment. As the latter accelerates, it creates a new basis for additional real assets on which to create further financial assets. It may thus artificially stimulate real asset investment to a degree. But as will be described shortly, increasingly over the boom cycle speculative asset investing becomes based less on real asset investment but more on previously created financial assets. As a consequence of this shift, disproportionality grows between real asset investment and speculative asset investment.

SPECULATIVE INVESTMENT AS THE BASIS FOR SPECULATIVE INVESTING

The preceding described how the real asset provides the basis for a speculative financial asset. The house creates a first-tier 'mortgage' and mortgages of various homeowners are bundled to create a 'mortgage bond' (RMBS), a second-tier financial instrument. But there are further tiers.

A third and even fourth tier occurs when yet another layer of financial instrument is created on the preceding layers. Stimulating the demand for third- and fourth-tier financial assets are the availability of extreme 'leveraging,' as well as the spread of securitization and widespread availability of secondary markets in which to sell the third- and fourth-tier of financial products.

In the third tier, previously created second-tier financial instruments are repackaged, then mixed with other short-term financial issues like asset-backed commercial paper (ABCP). The new repacked financial issue is marked up in terms of price, and then resold once again in other secondary markets. These resales are often global, since the product itself has no distribution costs and is available electronically. These financial 'products' also have virtually no production costs. Supply is not a factor and plays little or no role in pricing of these products. Price movements of third-tier instruments are even more independent of the original real asset. They become virtually demand driven, and thus quite unlike prices for real asset products, where tightening supply and slowing demand over the course of a business cycle eventually constrain further price increases. Financial asset prices, in contrast, have no supply constraints and are driven by ever greater demand almost exclusively.

As prices for second- and third-tier financial assets begin to diverge from real asset prices, supply and demand forces begin to slow real asset price increases as expectations of profitability weaken and decline. Declining expectations for profitability leads to slowing real asset investment. Real asset investment slows, just as financial asset investment begins to accelerate. More liquidity and credit subsequently flows into speculative investing and out of real asset investing. In other words, an imbalance and disproportionality begins to emerge between real asset investment and more speculative forms of financial asset investing, as well as between their respective price systems.

In this situation, creators of financial instruments are confronted with a dilemma: either get more physical asset investment into the pipeline, or create more speculative financial instruments from other financial instruments. This is precisely what occurred during the subprime mortgage boom in the U.S. Banks and other financial intermediaries in the U.S. needed a continued flow of mortgage loans in order to create their residential and commercial property mortgage-based bonds, RMBS and CMBS financial instruments, to securitize and resell into secondary markets. So they sent people into the field to instruct mortgage lenders how to develop a greater volume of mortgages and loans. This was called 'originate and distribute.' The quantity of mortgages was all that mattered, not quality.

First- and second-tier financial assets are mortgages, bonds, stocks, etc., whereas third-tier financial assets are even more highly leveraged, further securitized, and resold in global secondary markets. These typically include CDOs, CLOs, ABCPs, and ABSs.

There is a fourth tier of financial instruments as well, however. That is the creation of CDSs and other insurance instruments as cover for the increasingly risky character of second- and third-tier instruments' quality and quantity. But CDSs quickly become more than mere insurance. There are, in effect, essentially 'bets' on the likely degree of failure of the prior tiered instruments. As profitability from financial speculation rises with financial asset inflation, it in turn fuels even more speculation in various 'higher level' derivatives like CDSs. Other fourth-tier instruments include interest rate swaps, currency swaps, and other over-the-counter derivatives. These are all forms of 'casino investing,' or investment as pure 'betting.'

To partly sum up, real asset investment initially enables speculative asset investment. But as the general business cycle develops, the much greater price-driven profitability of financial speculation begins to feed upon itself. Financial speculation creates more financial speculation, thus increasingly diverting capital from real investment just at a time when growing supply constraints begin to raise costs of real asset investment, to lower its expected profitability and, in turn, consequently to slow real asset investment. The falling real returns, actual and expected, from real investment diverts liquidity and credit leading to even more speculative investing, which drives the demand and price of the latter still further. Speculative asset prices begin to accelerate while real asset prices slow. The former become relatively and increasingly profitable and the latter less so.

As professional investors and their 'shadow' institutions grow in number, weight, and the amount of liquidity they control, the overall effect is an increase in demand for speculative assets and a slowdown of the demand for real asset investment over time. Speculative forms of investing over the longer run therefore have a relative net negative impact on non-speculative asset investment. It is not that speculative investment 'crowds out' real investment, but that it diverts and distorts it. It over-stimulates some forms of real investment, while it slows other forms of real investment while the net effect is negative. Major disproportions and imbalances are the consequence—which become major contributing forces to financial instability.

SPECULATION AND ACCELERATION OF DEBT

There are at least two ways in which speculative investing accelerates the accumulation of debt. It does this first by transforming debt simple leveraging into a kind of super 'layered leveraging.' By layered leveraging is meant securitized leveraging. As previously noted, speculative investing by definition relies heavily on leveraging per se, just as it does on opportunities that are short-term and price-driven. However, securitization significantly increases leveraging even further (and thus levels of debt) by enabling multiple 'tiers' of leveraging. That is, at each tier of financial investment, the purchase of each repackaged financial asset is leveraged. Leveraging thus occurs multiple times. For example, mortgage bonds are rolled into collateralized debt obligation, CDO, securities. Those CDOs are repacked into and resold as part of a 'synthetic' CDO—a CDO created out of bundling other CDOs. Credit default swaps, CDSs, are created to 'insure' against the risk of the preceding. Along this chain of 'financial instruments created out of financial instruments,' additional leveraging and borrowing—and thus debt creation—takes place at each level. In short, securitization multiplies the volume of debt by enabling levels or tiers of leveraging. We have debt and leveraging based upon previous leveraging and debt.

Securitization additionally promotes greater investor risk-taking, all things being equal. With the possibility of quickly selling the asset after a short term on a secondary market, the investor develops a false sense of reduced risk that encourages further speculation and leveraging. If there's a secondary market, investors believe they can quickly dump the asset by reselling it should its price stop rising or begin to fall. The very existence of secondary markets for securitized assets therefore encourages excess risk-taking. As Keynes put it, they believe they can determine what the average investor will do better than the average investor can and that they can 'get out' before the market slows or collapses.

In short, securitization and secondary markets serve to increase the trend toward speculative investing by appearing to reduce risk and by enabling layered-leveraging. The greater leveraging and false sense of reduced risk translate into a greater volume (and reduced quality) of debt than otherwise would occur. The problem is that secondary markets for securitized assets work as an exit only when asset prices are rising. As soon as asset prices begin to fall rapidly, there is no secondary market in which to exit from. Everyone is trying to sell and no one is buying—and by definition there is no market when no one buys and everyone tries to sell.

DEBT AS THE DRIVER OF DEFLATION

The prior debt levels created by excessive leveraging and the shift to speculative investing over the business cycle mean that, once prices of speculative assets begin to fall, the greater volume of debt previously accumulated over the cycle will result in a longer fall in the price of the assets. And the poorer the quality of that debt, the more rapid the fall. Thus the level and quality of the accumulated debt will determine the asset price deflation. Speculative investing works through the medium of accumulated debt to cause asset price inflation, by creating excess debt as a result of creating tiers of speculative instruments, layered leveraging, and creating a false sense of reduced risk. Details of the debt–deflation process work something like this: During the boom cycle, debt servicing payments are not considered a major factor to the investor. He/she intends to sell the asset after a price rise before the debt payments are due in any great volume. But this works only so long as the price of the asset continues to rise. When it doesn't, if it declines, and sometimes even if it just slows in its rate of rise, then debt servicing payments come due and may become a burden. That debt servicing cost burden may prove significant if a large volume of debt was taken on in the original process of asset purchase and/or if the additional debt over time was of a poorer quality (i.e. shorter term and higher interest). Rising debt servicing costs may represent only one part of the growing cost pressure on the investor. Terms of borrowing for investors are often such that, should the value of the asset purchased fall below its original purchase price, the borrower is required to 'make up the difference'; i.e. put in more money assets or put up other assets as collateral. When that point is reached, the investor typically tries to 'dump' the asset and sell it. But that may pose a problem as well, when most investors are trying to dump the asset and sell it at the same time. The more savvy investors quickly exit the market early in order to avoid the inevitable rising debt servicing cost and losses and write-downs that can quickly follow once prices start falling. Their exiting, however, accelerates further declining asset prices and rising debt servicing costs. Unable to sell the assets for which prices are deflating, the investor may turn to selling off 'good' assets (i.e. other classes of assets not losing value due to price declines) in order to make the rising debt servicing costs. In this manner, asset price deflation may spread between classes of assets as well. A company as an investor, for example, may have to sell its better assets in order to raise cash with which to service its rising debt costs. It can all become a self-fulfilling downward spiral; general asset price deflation can quickly set in.

DEFLATION FEEDBACK EFFECTS

It has been explained how, in the run-up of a financial boom, rising debt and excessive debt leveraging may result in excess demand for financial assets that drives asset price inflation to extraordinary levels. But speculative investing may also drive product price inflation in several ways. Speculation in food commodities and oil drives up futures options prices for these commodities which are passed on to what is called 'core inflation,' energy and food prices, at the food and energy wholesale and consumer levels. Rising commodity prices for metals also causes a rise in product prices of crude, intermediate and finished producer goods, as metals and other raw materials prices are passed through producer goods prices. In turn, rising producer goods prices are eventually passed on in part to consumer products made from those producer goods. The consequence is a speculative investing and debt-driven asset as well as product price inflation. Rising debt thus drives inflation. But the opposite may occur as well; i.e. asset as well as product price deflation may actually result in a still further rise in real debt levels and thus debt servicing stress.

The reverse scenario, in which falling prices result in rising debt, works something like the following: Once a financial bust and crisis has occurred, businesses don't always sell assets that have started to collapse in price. First, the assets rapidly collapsing in price may prove difficult to sell. The prices of the falling assets may have declined so far that their sale provides little revenue gains with which to make debt service payments. So the company may simply hold on to the asset that might be now virtually worthless instead of selling it. That is what, in effect, happened to many banks and shadow banks after 2007 that were caught holding collapsed securitized assets. The dollar value had fallen to as low as 10 cents on the dollar. In that situation, banks just held on to the collapsed and now nearly worthless assets. But they still had to make debt servicing payments, and perhaps also make up for the lost value on those collapsed assets on their balance sheets. They therefore first sold other 'good' assets that had not yet fallen in price. That applies to non-finance companies that found themselves in a similar situation. For example, GMAC, the financing arm of General Motors, had speculated in securitized assets and lost billions. It played a major role in GM's ultimate financial decline. GMAC had to sell off 'good' assets to compensate for the collapse in value of the 'bad' assets it couldn't sell. Similarly, GM itself had to sell at 'firesale' prices real assets of several of its product divisions to cover the losses in assets at GMAC.

This, by the way, is also an example of a transmission mechanism illustrating how asset price declines can spread from asset class to asset class, eventually infecting good assets and setting off a general asset price decline. Cash flow must be raised in some manner in order to service debt payments coming due from debt accumulated during the boom phase. Selling 'good' as well as 'bad' assets is one response. But selling company assets, good or bad, is not the only way to raise cash with which to cover debt payments coming due. Reducing product prices to raise revenue and cash flow is another.

If the company is a non-financial institution, another alternative is to sell more of the company's inventory of real products in order to raise cash to make debt payments. But with a weakening real economy, selling more products requires lowering the prices of those products in order to increase sales revenue and raise the needed cash flow for debt servicing. This is an illustration of another transmission mechanism describing how asset price deflation can spread to product price deflation.

But lowering product prices in order to raise cash to service debt payments means the company's real debt levels rise. Specifically, falling product prices results in rising *real* debt and thus a rise in the servicing costs of that real debt. The company's original debt obligation and payments have not risen, but the company's income and available cash flow with which to make the debt payments has fallen—i.e. the real debt load for the company has risen. Sometimes referred to as the 'Fisher Effect,' this is an important process by which paying off debt by raising cash by lowering prices actually results in rising debt. It represents the process by which deflation can feed back and cause a rise in (real) debt, just as debt can result in deflation. If left unchecked, deflation results in a spiraling down of debt and deflation as they both feed upon and further exacerbate each other.

This debt-to-deflation and deflation-to-debt spiral is typical of Epic Recessions. If not checked early in the process, it may lead to a deepening and extending of Epic Recession. And if allowed to become particularly severe and protracted, it can play a central role in transforming an Epic Recession into depression.

Asset and product price deflation may also 'spill over' into wage deflation, further exacerbating the process. As product price deflation occurs and company revenues and cash flow eventually decline further, the natural management response is to cut operating costs as well—typically, employment and wages for those left still employed after layoffs. In fact, it is not necessarily sequential—i.e. asset firesales leading to product price deflation then to wage deflation. A company facing particularly severe debt servicing stress may engage in all three forms of deflation more or less at the same time, selling assets, reducing product prices to raise more revenue, and cutting operating costs. However, cutting product prices will eventually lead to wage deflation; first, as reductions in hours of work for a company's labor force and in the form of layoffs. Both constitute forms of wage deflation for the general labor force at large. Total wage payments decline for workers as a group. For those still employed, wage deflation can assume more traditional forms of hourly wage rate reduction, suspension of bonuses, reductions in company contributions to benefit plans, etc. In Epic Recession, resort to non-traditional forms of wage-cutting frequently occurs as well, such as forced monthly furloughs (days off without pay); cuts in paid sick leave, vacation, and holiday pay; and other forms of supplemental compensation. The key point, however, is that product price deflation eventually spills over to wage deflation in a general way in Epic Recessions.

Wage deflation also has the effect of feeding back upon and exacerbating debt. In this case it is consumer debt levels that are affected. When workers experience reduced income from job loss and wage-cutting, in effect their 'cash flow' also is reduced. Their real debt thus rises as well, as does their debt servicing stress. There is also a further feedback effect. Rising real debt for consumers means less consumption and therefore less demand for products. Product prices are in turn reduced further, causing additional rising real debt for business. In other words, rising real consumer debt results in a further rise in business real debt. Debt drives debt.

Finally, as business real debt rises and reducing product prices reaches its lower bound limits, businesses' only option is to turn to selling more assets. Thus, deflation in wages and product prices drives a second round of asset price deflation. We now have a generalized process of the three types of prices—asset, product, and wage—each driving the other in a downward spiral through the medium of rising real debt for each. The more generalized and the more multiple feedbacks that occur, the more severe the condition of Epic Recession.

DEBT–DEFLATION AS THE DRIVER OF DEFAULT

These processes of deflation and debt ultimately lead to a condition of default. When a business can no longer reduce wages (beyond a certain point, it results in an insufficient workforce to produce its product), can no longer reduce product prices (further reductions would mean producing products for a price consistently below the cost of producing those products), and has few or no remaining real assets to sell to raise cash flow to finance debt payments, then the only alternative for the business is to default. That default may be on its debt servicing payments, or it may take the form of a more serious company level default, meaning bankruptcy.

Default may be postponed, however, by various means. Lenders may allow the business to 'roll over' its debt due—in effect, reducing its debt payment levels in exchange for a longer-term debt obligation. The business may simply borrow additional debt in order to make the payments on the original debt. Or it may convince lenders to accept stock in exchange for debt. If it is fortunate enough, it may invoke prior covenants that allow it to suspend or slow its debt payments. Or perhaps the company's original lender (financial institution) is itself near-insolvent so it chooses not to take the company into bankruptcy court in response to the debt default, since doing that would require the lender to register even greater losses on its own balance sheet which it may be loath to do. There are a host of measures that are designed to 'buy time' for a company facing default as bankruptcy. However, most measures take the form of the company taking on additional levels of long-term debt amortized over a longer period in order to pay for increasingly unaffordable short-term debt. A favorite option in 2009, for example, was for companies having difficulty making debt payments to sell more junk bonds to cover immediate debt. But this represents a temporary solution only. It means raising long-term debt levels in order to finance short-term debt payments.

A similar process to that described above occurs for consumers and consumer default. Falling consumer income from job losses, wage cuts, and growing inaccessibility to credit (wage deflation) means a greater difficulty paying for debt incurred during the boom phase (real debt rise). However, unlike businesses, there are fewer temporary solutions available to consumers facing default on their debt as debt servicing burdens rise dramatically. Their options are default via foreclosure, default via credit card non-payment, default via auto repossession, or default on student loans resulting in wage-garnishing by the lender.

Unlike non-financial businesses and consumers, the so-called 'big 19' U.S. banks and shadow banks avoided default because the U.S. Federal Reserve or Treasury gave them interest-free loans to cover their debt payments (and then some). In fact, frequently the Fed 'paid' banks to take its loans, in effect offering them negative subsidized interest loans. This amounted to the U.S. government making the debt payments for the banks. This largesse did not extend, however, to the 8,200 smaller regional and community banks, several hundred of which by the end of 2009 were allowed to default and were subsequently reorganized by the Federal Deposit Insurance Corporation (FDIC).

Notwithstanding possible short-term or government-subsidized solutions, the more protracted the period of deflation, and the greater the prior debt levels and poorer the debt quality, the more likely is default—either in its severe form of company asset liquidation or in the partial form of company restructuring involving selling off some assets and downsizing. Once again, the medium by which the rising debt is transmitted into default is deflation in either or all of its three price systems.

DEFAULT FEEDBACK EFFECTS

Defaults in turn provoke further price deflation. For example, bankruptcy means severe asset firesales. Bankruptcy in the form of a total liquidation of a company means that all the remaining assets of the company are sold at auction at firesale prices. A good example is the late 2009 liquidation of the once $100 billion-valued communications equipment company, Nortel Inc. It sold its assets for less than $900 million in late 2009. Bankruptcy in the form of partial reorganization of a company, instead of total liquidation, also results in asset sales determined by the bankruptcy courts. The asset price deflation is not as severe, but is still quite significant. The very best assets are typically sold off at well below market prices.

Reorganizations also almost always result in a major downsizing of the company's workforce and thus major layoffs of employees. The remaining workers are thereafter generally paid at reduced wages and extremely reduced benefits. Wage deflation thus occurs as jobs, hours of work, and earnings are reduced. As the restructured company re-enters the market, it typically must offer lower product prices in an effort to re-establish a new foothold once again in the market. Defaults therefore translate into more intensified deflationary pressures across all three price systems—asset, product, and wage.

While a restructured and reorganized company no longer has the burden of excessive debt and debt servicing payments, employees of that company— those laid off and those remaining—in contrast end up with less income. Their income is less but their prior incurred debt levels have not changed. In other words, their real debt has risen and their debt servicing difficulty has grown. All things being equal, employees of the company must reduce their level of consumption. Lower consumption feeds back into lower product demand and further pressure to lower product prices and cut wages.

Non-bank defaults can provoke bank defaults, as well as vice versa. When a non-financial business defaults, it means that the debt previously borrowed from its lender, a bank or other financial institution, becomes virtually worthless. The bank lender must then write off the now 'bad' debt on which the non-bank defaulted. With a loss now on its own books, the bank needs to make up the loss by either adding more capital, selling more of its stock, borrowing from the government (i.e. the Fed), or getting bailed out by the U.S. Treasury. Sufficiently widespread and numerous defaults by companies it lent to may result in the bank/financial institution itself defaulting. Until its losses can be offset by other measures, like asset sales, the bank or financial institution in question is generally reluctant to loan or issue credit to its business customers. Unable to obtain credit, the non-financial customers necessarily turn to asset, product, and wage deflation solutions, thereby continuing the cycle. In short, debt drives deflation, which in turn drives defaults that subsequently feed back upon deflation.

A rising level of consumer defaults—housing, auto, credit card, other loans— may lead to losses and write-downs and subsequent defaults of financial institutions as well. But consumer defaults more often negatively impact secondary levels of the banking system—i.e. thrift institutions, credit card companies, smaller community and regional banks, auto finance companies (GMAC, Ford Credit), credit unions, small business and consumer installment credit, etc. The effects are thus not necessarily direct on the tier-one banking and financial institutions. They also impact what are called secondary credit markets as well. In the U.S. these include the securitized markets for credit card, auto, student, and other loans which after 2007 virtually shut down and, at the present, have yet to revive.

Epic Recessions occur when the debt–deflation process results in an increase in defaults that are sufficient in scope and magnitude to feed back upon and exacerbate debt and deflation—and in turn cause a further deterioration in both financial and consumption fragility. An Epic Recession evolves and grows in momentum, bringing it closer to depression, when the scope and magnitude of defaults significantly exceed historic averages, and when business and consumer defaults feed back upon financially fragile banks and institutions and precipitate a second round of major financial instability. In contrast to Epic Recessions, depressions are characterized by a series of banking-financial crises that take place in the context of a further deteriorating financial and consumption fragility.

THE DEBT–DEFLATION–DEFAULT NEXUS AND FINANCIAL FRAGILITY

This dynamic interaction and the feedback effects between debt–deflation and as debt–deflation intensifies between debt–deflation and default as well, result in a further deterioration of both financial and consumption fragility.

Recall that both forms of fragility are a function of levels of debt, of the quality (terms and cost) of that debt, and of cash flow (business) or disposable income flow (consumer)—all three factors ultimately combine in the ratio of debt servicing to available cash income flow. As debt rises or deteriorates, financial fragility rises; as the latter (cash flow) slows or declines, financial fragility rises as well.

Asset deflation drives a company toward more debt accumulation, thereby raising financial fragility. When a company's assets are declining in value, it is not able as a rule to raise liquidity through new stock issuance. Existing stock prices in such situations are normally stagnant or declining due to public negative perceptions of the company's future economic performance potential. Thus the door to raising cash flow to make debt payments is largely closed. In addition, the company by definition lacks the necessary internal funds in such conditions. If it had sufficient internal funds it wouldn't have to sell off assets in the first place to make debt payments.

Without internal funding or stock equity funding available, the company is necessarily driven to debt financing. Declining asset prices thus mean that the company must seek more debt financing in order to make debt servicing payments. New levels of debt are added to existing debt. And if the company is already overloaded with debt in the first place, new debt is normally only obtained at greater cost than the old debt, which means debt quality declines and fragility rises as well. The company becomes even more financially fragile over time from debt, as asset deflation eventually forces it to acquire more debt.

But product price deflation similarly results in more financial fragility. Price deflation works on financial fragility from the cash flow side. If a company chooses to reduce product prices instead of selling assets to raise necessary cash flow, it may increase revenue and improve cash flow in the short run in order to service debt payments, but it does so by weakening its revenue base and future cash flow in the longer run. Albeit not as rapidly as asset price deflation, product price deflation therefore also eventually results in reduced cash flow to finance debt and consequently a deterioration in financial fragility.

The company can buy some time from having to resort to asset or product deflation. It may avoid reducing product prices initially by reducing planned real investment or by cutting production and operating costs, especially labor costs. Yet all three—suspending planned investment, cutting labor costs, and cutting other costs of production—also translate sooner or later into reduced revenue and cash flow. Wage-cutting and wage deflation may serve as a temporary substitute for price deflation and thus delay a further deterioration of financial fragility in the short run. But wage deflation will eventually result in less productivity and thus higher costs and less cash flow. Cutting back on new investment and production also reduces productivity, with the same effects on rising costs and less cash flow. Because wage deflation's impact on cash flow is less immediate than product price deflation, businesses typically pursue wage deflation first before product price-cutting; and wage cost reduction via layoffs before other forms of wage-cutting, since layoffs affect the productivity of the remaining employees less than wage-cutting for those that remain.

To summarize, there are a combination of effects from the interaction of debt–deflation–default that result in a deterioration of financial fragility. Selling off assets is the quickest way to raise liquidity with which to make debt service payments. But asset sales and asset deflation eventually lead to the need to raise more debt, locking the company in a cycle of asset sales to offset rising debt. Reducing product prices is an alternative to raising cash to cover debt payments. But it takes longer than asset sales to raise the cash and is also more uncertain. It also means in effect that the company's real debt servicing rises. Paying debt by product deflation means raising real debt. Companies, if possible, therefore initially turn to shutting down planned real investment and cutting operating costs, especially labor costs—first by reducing hours of work, then by layoffs, then by other forms of wage cuts. However, all three of these measures may result in immediate cash with which to service debt, but ultimately result in a reduction of cash flow. All forms of deflation therefore exacerbate debt and debt servicing problems. In the real world, companies with rising debt servicing stress and facing default undertake all measures in some combination, as well as seek to raise more debt (even if more costly) and delay making debt payments, if possible.

THE DEBT–DEFLATION–DEFAULT NEXUS AND CONSUMPTION FRAGILITY

The situation is not dissimilar for consumers and consumption fragility. Consumer debt takes the form of mortgage debt, installment loan debt like auto loans and other 'big ticket' items, credit card debt, student loan debt, and other forms of personal loans and debt. While not as massive as financial institution debt accumulation, or non-financial corporate debt growth, in the ten years leading up to the 2007 financial bust, household mortgage debt nonetheless increased by around $7 trillion in the U.S. and consumer credit from around $1.3 trillion to $2.5 trillion.[17]

The ratio of household debt to income in the U.S. rose to 140 percent in 2007, and two years later it was still at around 130 percent.[18] This compares to the ratio's long-run historic average of around 100 percent, last recorded in the late 1990s. What this means is that consumers have been unable to reduce debt in any significant way since the financial crisis and recession began. They will likely remain unable to do so for some time, especially given continuing trends involving home foreclosures, rising job losses, rising credit card rates and terms, record income losses for the millions of very small unincorporated businesses, negative wealth effects due to one-fourth of home values now 'under water' (i.e. negative equity), the general failure of 401k retirement plans to recover lost values—to name only the more significant factors continuing to impact upon consumer disposable income (i.e. consumer cash flow). The problem for consumption fragility is therefore debt, but, even more fundamentally, weak disposable income—especially for the bottom 80 percent of the households whose ratios are much worse than the 130–140 percent noted above, which includes wealthy households as well as the bottom 80 percent.[19] Furthermore, for the 80 percent at least, the problem of rising debt is a consequence, to a significant extent, of declining real disposable income.

It is important to note that this consumer debt run-up was not the result of some profligate cultural attitude change. It's not primarily that American consumers all of a sudden became reckless spendthrifts. At least not for the average American middle- and/or working-class family in the bottom 80 percent households, and in particular for the roughly 110 million who constitute the category of 'non-supervisory production and service employees.' Their resort to credit is one of the few ways that 110 million maintained their standard of living in the face of stagnating real weekly earnings and incomes over the past three decades, and since 2000 in particular. Real weekly earnings in 2007 for this group, who constitute the vast majority of consumers in the economy, were less in 2007 than in 1982, a quarter of a century earlier, when measured in terms of 1982 dollars. Working-class living standards were propped up by credit due to a long period of wage and earnings stagnation.

The other ways in which stagnating real income was offset for a quarter of a century include this group's additional hours worked on a family basis, as spouses were sent into the labor force in record numbers and second part-time jobs were taken on by primary heads of households. The group also reduced savings and even depleted retirement funds to maintain living standards. They entered the recent crisis and Epic Recession with very little in the way of income reserves and very heavy debt loads—i.e. historically severe consumption fragility. It is therefore not surprising that overall consumption in the U.S. economy nearly collapsed in late 2009 when this group was heavily impacted by massive reductions in working hours, millions of layoffs for six months running, an acceleration of wage-cutting in the form of furloughs, elimination of paid leave, benefit cuts, etc., plus an escalation of home foreclosures in the millions and tens of millions of home values thrown 'under water.' Something similar in terms of growing debt-driven and income-stagnating consumption fragility occurred in the 1920s and through 1929–31, according to other studies.[20] The banking panic of September–October 2008 was an indicator of the fracturing of financial fragility. But less attention has been (and unfortunately still is) given to the fracturing of consumption fragility that quickly followed in less than a month in late 2009 as mass layoffs began.

On the income side of deteriorating consumption fragility, there have been various causes of the real earnings stagnation since the 1980s: de-unionization of the general workforce, atrophy of the real value of minimum wage, free trade and the relocation of much of the high-paying manufacturing sector offshore and replacement of higher-paying export jobs with lower-paying import employment, the shift from manufacturing to low-paying service jobs, accelerating displacement of labor with technology, major shifts in labor market conditions from full-time permanent work to part-time temporary 'contingent' work, the shifting of costs of health care and retirement from businesses to workers, and other lesser but numerous real developments—all having some negative effect on wage and earnings levels for the 110 million in particular. These real causes better explain the shift of consumers to record levels of debt than do arguments based on consumer attitude changes.

The rising debt impact on consumption fragility is obvious. Less so is the effect of deflation. Asset deflation has little influence on consumption fragility for the bottom 80 percent of households, since they hold virtually no assets apart from some minor amounts in pension plans, which have declined in total value (and thus has had some effect). Product price deflation does not impact consumption fragility directly, but does so indirectly. Companies that engage in product price cuts to cover debt almost always introduce cuts in operations costs and labor costs. Product price deflation almost immediately results in wage deflation—i.e. layoffs and wage-cutting that directly impact disposable income. Thus, rising joblessness, reduced hours of work, and wage and benefit cuts translate directly into rising consumption fragility from the disposable income side.

Defaults for households and consumers take the form of foreclosures, auto repossessions, credit card suspensions and card rate charges and fee increases, garnishment of pay for student loan default, credit score reductions and elimination of credit availability, and ultimately in personal bankruptcy filings. Default in any of the preceding forms has a major effect on the individual and household's consumption fragility.

As consumer fragility deteriorates from rising debt, deflation, and default, it feeds back upon all three elements of the critical debt–deflation–default nexus. Increased fragility means an inability to cover debt payments in a timely manner and a need to borrow further to supplement insufficient household income flow. It means less consumption demand, which results in further downward pressure on product prices. And in the severest situations, it translates into default—for debt payments due on mortgages, autos, or student loans, or credit card payments.

As in the case of financial fragility and its interaction with the debt–deflation–default nexus, consumption fragility similarly feeds back on the elements of the nexus, which, in turn, results in a further deterioration of consumption fragility. A dangerous potential downward spiral may subsequently set in.

FINANCIAL AND CONSUMPTION FRAGILITY FEEDBACKS

Financial fragility and consumption fragility also mutually determine each other, while each simultaneously reacts upon debt–deflation–default as well.

The main financial fragility to consumption fragility transmission mechanisms are layoffs, reductions in hours of work, and wage-cutting for those remaining employed. To recall, non-financial companies facing increasing difficulty in making debt service payments may either sell assets, reduce product prices, or cut labor and other production costs; in short, resort to deflation in one or all the three forms in order to raise cash flow to service debt. Reducing operations and, in particular, labor costs are the quickest ways to supplement liquid assets on hand. Selling inventories of products at lower prices and resorting to asset firesales may serve the same purpose. But those alternatives make it more costly and difficult to raise further business debt if that proves necessary. It is generally easier and less costly to replace labor than it is to replace assets and inventory. So businesses typically resort to wage deflation first (although a company in a severe economic situation may undertake all three measures simultaneously).

Wage deflation in all three forms—i.e. layoffs, reduction of working hours, and direct wage and benefit cuts—serves to reduce real disposable income for the company's workforce and the labor force at large. Consumption fragility subsequently grows. When wage deflation occurs broadly in scope and magnitude, when tens of millions are laid off and converted to part-time work, when benefits cuts and furloughs, bonus cuts, paid leave reductions, and other forms of wage-cutting occur, then the increase in consumption fragility becomes widespread and a major economic factor.

Financial fragility feeds consumption fragility from the debt side as well, from the direction of a contraction in bank credit and lending to consumers, which means a higher cost of borrowing for consumers. For example, credit card rates and fees rise for consumers, both for existing and future credit. Borrowing rates for consumers attempting to refinance mortgages that are delinquent, or for home values that are 'under water,' rise as well. The unemployed consumer must pay higher rates for auto loans. Penalties for late payments on loans and credit cards are increased more aggressively and frequently. In general, the cost of credit for consumers who have no alternative but to raise more debt to cover costs becomes more expensive, while at the same time their real disposable income may be declining. Both 'sides' of consumption fragility therefore deteriorate as a consequence of financial fragility.

A reverse effect can also occur—consumption fragility may exacerbate financial fragility. The most obvious example is consumers who, as homeowners, default on mortgages, resulting in foreclosures. Banks and financial institutions must thereafter write-down or write off the loss from the defaults. Their financial fragility rises. More than $1 trillion in subprime and other mortgage write-offs has occurred in the U.S. thus far in the cycle.

Credit card debt is another consumption to financial fragility mechanism. Consumers defaulting on credit card debt results in credit card companies 'charging off' the debt, thereby themselves becoming more financially fragile. The corporate rating agency, Moody's Inc., estimates, for example, a 12 percent credit card charge-off rate by 2010 in the U.S.[21] That's nearly $150 billion in credit card loss write-offs. Card companies in response have begun raising rates on consumers still with cards to make up for the losses, even charging interest to card holders who pay off their balances monthly—all of which results in reducing consumer disposable income and increasing consumption fragility. With credit cards as a source of credit sharply reduced, and cost of usage rising rapidly, consumers are driven to default on other debt. According to some estimates, the 'big five' credit card companies, in order to reduce their own financial fragility, plan to cut $2.7 trillion in credit card lines of credit; i.e. by more than half the estimated $5 trillion total available card credit outstanding.[22] These draconian measures by big credit card companies represent efforts to, in effect, transfer their own financial fragility to consumers in the form of raising consumption fragility.

Just as the Fed and U.S. Treasury's bailout of the 'big 19' banks represents a transfer of bank financial fragility to the U.S. government's balance sheet, the response by banks and financial institutions, like credit card companies, to make consumers pay more for remaining credit represents a transfer of banks' and card companies' financial fragility to the consumer and consumption fragility.

What was described in the preceding paragraphs is not only how consumption fragility can exacerbate financial fragility, or how financial fragility in turn exacerbates consumption fragility, but how the two may continually impact each other in a negative fashion. A continuing, mutually sustaining process may potentially occur. In Epic Recessions this 'mutuality' of process takes place to some degree. When it especially intensifies, the momentum toward depression grows. Moreover, the linkage, or economic glue, between the two forces of fragility are the mechanisms of debt–deflation–default.

FRAGILITY AND THE REAL ECONOMY

Financial and consumption fragility not only partially determine each other and provide feedback on debt–deflation–default processes, but both forms of fragility drive the decline in the real economy as well. Both forms of fragility, in different yet similar ways, negatively impact real economic indicators like consumption, real investment, industrial production, exports, and employment.

Financial and consumption fragility are also the key aggregate variables that connect the processes represented by the interactions between debt–deflation–default, on the one hand, and real economic indicators like investment, consumption, production, exports, employment, on the other. It is financial and consumption fragility that determine the depth, degree, and duration of those indicators that define the characteristics of Epic Recession described in Chapter 1.

The origins of Epic Recession ultimately lie in the relationships between liquidity, the global money parade, and the growing relative shift to speculative investing. But the dynamics and the evolution of Epic Recession lie in the relationships between speculative investing, the processes of debt–deflation–default, and the conditions that define financial and consumption fragility. The processes and conditions of fragility appear (i.e. are reflected) in real economic indicators such as consumption, investment, production, export, and employment. But the essential forces and variables are those addressed in this chapter, those that produce the changes in scope and magnitude of those economic indicators that measure and differentiate an Epic Recession from a normal recession.

Perhaps the most obvious impact of fragility on the real economy is the direct, negative effect of consumption fragility on the level of consumption demand in the economy. Consumption represents more than 70 percent of the U.S. economy today. Growing consumption fragility slows consumption over the long run, since by definition it signifies both rising debt servicing requirements and lower real disposable income. As was shown in Chapter 2, consumption fragility for the vast majority of consumers in the U.S. today, the bottom 80 percent households, has been rising significantly due both to stagnating or declining real disposable income and to rising debt levels and debt servicing requirements. Two years after the start of the current economic crisis, consumer debt to disposable income as a percentage has barely fallen, from around 140 percent to only 130 percent. And that's for all households, including the top 20 percent. Consumers are clearly experiencing great difficulty in retiring debt and/or raising disposable real income.

Adding consumer debt in the short run to make debt payments—which has been the rule for two decades now for many consumers—only temporarily addresses the problem of consumption fragility in the short run, while actually exacerbating that fragility in the longer term. Increasing debt as a way to offset weakening real disposable income not only represents a temporary solution to weakening disposable income, it is at the same time a solution that exacerbates the problem of disposable income in the longer run. Assuming more debt may raise consumer income flows to enable servicing debt in the near term, but more debt raises the level of cash income needed to pay for what will necessarily become a still larger debt servicing requirement in the longer term. Over the longer term, then, rising debt actually reduces disposable income and, as a consequence, steadily slows consumption demand over time. That is why taking on more debt as a solution to lagging disposable income and consumption—the practice in recent decades—usually results in the need to take on even more debt over time. Growing consumption fragility is a reflection of this dilemma that exists in the contradictory relationship between debt and real disposable income over time.

Consumption fragility not only has a long-term negative impact on consumption demand, but in times of economic crisis, consumption fragility may deteriorate rapidly. When it does, it precipitates an abrupt shift in consumption demand to a lower level than had existed previously, at which it may then more or less stabilize for an extended period. This condition may be described as a 'fracturing' of consumption fragility, following which its feedback effects on other processes and variables intensify.

There is an additional effect. A fracturing of consumption fragility, and consequent decline in consumption, also reduces business planned real investment, production, and, in turn, employment. Business expectations may shift, anticipating a lower level of future sales and rate of return (profitability) from consumers as consumption becomes more difficult to sustain. In this scenario, consumption fragility feeds back on economic indicators through the business-investment channel, as well as directly via consumption, as described previously. Weakening consumption can also drive companies toward allocating a greater proportion of available liquid assets to speculative forms of investing, since speculative investing depends less on (now weakening) domestic consumer demand and more on (now growing) worldwide global investor demand. That, too, diverts liquidity from real investment that might otherwise result in increased production and employment. So consumption fragility affects consumption directly, as well as real investment indirectly as that real investment slows or is diverted in expectation of lower levels of consumption.

Like consumption fragility, financial fragility also has both direct and indirect effects on the real economic indicators. It, too, may 'fracture' from time to time. Financial fragility fracturing is represented by banking panics, such as the one that occurred in September–October 2008 in the U.S. Just as in the case of the fracturing of consumption fragility and the subsequent abrupt decline in consumption spending, financial fracturing is represented by an abrupt decline in bank spending—i.e. bank lending—that follows the banking panic. That bank lending, like consumer spending, may settle in at a lower level for an extended period—until policies generate a sufficient return to higher levels or until another 'fracturing' event takes place. Whether consumption or financial fragility, fracturing does not take place in normal recessions. Depressions are characterized, in contrast, by a series or sequence of repeated fracturing events.

Considering once again the possible specific impacts of financial fragility on the real economy, an abrupt decline in a company's cash flow amidst rising debt and debt servicing costs will first translate, in most cases, into a suspension of real investment projects in progress and a cancellation of future planned investment. Both actual and planned investment are thus negatively impacted from the outset should cash flow drop precipitously, especially when a recession is underway or imminent. A similar suspension and cancellation of investment may result from a company raising significant amounts of additional debt. Either/both a sharp rise in debt or an abrupt fall in cash flow can have the same investment suspension effect. Financial fragility thus tends to have a first, and often immediate, effect on real investment. Investment is suspended or cancelled to divert needed liquidity to cash flow and debt servicing.

Concerning current production and output, it is typically the next casualty of financial fragility. Cutting operating costs, in particular labor costs, takes a little longer to implement but is also a preferred means by which to generate cash flow. Renegotiating contracts with suppliers, delaying payments for materials, reducing hours of work, converting full-time employees to part-time status, layoffs, and eventually other forms of direct wage reduction are alternative approaches to raising cash flow. But these measures have consequences in turn for consumption and consumption fragility. They increase the latter and reduce the former, for both those laid off and those who remain working with less income flow. So financial fragility works directly on investment, as well as indirectly on consumption by causing a further deterioration of consumption fragility by lowering disposal real income.

After reducing investment and production, after cutting operating and labor costs, a company that still faces severe problems of financial fragility—whether due to a collapse of sales revenue, a major credit contraction, a refusal by banks to extend credit, or lending at sharply higher interest rates—that company may also have to sell assets at reduced prices or sell inventory of products at below market prices in order to quickly raise necessary cash flow. The need to raise additional cash might also result from a large collapse of asset values on the company's balance sheet as a result of prior bad investments that failed. Resorting to deflation solutions involving asset firesales or product inventory price-cutting has a long-run negative impact on investment. Selling assets usually means selling the company's better, more productive, and well performing assets. Those who buy the assets of a debt servicing stressed company are not generally interested in buying the worst performing assets, but rather the best performing ones. The loss of preferred assets usually means a weakening in productivity and thus rising costs in the longer run—with greater negative pressure on cash flow. Selling product inventory at below market prices may also initially raise additional cash, but with longer-run negative consequences. Cash flow is obtained in the short run, at the expense of profitability and therefore cash flow levels in the longer run.

If sufficiently widespread among sectors and industries of the economy, the wage deflation solution to financial fragility can also have long-run, offsetting, negative consequences. Should mass layoffs occur across industries, hours of work become reduced in general, and wage-cutting spread as rule, then consumer demand decline will also have a feedback effect on investment, production, and employment levels once again.

The general scenario described is one in which financial fragility impacts investment negatively in a direct way in the shorter run, and investment is impacted negatively through consumption fragility and consumer demand in the longer run; conversely, consumption fragility directly affects consumption negatively in the short run, and consumption is impacted negatively through financial fragility and investment in the longer run. The two forms of fragility are in ways mutually reinforcing. They both together affect real indictors like investment, consumption, production, exports, and employment levels.

These real indicators in turn feed back upon the general process, as well as through both forms of fragility. The cycle is reinforced by both financial and consumption fragility feeding back upon the threefold processes of debt–deflation–default. The latter, in turn, exacerbate financial and consumption fragility, and so forth.

What this all produces is a tendency for the real economy to proceed in a downward trend or cycle. That trend may not be perfectly smooth; i.e. it may accelerate at times of fracturing, and may thereafter settle into an extended period of stagnation. That stagnation may itself also not be perfectly linear. It may be represented in a series of short, shallow, economic growth periods, with which may occur similar short and shallow periods of economic decline: a 'bumping along the bottom' with periodic bounces up and weak bounces down.

From a policy perspective, this scenario suggests that checking or containing Epic Recessions, and avoiding the extended stagnation or a further descent into depression, requires policies that directly confront the key variables of financial and consumption fragility, debt–deflation–default, and the shift to speculative investing. For banks, financial institutions, and business in general, it means that debt must be 'expunged' and not simply offset with liquidity injections by central banks. It means that cash flow needs to be stabilized, not allowed to swing widely due to speculative bubbles and busts. It means that consumer disposable income must be fundamentally restructured. That cannot be accomplished without some fundamental redistribution of income on a permanent footing. Consumer credit must also stabilize and not be allowed to negate consumer income. Stopping deflation in either of the three price systems is a requirement of sustained recovery. And defaults, consumer and business alike, must be prevented. Not least, the ultimate solution requires that the shift to speculative investment is reversed and the global money parade is eventually tamed.

Part Two (Chapters 4, 5 and 6) addresses empirical evidence in the historical record of depressions and near depressions in the nineteenth and twentieth centuries in the U.S. To what extent do the three great depressions of the nineteenth century conform to the analysis presented in Chapters 1, 2 and 3? And what of the two closest examples of Epic Recession in the U.S. in the twentieth century—the financial crisis of 1907–14 and its aftermath, and the initial phase of the depression of the 1930s, the 1929–31 stage? Both constitute forms or 'types' of Epic Recessions that have occurred. In Part Three (Chapters 7, 8 and 9), Chapter 7 discusses how the current crisis and economic contraction, 2007–10, qualifies as an Epic Recession, and how it is similar and different from 1907 and 1929–31. Chapter 8 confronts the question of policy, solutions, and programs. To what extent have the U.S. Federal Reserve, the U.S. Treasury, Congress, and the President provided solutions that confront fragility, the debt–deflation–default processes, and speculation and the global money parade? Are they addressing today's Epic Recession as if it were simply a moderately more severe normal recession? Our conclusion is they have not, are not, and likely will not correctly address the problem. If not, the dynamic of Epic Recession will continue. What is necessary to successfully address the unique character of the current crisis is suggested in the final chapter.

Part Two

History

4

U.S. Depressions in the Nineteenth Century

Mainstream economists today make little, if any, distinction between the causes of normal recessions and depressions—and no consideration whatsoever of 'intermediate' stages such as Epic Recession.

THEORY VERSUS HISTORY

One wing views all economic contractions, whether normal recession or depression, as the outcome of either 'external shocks' to the economic system or 'external' policy errors by government. There is nothing 'internal' to the capitalist economy that is responsible for any form of contraction—normal, Epic, or depression. External shocks may take the form of supply disruptions such as a global crude oil price hike; or a demand-based price surge due to inflationary expectations; or a political or natural event, such as war, a bad harvest or a weather catastrophe. The external causes may assume different forms, but external shocks are never intrinsic to the nature of the investment process or the economic system itself.

But the most preferred form of 'external' explanation is failed government policy action as a cause of contraction. Whether recession or depression, economic contraction is due to, or exacerbated by, faulty central bank (Federal Reserve, or Fed) policies or fiscal policy meddling by Congress or other government institutions. As the arguments go, the Fed reduced the money supply and raised interest rates when it shouldn't have, or else failed to increase that supply and lower rates when it should have. Central bank policy failures either precipitate the downturn or accelerate it once a decline was already in progress due to a prior external supply or demand external shock. When such errors are repeated, error on top of policy error transforms a normal recession into a bona fide depression. Similarly, fiscal policy is applied pro-cyclically due to government policymakers' inability to predict the future accurately given the lag times for such policies to take effect.[1] Like central bank (Fed) monetary policy, fiscal policy errors often cause and almost always exacerbate a recession. Repeated policy errors produce a depression when a normal recession might have otherwise occurred.

Another wing of mainstream economics sees contractions as simply the result of imbalances in the economy that are normal and correctable with traditional fiscal (taxes and spending) and/or monetary (interest rate adjustments) measures. The economy is like a black box, with a simple hydraulic system within. Just adjust the proper fiscal or monetary knob on the box and the gross domestic product (GDP) that flows from the box will grow or decline in a linear, predictable fashion.

What all these perspectives share, however, is the failure to distinguish normal recessions from depressions and, in particular, Epic Recessions from both normal recessions and depressions. External shocks and policy error-driven contractions are the only form of contractions. There is no analysis of economic contraction precipitated or caused by 'internal' financial booms, busts, and instability events. Indeed, financial variables and forces are virtually ignored by either wings of mainstream economic analysis in explaining a crisis. By ignoring financial forces, both wings are unable to provide an adequate differentiation of normal recessions from depressions. The latter are simply the former 'writ large.' Moreover, Epic Recession as a distinct stage between normal recession and depression is also left out.

External shocks and policy errors may precipitate, and even exacerbate, normal recessions. But it is an error simply to extrapolate causes of normal recession to Epic and depression events.[2] Epic Recessions and depressions are not simply normal recessions writ large. They are fundamentally different economic animals, driven principally by internal, not external, forces.

The historical record contains ample examples of severe financial instability events that precede depression. Conversely, it is equally clear that normal recessions are never preceded by bouts of severe financial instability. Normal recessions may exhibit financial stress in localized markets. But the financial instability follows, not precedes, the economic contraction, and is relatively moderate in scope and magnitude as well. In contrast, severe financial instability is typically associated with both Epic Recession and depression, although that financial instability need not lead inevitably to depression. It may instead produce an interim condition, an Epic Recession.

As proposed elsewhere, to recall, there are two basic types of Epic Recession. In the first, 'Type I,' Epic Recession is set in motion by a severe financial instability event, results in significant contraction of the real economy, but thereafter dissipates into a period of extended stagnation. In the second 'Type II,' as debt unwinds in the economy and credit contracts sharply for an extended period, deflation and defaults spread and deepen. Should these processes continue unabated and unsuccessfully checked and contained, Epic Recession dynamics continue to evolve and transform into depression. In the first, Epic Recession is a kind of residual that settles into an extended stagnation period. The decline of the real economy is checked and contained, but no sustained long-run recovery occurs thereafter. In the second, efforts to check and contain fail, setting off a series of financial and consumption 'fracturing' that drives and transitions the economy toward depression.

The severity of the initial financial instability event is critical to whether just extended stagnation follows or whether the economy continues to further contract. Or, to express the same alternatively, the level and composition of debt build-up leading to the financial crisis is key to the severity of financial instability and subsequent downturn. This is represented by the notion of financial fragility expressed in the preceding theoretical chapters of this book.

Equally critical is the corresponding notion of consumption fragility discussed earlier. The degree of consumption fragility at the time of the financial crisis event may also determine the severity of the collapse of the real economy in response to the severity of the financial instability that sets the crisis and contraction in motion initially.

Once the financial crisis erupts (fractures) and the real economy declines, deflation and defaults play a major role in subsequently provoking a fracturing of consumption fragility. If and when both forms of fragility in effect fracture, at that point it is usually clear that the contraction of the economy has attained Epic dimensions. Whether Epic Recession evolves toward depression depends on the continuing processes of debt–deflation–default, and whether those processes evolve to a point that financial and consumption fragility deteriorate further to such a degree that subsequent fracturing of either or both follows. Multiple fracturing events build significant momentum toward depression.

The evolution of Epic Recession is also influenced in part by the character and magnitude of central bank and government monetary and fiscal policy responses. An aggressive monetary response designed to prevent a collapse of the banking system may stabilize that system and slow the development of Epic Recession. It may put a floor under the contraction, but will not succeed by itself in generating a sustained economic recovery. It thus increases the likelihood of a Type I Epic Recession. A deficient fiscal policy response will have a similar effect, i.e. putting a floor under the contraction but not generating a sustained recovery. Only a massive injection of government spending and/or tax cuts can succeed in generating a possible sustained recovery. To provide one historical example: during the 1929–35 period of the Great Depression in the U.S. the financial system was finally stabilized only in 1934, almost five years after the initial financial instability event of 1929 and after several subsequent banking crises that followed (i.e. after multiple financial 'fracturing' events). At the same time, circa 1935, federal government fiscal policy raised government share of GDP from 3 percent in 1929 to around 17 percent in 1935. But the stabilization of the banking system and insufficient magnitude of government fiscal policy succeeded only in stabilizing the economic collapse. Policies did not generate a sustained recovery. It was not until federal spending as a percentage of GDP rose to 40 percent in 1942 that the depression finally ended. In the case of a less severe than depression situation that characterizes Epic Recession, it is therefore likely that fiscal policy would have to produce a rise in government's share of GDP to around at least 30 percent.

NINETEENTH-CENTURY FINANCIAL CRISES AND DEPRESSIONS IN THE U.S.

The nineteenth century was full of financial instability and economic contractions, many of which were normal recessions, several of which were clearly depressions, and a few that possibly qualify as Epic Recessions. However, it is difficult to determine the scope and magnitude of contractions during the century. Data required to estimate quantitative characteristics of depth, duration, deflation, and default outlined in Chapter 1 of this book are simply not available. Economy-wide data are often extrapolated from limited state or local sources, while other data are derived from questionable statistical manipulation undertaken by contemporary economists.[3]

Despite the data limitations, it is possible to identify what were clearly financial crises and subsequent depressions in the nineteenth century. For the latter, the National Bureau of Economic Research (NBER) has identified depressions occurring in 1837–43, 1873–78, and 1893–98. Each was preceded and to some extent precipitated by financial crises. In addition, there were other financial crises that did not result in a major economic contraction, which happened in 1857 and 1884. However, these were localized and not sufficiently generalized to precipitate a descent into depression. And in the case of 1857, its aftermath was dampened by a major shift in government fiscal policy in 1860–61.

The depression of 1837–43

The period leading up to the dual financial panics of 1837 and 1838 was one of intense speculative investment and inflation. Speculation focused on western land, in the south, the Great Lakes region, and the Mississippi valley, on inland canal bonds and stocks, the first wave of limited railroad construction in the east, on state government bonds, and in bank stocks accompanying the explosion of new bank charters in the late 1820s to the early 1830s. As one commentator remarked, "The increase in enterprise which was normal and represented increasing wealth was attended by speculation everywhere… Speculative operations attained a volume not known before."[4]

Commercial bank charters, which were exclusively issued by the separate states at the time, grew in number from 330 in 1830 to more than 700 by 1835, and with them an explosion in money creation and liquidity, which became an important basis for the subsequent intense speculation in land, transport, bonds, etc. With the demise of the Second U.S. Bank, state-chartered banks increased their bank note issues at will. Bank creation and corresponding bank stock issuance raised liquidity further. While other forms of stock existed at the time, "banks were undoubtedly the largest component of the early U.S. stock market."[5]

Parallel to the surge of growth in unregulated state chartered-banks was a simultaneous expansion as well of thousands of non-chartered private banks and savings institutions, as well as the state governments themselves acting as quasi-financial institutions—all representing in a fashion the 'shadow banks' of their time. They, too, issued their own paper money and currency, in addition to the chartered banks.

State government-provided liquidity originated from governments' issuing state bonds in order to obtain an income flow from bond interest, since most state governments derived little if any income from taxes. Bond income was thus an alternative to unavailable tax revenues. State bond issues rose from $40 million in 1830–35 to $108 million in 1835–38.[6]

Added to these sources of excess liquidity from domestic sources were major inflows of gold from Europe, London in particular. Mexico silver inflows and payments by France to settle claims for shipping losses during the Napoleonic Wars boosted liquidity further still.[7] The U.S. gold and silver ('specie') stock (i.e. money supply) escalated from $30 million in 1832 to $89 million by 1837, nearly tripling, from the various sources. The money stock thus rose 250 percent.[8] And state bond issues rose from $40 million in 1830–35 to $108 million in 1835–38.[9]

The U.S. federal government also contributed to the explosion in liquidity. The then President, Andrew Jackson, broke up the Second Bank of the U.S. and distributed the deposits of the U.S. Bank to state banks, further increasing the money supply. Jackson then distributed the federal government's surplus from preceding record speculative land sales of the previous decade. Both distributions resulted in still further growth in available liquidity.

The primary speculative instruments at the time were bonds for canals, railroads, and banks, and bank and canal stocks. Another favorite financial instrument were call loans (loans on stocks) issued by banks to speculators, who borrowed in order to speculate in the transport and land markets. With no bank regulation to speak of, the instruments soon proliferated and banks held little or no reserves as guarantees.

The result of the explosion in liquidity, thousands of new unregulated financial institutions, and new financial instruments (call loans) was unrestrained speculation in commodities, land sales, cotton, wheat, and general inflation. After remaining largely stable from 1825 to 1834, prices shot up more than 30 percent in a matter of a few years between 1834 and 1837.[10]

The speculative boom turned into a bust in May 1837 when banks suspended payments of gold for their (over-issued) paper bank notes. Immediately, severe asset price deflation set it, followed by more bank suspensions (i.e. defaults) in 1838—a pattern repeated in other depressions to come. Precipitating the first bank crisis in May 1837 were the U.S. government's decision to accept only gold for future purchases of U.S. land, and the decision of the Bank of England to raise its interest rates. The latter resulted almost immediately in a major outflow of gold from the U.S. to England and a contraction of liquidity and dampened investment in the U.S. Without credit and borrowing, speculative prices no longer rose, investors pulled out, and the downward spiral in various asset prices began, followed in turn by general asset price deflation.

Land prices, in particular, fell rapidly. And the general price level contracted 33 percent from 1839 to 1843.[11] So did export prices. Bank failures in 1839 were even greater in number than in 1837. Bank defaults and failures led to a sharp reduction in available credit to other banks and non-bank businesses. Gold outflows from the U.S. to London accelerated, further reducing credit availability in the U.S. The huge volume of debt that accumulated during the boom phase leading up to 1837 meant heavy debt servicing payments amidst an inability to obtain new credit and falling prices. Financial fragility thus escalated. Many companies ended up in default. State governments that had participated in the speculative frenzy ended up repudiating their debts. Thus states defaulted as well as banks and non-bank businesses.[12] Real asset investment fell sharply in the commercial and industrial sectors of the economy. The outcome was that "it appears that there was a severe and protracted depression."[13]

One later nineteenth-century analysis raised the question of the possible relationship between excessive speculative investment and its impact on the real economy in the period preceding the initial financial collapse of 1837. In the First Annual Report of the United States Commissioner of Labor, written in 1886, it was noted how, in the 1830s, excessive prices, liquidity, and profits from speculation led to further borrowing. As a result, "men were taken from productive and put to work in non-productive undertakings... the natural result of the transfer of labor from productive to non-productive enterprises was the cessation of the production of the commodities of life... These conditions existed until the crash came."[14]

As early as the 1830s depression, there occurred the familiar pattern of exploding liquidity, formation and expansion of virtually unregulated shadow banks, the issuing of new kinds of financial instruments, land speculation, construction and infrastructure building, upon which financial instruments proliferated as 'speculative plays' in addition to the real investment. Escalation of debt and inflation was followed by a financial bust and deflation and defaults.

The financial crisis of 1857–59

A subsequent financial instability of some significance occurred in 1857. But unlike 1837–38, it did not lead to a depression. Erupting in August 1857, the basis for the speculative excess was the railway expansion boom of the early 1850s. It was financed almost exclusively by bonds, with heavy involvement by foreign investors, especially London. But the expansion was limited mostly to Midwestern railroads and was therefore relatively localized. The precipitating event was the failure of the Ohio Life Insurance and Trust Company. Life insurance companies were the new shadow banks of the period, just emerging. They would play an even greater role in later financial panics.

According to one nineteenth-century report, "Speculation, extension of credit, and all the usual accompaniments of financial disturbances ushered in the period."[15] The real economy quickly contracted in the wake of the 1857 financial panic, reaching a low point in 1859. Business defaults and failures, according to R.G. Dun & Co., a major business conditions reporting service, rose considerably—from 4,225 business failures in 1858 to 6,993 in 1861, which in terms of total asset values reflected a rise in losses ranging from $95 million to $207 million between those years.[16] The crisis was prevented from expanding and deepening into the real economy by the onset of the Civil War. That raises an important question as to the effect of massive fiscal spending on checking and containing the transmitting of financial instability to the real economy. As noted by one economic historian, "The great demands incident to the war and the general employment of labor caused by these demands...prevented the possibility of depression. The issuance of paper money (once the war began)…made the payment of debts easier, and tended to prevent bankruptcies."[17]

The regional character of the 1857 event and the role of war and massive government spending raises the question of whether a serious financial panic and subsequent economic contraction like that of 1857–59 might otherwise have evolved into an Epic Recession—or even depression—were it not for the fiscal impact of war spending? What is the magnitude of fiscal spending required to check and contain Epic Recession or depression? The massive spending of the civil war, plus the U.S. federal government's flooding the economy with paper currency (the 'greenback') once the war started, was clearly sufficient to check and contain the financial crisis. But it was a very significant monetary expansion, and an even more massive incidence of government fiscal spending.

The depression of 1873–78

A second, serious financial collapse came with the financial panic of 1873, which was followed in 1873–78, by the most serious U.S. depression to date, sometimes publicly referred to at the time as the 'the great depression.'

While the Civil War of 1861–65 dampened the effects of the crisis of 1857–60, it simultaneously provided a new boost to investment, particularly in war contracts. The war also unleashed significant inflation, one of the key elements underlying speculative activity. Out of government war bond trading was also born the modern bond market. Major figures associated with wartime U.S. government bond issues were Jay Cooke, James Fisk, and others. Once the war ended, they quickly became leaders in the newest emerging bond speculation opportunity—the railroads. A second great wave of railroad building (that began in the 1850s but was initially interrupted by the war) was unleashed in the late 1860s. Railroad bond speculation dovetailed nicely into two other areas of classical speculative investing—land and urban residential and commercial properties. Thus three major forms of speculative investing converged in the late 1860s and early 1870s.

New forms of shadow banks also emerged concurrently. Some had origins in the pre-war period and now reorganized in new roles, like the trusts and investment banks. Pre-war, trusts focused on purchasing securities 'in trust' for their wealthy depositor-investors and offering insurance; postwar they transformed into investment houses, taking collateral and lending and buying commercial paper. Investment banks also shifted activity after the war, marketing U.S. securities directly to customers in the U.S., not just to European investors as before. Meanwhile, new players becoming a factor for the first time included insurance companies acting as investors, mortgage brokers and banks, and early forms of private banks, of which very little was recorded or known at the time. State banks also exploded in number after 1870, and were destined to play a key role in local land speculation. National banks were chartered for the first time in 1864, but were not allowed to invest locally in mortgages and real estate. So state banks had a clear field of play in local land speculation. State regulations were watered down, allowing state banks to hold virtually zero reserves in many cases, to pay no taxes, and to set up with very minimal capital—i.e. the financial deregulation movement of its day. No reserves and low capital meant the likelihood of bank runs at the first sign of any financial instability, which was precisely what would soon happen.

New financial instruments were once more created: Commercial paper, tontine insurance,[18] and futures trading. Call loans were now employed as a way to leverage stocks in particular. But the big speculative instrument was railroad bonds.

Real investment in railroads expanded dramatically, doubling the size of total rail mileage in the U.S. and creating a then immense value of $1.5 billion by 1873. Railroad bonds that financed that investment were a classic speculative instrument. The post-1865 railroad building boom was driven not in anticipation of creating an income stream from shipments of agricultural goods and related fees; the real money was to be made in land sales and land speculation for the towns that would arise at the junctures of the railroad lines. The construction of railroads therefore preceded the development of farming and agriculture in the deep Midwest. Railroad construction was an end in itself, to feed the speculative gains to be realized from the bond sales—not the fees charged to transport produce. They were the nineteenth-century counterpart to the twenty-first century of building bridges in Alaska that 'went to nowhere.'

Railroad bond speculation even developed a kind of early form of multi-tiered speculation. Capital raised from initial bond sales was in turn 'paid' to the railroads' own construction companies. The construction companies made the money, not the railroads. This required the railroads to continually issue more and more bonds in order to keep the railroad construction going. Continuing railroad construction was necessary to enable the further issuing of bonds. Debt piled upon debt. And so the consequent cost of financing that debt also grew over time. Another variation on speculation involved railroads selling parcels of land paralleling their track lines. Questionable marketing tactics drew even more investors into railroad bonds. But the big gains were from urban land speculation. In this venture, local country banks, state banks, private banks, mortgage brokers, and others participated as well. Infrastructure bonds to build docks and ports on the eastern and southern U.S. coasts were additional speculative investment opportunities at the time.

The liquidity for all this came from multiple sources. Foreign investors financed a large portion of railroad bonds with their gold. The U.S. Treasury injected sizable amounts of cash into the economy at the time in the late 1860s through its retirement and sale of civil war debt. Paper currency, the greenbacks of the war, also still floated around in sizable quantities. State banks joined the liquidity explosion by issuing inconvertible (to gold) paper notes, while regional and community banks lent out all their available reserves to leverage their land speculation ventures.

Constantly rising bond issues and higher interest costs meant that financial institutions were growing increasingly fragile. The financial crash came in 1873. The precipitating event was when the biggest railroad bond speculator,

Jay Cooke, could no longer sell new bonds for his Northern Pacific Railroad. Cooke also owned banks. His New York, Philadelphia, and Washington D.C. banks purchased more than $100 million of the Northern Pacific Railroad bonds, and then 'borrowed' from their depositors' accounts to cover losses. When the Northern Pacific went bust, so did Cooke's banking empire in all three cities. This led to a classic 'run' on other New York banks. Within a few days more than 40 New York banks and brokerages collapsed, followed quickly by the New York stock market, which was built upon the shaky edifice of call loans. Stock prices plummeted along with bond asset prices. The stock market closed for ten days—the first time since its formation in 1819. The remaining banks suspended payments to depositors attempting to withdraw cash. Multiple bank runs followed, spreading out of New York along the eastern seaboard, throughout the Southern states, then the Ohio valley out to Chicago. A fracturing of financial fragility had clearly occurred. A full-fledged banking panic was underway by October 1873.

Defaults followed in large number. In September 1873 alone, more than 100 banks closed, of which 16 were national banks and 11 were state banks. The remaining closures were other shadow banks.[19] It is estimated that as many as 50 New York brokerages also collapsed.[20] However, these numbers do not include the hundreds, perhaps thousands, of local community banks. These numbers also fail to include the banks and other financial institutions that did not close, but temporarily shut down, i.e. were 'suspended,' and later returned to operation. There were countless 'runs' on banks by depositors. Twenty-five railroads defaulted on debt payments between January and September 1873, right before the financial crash; railroad bankruptcies also occurred thereafter by the dozens.[21] It has been estimated that 18 percent of all railroad mileage defaulted and went into receivership following the second crash in 1877, as well as 18 percent of all railroad bonds.[22] General business failures in the wake of 1873 were also impressive. In 1871 a total of 2,915 enterprises worth a value of $85 million failed; in 1878, 10,478 worth $234 million failed.[23]

As one of the most respected economists on business cycles at the time noted, "this industrial depression was far more severe than any that preceded it" and was clearly "ushered in by financial disturbances."[24] The relationship between financial instability and the depression that followed was also noted by another economist, Rendig Fels, who, in later years, writing on the business cycle of 1865–79, noted, "The panic was the proximate cause of the business downturn…Even without a decline of long term investment prospects to reinforce it, the panic by itself could have started a cumulative cyclical decline."[25]

By a whole host of measures, quantitative and qualitative, the 1873–78 event was clearly a depression. In terms of duration, it lasted nearly five and a half years. After experiencing significant inflation from 1871 to 1873 during the speculative boom, the U.S. economy underwent serious deflation after mid 1873. Deflation was deep and lasting, and extended well beyond asset deflation in real estate, stocks, and other securities, to commodity prices, general prices, and wage deflation. The wholesale price index fell by about a quarter from 1873 to 1878.[26] General prices fell, according to conservative estimates, by around 16 percent, and more liberal estimates put the figure at just over 20 percent.[27] Money wages declined by around 20 percent as well.[28] Real wages would continue to fall into the first half of the 1880s and not recover to their 1870–73 levels until the early 1890s.[29] Lending by financial institutions contracted sharply during the decade, by as much as 40 percent or more. Defaults involving banking, financial, and non-financial companies were previously noted. Investment is generally recognized also to have declined significantly. On the other hand, the manufacturing sector, new and growing in weight in the economy at the time, appears to have been somewhat less impacted after 1876, but mining, railroads, and building construction in particular appear to have been hard hit by the financial fallout throughout the 1873–78 period.[30] Data for unemployment and GDP are less reliable or else unavailable.[31] But perhaps a useful indirect indicator of the rise in unemployment is data on immigrant labor. In both 1872 and 1873, an average of 435,000 immigrant laborers entered the U.S. seeking work, thus indicating that jobs were most likely plentiful and unemployment was low. But after 1873 the numbers consistently fell, and by 1878 the number of immigrants entering the U.S. had declined to only 138,000, indicating, conversely, that jobs were likely unavailable and unemployment was relatively high.[32]

The financial panics of 1884 and 1890

Not all banking or financial panics necessarily led to depressions in the nineteenth century. Unlike 1873—and 1893–98 to follow—financial instability in 1884 and 1890 did not result in a major contraction of the real economy. Financial instability may be necessary, but not sufficient, for the emergence of depression. Or, to put it another way, financial fragility is necessary, but consumption fragility is equally necessary for a crisis to evolve to depression stage.

It is necessary to differentiate between a full financial *crisis* and a banking *panic* that is localized geographically or to limited sectors of the financial system. There is also a difference between a localized banking panic and an even less severe banking *stringency*, as it was called at the time. The financial instabilities that erupted in 1884 and 1890 were not full-fledged financial crises. They were either a localized banking panic (1884) or a banking stringency (1890).

A full financial crisis embraces not only commercial banks but most other financial institutions as well. It includes bank runs (represented by either retail consumers withdrawing deposits or wholesale runs as institutions to withdraw funds), bank suspensions, and bank failures or closures. A full financial crisis occurs not simply in a single city (e.g. New York) or even several cities (Philadelphia, Washington D.C., etc.) but in the 'interior' of the economy as well. Banks, credit markets, and stock and money markets are all impacted to some degree. Credit availability and bank lending significantly contract as a result, with subsequent serious consequences for non-financial companies and for the real economy. Epic Recessions are characterized by full financial crises; depressions by a series of the same. A fracturing of financial fragility is necessary to produce a true financial crisis event. That does not occur in the case of a banking stringency.

In 1884 the banking panic was limited to relatively few banks and brokerages in New York and in a few other cities. The stock market did not fall more than 10 percent. Depositor 'runs' were limited to the few institutions specific to the event and did not spread to other banks or financial institutions. Relatively few bank suspensions occurred. It may have been a banking 'panic,' but not a more general financial crisis.

1890 was again localized to New York with a couple banks in Philadelphia and Richmond, Virginia. Most of the failures and closures appear to have been state banks, private banks, savings institutions, and brokerages—i.e. shadow banks rather than mainline commercial banks. Like 1884, in 1890 the stock market fell by less than 10 percent. In both cases, 1884 and 1890, the impact on the real economy was apparently minimal by most accounts.

There was likely inadequate time between 1879, the end of the prior depression, and 1884 for banks to accumulate the necessary excessive debt and financial fragility required to result in a full-fledged financial crisis in 1884. The same point applies to the run-up to 1890.

The banking system's response to the problems in 1884 and 1890 may also have played an important role in preventing a full-fledged financial crisis during those years. The events of 1884 and 1890 were successfully contained geographically to a few cities. The major New York banks quickly formed a 'clearing house' and provided emergency funding to other banks in trouble that limited bank runs and further instability. The panics thus did not generalize and grow to crisis dimensions. The more limited initial magnitude of the financial eruptions in 1884 and 1890 also permitted bank cooperative efforts (clearing house, interbank emergency lending, etc.) to prove more successful. Had the initial financial eruption been more serious, it is debatable whether banks would have collectively pooled their resources to aid one another. A more severe crisis, caused by a longer and deeper debt run-up to the implosion—i.e. characterized by great financial fragility—might have overwhelmed the self-help efforts between the banks.

The lesson of the experiences of 1884 and 1890 is that voluntary measures by banks themselves to contain an initial eruption of financial instability only work when the magnitude of the crisis is not particularly severe. Voluntary responses in which the banks attempt to act as their own 'lenders of last resort' amongst themselves do not work in cases where severe financial fragility has accumulated in the boom phase. But when the initial financial bust is more severe, as in 1873 and 1893, the voluntary approach fails. Even the 'good' banks were not able to raise sufficient funds to stabilize the system.

One final comment concerning 1884 and 1890: the relatively minor impact of the banking panics of 1884 and 1890 on the real economy was due only in part to the moderate nature of the financial instability during the decade. The non-financial economy was also less impacted due to other countervailing forces pushing economic growth at the time. The real economy was being driven increasingly during the 1880s by the rapid growth of the manufacturing sector in the U.S., as well as by a higher than normal demand for U.S. agricultural exports from Europe. Also, early manufacturing growth in the 1880s was possibly less dependent upon debt financing than it would be in later decades. And agriculture was clearly driven by foreign demand and foreign credit for U.S. exports by a booming European economy in the 1880s.

In other words, the speculative debt-driven excesses that were continuing to grow throughout the 1880s were muted by significant real asset investment in manufacturing and agriculture that was also taking place more or less independently at the same time. Therefore, not only may speculative investing not have had time to develop financial fragility to sufficient levels to produce broader and deeper financial crises in 1884 and 1890, but the expansion of manufacturing and agricultural production was sufficiently robust to shield the real economy somewhat from the credit contraction that followed the financial events of 1884 and 1890, contractions which themselves were not that serious given the relatively moderate financial instability of 1884 and 1890 in the first place.

The depression of 1893–97

The depression of 1893–97 was serious, and perhaps in ways even more serious, than the depression of 1873–78. Like 1873—and unlike 1884 and 1890—it was precipitated by a banking panic and a full financial crisis. The banking panic that erupted in April 1893 was followed by a major decline in the New York stock market on May 3, 1893. The collapse of the Philadelphia and Reading railroad as well as the failure of the major industrial company, National Cordage, set off the panic. The latter was the focus of particularly intensive speculative investing activity in the months leading up to its collapse. Bank credit and lending had already begun declining from January 1893 and gold began flowing out of the U.S. to Europe as well before that spring, a harbinger of a further constriction of bank credit and lending to come.[33] U.S. Treasury gold stocks also fell to record levels, exacerbated by misstatements by Treasury officials that further contributed to a rapidly declining general state of confidence in the economy. Initially, it was banks and shadow banks (i.e. brokerages, private banks, trust companies, investment banks, commercial paper dealers, etc.) in New York that were impacted. But after May the banking crisis generalized and spread to the interior of the country, in particular to the Midwest (Chicago, St. Louis, Milwaukee, Kansas City, Denver), cities of the southern Great Lakes region, and eventually to the Pacific Coast as well (Los Angeles, San Diego, Portland). Between January and August 1893 alone, a total of 536 banks suspended operations, the majority of them in the Midwest–Pacific. Located in the interior, most were largely state banks (many of which retained little or no reserves) and other forms of shadow banks.[34] Initial bank suspensions and failures in New York were also largely investment banks, brokerages, and private banks.

A second round of bank runs occurred in July–August 1893, when most of the interior banks failed or were suspended. As this occurred, they withdrew what reserves they had on hand with national banks, predominantly in New York, which precipitated a further crisis in the New York banks. The result was a second bank panic in New York in July–August, followed by a decision by New York banks to suspend cash payments to depositors, as well as delay transfer of reserves requested by banks in the interior. The crisis was too large, in other words, for bank voluntary cooperative efforts to succeed. And unlike 1884 and 1890, they didn't even try.

1893 was clearly a generalized banking and financial crisis. Its 'center' was the interior, not New York. That was new—and a foreshadowing of bank crises to come in the twentieth century. The smaller, more exposed and less regulated interior banks—i.e. the same banks more apt to invest in the otherwise more volatile and speculative sectors of land, construction, and mortgages—were the banks more seriously impacted by the crisis. The New York banks delayed much-needed currency transfers to the interior banks and also decided not to extend emergency liquidity to them—in contrast to what the New York banks had done amongst themselves within the New York market during the 1873 banking panic. The result was a more serious crisis in the interior that fed back ultimately upon the New York banks in turn once again. The 'drying up' of interbank lending that occurred in 1893 is another characteristic of a more serious financial crisis, and ultimately the consequence of the greater financial fragility that preceded the crisis among banks in general. The more widespread nature of the banking crisis in 1893 also contributed significantly to the more serious decline of the real economy that followed. The contraction of bank credit to non-financial companies was also more generalized, and it continued long after the banks themselves appeared to have been stabilized. The run-up to the financial crisis of 1893 was fueled by an extended period of excessive speculative investing. Once again it was railroad bond speculation, as the final phase of 'feeder' lines were built throughout the main railroad network created in the late 1860s to early 1870s. Overlaid on this, however, was an explosion in farm mortgages, urban construction in the towns along the feeder lines, and land speculation. A major wave of industrial mergers simultaneously took place in the 1880s as the manufacturing base of the economy expanded rapidly during the decade. Here speculation centered on the stock market, as newly emergent investment banks and other shadow banks financed the mergers movement in manufacturing with massive new stock issues. As later reported by the National Monetary Commission, "activity on the stock exchange was largely in connection with speculation in industrial companies and the financing of various combinations."[35] Stock speculation took another new twist, based on the idea of the 'holding company.' Stock was issued on both the primary company and the holding company owning it as well, a kind of double stock issue based on the same foundation of real physical asset. The total value of industrial corporations (excluding railroads and utilities) as a group rose from $216 million in 1887 to $1.2 billion in 1893, a sixfold increase. That would grow to $4.4 billion by 1900.[36] The practice of 'watered stock' was also introduced around the same time. Previously, stock issued by a company did not exceed the market value of its assets. Watered stock meant more stock was issued than the company's value. This was typically accomplished by issuing common stock equal to the value of assets, but then further issuing preferred stock also equal to asset values. Thus at least twice the value of assets was issued in stock. In 1887 it was estimated that 40 percent of industrial companies had issued watered stock in this manner. By 1892 it was 90 percent.[37]

Another major speculative play was in gold and gold-denominated securities. In 1890 the Sherman Silver Purchase Act was passed by Congress, establishing silver as specie alongside gold. Along with major inflows of specie from abroad, the silver Act significantly expanded available liquidity, providing further basis for debt and speculation. It also opened direct opportunities for speculating in silver prices, as well as in falling gold prices. Under the Act, the U.S. Treasury was obliged to purchase 4.5 million ounces of silver a month, paid for with the new Treasury Notes of 1890. Available liquidity in the U.S. rose by $100 million in just the last six months of 1890.[38]

The explosion in issues of industrial stock, holding company stock, and gold- and silver-denominated securities, was enabled by a major increase in borrowing and debt in the form of call loans by brokers. Call loans enabled a sharp increase in debt 'leveraging,' another key element of speculative investing.

Added to all this stock speculation was bond speculation—not just in railroads but to finance various new technologies and industries that arose in the 1880s. It was during this period that most cities began developing gas, electric, water, electric railway systems, and other utility infrastructures. Many community and regional state and private banks funded these projects. But they were often overbuilt, with multiple similar utility companies per town. The intense competition meant that many would fail, and thus bring down the local banks that loaned money to them. But while it was all underway, gas, electric, and water utilities were the 'internet-like' hot investment opportunities of their day.

The general picture leading up to the financial crisis of 1893 was therefore one based on a high degree of speculative investing—in railroads, mortgages, local business and utility infrastructure, land speculation, grain commodities, in "gold and gold-denominated assets," and growing stock speculation driven by industrial mergers and holding companies.[39]

Both old and new forms of liquidity and credit fed the speculative boom. There were the periodic gold inflows from Europe that rose significantly during the 1880s then fell in 1890 as Europe entered a depression of its own and foreign investors cashed in U.S. securities for gold. There was the U.S. Congress and Treasury purchasing silver with Treasury Notes at the rate of $7–8 million a month after mid 1890, and the record issues of new stock to finance the growing industrial merger movement. An unprecedented level of money, credit, and liquidity thus entered into the economy during 1886–93.[40]

The institutions driving it all were similar to those of the early 1870s, but now even larger in number and with some newcomers as well. The system of state banks had grown appreciably, but so too did the various forms of shadow banks—in particular the investment banks and trust companies that drove the industrial mergers speculative wave. The expansion of shadow banks was another notable feature of the years immediately preceding the financial crisis of 1893, especially the new trust companies and other private banks. Numbering roughly only around 40 in 1886, trust companies grew in number to more than 200 by 1893 and 390 by 1897.[41] Mutual savings banks and life insurance companies—also shadow banks by our definition—also grew in number and assets relative to commercial banks in the concluding decades of the nineteenth century.

Following the financial crisis in the spring of 1893, a decline in the real economy intensified around August–September 1893. About that time the interior banks began to run out of currency to loan clients to cover business payrolls. Prior to August, 3,401 defaults and failures of non-financial companies occurred from January through June 1893.[42] But for all of 1893, business failures totaled 15,242, with a corresponding increase in lost value of $346 million, an increase of 300 percent compared to the preceding year. The failures and losses declined in 1894–95 to around 13,000 and $170 million, but rose sharply once again in 1896 to more than 15,000 and $226 million.[43]

The rise and fall and rise in business failures suggests that the 1893–97 depression was 'W'-shaped with two downturns—i.e. a feature not untypical for depressions or Epic Recessions. The real economy declined from January 1893 through June 1894, then rose slightly in June 1894 to December 1895, then collapsed again from December 1895 through June 1897. A sustained recovery did not occur until 1898. Like the financial panic of 1857 that was cut short in terms of its real economic impact by the Civil War, the depression of 1893–97 was only fully terminated in 1898—i.e. the year in which the Spanish-American War began. This pattern would also replicate in the twentieth century.

In terms of debt, deflation, and default, more than 500 bank suspensions and failures occurred in the first year, 1893, and tens of thousands of non-bank failures followed annually each year between 1893 and 1897. More than 40 percent of all railroad mileage defaulted during the depression that followed the financial crisis of 1893. Deflation was more or less constant throughout the period. Unemployment, by one estimate, reached 18–19 percent in 1893–94 and remained at around 14 percent into 1898.[44] Bank lending contraction was the most severe of any crisis to date, falling 14.7 percent in just five months from the date of the stock market collapse, May 3, through October 4, 1893. This compared to a lending contraction of 5 percent in 1873.[45] An index of industrial production fell –8.7 percent in 1893 and another –7.2 percent in 1894, rose slightly in 1895 and fell again in 1896.[46]

By August–September 1893 the banking system was beginning to stabilize, but the real economy's descent was just beginning. According to one estimate, $300 million was injected into the banking system to stabilize it.[47] But it had little effect on the real economy's descent into depression, thus once again raising the question of whether monetary policies can only check the financial downturn and cannot generate a sustained recovery of the real economy once in a depression. The situation was perhaps best summed up by one of the leading business sources of the time, the *Commercial and Financial Chronicle*, which, on September 16, 1893, reported:

> Never before has there been such a sudden and striking cessation of industrial activity. Nor was any section of the country exempt from the paralysis: mills, factories, furnaces, mines, nearly everywhere shut down in large numbers, and commerce and enterprise were arrested in an extraordinary and unprecedented degree...so that our internal trade was reduced to very small proportions—in fact, was brought almost to a standstill—and hundreds of thousands of men thrown out of employment.[48]

OBSERVATIONS ON NINETEENTH-CENTURY DEPRESSIONS

There were at least 24 identifiable economic downturns in the nineteenth century. But the three periods 1837–43, 1873–78, and 1893–97 were exceptionally deep and of sufficient duration to qualify as depressions. Two of the three depressions—in the 1830s and 1890s—were also 'double-dip' ('W'-shaped). In contrast, the 1873–78 depression was a steady and long decline, beginning in late 1873 and continuing into 1876, after which it simply leveled off and remained at that lower level for another two years before recovery began in early 1879. None of the depressions of the nineteenth century were what might be called 'V'-shaped; i.e. a rapid and deep but short decline followed by an equally rapid and short upturn. Bona fide depressions, in other words, do not end quickly and may appear to have several false recoveries that dissipate along the way as well.

In the 1830s the primary institutions participating in the speculative build-up were the essentially unregulated state banks, state governments themselves as speculators, private banks, and early savings institutions. The speculative 'plays' included land sales, state bonds, canal stocks, cotton, and the first railroad construction wave. Excess credit creation feeding the speculation came from numerous sources: foreign gold flows and investment, U.S. Treasury distributions, state bond creation, and paper money creation virtually at will by the then predominant and essentially unregulated state banks. The financial 'instruments' employed were transport bonds, bank stocks, and call loans.

In the 1870s financial intermediaries and shadow banks blossomed still further, now including insurance companies, mortgage brokers, private banks, investment banks and brokerages, savings banks, and the new emerging 'trusts.' The speculative opportunities were once again land sales, railroad bonds and stocks, farm mortgages, new forms of insurance, commercial paper, government bonds, and stock market call loans. Futures trading had also begun on a larger scale. Excess credit creation was once again feeding the opportunities, enabling the borrowing and debt that fueled the speculation; foreign bond investors, U.S. Treasury distributions again, greenbacks, and other inconvertible paper issues, and state banks creating money based on virtually zero accompanying reserves.

In the 1890s, the new institutional forms were loans and trust companies, private banks, savings banks, and investment banks, now growing rapidly as a result of speculative activity associated with the industrial merger movement. State banks also proliferated by the thousands over the period. Railroads, farm mortgages, the manufacturing-industrial mergers movement, holding company stock, call loans, and an even greater role for the stock market as larger sections of the populace began buying stocks for the first time. Credit and liquidity from gold inflows, silver added to the currency by act of Congress, massive stock equity creation including 'watered' stock—all fed the excess speculative investing that led to an even greater debt overhang and subsequent financial implosion in 1893.

Some more generalized observations on the three depressions are as follows:

All three depressions in the nineteenth century were preceded, and indeed precipitated, by initial financial crises. Although data on debt levels and quality is not readily available, secondary sources, press commentaries, government reports, and anecdotal observations by participants and those writing at the time, confirm that debt and speculative excesses played key roles leading to the depressions that followed.

A major expansion of liquidity occurred in the run-up years preceding the financial eruptions that precipitated the depressions. Much of this excess liquidity creation was the product of two major forces: first, major inflows of gold and capital, particularly from London. Given the gold standard system at the time, gold flows often swung widely back and forth as conditions in England and Europe shifted as well. The second major force driving liquidity expansion in the century was the banking system itself. With no central bank, money creation as paper currency was largely at the whim of the thousands of separate state banks, both chartered and non-chartered. Many simply created paper currency at will, as investment opportunities for speculation in land settlement, transport infrastructure, and as bond and stock markets expanded rapidly and they rushed to exploit them.

Before the 1860s there was no semblance of any regulated commercial banking system, once the early vestige of central banking in the form of a First and Second Bank of the U.S. was allowed to disappear in the 1830s. The private state-chartered banks shared characteristics of both commercial and shadow banks, while the state governments that participated directly in canal and land speculation in the 1820s and 1830s by issuing bonds themselves acted as a de facto form of shadow banking institutions. When 'free banking' replaced chartered banking after the 1830s depression, it opened a period of 'Wild West' banking where almost anyone could form a bank with little or no reserves or capital and where there was no regulation to speak of to ensure adequate reserves were kept. Prior to the Civil War, banks therefore created currency more or less at will, expanding liquidity in the process, as opportunities for speculative investing proliferated in the run-up boom phases preceding financial crises.

The Civil War thereafter unleashed a variety of new financial institutions, financial instruments, and speculative opportunities. Institutionally the war gave birth to investment banking and eventually to the formation and spread of shadow banks called 'trusts.' Both later played a major role in financial instability in the post-Civil War period. Liquidity expanded exponentially during the war, and in the post-Civil War economy, as even greater foreign inflows of gold occurred, excess greenbacks created during the war by the federal government continued to circulate, government bond brokers turned to new forms of bond creation, and silver was introduced as money alongside gold. It all meant a major expansion of liquidity once again in the post-Civil War period, which the new institutions and instruments readily exploited. The 1880s and 1890s were also the period in which common stock speculation truly came of age, driven first by the real asset growth in manufacturing and distribution and new power technologies, and thereafter by the creation of securities built upon the real assets.

The closing decades of the nineteenth century provide a useful illustration of the relationship between real asset investment and speculative investing. As described previously, speculative investing is initially dependent upon real asset investment but eventually expands beyond the value of those real assets as speculative investing is driven increasingly by its own internal forces. Eventually, it is speculation that drives speculation; i.e. there are no supply constraints to the creation and marketing of speculative instruments, the demand for which feeds further demand in a reinforcing fashion. Debt and leveraging enable the acceleration of the process. Speculative investing, driven by inflation, in turn drives asset inflation to further extremes. The spiral only ceases when expectations of continued price-driven profitability break the cycle. The more prescient of investors in the global money parade first pull out and shift their liquid assets to other opportunities. Latecomers follow, sending asset prices plummeting. Finally, the investor 'herd' that remains responds last and attempts to sell off assets into what is now a rapidly falling market. Asset prices then crash, spilling over with similar effect to other classes of assets. This is essentially what happened leading up to and following the panic and crash of 1893.

Liquidity was excessively available from various sources in the run-up to financial crises phases for all three depressions. Multiple new forms of shadow banks developed in each case. Speculative investing based on canals, railroads, land speculation, farms and residential construction, new industries and technologies, new innovations in stock issuance (watering, holding companies, call loans for stock, etc.), grain commodity sales to Europe, and silver and gold price movements all drove speculation to a fever pitch preceding each of the financial crises. Unregulated borrowing and debt accumulation undoubtedly drove financial fragility to an extreme in the process. When the financial eruption finally came in 1837, 1873, and 1893, deflation quickly set in rapidly—first in asset classes, then product prices, and subsequently wage deflation as well. Defaults by financial institutions and non-financial companies followed quickly, exacerbating debt and deflation in turn. The real economy subsequently collapsed and then either stagnated over a relatively long term ('U'-shape) or recovered only to fall once again ('W'-shape).

With no central bank 'lender of last resort' or federal government fiscal stimulus to speak of available, asset values continued to collapse until written off as banks and non-banks defaulted and failed in great number. Debt was successfully 'unwound' or expunged in the process. With general deflation also having occurred, opportunities now once again presented themselves for renewed real and speculative investing. Foreign capital once again flowed into the country and was also created by the new financial institutions. New technologies, inventions, and industries arose. New stock issues and speculation began once again. Such was the cyclical nature of the nineteenth-century U.S. economy.

Some other perhaps useful observations on the nineteenth century include the following:

In all three depressions, the initiating financial crisis and bank failures were contained but the real economy continued to decline for years thereafter. This raises the important point that stabilizing the banks may prevent a further collapse of the financial system, but may not necessarily generate a sustained recovery of the real economy. Stabilizing the banking system is not the same as getting that system to freely lend once again and thus provide credit and liquidity to non-financial institutions. There may be a long lag between stabilizing and the free flow of credit. The longer that lag, the more deflation may damage the non-financial sector. The more cost-cutting by non-financial companies may deepen and the more layoffs occur, the more general consumption declines and drags real investment with it. When banks finally return to a willingness to lend and supply credit, the demand for loans and credit by non-financial companies may have fallen to such a point that they cannot afford to borrow. In short, factors other than banking stability take over as the drivers of the depression trajectory. A kind of extended economic stagnation may then take hold (i.e. 'U'-shaped conditions emerge). In contrast, a 'W'-shape may occur when government policy—monetary or fiscal—may prove sufficient to generate a limited temporary recovery but not sufficient to ensure that recovery becomes self-sustaining. Or, alternatively, a recovery begins and then policymakers choke it off by reducing the stimulus prematurely.

Banks in all three depressions were stabilized relatively quickly, in one to two years, but the depression continued for two to four more years thereafter. In all three depressions a severe financial crisis erupted, banks failed, credit was constricted, deflation accelerated, and defaults spread from the financial-banking sector to the real economy. The banks and financial institutions were subsequently refloated with liquidity, stabilized, and the bank failures and suspensions were abated. But the real economy continued to decline nonetheless for quite long periods thereafter; or else declined, then briefly recovered, then fell again (i.e. a 'W'-shaped trajectory depression)—as occurred in 1837–43 and 1893–98. In other words, checking and containing a financial crisis—i.e. stabilizing the banking system—does not necessarily prevent a consequent depression.

Depressions in the nineteenth century were at least in part determined by international economic factors affecting the availability of liquidity and credit. Foreign gold inflows fed the excess liquidity, asset inflation, and speculation leading to the financial break. Gold outflows exacerbated the contraction of credit, the asset deflation, and the decline in the real economy.

Wars and their associated government spending may have blunted the effects of an initial financial instability on the real economy. This was clearly the case in 1861 in relation to the crisis of 1857–60, and may have also been a factor in 1845 (the Mexican-American War) and 1898 (the Spanish-American War), both of which coincided roughly with the ending of depressions in 1844 and 1898, and helped bring those depressions to an end. New invention, technology innovations, and new industries that arose in the 1880s may have also played a mitigating role on the transmission of the financial instability to the real economy. New gold field openings (1849, 1898), and new markets may have also played a role in bringing depressions to a close.

The above two developments—the role of wars and of the advent of new technologies and industries—together raise a subject of relevance to contemporary policy in the post-2007 economy. Is it massive government fiscal spending that ends a depression, given that monetary policy can only stabilize the banking system but not generate a sustained recovery? Or is it the creation of new technologies and industries that regenerate real investment required for real sustained recovery? Or, perhaps, can the solution also take the form of a combination of the two—i.e. massive government spending to jump-start new technologies and industries; i.e. a sharp increase in government spending as a share of GDP, but not necessarily on war production?

The next chapter will explore how these apparent patterns in the nineteenth century played out in the twentieth century. Two specific periods and events stand out in the first half of the twentieth century. Both were precipitated by severe financial instability and crisis. One resulted in depression and the other didn't. As this book argues, however, both periods produced an Epic Recession. In the first Epic Recession case, 1907–14, Epic Recession did not descend into depression. The prolonged stagnation was ultimately resolved by the onset of World War I. The second was the Epic Recession of 1929–31, which followed the financial crisis of 1929. Unlike 1907–14, the experience of 1929–31 transformed into a bona fide depression. Thus the first might be considered an Epic Recession that 'failed,' while the second might be thought of as an Epic Recession that 'succeeded.' In other words, just as depressions can take different forms, so may Epic Recessions. Understanding these two cases is essential to understanding the current Epic Recession of 2007–10 in general, and for considering the important question of whether the current downturn of 2007–10 will result in a protracted period of stagnation of the real economy, as in 1907–14, or end up in a 'W'-shaped event and an eventual descent into depression once again, more similar perhaps to 1929–31.

5
'Type I' Epic Recession: 1907–14

This chapter and the next explore two specific financial crises and subsequent economic contractions, 1907–14 and 1929–31. Both represent two different forms of Epic Recession in the twentieth century. The first, a 'Type I' Epic Recession, takes the form of an initial financial crisis, followed by contraction of the real economy, that becomes an extended economic stagnation; the second, a 'Type II,' assumes the form of an initial crisis and contraction that declines, instead of stagnates, and subsequently evolves into a bona fide depression. In Type I that subsequent real economic decline flattens out long term, but the stagnation may appear as short and shallow recoveries followed by similar short-shallow contractions, that is a variant of a 'W'-shaped double-dip trajectory. The extended stagnation period may last well beyond two years or more. In Type II, the real economy's decline results in continuing deflation and defaults that feed back on the initial financial instability, creating a second and subsequent series of financial crises that drive the real economic decline still deeper. The subsequent financial crises precipitate a classic depression.

In a Type I, monetary policy succeeds in stabilizing the financial system but is unable alone to generate a sustained recovery. Subsequent banking crises are thus averted, but long-run recovery is not forthcoming. Debt is not removed sufficiently or quickly enough from the system and it remains a major drag on real investment. Deflation and defaults slow, but bank lending for real investment does not recover. Government fiscal policy stimulus is not aggressive or large enough to stimulate real investment, given the financial system's inability to revive on its own due to remaining high debt levels for banks, businesses, and household balance sheets. Excessive debt lingers and serves as a serious drag on investment and consumption. Financial and consumption fragility does not deteriorate significantly, but neither does it improve significantly.

In a Type II, monetary policy only temporarily stabilizes the financial system. Debt levels continue to rise and income levels (cash flow and real disposable income) fall. Both financial and consumption fragility deteriorate and feed upon each other, provoking further deflation across all three price systems (asset, product, and wage) and business and household defaults. The real economy continues to decline instead of just stagnate. A subsequent banking crisis eventually occurs as asset deflation and defaults rise. Credit and lending decline still further in the wake of the second financial crisis, contracting the real economy still further in turn. Fragility and debt–deflation–default feed into each other in a downward spiral. The process continues until such time as government policy intervention is massive enough to interject and disrupt the downward spiral at one or more of its points—either by eliminating debt levels, by subsidizing income (business or consumer) loss with bailouts and work programs, by stopping deflation with sufficiently large government spending programs, or by programs that suspend defaults.

Monetary policy may serve to postpone bank defaults by liquidity injections to offset debt on bank balance sheets, but such action does not necessarily result in an increased flow of bank lending. Banks' bad assets are not removed and balance sheets are not cleaned up, only contained. Preventing further debt deterioration puts a floor under financial fragility, but does not improve it. The income side of fragility may continue to deteriorate. Similarly for consumption fragility, which may be temporarily stabilized in terms of debt decline but not in terms of income recovery.

In other words, sustained recovery in each type of Epic Recession does not fully occur until fiscal policy action of appropriate scope and magnitude takes place. Monetary policy may stabilize debt deterioration, but only fiscal policy of adequate dimension can successfully stabilize the income element of fragility. The degree of fiscal stimulus required depends upon the degree of fragility in the system, the strength of the deflationary pressures transmitting between the three price systems, the scope and magnitude of defaults, and the intensity of the causal effects and feedbacks between the debt–deflation–default processes. Historically, in either type of Epic Recession, the extraordinary levels of government spending that eventually occurred, and thus succeeded in generating sustained recovery, occurred as a consequence of war spending: in the case of Type I (1907–14), World War I, and in case of Type II, World War II.[1]

THE BOOM–BUST PROCESS

In the run-up or boom phase, the processes by which financial and consumption fragility develop and deepen begin with the growth of excess liquidity that feeds the relative shift in favor of speculative forms of investing. Debt levels build up and debt quality deteriorates. Rising debt servicing costs and declining profitability from real asset investments, as well as other forces, result in a decline in cash flow. Financial fragility intensifies. A similar parallel process occurs for consumption fragility, in which consumer household debt rises while household real disposable income (i.e. household cash flow) tends to decline. Rising asset price inflation and increasing use of 'leveraging' feed the debt accumulation process. Profitability and returns from asset speculation rise relative to declining profitability from real investment, further driving the shift.

In the transition to the financial bust, the advance guard of speculators withdraws from one of the asset bubbles, precipitating a withdrawal by second-tier investors as well. Asset inflation slows, stops, and then reverses. 'Herd' investors quickly follow and prices for the asset in question begin to collapse. Prices of other asset classes follow into decline. Losses are incurred, written down or written off.

Following the financial bust, the creation of excessive credit, borrowing, and debt accumulation during the run-up phase is reversed. Once-abundant and available liquidity becomes increasingly a liquidity shortage. Excessive credit becomes a credit contraction for financial and non-financial companies alike. Ease of borrowing becomes an inability to borrow. Debt accumulation becomes debt unwinding. Accelerating asset price inflation becomes asset price deflation spreading across asset classes then spilling over to product and commodity price deflation, and then wage deflation. Rising real debt levels and falling prices in turn provoke defaults. The depth and extent of the deflation and consequent defaults define the depth of the subsequent contraction of the real economy, which may continue for months and even years. When debt–deflation–default interactions attain a certain threshold, the consequence is a contraction in the real economy of depth and duration that qualify as Epic proportions.

Continuing deflation and defaults also undermine the effectiveness of efforts at economic recovery. Policymakers, both monetary and fiscal, who respond with countermeasures 'too little too late,' do not promptly or adequately contain the real economy's contraction, thus producing an extended stagnation Type I Epic Recession. If the debt–deflation–default processes are of particular significant initial magnitude and the policy response is delayed, misdirected, or of an inappropriate composition, then a further series of financial banking crises may follow, accelerating the transformation of the initial Epic Recession into a bona fide depression.

Weak and/or delayed responses by monetary authorities delay the stabilization of the banking system, allowing deflation–defaults to spread and deepen. Relatively prompt and sufficient action by monetary authorities may stabilize the banking system, resulting in diminished deflation–defaults pressures. But that only stops the collapse. It does not generate a sustained recovery. Weak and/or delayed fiscal stimulus produces weak and temporary recoveries and a continuing extended period of stagnation of the general economy. Something like this occurred, in fact, following the major financial crisis known as the 1907 financial panic.

THE FINANCIAL PANIC OF 1907

The financial panic that erupted in October 1907 was the consequence of speculative investing activity by 'shadow' banking institutions. The predominant shadow banking institutions at the time were the 'trusts' and the investment bank brokerages (I-banks) of the day. Originating in the post-Civil War period and especially in the 1880s, the trusts and I-banks became a force nearly equal to the traditional banking system. Unlike banks, they were unregulated and maintained little or no reserves on hand in the event of a crisis and depositor withdrawals. The central role played by the trusts and other shadow financial institutions at the time led commentators to refer to the crisis as 'the trust company panic of 1907.'[2]

Originally focusing on conservative investments for private estates and corporations in the late nineteenth century, trusts quickly evolved to assume the functions of commercial banks. They also played a major role in railroad speculation and manufacturing company mergers, which accelerated in number and volume at the time. Paying depositors higher interest rates, and able to engage in more risky speculative ventures without oversight by government agencies, as a rule they provided greater returns for their investors than most commercial banks. The trusts were de facto hybrid investment-commercial-private banks.

In the decade leading up to the panic of 1907, the trusts and other shadow banking institutions grew tremendously. In New York alone, trust assets quadrupled over the preceding decade, growing two and a half times as fast as those of national banks, and by 1907 they held the equivalent of nearly three-quarters of the total assets of national banks. Together with the state banks, whose assets also doubled over the same period, the combined trust–state bank asset total exceeded that of the New York commercial banks.[3] In other words, the relative assets of the shadow banking system were roughly equal to that of the traditional banking system. This growing relative weight and mix in favor of shadow banks diverted ever-larger quantities of assets into speculative investing. Trust company loans and credit issued grew to $610 million, compared to $712 million by the national banks by 1907.[4] And this is just for the trusts, and does not include credit extended by other private banks, I-banks, insurance companies, and other shadow financial institutions at the time. Clearly, by 1907 the shadow financial system had grown at least as large as, if not larger than, the national commercial banking system itself. With its rise, so, too, grew the share of speculative forms of investing in the total investment mix.

The trusts and shadow banking system competed with the traditional national banking system. But at the same time they were deeply integrated with the commercial, national bank system. The national banks, centered in New York City, often set up their own trusts and transferred loans to them in order to maintain more reserves and lending on the commercial bank side—much as, decades later, after 2000, commercial banks would set up 'structured investment vehicles' (SIVs) and other 'conduits' off their regular bank balance sheets in order to maximize lending potential and provide a cover for the true extent of speculative investing. Trust companies also deposited huge sums with the banks, "but as few of the trust companies held cash reserves, in receiving deposits from them the banks were assuming a risk of a particularly explosive character."[5] This deep interpenetration of the two banking sectors meant that when the unregulated trusts encountered 'runs' and liquidity problems, those problems quickly spread to the national banks as well.

Like the trusts, the state banks were 'outside' the national banking system, located largely in the interior, and had grown tremendously in number in the decade leading up to 1907. They doubled in terms of assets. Like the trusts and I-banks, the state banks typically kept few, if any, reserves on hand, transferring these reserves to the New York centered banks. This increased the linkages and dependencies between the state banks and the national, commercial banks centered in New York and other big eastern cities. Linkages and interpenetration between the state banks and New York banks, as well as between trusts/shadow banks and the New York commercial banks, effectively spread financial fragility throughout the general banking system once the crisis erupted, making "the banking panic of 1907 the most severe of the national banking era panics."[6]

The crisis and panic that erupted in October 1907 had its roots in the preceding decade. Sources of liquidity expanded dramatically over the period, providing a rapid growth of credit (and debt) and serving as the basis for the speculative excesses in the speculative boom phase of 1898–1907. Thus, gold flowed into the U.S. from Europe in significant quantities as U.S. agricultural exports surged to Europe. U.S. gold production also increased. Added to this, the currency Act passed by Congress in 1900 stimulated the issuing of bank notes in circulation, which rose from $204 million to $551 million by 1907. Further actions by the U.S. Treasury also added to the liquidity and credit explosion. As one economist wrote at the time, the U.S. Treasury injected money into the banks without sales of government bonds as collateral. It additionally "exempted the banks from maintaining the legal reserve…and transferred to the banks other public money which had already been turned into the Treasury."[7] All these measures enabled an increase in loans and credit that reached record levels by 1907 and over-stimulated speculative investing in the process.

The composition of speculative investing during the first decade of the century had shifted in important ways differently from that which occurred prior to other financial crises in the nineteenth century, in 1872–73 and 1893. Now railroads and railroad bonds were no longer central. Land speculation associated with farm and business mortgages and urban development were involved, but were only secondary. The stock market and stock speculation were primary. As one historian of the period noted, "This was speculation of the traditional kind, speculation for profits from increasing stock prices in a market characterized by new conditions like…the abundant flow of securities issued by new kinds of corporations and frenzied buying and selling. It rode up and down in several waves and collapsed with the Panic of 1907."[8] The composition of speculation changed in other ways as well. Speculation now was in common stocks, with margin and futures trading. It sucked in new layers of middle-class investors for the first time.

The escalation of stock prices was based at first on the rapid growth of manufacturing and industrial mergers that began to emerge in the late 1880s, slowed only somewhat in the early to mid 1890s, then accelerated rapidly in the decade following 1897. Stock speculation after 1897 began increasingly to feed off of itself. Stock price rises drove stock prices, as the creation of holding companies and mergers continued to gain momentum after 1900. Investor expectations of continuing, and even accelerating, stock price appreciation gave "encouragement to the unbridled optimism which was already too much in evidence…which was made possible through credits granted by the banks."[9]

The trusts, I-banks, and state banks participated particularly heavily in the stock market, as a consequence of their providing call loans to investors for the purposes of stock speculation.

By mid 1906, however, there were growing signs of a slowdown in the real economy. Industrial production had doubled over the preceding decade as tens of thousands of new manufacturing companies were formed. The issuing of new stock issues slowed briefly in 1906 as the growth of liquidity and credit availability temporarily slowed. The slowdown was quickly offset in late 1906 by Treasury action and gold inflows. However, in late 1906 credit growth slowed once again as the Bank of England put a virtual halt on gold outflows to the U.S.

In February 1907 the initial warning signs of a possible crisis occurred but were generally ignored. Credit and loan contraction set off what was then called the 'rich men's panic' on the stock market in March 1907, eliminating $2 billion of stock value. A second important warning came in June with the failure of New York City to sell its bonds on two separate occasions. In addition to the March and June warning signs, indications of potential problems with utilities and shipping began to emerge. Stock markets in Europe and Japan also began to weaken. But the speculative momentum and euphoria was too great. The U.S. stock market rose again as asset and commodities price inflation continued into the summer of 1907. So long as prices continued to rise, so the euphoria and speculation would continue.

The real economy in the U.S. cooled abruptly in the summer of 1907, which resulted in August 1907 in yet another sharp stock market correction and decline. The more savvy investors realized that the real basis for the speculative boom was weakening and that "the outlook for the future was not promising in many basic industries."[10] They began leaving the market and cashing stocks and other assets. The financial boom turned to bust with a precipitating event in October 1907. Speculation in copper commodity prices imploded one of New York's largest 'shadow' banks at the time, the Knickerbocker Trust, which in turn quickly dragged a number of New York commercial banks and other trusts down with it.

When the financial crisis initially broke, a consortium of New York banks quickly bailed out several banks closely tied to the Knickerbocker Trust. But even though Knickerbocker was a member of the club of elite New York banks called the New York Clearing House (NYCH) system, and despite Knickerbocker's 18,000 depositors and $65 million in assets, the clearing house banks refused to bail it out as well. That led quickly to major depositor 'runs,' first on Knickerbocker itself, then on dozens of other trusts in New York which also had ties to other banks. Bank runs spread in New York from the trusts to various I-banks and brokerages, and eventually to other commercial banks. A full-fledged banking panic followed.

An emergency group of big bankers led by the famous J.P. Morgan quickly raised money to bail out two other large trusts—the Trust Company of America and the Lincoln Trust—to avoid a total collapse of all the trusts and the shadow banking sector. But runs on trusts and other New York banks continued nevertheless. More than two dozen banks and trusts collapsed in a matter of days in New York, and scores more brokerages and private banks. Credit to financial institutions effectively dried up and interbank lending ceased. Another $40 million was raised by Morgan, which barely averted the collapse of more than 60 brokerage houses.

By this time the banking panic and runs on the banks spread to the interior of the country, where more than 15,500 remaining banks were located. State banks that had previously deposited most of their reserves in the New York banks demanded their reserves returned from New York. The New York banks, however, suspended transfers for the moment and began hoarding their reserves and cash. This caused further crises in the interior banks in Chicago, St. Louis and elsewhere, which in turn suspended cash payments (i.e. withdrawals) to their local customers. In a matter of a few months, the situation had shifted from a large excess of available liquidity and credit to a general lack of credit throughout virtually all regions of the U.S. economy. Since most non-financial businesses rely on credit to cover basic operating costs and working capital, when lending from their local banks ceased, many started to fail. In October alone nearly 1,000 non-bank companies failed.[11] Tens of thousands more followed in the next 18 months in what would prove to be the second largest number of bankruptcies in the history of the U.S. up to that point.[12]

Various emergency measures were introduced in order to address what was quickly by late October 1907 a growing severe credit contraction. A total of 71 of the largest 145 U.S. cities resorted to money substitutes and to printing special local government 'checks' in lieu of currency now in growing shortage. Two-thirds of all cities with a population over 25,000 were impacted in this way in some manner. To counter the problem of both credit and cash drying up, new liquidity amounting to $238 million in the form of emergency 'certificates' for loans just between banks were issued by clearing houses in New York and other major cities.[13] The U.S. Treasury also assisted by distributing tens of millions of dollars more to large banks in the interior cities, depleting its total reserves down to only $5 million. The U.S. Treasury thus nearly went broke in trying to aid the big banks and restore liquidity to the national banking system.[14] The Treasury further sold $40 million more in special bonds using the Panama Canal as collateral, which allowed banks buying the Canal bonds to issue currency based on them at full purchase value. Gold inflows to the U.S. were also arranged to help to alleviate the liquidity shortage, as U.S. banks still continued to hoard cash for months after the financial crisis of October 1907 and refused to lend. A gold inflow amount of $96 million was arranged in November–December 1907, which compared to a paltry $4.5 million gold inflow in August–September.[15] J.P. Morgan and his emergency rescue committee raised an additional $30 million to stave off the collapse of the New York stock market, plus an additional $30 million to bail out the City of New York.

Despite all these bailouts, rescues, and liquidity injections, a general crisis of confidence in the banking system grew throughout October, reaching a peak in early November. The implosion of the shadow banking sector shifted thereafter from the trusts to another sector, the large brokerage houses. At the center was the major brokerage firm, Moore and Schley. It had financial tentacles into many directions, including many major industrial companies. Testifying four years later to Congress, J.P. Morgan explained that if Moore and Schley had also been allowed to fail following Knickerbocker, it would have provoked an even more serious financial crisis. As Morgan put it, "If Moore and Schley go there is no telling what the effect on Wall Street will be and on financial institutions in New York, and how many other houses will drop with it, and how many banks might be included in the consequences."[16] The brokerage was bailed out in a convoluted deal involving the sale of U.S. Steel mortgage bonds in which principals in several companies, including Schley himself, made millions.

The huge injection of liquidity from multiple sources stabilized the initial banking panic by the end of December. But not before 73 banks failed in the final months of 1907 with liabilities of roughly $200 million—which represented a smaller number of banks (which were mostly trusts) but a much larger volume of losses, when compared to the previous financial crisis in 1893. The impact on the interior banking system was also greater in 1907 than in 1893. Despite massive liquidity injections of various types arranged by the NYCH, by J.P. Morgan and his rescue committee, by the U.S. Treasury, and by interior financial institutions innovating with 'cash substitutes,' the big New York banks continued to refuse to lend for months after the financial crisis peaked and ebbed. Not only did they refuse to lend, they also refused to allow withdrawals and even suspended cash payments owed to non-bank businesses. The big New York banks simply refused to reinstitute cash payments and sat on reserves of as much as $250 million until as late as January 2008, three months after the panic initially began in early October 1907 and well after they, the banks themselves, had been stabilized.[17] It was the suspension of cash payments that particularly devastated non-financial companies.

The main historian of the 1907 panic, O.M. Sprague, noted in 1910 that the New York banks for months thereafter continued to hoard the massive amounts of reserves that had been pumped into them during the crisis months. By way of comparison, the Bank of England at the time had bank reserves of only $24 million—not $250 million—but nevertheless disbursed $7 million in early November 1907 without suspending cash payments.[18] The refusal of the big New York banks to lend despite restored liquidity was a major cause of the subsequent severe contraction in the real, non-financial economy that spread to the interior and throughout the country in 1908.

THE 1907 AND 2008 BANKING CRISES COMPARED

The financial panic of 1907 shares notable similarities with the recent financial crisis that began in 2007.

In both early 1907 and 2007 there were growing signs of financial instability. The real economies in both periods were slowing down in the months immediately preceding the financial crisis. The stock markets declined sharply on several occasions before each crisis, only to recover again briefly as speculators refused to acknowledge the growing instability so long as asset and commodity prices continued to rise. Corrections in the markets went unheeded. A second round of visible problems arose in June in both periods: in 2007, leading mortgage companies and hedge funds began to fail and the stock market became increasingly volatile; in 1907 further problems visibly arose in New York city bonds and speculation in utility stocks. Hedge funds' speculation in subprime mortgages and trusts' in utilities played similar roles. Stocks fell again after June and recovered once more, as signs of the real economy's weakening continued to appear.

The subprime mortgage market blew up in early August 2007 and in stages began to drag the shadow banking system down with it in a matter of a few months, spreading the crisis to commercial banks and various credit markets before the end of the year. By December, interbank lending was in trouble. It took three more months thereafter for the unraveling of the shadow banking system to evolve to a further stage with the collapse of investment bank Bear Stearns in March 2008. That collapse set in motion events that would lead to the next benchmark event—the collapse of Lehman Brothers in September 2008 that in turn set off the deeper banking panic of October 2008. October 2008 closely resembles that of the panic of October 1907.

The Federal Reserve, the central bank of the U.S., did not exist in 1907. The weak counterpart to the Fed in 1907 was the New York Clearing House group of elite banks that made a feeble attempt to function as a 'lender of last resort' to other banks. Once the crisis deepened, however, the NYCH abandoned this role and protected its members' assets first. A kind of lender-of-last-resort authority shifted to the pre-eminent banker of the period, J.P. Morgan, who pooled bailout money among the trusts and then played a pivotal role in getting Treasury funding to bail out the remaining banks that were in trouble. The Treasury thus played a key funding role in both crises, with J.P. Morgan functioning as a kind of de facto Fed chairman.

Fed actions from August 2007 to March 2008 were consistently behind the curve of events and insufficient to prevent the shadow bank implosions that began to occur in March with Bear Stearns. However, the Fed's participation in the Bear Stearns' bailout in March and other actions at the time in effect delayed the process by which other I-banks and other segments of the shadow banking sector would inevitably implode. The Fed did not prevent the I-banks implosion but slowed the process by several months between March and September 2008. In contrast, with no central bank on the scene in 1907, the process of financial collapse accelerated.

The collapse of the shadow bank, the Knickerbocker Trust, in 1907 played a precipitating role in the crisis similar to Bear Stearns in 2008, except that the former went under, while the Fed bailed out the latter. The bailouts of Fannie Mae and Freddie Mac in July–August 2008 might also be compared to the bailout of two brokerages, Gross and Kleeburg and Otto Heinze and Company, that occurred at the very beginning of the October 1907 panic. The collapse of other trusts that followed were similar perhaps to the collapse of the other I-banks, like Lehman Brothers, in September 2008. Subsequently, the spread of the financial crisis to the commercial banks in October 1907 parallels the spread to other commercial banks like Bank of America, Citigroup, and others in 2008, while the spread of the crisis to the interior in 1907 shows similarities to the propagation of the crisis internationally in 2007–08.

While making such comparisons might seem too simplistic, nonetheless the parallels between the two financial crises are too striking to dismiss. A precipitating financial institution's collapse, followed by a rapid spread of the crisis to other sectors of the shadow banking system, followed by a spread to the commercial banking system. A scurrying for sources of liquidity to shore-up bank balance sheets while interbank lending dries up. A patchwork of bailouts. A spread and propagation of the crisis geographically. A severe contraction of credit not only to other banks but to non-financial companies as well. While the pattern is not perfect, it is nonetheless something of a pattern. And it occurs whether or not there is a Fed, a central bank—a point that suggests that even the presence of a central bank acting as a lender of last resort may not enable, at first, the prevention of the financial crisis but may only, at best, slow its progression as it unfolds.

There are other similarities between the two crises, 1907 and 2007–08. What stands out in particular is the refusal of the NYCH (that functioned as a kind of proto-Federal Reserve 'lender of last resort' at the time), to bail out the third largest trust (i.e. shadow bank), the Knickerbocker Trust. This event was perhaps similar to the refusal of the central bank and the U.S. Treasury to bail out the big investment bank, Lehman Brothers, in September 2008. The failure to rescue Knickerbocker and Lehman Brothers precipitated the respective general banking panics that followed: in 1907 in October and in 2008 in late September and October. Once again the collapse spread more quickly in the earlier period, while it was dragged out into December in 2008. This parallel suggests that institutions and managers who function as lenders of last resort typically underestimate the depth and momentum of the crisis, respond with too little too late at first, and resort to traditional rather than extraordinary measures initially that prove relatively ineffective.

Another similarity is that runs on the banks occurred in both periods. However, in the earlier period they were predominantly retail depositor runs, while in the latter they were mostly wholesale (institutional) depositor runs due to the availability in 2008 of Federal Deposit Insurance Corporation (FDIC) guarantees for retail depositors. Institutional runs in 2008 took the form of, first, hedge funds withdrawing and refusing to deposit with the I-bank, then other shadow institutions following suit, and finally commercial banks refusing to provide overnight loans to the faltering Bear Stearns or Lehman Brothers.

Recognizing their strategic error in allowing Knickerbocker to fail led to a quick reversal by the NYCH, J.P. Morgan, and the U.S. Treasury, who then bailed out the two equally large trusts, the Trust Company of America and Lincoln Trust. In similar fashion, recognition of the serious consequences of having failed to bail out Lehman Brothers in September quickly led in 2008 to the Treasury and the remaining large banks 'rescuing' the insurance giant, AIG, in early October.

In both crises, the formal institutions serving as potential rescuers (i.e. lenders of last resort) procrastinated, delayed, and generally fell behind the curve of events at the outset—in 1907 the NYCH, and in 2007 the Fed. The U.S. Treasury also played a delayed response role in 2007–08, only entering the fray in July 2008 to prevent the collapse of Fannie Mae and Freddie Mac in order to allay the fears of foreign bondholders.

In the midst of the 1907 crisis, J.P. Morgan brought together in his office all the presidents of the trust companies and 'forced' them to pool funds to help rescue other trusts, I-banks, and institutions. Similarly, Treasury Secretary Henry Paulson did the same with leading bank presidents in October 2008, although this time they were 'forced' to take $125 billion of taxpayers' money from the $700 billion Troubled Asset Relief Program (TARP) fund provided by Congress.[19]

Both financial crises were preceded by extraordinary growth in liquidity that fed the speculation and debt and, once the crisis began and credit dried up, both crises were followed by massive injections of liquidity into the banking systems (commercial and shadow). In 1907 the liquidity was arranged by the NYCH providing liquidity in the form of special certificates to reopen the interbank lending market, and in 2008 by the Fed through a proliferation of 'emergency auctions' and discount loans to banks and shadow banks available at near-zero interest rates.

Another similarity is the U.S. Treasury's commitment of virtually all its available capital (less $5 million) and mortgaging the newly acquired Panama Canal to help J.P. Morgan and the NYCH bail out their colleague banks. In 2008 the counterpart was the Treasury and the Fed providing $3 trillion in taxpayers' money and public debt to assist the bailout.

A notable difference between the periods, however, was the international gold standard in 1907 which did not exist in 2008. In the earlier period, the restoration of liquidity was in part enabled by accelerating U.S. farm exports and thereby obtaining extra gold inflows to the U.S. economy. In 2008 the dollar had replaced the gold standard. Increasing exports to obtain gold and liquidity was therefore not possible in 2008. But foreign investors, public and private, buying massive amounts of U.S. Treasury bonds effectively played the same role injecting liquidity into the U.S. banking system through the Fed as a conduit as they purchased U.S. government bonds in record volume. The flow of dollars was reversed somewhat in 2008, as the Fed pumped more than $600 billion of liquidity into foreign banks needing to cover dollar-denominated debts and withdrawals.

The pivotal event in 1907, the bailout of the big I-bank, Moore and Schley, has perhaps its equivalent in the dual bailouts of the giant Citigroup banking empire and, nearly as large, Bank of America, that occurred in stages from October 2008 through January 2009. As in the case of Moore and Schley, had Citigroup in particular been allowed to crash in 2008 its global multi-trillion-dollar balance sheet would have undoubtedly caused a global banking collapse of immense proportions. More than $500 billion of direct and indirect credits by the Fed and the Treasury were consequently pumped into Citigroup to keep it afloat (while Citigroup remained technically insolvent). Millions of dollars were similarly pumped into Moore and Schley, without which, according to J.P. Morgan, the collapse would have become in general much worse.

Further post-bank stabilization similarities also exist for 1907 and 2008. Both periods illustrate that even once the banking system is 'stabilized' in the sense of containment of further bank failures, an extended period follows during which bank lending continues to contract with a subsequent serious impact on the real economy. For twelve months after September 2008, bank lending to non-financial business continued to contract. It takes a significant period after a crisis for the financial system to recover fully. During this period lending is insufficient, and recovery of the real economy is therefore spotty, weak, and tends to falter. This extended period of slow recovery reflects the fact that debt and balance sheets take time to 'clean up' after the crisis, and banks are reticent about lending until that happens. This happened in 1908 and after. It also happened in 2009 as the multi-trillion-dollar annual securitized markets failed to resurrect after even two years, as consumer credit markets continued to tighten, commercial property markets remained in decline, residential mortgage problems spread to other stable housing segments, rising failures in the 'interior' impacted smaller regional banks, and the possibility of sovereign debt crises loomed in the periphery of Europe and elsewhere. Thus both crises show that a kind of 'stop–go' scenario in the real economy following a financial bust may be not untypical of Type I Epic Recessions.

THE REAL ECONOMY AFTER 1907

The 1907 financial crisis had severe effects on the real economy. Credit contracted sharply, not only to banks but to non-financial businesses as well. An indication of the severity was the widespread local creation of 'scrip'[20] as a cash money substitute. New York and other money center banks hoarded cash by refusing to send reserves to the interior banks and by suspending cash payments. Many cities simply ran out of money. Credit is one of the main mechanisms by which the financial crisis is transmitted to the real economy. Major financial crises that produce Epic Recessions are associated not only with credit contractions but virtual credit crashes. Credit crashed in 1907, especially for the interior. Considering just the trusts segment of the shadow banking sector, for the New York City region alone from August 27 to December 10, 1907, the panic resulted in a "33 percent decline in total deposits, 43 percent decrease in loans, and a 20 percent decline in cash reserves. Total resources contracted by $362 million," according to one well respected contemporary economic historian.[21]

Apart from cash shortages or the decline of available bank credit, the crisis was transmitted from the financial system to the real economy in other ways as well. Excess debt accumulated during the speculative investment binge run-up phase must be 'worked off,' for financial and non-financial companies alike. Debt requires debt servicing, and often the first casualty of the need to service debt is the suspension of investment projects. The second is a reduction in levels and activity of production. The precipitating event of a financial crisis may occur and failures and suspensions abate after an initial surge, but this doesn't mean the financial crisis is over. In fact, in several ways it is just beginning. The debt levels accumulated during the boom phase do not disappear overnight, and take months and even years to work off. For banks this means an extended period of falling lending. For non-banks this means suspension, postponement, or even cancellation of investment that might otherwise produce jobs, or production cutbacks, which cause the loss of jobs. The greater the excess debt, the more difficult and extended the period of debt unwinding. Debt drives non-financial businesses to contract, apart from whether or not they are able to obtain credit. That contraction may take various forms: bankruptcies, reorganizations, mergers, cost-cutting, asset and product firesales, etc.

Debt unwinding and deflation, if unchecked and uncontained, eventually leads to rising business defaults. If prolonged and deep enough, the debt–deflation–default processes can feed back on the financial system itself in a second and third round of financial banking crises. If the debt–deflation–default processes are unchecked and continue to gain momentum, this can lead to subsequent financial crises and, ultimately, to depression. If they are partially checked and contained, a period of extended stagnation may instead take place. Something like the latter occurred after 1907.

Modern data sources begin in the U.S. with the creation of the National Bureau of Economic Research (NBER) in the early 1920s. But useful NBER data was lacking prior to the 1920s. This has led contemporary economists to try to reconstruct statistics for 1907–14. The reconstructions come up with different and contradictory results.[22] And none seem to account for the 43 percent fall in bank loans to business, various reports of the slowing economy in 1906 and in 1907 even before the financial crisis of October, and the widespread resort to cash substitutes and scrip in the interior as cash and credit virtually vanished after the bank crisis erupted. Comments by economists and informed observers writing at the time in the two leading business journals of the day, *Bradstreet's* and the *Commercial and Financial Chronicle*, report a deep and serious contraction of the real economy following what was a major financial crisis in 1907.[23] One leading economist at the time, Alexander Noyes, referred to the post-financial bust period in 1908 as a "reaction in trade, consumption, and production, after the panic of 1907, [that] was so extraordinarily violent that…at the opening of the year, business in many lines of industry was barely 28% of the volume of the year before."[24] By June 1908, gross national product (GNP) was still 50 percent of the previous year. Later studies in the 1930s that compared that period to 1907–14 referred to 1907–08 as "the depression of 1907–1908" that "was of very considerable depth."[25]

EPIC CHARACTERISTICS OF THE 1907–14 RECESSION

In terms of quantitative characteristics of Epic Recession stated in Chapter 1—i.e. GNP, employment, industrial production, the stock market, and exports—the first phase of the 1907–14 contraction qualifies as an Epic Recession.

To recall, to qualify as an Epic Recession, GNP (or gross domestic product, GDP) must decline by at least –5 percent for two consecutive quarters. Independent studies show that GNP declined in 1907 at a –1.6 percent *annual* rate and an additional –5.5 percent *annual* total for 1908.[26] Since no data were kept for quarterly periods at that time, it is almost certain that the economy declined more than –5.0 percent in the last quarter of 1907, given that the previous three quarters of 1907 were growth quarters. Similarly, the –5.5 percent fall in GNP for all of 1908 must have included a contraction of –5.0 percent or more in early 1908, given the temporary recovery that occurred in the second half of 1908. So two consecutive quarters of decline—i.e. the last of 1907 and the first of 1908—easily exceeded declines of –5.0 percent each quarter. The decline in the last quarter of 1907 might have been even significantly greater than –5.0 percent. For example, bank clearings in November and December 1907 fell by nearly –19 percent. That precipitous a drop almost certainly means fourth-quarter 1907 GNP fell perhaps as much as –15 percent in just that quarter![27]

In Epic Recessions, industrial production declines by –10 percent to –20 percent over a twelve-month period. A study in 2004 of industrial production decline during 1908 indicated a collapse of –21 percent in 1908 alone.[28] This compares with an industrial production decline for the depression of 1893–97 of about –30 percent and for 1873–75 of –11 percent, according to the same study.[29] So the 1907–08 real economic contraction was worse than the 1870s depression but not as bad as the 1890s depression, when measured in terms of industrial output in 1907–08. When measured in terms of industrial production, the 1907–08 real economy's contraction therefore certainly ranks as Epic in magnitude and, one might argue, even borders on depression.

Employment data for 1907–08 also indicate a near-depression condition. In Epic Recession, unemployment levels range between 10 percent and 20 percent. Although available data are sparse, from what is available it is likely that joblessness levels fell sharply through the first half of 1908 in particular. At least that level is likely to have been attained for the first half of 1908, given the near-collapse of the real economy in the final months of 1907 and the continuing decline through the first half of 1908. The unemployment rate for the last quarter of 1907 and the first half of 1908 was thus easily more than 10 percent and probably in the 15 percent or more range.

Stock market declines are associated with falls of –40 percent to –60 percent in Epic Recessions. The retreat of stock prices from the peak in September 1906 to the trough in December 1907 was –34 percent for common stocks overall, and a slightly higher –38 percent for industrial stocks.[30]

Declines in exports must reach –10 percent to qualify as Epic Recession levels, and came close at –9.2 percent in 1908 followed by –8.4 percent in 1909, just short of the –10 percent threshold, but a still respectable magnitude given Europe's continuing heavy demand for U.S. agricultural raw and semi-finished materials that prevailed throughout the early twentieth century.[31] Global forces (i.e. demand for U.S. exports) apparently played some role in the U.S. real economy's decline at the time, although it is not clear that the U.S. Epic Recession was part of a synchronized global decline.

The preceding data measure quantitative characteristics for the period 1907–08, the first phase of the Epic Recession. But Epic Recession includes subsequent phases as well. When the broader period of 1908–14 is considered, the case for Epic Recession becomes even stronger.

The 1907–14 period represents a Type I Epic Recession—i.e. one in which a sufficiently deep and widespread financial crisis sets in motion a contraction of the real economy significant enough to push it to Epic dimensions. A partial recovery occurs that is short in duration and shallow. However, a sustained recovery does not take place. Rather, a period of extended stagnation occurs. This stagnation may take the form of a series of shallow growth periods and contractions, or it may take the form of 'W'-shaped recoveries that are sharper and brief. At the end of the extended period of stagnation, the real economy is roughly where it was when the stagnation period began.

Evidence that the period 1907–14 was a Type I Epic Recession characterized by a financial crisis followed by a sharp contraction of the real economy, and an extended period of relative stagnation thereafter, is provided by the NBER. For example, the NBER describes the period in GNP terms as having three relatively brief declines and three recoveries of roughly the same dimensions: There's the initial 13-month contraction bottoming out in June 1908. From July 1908 through December 1909, there's an 18-month recovery again, followed by a second 24-month decline from January 1910 through December 1911. 1912 was another brief twelve-month recovery, followed by a 23-month second decline from January 1913 to December 1914.[32] The brief recovery phases pretty much 'net out' the decline phases, leaving a period of extended stagnation from 1909 through 1914. As one commentator described it, "one result of the Panic of 1907 was seven more or less lean years in America."[33]

The three fluctuating GNP recoveries–declines, netting out as a stagnation, are corroborated by three similar employment growth–decline periods, in fluctuations in bank suspensions and general business failures, in product price swings, and in stock price volatility.

The characteristic requirement that Epic Recessions have a duration of 18–24 months is not rigidly applied in the case of Type I Epic Recessions, like 1907–14, that have extended stagnation periods. Thus the *initial* phase of the real economy's downturn need not necessarily have a duration of a consecutive 18–24 months, but that duration might be intermittent throughout the longer extended stagnation period with a series of 'W'-shaped gains and declines. When viewed from this latter perspective, the 1907–14 extended period qualifies as Epic in character.

LIQUIDITY AND SPECULATIVE INVESTING

The decade leading up to the 1907 financial crisis was marked by extraordinary liquidity growth. Gold inflows from Europe, gold production following the 1898 Alaska–Yukon rush, the U.S. currency Act of 1900, Treasury injections into the banking system, a reduction in reserve requirements to virtually zero by the Treasury—all fed the debt accumulation process. Much of it found an investment outlet in industrial stocks and stock market speculation. But food and metal commodities were favorite speculative markets as well. The 1907 panic itself was, to recall, set off initially due to an attempt by trust investors to corner the 'copper' market, which was in turn being driven by the new electric industry-based utilities and manufacturing. For stock market speculation, call loans enabled the excess leveraging and drove a good deal of the debt accumulation. Margin buying and futures trading also accelerated the process. New layers of 'herd' investors from the middle classes entered the stock market and fed the speculative euphoria.

The new forms of shadow banking facilitated the speculative run-up, at the forefront of which were the newly transformed trusts, as well as I-banks and brokerages, life insurance companies and mutual savings banks. Highly leveraged and not required to maintain reserves, these institutions became increasingly financially fragile institutions and as their numbers and assets grew, so the financial system itself became increasingly fragile. The close integration between the trusts and the commercial banks increased that general fragility, as did the practice of the interior banks in keeping their reserves with the New York money center banks. High leverage and low or no reserves was not a problem so long as asset prices continued to rise. But that changed abruptly as soon as the asset inflation ceased, or even began to slow. The leading shadow institutions, the trusts, saw their assets and numbers especially rise rapidly in relation to the commercial banking system. While there are no firm data on what the share of speculative investing to total investment might have been at the time, with the trusts' share of total assets growing to 27 percent of commercial banks', the speculative investing behind that 27 percent must certainly have been rising significantly along with that rise in assets to 27 percent.

The 'global money parade' was not nearly as large in that first decade of the century as it would be in later decades. The numbers were no doubt concentrated in London and New York, with perhaps a smaller number in Paris and a few other lesser world financial centers. But the growth in total volume of new investing in the stock and commodities markets by this parade was not insignificant. It was sufficient to cause a near complete collapse of the trusts' sector in New York, which pulled in other shadow banking institutions and subsequently commercial banks as well. The nature of the responses of the commercial banks in money centers like New York in turn also dragged down highly leveraged state banks in the periphery or 'interior.' Debt unwinding, asset deflation, and defaults followed.

DEBT–DEFAULT–DEFLATION PROCESSES

The debt characteristic is difficult to verify quantitatively or the Epic Recession of 1907–14, given the lack of appropriate data. On the one hand, there is no lack of direct, eyewitness and participant accounts of the 1900–07 boom period as one of excessive speculative activity. To recall, this was a period in which the main locus of speculative action was the stock market itself. The price index for common stocks rose by more than 30 percent in the period immediately preceding the panic of 1907. There is also general acknowledgment among chroniclers of the period of the crisis of the central role played by trusts and other financial intermediaries in excessively stimulating credit (thus creating excess debt) during the speculative run-up phase of 1899–1907. But credit comes in various forms: bank loans, commercial paper issues, bond issues, call loans on stock purchases, etc. And there simply is no reliable aggregate database on credit in general for the first decade leading up to World War I. That would have to await the 1920s. So the overwhelming anecdotal evidence must suffice for claiming that the 1907–14 period satisfied the debt characteristics of Epic Recession.

The presence of deflation is more easily verified. Deflation under Epic Recession conditions has three measures: asset price deflation, product prices, and wages. Asset prices fall in Epic Recessions between 10 percent and 40 percent, product prices by 2–7 percent, and wage deflation begins.

In 1907–14, asset prices collapsed dramatically on numerous fronts. Stock prices alone fell by 34 percent in the first year. The shifts in the index of common stock prices that occurred during 1906–14 support the claim of a 'double-W' extended stagnation following the panic of 1907. The index of stock prices fell 34 percent by late 1907, recovered the entire 34 percent by 1909, remained flat year to year on average from late 1909 through the end of 1912, before falling 22 percent again in 1913–14.[34] Product prices, according to an NBER index, accelerated by more than 40 percent in the three years prior to the 1907 financial panic. Then followed the familiar 'double-W' pattern followed by GNP and stock prices. Product price deflation fell by 32 percent in the six months after the panic of 1907, fully recovered that loss by the end of 1909, fell again in 1910–11 by 23 percent, recovered again to prior levels of 1909, and fell a third time in 1913–14.[35] Wage deflation appeared to follow a different pattern. There was no volatile fluctuation in wages like there was in GNP, asset, or product prices. They remained largely stagnant from 1909 to 1914.[36] Thus general wage stagnation was the rule after 1907.

Default data for banks and general businesses in the initial year of the crisis, 1907–08, were presented earlier. For bank suspensions during the extended period, 1907–14, the premier business publication at that time, *Dun's Review*, recorded a total of 1,008 bank suspensions from the fourth- quarter 1907 financial eruption to the end of 1914.[37] In terms of general business, a total of 958,485 failed from the fourth quarter 1907 through 1914.[38] Both bank suspensions and business failures tracked the fluctuating rise and fall of GNP and prices. Not surprisingly, business failures spiked significantly in 1908, moderated in 1909–10, only to rise steadily once again from 1912 on until peaking in 1914 with nearly 17,000 failures. The period of 1907–14 is thus generally overlooked as quite volatile in terms of the real economy, deflation, defaults, and other indicators. It is certainly not characterizable as a period of sustained recovery. Post-1907 recoveries were short and shallow, followed by similar decline periods. The volatility lasted until the onset of World War I.

The experience of 1907–14 satisfies many of the qualitative characteristics of Epic Recession as well. The run-up in debt was significant, as was the deflation and defaults that followed after the panic of 1907. Bank suspensions, capital loss, bank runs, or unavailability of credit—all occurred in Epic Recession dimensions between 1907 and 1914. Loan contractions of 43 percent, the collapse of scores of trusts, I-banks, and brokerages, New York banks' refusal to return reserves to interior banks, the suspension of cash payments to the interior, local banks resorting to payment in scrip to customers, depositor runs on banks throughout the interior, the rising importance of shadow bank categories like trusts and I-banks, the growth and spread of common stock speculation, the increasing fragility of financial institutions—all were classic qualitative characteristics of Epic Recession.

FINANCIAL AND CONSUMPTION FRAGILITY

If fragility is a function of debt, income flows, and consequent debt servicing difficulty, the period after 1907 witnessed continuing financial fragility. Despite the lack of direct data to measure fragility at the time, the significant number of non-bank business failures that occurred throughout 1907–14 certainly reflects what must have been chronic difficulties in servicing debt. The repeated bouts of product price deflation followed by only brief periods of price recovery must have meant significant downward price pressure on business revenues and cash flow. Bank and financial institutions' fragility may not have worsened appreciably after 1908, but it does not appear to have recovered either. There was no subsequent, second banking crisis after 1908, which prevented a descent into a full-blown depression. But bank stability must have remained an issue. It was only after 1912 that bank and government support for creating a Federal Reserve finally reached a point sufficient to push through legislation in Congress to create the Fed. The Fed only became a reality in 1913–14, not immediately in the wake of 1907. It may have been growing concern for a second possible financial crisis after 1912 that finally spurred the creation of the Fed. Fears for a growing financial fragility of the system by 1914 may also explain in part why the New York stock market was shut down when World War I erupted in Europe in August 1914, and the market remained closed for a record three months, and only reopened in December, perhaps not coincidentally when the Fed began functioning. So financial fragility may not have deteriorated to the point necessary to provoke a second banking crisis before 1914, but that fragility did not dissipate sufficiently to produce robust bank lending to general business and a consequent sustained recovery.

Continuing consumption fragility after 1907–08 is more difficult to verify. As noted, wage data are unreliable. But data that do exist suggest that wages were largely stagnant until 1914 and therefore real disposable income likely did not rise much, if at all. Debt was not a factor for most working-class consumers since it was not available. That would have to wait until the 1920s to become a factor in consumption fragility. However, debt may have been of relevance for small farmers. But wage stagnation certainly served to cause consumption fragility to worsen. Both forms of fragility would be reduced by the onset of world war, as incomes would rise both for businesses and consumers, although so too would debt levels.

A SHORT INITIAL NOTE ON WAR AND RECESSION

Wars have a double-edged impact on Epic Recessions and depressions. War unleashes and accelerates speculative investing to new levels. The Civil War played such a role, creating many new opportunities, new shadow institutions, and speculators. Wars also appear to dampen and contain contractions of the economy precipitated by financial crises. The financial panic of 1857 was cut short by the onset of the Civil War, which clearly dampened the potential impacts of the panic of 1857 on the real economy. The timing of the Mexican-American War in 1845 has yet to be analyzed as to its role in ensuring the end of the depression of 1837–43. Similarly, the Spanish-American War in 1898 perhaps not accidentally coincides with the ending of the depression of 1893–98.

Unlike 1845, 1865, and 1898, the role of World War I in putting a definitive end to the Epic Recession of 1907–14 is less debatable. The war put a definitive end to the extended stagnation period of 1908–14. The same claim is possible for another, even greater Epic Recession. Epic Recession in 1929–31, unlike 1907–14, did not stagnate but continued to spiral lower, precipitating a series of follow-on banking and financial crises until 1933. In the latter example, both financial and consumption fragility continued to deteriorate—driven by the cumulating processes of worsening debt, deflation, and spreading defaults, financial and non-financial alike. In the next chapter, it is the 'Type II' Epic Recession of 1929–31 to which our analysis turns.

6
'Type II' Epic Recession: 1929–31

Financial crisis starts with an expansion of liquidity and excess credit. Epic Recessions that follow involve the collapse of that liquidity and the contraction of credit. It is liquidity and credit that initially enables excessive borrowing and consequent debt accumulation. Speculative investing creates multiple opportunities of borrowing and debt as a result of leveraging, the tendency toward layers of borrowing and leveraging, and the nature of short-term unlimited demand and asset inflation intrinsic to speculative investing and markets. Shadow banking institutions engage disproportionately in speculative investing. So as their numbers and total assets grow, so too that growth adds to the weight and mix of speculative investment. If short-term demand, inflation, leveraging, and layered leveraging all lead to excess borrowing, debt, and debt servicing loads, then growing numbers of institutions and investors that target speculative markets all add to the total load of debt as well. But it all begins with the availability of excess liquidity and credit creation. The analysis of Epic Recessions therefore begins with understanding how and why liquidity and credit creation at times expand to extraordinary levels, and in the process result in excessive debt that leads to financial instability and crisis.

Liquidity and credit may originate externally or internally within the financial system: from a central bank like the Federal Reserve (Fed) increasing the money supply, from international gold flows into the economy if there's a gold standard system in effect, from internal sources within the banking financial system as shadow banks and traditional banks create and issue new forms of credit and securities independent of central bank policies, and from the growth of income by investors—i.e. profits and retained earnings by corporate investors and personal income growth by wealthy individual investors. Borrowing and debt accumulation take place in the run-up or boom phase. The unwinding of excess debt and credit contraction occurs in the bust phase of the financial crisis. Unwinding here means the expunging, writing-down, writing off, or otherwise removal from balance sheets, of that excess debt.[1]

Should debt unwinding proceed too slowly following a financial bust (or virtually not at all if Fed liquidity injections eliminate the need to unwind debt), banks are reluctant to issue new credit and loans to non-bank businesses. That means new real investment may stagnate or at best grows weakly and slowly in the recovery stage. Fed policies may even result in reigniting speculation. With excess debt remaining on balance sheets in the form of 'bad' assets, banks may prefer to lend to speculative projects more than real asset investment since returns on the former are quicker and greater than the latter.

Thus a return to prior levels of real investment will not take place without the elimination of the excess debt hangover. Lingering bad debt thus become a significant drag on recovery if not expunged or removed in some manner, not merely 'offset' by liquidity injections. The 'natural' unwinding of bad debts and assets can take years. Together with liquidity injections, that slow, natural unwinding may condemn a recovery to what looks much like a period of extended stagnation. That is what essentially occurred in 1907–14. On the other hand, if there is no unwinding, but an actual continued accumulation of real debt as deflation accelerates, and if no liquidity injections take place, the outcome eventually is a subsequent financial banking crisis. This is what happened in mid 1931, and again at the close of 1932. At that point, mid 1931 Epic Recession had descended into a bona fide depression.

STRATEGIES FOR DEBT UNWINDING: LIQUIDATION VERSUS REFLATION

Is it necessary for debt to unwind before recovery can begin? Should the real economy be allowed to collapse to eliminate the excess debt—no matter what the real costs? This was the very position taken by one wing of government policymakers in the initial years of the Great Depression of the 1930s in the U.S. It was called the 'liquidationist' view and was promoted by then Treasury Secretary Andrew Mellon circa 1930. Mellon advised then President Herbert Hoover to 'liquidate the farmers, liquidate the banks, liquidate labor.' What Mellon meant was to let deflation run its course—which he maintained was a necessary prelude to any real recovery. This view further suggests that attempting to restimulate the economy prematurely, before bad asset values had sufficiently collapsed (i.e. excess bad debt had unwound), would prove largely futile and have little effect in generating an economic recovery.

Whether in response to Mellon's proposed policy, or other factors unrelated, the Hoover administration in effect presided over such a policy. Assets were liquidated; i.e. collapsed in value to where they were essentially worthless, and were then removed from bank and other business balance sheets. With that came the additional 'liquidation' of thousands of businesses, jobs, and incomes. Roosevelt's first two years in office, 1933–34, did little to reverse the liquidation process.

In those first two years of his first term in office, Roosevelt focused on stabilizing the banking system, while attempting to stop general deflation by suspending prior Antitrust laws in order to allow business to raise prices. Whereas Mellon's proposed intervention to break the debt–deflation–default cycle was to allow deflation to run its course, at which point the process would end, Roosevelt proposed to intervene by engineering a price inflation. It was hoped that price inflation would provide additional income and cash flow to businesses that would prevent defaults that would exacerbate the debt–deflation–default nexus. This approach was embodied in legislation passed by Congress at the time called the National Industrial Recovery Act (NIRA). The NIRA would replace product price deflation with product inflation. For asset price deflation, Roosevelt's policy was a series of banking stabilization measures introduced in the first 100 days. In contrast, no policy was introduced to directly confront household (i.e. consumer) defaults or wage deflation.

The NIRA proved a dismal failure. Roosevelt may have stabilized the banking system in 1933–34, but his reinflation policies of the first two years produced no sustained recovery of the real economy. The financial banking system was stabilized, but that was insufficient to generate recovery, and the rest of the real economy continued to stagnate in 1933–34, neither collapsing further as in 1929–33 but not recovering either.

The famous economist, John Maynard Keynes, in a series of written communications with Roosevelt through his immediate advisors and in open letters to the President, warned that the NIRA did not constitute recovery "and probably impedes recovery." Nor did Keynes believe that merely bailing out the banks by injecting them with government-provided liquidity would resolve the economic crisis. As he put it: "Some people seem to infer from this that output and income can be raised by increasing the quantity of money. But this is like trying to get fat by buying a larger belt."[2]

It wasn't until 1935 and Roosevelt's 'New Deal' that the depression's declining trajectory of 1929–32, and leveling off of 1933–34, would finally reverse. However, the New Deal was not sufficient to generate a sustained recovery either. Roosevelt's fiscal policy was inadequate to the task. Roosevelt's bank bailout program put a floor under the collapse of the banks and thus financial fragility. His New Deal put a floor under the collapse in general consumption and thus consumption fragility. But neither financial nor consumption fragility was reversed, but only prevented from significant further decline; enough to check further downturn, but not enough to generate robust recovery. Then the rug was lifted and removed from the consumption floor in 1937 and the economy quickly and sharply fell once again, in terms of gross national product (GNP), employment, production, and other indicators.

PHASES AND STAGES OF THE GREAT DEPRESSION

A widespread and incorrect popular impression is that the depression of the 1930s started with the stock market crash of October 1929, continued until Roosevelt was inaugurated in March 1933, and that once Roosevelt's New Deal programs were quickly implemented in his first 100 days in office in early 1933, a general, sustained recovery thereafter began. None of these points are accurate, however.

The depression was not a single, monolithic event but consisted of several phases and included stages within the phases. Failure to see the depression thus, leads to distinguishing the early period of the Great Depression as an Epic Recession stage. The first phase of the depression was the period of general decline from 1929 through the initial months of 1933. But within 1929–33 are several identifiable stages, punctuated roughly by a series of four banking crises, each progressively worse than the preceding. The four banking crises occurred roughly in November–December 1930, April–September 1931, and

June–October 1932, culminating in the near collapse of the entire financial system in March 1933.[3]

A second major phase of the depression occurred from the beginning of the second quarter of 1933, the so-called 'banking holiday' in which Roosevelt shut down the banks and his first 100 days in office, through to the summer of 1935—a little over two years. During this phase the debt–deflation–default process driving the economy was partially stabilized, but no recovery occurred in its wake. The real economy did not continue to contract at previous rates, but stagnated more or less. Movement toward recovery did not begin until late 1934.

By early 1935 a third phase of the depression began, and continued for another two years, lasting roughly until late spring 1937. During this period the Roosevelt New Deal programs were in full effect.

A fourth phase occurred with the beginning of the retreat of the New Deal and the federal government's reduction of fiscal spending and tightening of monetary policy around mid 1937. As noted previously, it was at this point that the partial dismantling of the New Deal began. Starting from a collapse of 89 percent, the stock market underwent one of its greatest boom and growth periods in 1935–37. Prematurely assessing that the depression would soon be over, business interests began pressing vigorously for repeal of the New Deal.

In a false belief that a rapid 'V'-shaped recovery was underway, the Roosevelt administration began paring back the New Deal while reducing prior fiscal and monetary stimulus as well. These premature pullbacks resulted in a re-collapse of the economy in 1937–38 and a return to conditions approaching (though not quite attaining) those of 1933–34. Unemployment, for example, quickly surged back up to more than 15 percent. Consumption of durable goods fell 18 percent and private investment by 33 percent compared to the previous year.[4]

A final fifth phase of the depression was the partial recovery in 1938–40 from the 1937–38 relapse. The tightening of fiscal and monetary in 1937–38 was again quickly reversed by Congress and the Fed. A partial recovery followed in late 1938. The economy still languished, almost stagnated, between late 1938 and 1940. Full recovery did not take place until 1941–42. The complexity of the depression's 'long decade' of 1929–40, with its internal mini-cycles of phases and stages, has meant that even today, after more than 70 years, economists writing on the topic still do not agree on what precisely caused the depression. And they agree even less so on what truly ended it. That lack of unanimity is due to various reasons, not least of which is the inability of most economists to understand the role of finance and speculation in the general collapse.

This chapter explores the first 'phase' of the depression, 1929–33, and in particular the initial stage, 1929–31, within that phase. That stage of 1929–31 is the period of Epic Recession within the broader event of the Great Depression. It dates roughly from around May–July 1929 up to the event that is sometimes referred to as the second banking crisis that occurred as a 'rolling event' of sorts through the summer of 1931 to September–October

1931. It was during this period, April–October 1931, that Epic Recession began the transition to a classical, bona fide depression.

To begin to understand the Epic Recession of 1929–31 and its transition to depression properly, however, it is first necessary to examine what happened in the run-up over the decade of the 1920s. The roots of the Great Depression lie in the preceding decade of the 1920s. In considering the 1920s, there were two important periods in question: that from the end of World War I, 1918, through the steep downturn of 1920–21; and from 1922 to the summer of 1929.

FROM POSTWAR TO THE 'DEPRESSION' OF 1920–21

World War I resulted in massive inflow of gold, increasing the U.S. money supply, and contributing to a subsequent rapid acceleration of prices. Fed policies, government war spending costs plus pricing, and banks' credit creation, further stimulated inflation. Near-zero in 1914, consumer prices accelerated to double-digit levels by 1916 and peaked at more than 20 percent annually in 1918. Wholesale prices doubled over the war period. Real GNP rose 5–15 percent between 1916 and 1918, and industrial production by approximately 70 percent. GNP expanded for 44 consecutive months, just shy of the prior civil war record of 46 months.

Out of a labor force of 37.7 million with 7.9 percent unemployed in 1914, unemployment fell to only 1.4 percent of the labor force of 40.3 million by 1918. Money wages rose significantly during the course of the war, although real wages adjusted for inflation increased a much more moderate 5 percent over three years for factory workers and barely at all for agricultural workers. Manufacturing wages rose 38.8 percent from 1916 to 1918, but inflation increased by nearly as much, 32.3 percent. Real wage gains during the war were therefore minimal, despite coming off a period of stagnation or decline from 1907–14.

Given a 57 percent increase in the money supply (M2), a doubling of currency held by the public, and major gold inflows from Europe during the war, available liquidity rose significantly. And with excess liquidity comes excess credit creation, leveraging by investors, a rise in the relative weight of speculative to total investment, and an eventual sharp rise in debt. Like most wars, World War I was a speculator's paradise. Opportunities especially abounded for speculating in currencies, gold futures, in the new government bonds financing war spending, in corporate stocks in the now booming defense industries, and in a return to the mergers and acquisitions (M&A) movement of the early first decade prior to the 1907 bust.[5]

However, the speculative boom was not of sufficient magnitude or duration to provoke a financial crisis. Contraction would come in late 1920–21. But it would not be precipitated by financial crisis. Known at the time as the 'depression of 1920–21,' the downturn did not have its origins in a financial banking blow-up originating from endogenous and internal forces within the U.S. economy. The contraction of 1920–21 was therefore a severe normal recession, not an Epic Recession. It was due instead to four basic 'external' causes.

The first of the four external events behind the contraction was a sharp and rapid reduction of government spending after the war. From a federal deficit of $25.4 billion in 1919 (which rose from only $2.9 billion in 1917), the federal government shifted abruptly from massive deficit spending to a surplus in 1919 and 1920.[6] At the same time the Fed reduced the money supply by the largest decline in a single year up to that time, 9.4 percent, and raised its discount rate in just a matter of four months from 4 percent to 7 percent.[7] At the same time, U.S. gold reserves shrunk by 10 percentage points. In response to this general contraction of liquidity, banks began to recall their loans to businesses and to dump bonds, further exacerbating the contraction. On top of all this, exports to Europe contracted, especially in the area of agricultural goods. U.S. agriculture was already in trouble, having added excess production capacity during the war to satisfy U.S. and European war demand for agricultural products. Now the excess capacity faced the problem of collapsing demand. Congress then exacerbated the softening exports problem further in 1921 by initiating an emergency tariff. What followed in 1920–21 as a result was a very sharp 'V'-shaped economic contraction that was short, brief, but deep.

The severity of deflation, unemployment, and production cutbacks that followed made it feel very much like a depression. Unemployment rose from the 1.5 percent wartime low to 9 percent by 1921.[8] Wholesale prices fell 46 percent. Consumer prices by 10.8 percent. And already weakened farm prices fell by 53 percent.[9] Workers' weekly wages and earnings declined by 21.2 percent.[10] Deflation was indeed a factor. Nevertheless, this wasn't a depression. There was no precipitating financial crisis behind the contraction, and debt and defaults were not extraordinary. The general process of debt–deflation–default that drives more extended and longer contractions characterizing Epic Recessions and depressions was not at work. As a consequence, neither financial nor consumption fragility contributed to extending the downturn.

Pre-war financial fragility was shaken out by wartime profits gains, improvements in business income, and cash flow stabilization. Wartime speculative investing, though significant, was not of sufficient duration to produce the excessive debt build-up necessary for a subsequent financial crisis. It is likely, therefore, that financial fragility in net terms may have even improved for reasons of both debt and income.

For example, bank loan volume—and thus credit and debt—increased after 1919 but nothing like what would occur from 1923 to 1929. Total corporate domestic securities (long-term bonds, short-term notes, preferred and common stock) issued between 1919 and 1920 rose a moderate 6 percent.[11] Stock speculation was therefore not a significant factor. There were no notable bank runs associated with the contraction of 1920–21. Beginning in late 1920, there was a modest rise in bank suspensions through 1921, but the numbers were not particularly excessive. They were no larger than the average number of annual suspensions recorded during the first half of the decade. This suggests that secular forces were driving the bank suspensions more than the cyclical conditions of 1920–21, most likely having to do with problems with farm mortgages throughout the decade. Bank suspensions in 1920–21 were less than half compared to bank suspensions that would occur in each year between 1924–29.[12] In contrast, more than 1,000 banks would later fail in 1926 alone, a clear sign that financial fragility began to deteriorate later in the decade, but not immediately prior to or during 1920–21. The picture was similar for general business failures. They were no larger in number in 1920–21 than occurred annually throughout the remainder of the decade.[13]

The picture is similar for consumption fragility. It is not likely that it deteriorated during the war compared to pre-1914, and may have actually improved. Jobs were plentiful and money wages rose significantly after 1914, even if real wages did not. Real disposable income, at worst, remained stable for the industrial workforce and probably rose for consumers not in the industrial or agricultural workforce. Once again, consumer credit and debt were not yet important elements of consumption fragility. Except for small farm mortgages, consumer and household debt was not yet the problem it would become later in the decade. Thus neither consumer debt nor disposable income likely grew worse in the run-up period to 1920–21. As with financial fragility, consumption fragility most likely did not appreciably deteriorate prior to 1920–21.

With neither excessive debt, nor either form of fragility, playing major causative roles, defaults were similarly not a major factor in 1920–21. As the data show, deflation was a factor in 1920–21, but deflation need not necessarily occur due to financial crisis and debt unwinding. Nor did it at the time. But when deflation is closely integrated with debt unwinding and related defaults, deflation is exacerbated. Deflation itself can thereafter feed back upon and cause a further deterioration in terms of debt and defaults. Both falling asset prices and product prices result in rising real debt and provoke defaults—which in turn generate even more debt stress and defaults. When debt and defaults are particularly large and severe, when the dynamic linkages between debt, deflation, and defaults are stronger and more mutually reinforcing, deflation is much more difficult to slow and reverse. However, such processes were not at work in 1920–21. In short, debt was not a key factor, nor were defaults, since neither financial nor consumption fragility had deteriorated significantly prior to the 1920 contraction.

Without debt and default to provide continuing momentum to deflation, the trajectory of price contraction in 1920–21 was sharp in terms of both decline and recovery—i.e. 'V'-shape. So were associated levels of production and output. As a consequence, 1920–21 does not satisfy the duration characteristic of either Epic Recession or depression. The severe recession of 1920–21 was thus a different 'economic animal,' with critically different internal dynamics, compared to 1907–14 and, later, 1929–31. Despite the popular reference to it as a 'depression' at the time, it was decidedly not—in terms of neither its quantitative characteristics nor its qualitative and dynamic processes.

The reinforcing dynamics of debt–deflation–default were not at work in 1920. Fragility was not a major force driving the debt–deflation–default nexus. Speculative investing had not yet driven financial fragility once again to extremes. It was still too early in the cycle. The 'money parade' had ample opportunities for excess profits realization from war goods production, i.e. a form of real asset investment. The build-up of excess liquidity and credit flowed into the latter first, and only began to flow into speculative forms when the war abruptly ended. And perhaps to some extent, government wartime regulation and controls may have inhibited speculation in war bonds, while the newly adopted personal income tax during the war likely diverted excess income and liquidity that might have stimulated further speculative investing.

So if the 1920–21 contraction was not an Epic Recession nor a bona fide depression, what, then, was it? Once again, it is perhaps best described as a severe normal recession, exacerbated by the abrupt and extreme shift in both government monetary and fiscal policy—i.e. external forces and policy 'shocks' which qualify it as a normal recession.

The extreme (both magnitude and timing) policy shifts also coincided with international contractions, gold-currency instabilities, and trade problems that immediately followed World War I. A kind of normal recession 'perfect storm.'

Such exogenous or external causes are hallmark characteristics of normal recessions. Internal or endogenous forces are hallmarks of Epic Recessions and depressions. In the case of Epic Recession and depressions, external factors and shocks may be contributory but are not fundamental causative forces. Epic Recessions are either flat 'U'-shaped or short 'W'-shaped events. The 1920–21 contraction was 'V'-shaped and recovered quickly. That rapid recovery was possible because financial instability, and therefore debt unwinding, was not central to the contraction; because bank losses and suspensions were not as severe or numerous, general business defaults were not as severe or widespread, and deflation was consequently quickly reversed; and because both forms of fragility had not deteriorated significantly in the run-up to the general contraction.

ORIGINS OF THE GREAT DEPRESSION: 1922–29

The preceding section provided an explanation of the fundamental forces and processes that drive an Epic Recession by contrasting those forces and processes to the actual historic case example of the 1920–21 contraction. The purpose was to show how the fundamental processes differ for Epic Recessions from 'normal' recessions, of which 1920–21, it was argued, was a specific, albeit virulent, form. Defining recessions or other forms of economic contraction like Epic Recessions and depressions cannot be adequately achieved merely by looking at quantitative indicators. Such indicators are not unimportant, of course. They are necessary, but are not sufficient. Qualitative forces and dynamic processes are just as critical to understanding differences in the nature of types of economic contractions. Economic analyses to date have been deficient in differentiating qualitative and dynamic factors in the different types of contraction. That is why academic economists are unable to distinguish between different forms of contraction and tend to see depressions as simply recessions 'writ large.' It is also why they generally have not been able to recognize the possibility of Epic Recession as a particular form of its own.

The remainder of this chapter now turns toward investigating a particular economic contraction that was quite unlike 1920–21, more like 1907–14 in some ways, but different once again from 1907–14 in other important ways as well. 1929–31 was also, like 1907–14, an 'Epic' recession. However, unlike 1907–14, it did not simply transform into an extended period of stagnation. Its processes and dynamics, in contrast, drove it to transform into a bona fide depression. How this process and transformation occurred is thus of some importance for understanding the nature of Epic Recession as a general economic phenomenon.

Liquidity

Liquidity grew rapidly during 1922–29. There were at least four fundamental sources of that growth at the time: Federal Reserve policies pumping money into the economy, chronic and major international gold inflows into the U.S., internal forms of credit creation within the financial system itself, and record growth of realized profits and income by corporations and institutional and wealthy individual investors.

Between 1922 and 1924 the Fed repeatedly increased the money supply and reduced interest rates, to as low as 3 percent. $510 million was injected into the economy just to help Britain to return to the gold standard. In 1926 the Fed briefly raised rates to counter growing speculation in real estate, but quickly reversed itself and increased the money supply and lowered rates to the 3 percent range once again. Over the period, in net terms, the Fed's action significantly raised liquidity available to banks, which thereafter extended additional credit, loans, and borrowing for speculative activity. The Fed's 'seesaw' response also stimulated speculation in gold prices and currency fluctuations.

A net inflow of gold to the U.S. further raised liquidity, as foreign investors took increasing advantage of stock and speculative opportunities in the U.S. Gold flowed into the U.S. not only to speculate in stocks and other markets but as a result of the U.S.'s growing export surplus—i.e. imports to foreign countries paid for by gold.

New stock and bond issues escalated, based upon the creation of new, fast-growth industries and holding companies. Companies in the new industries of autos, chemicals, electrical power generation, electrical appliances, furniture, radio, motion pictures, food processing, etc., often borrowed from banks, issued new stock, and then used the proceeds from sale of their stock to invest in the higher-paying call loans in the stock market. Corporate profits and retained earnings rose rapidly, as did the incomes and wealth of individual wealthy investors over the period. Corporate profits rose 75 percent over the period, while the incomes of the wealthiest 1 percent of households—i.e. investors whose earnings derived from capital incomes—rose from 16 percent to a 24 percent share of total income in the U.S.[14]

For corporations, record profits and retained earnings derived in part from the booming growth of new companies and industries. But the 75 percent increase in corporate profits was also enabled by major cost reductions in wages and from productivity. Much of the cost reductions were enabled by the destruction of unions over the course of the decade. Union membership fell from about 20 percent of the workforce at the start of the decade to around 9 percent at its end. That held wage gains during the otherwise boom period of the decade at or below the general rise of the price level. But cost reductions were no less achieved by the historic rise in labor productivity, which grew between 1919 and 1929 at an unprecedented annual rate of 5.44 percent. Record productivity gains also lowered corporate costs as never before. Both record productivity gains and union wage containment together boosted profits and retained earnings. Retained earnings meant, in turn, record dividend payouts and capital gains for wealthy investors with stock in those corporations. Corporations thus served as the conduit for corresponding pre-tax income gains of wealthy investors. Together, both corporate and individual investor income gains provided a major source of internal liquidity for the purposes of speculative investing.

Both corporations and individual investors especially benefited from the major shifts in the tax structure that occurred over the course of the decade. Top rates on the personal income tax were lowered in November 1921 from 65 percent to 50 percent, and the wartime excess profits tax was repealed. A second tax cut followed in 1923 that lowered the top rate still further, cut the capital gains tax rate, and reduced corporate taxes to only 2.5 percent.[15] A third cut followed in 1926, which reduced income tax, surtaxes, and cut inheritance taxes in half. In 1921 there were 6.6 million tax returns; by 1929 it had been reduced to only 4 million returns. A household with an annual income of $1 million paid taxes of $663,000 in 1921. By 1929 that was reduced to less than $200,000.[16] Thus, after-tax corporate profits and after-tax investor incomes also increased dramatically, as a result of the pro-corporate and pro-investor tax shift of the decade.

Credit

If liquidity is the enabler of credit, then borrowing based on credit is the enabler of debt. Credit may derive from several sources. It may be extended by banks or by 'shadow banks.' The Federal Reserve, the central bank of the U.S., also may extend credit to the banking system itself. The banking system then passes on the credit to borrowers in whole or part, in turn, subject only to keeping a part as reserves. But shadow banks keep virtually no reserves and loan it all out. Therefore, as shadow banks grow, so too does credit and debt overall grow at a faster rate. As shadow banks and speculative investing grow, respectively, in terms of number and assets over the cycle, typically bank regulators allow the commercial banking sector to keep less reserves over the cycle; i.e. just at that time when more, not less, reserves should be required. Finally, to get around even the reduced reserve requirements, commercial banks simply set up shadow bank subsidiaries 'on the side' and provide internal loans to those subsidiaries for the more speculative purposes. Credit is also obtainable from sources outside the U.S.; i.e. from offshore banks, shadow banks, and both institutional and individual investors.

A particular characteristic of credit, borrowing, and debt is that it is able to be leveraged. For example, banks borrow from the Fed at low rates, then loan the amount borrowed from the Fed to their shadow bank subsidiaries, who in turn loan out the total amount to corporations issuing new stock. The corporation pays a dividend of 4 percent on the new stock it issues, then takes the remainder and invests it in the brokers' call loan market at 15 percent. The brokers then provide the call loan to buyers of common stock who leverage the amount once again by purchasing stock 'on the margin.' This 'layered leveraging' scenario became quite common after 1927.

Debt accumulation

Excessive credit and leveraging fueled the increasingly speculative mix of total investment over the course of the 1920s, particularly after the mid decade. Debt grew over the decade to historic levels as a consequence, becoming increasingly costly and of poorer quality as well.

In the early to mid decade period, debt problems were especially concentrated in the farm and construction sectors of the economy. Farm mortgages in particular were a major problem, as was land speculation in suburban housing and urban commercial property development. In the second half of the decade excess debt accumulated in the stock and bond markets, representing common stock speculation and over-issuance of bond debt associated with mergers, new company and industries formation, and the creation of utility and other holding companies. Finally, for the first time on a major scale, consumer installment debt involving autos and durables became a factor. The debt side of consumption fragility was thus deteriorating progressively over the course of the decade.

With regard to agriculture and farm mortgages, debt levels rose during the war to finance the expansion of production as wartime U.S. and European demand for food grew sharply. Additional debt was then added as mechanization was introduced into agriculture immediately after the war. Costs for tractors and other farm machinery, related maintenance costs, parts, and fuel, all raised the cost of agricultural production. Total agricultural sector debt reached $11.4 billion by 1929. At the same time, record farm prices plummeted after the war and then fell even further during 1920–21. Annual net farm income collapsed from $1,395 to $517. Farm income declined by more than 20 percent over the decade. Deflation in farm product prices, in farmland values, and other farm assets meant that farmers could not generate enough income to service debt or obtain further loans to roll over existing debt. With the collapse of farm income came the collapse of farm land values (i.e. asset deflation), from $55 billion in 1920 to $37 billion in 1926.[17] Farm sector consumption fragility became severe as early as the mid decade. With fixed servicing payments, mortgages taken out to finance expansion and mechanization defaulted. Farms foreclosed in record numbers throughout the early to mid decade. Farm foreclosures were already a problem in the first half of the decade, rising threefold in 1921–25 compared to 1913–20.[18] And they continued to rise another 60 percent after 1925. Local banks and other financial institutions holding the mortgages had to write down the losses (i.e. more asset deflation). Financial fragility consequently deteriorated in turn. Most of the chronically high level of bank suspensions during the first half of the decade were associated with farm mortgage and land value declines. Farm mortgage debt continued to rise, to $9.5 billion in 1928.[19]

Yet another major area experiencing accelerating debt levels was non-farm residential and commercial mortgages. Here, shadow bank institutions were heavily involved: building and loan associations, mutual savings banks, life insurance companies, fire and casualty insurance companies, and other local banks and institutions. Non-farm mortgage debt stood at $9.6 billion in 1920. Real estate speculation and mortgages came in two waves, the first peaking around 1925, ebbing briefly thereafter, and accelerating again after 1927. By 1928, mortgages for non-farm real estate had risen to $29.5 billion, and escalated in one year alone, 1929, to $37 billion.[20] A good part of the real estate debt run-up was speculative in character. The most notable, perhaps, was speculation in Florida land values that collapsed in 1926. "As farmland fell and urban and suburban land rose in value, fortunes could be made simply from the subdivision, sale, and resale of land, particularly at the city's edge."[21] With 1930 as a benchmark index (1930 = 100), the volume of housing construction in 1925 was 252.3. As in the case of farm mortgages and land values, an early financial bust occurred in the construction sector before 1929 as well.

Investors and banks speculating in housing land values faced collapsing values and losses in various regional markets. Housing construction began to slow appreciably after 1927. New housing unit construction in 1929 was only half of the 1926 highs.

In addition to deteriorating consumption fragility, financial fragility was growing worse. Already banks in rural areas were beginning to default and fail by mid decade. No fewer than 1,000 banks went under in 1926 alone. The main causes were farm debt and default. Farm consumption fragility was severe, as collapsing farm prices eliminated nearly all disposable income as farmers' debt servicing loads and payments rose. As farms defaulted and collapsed, local banks took over their collapsing mortgage and land values. Many of them in turn collapsed. As local bank credit dried up, many smaller non-bank businesses were negatively impacted as well. The Great Depression of the 1930s came first to the 'interior,' to small businesses, banks, farmers, and workers—and came in the mid 1920s.

In addition to farm and non-farm real estate debt, corporate debt escalated rapidly during the 1920s peaking, in contrast to the farm sector, in the closing years of the decade. Total corporate debt rose from $2.9 billion in 1922 to $9.3 billion in 1929. These figures include all corporate domestic security issues, including long-term bonds, short-term notes, and preferred and common stock. The heavy weight of stock issues in the total corporate issues toward the close of the decade is of particular note (see Table 6.1).

Table 6.1 Total Domestic Corporate Issues, 1922–31 ($ millions)

	Total Corporate Issues	*Long-Term Bonds*	*Short-Term Notes*	*Stock**
1922	2,949	2,195	133	278
1923	3,178	2,262	180	735
1924	3,520	2,319	335	865
1925	4,222	2,667	308	1,246
1926	4,573	3,059	294	1,291
1927	6,506	4,466	302	1,837
1928	6,930	3,174	264	3,491
1929	9,376	2,369	250	6,755
1930**	4.957	2,810	620	1,526
1931**	2,371	4,628	400	343

* Includes both preferred and common issues.
**The years 1930 and 1931 are included for the purposes of contrast and for the discussion to follow.
Source: Irving Fisher, *Booms and Depressions*, Adelphi Publishers, 1932, Table 7, p. 175.

Commercial banking debt accumulation was no less significant over the decade. Loans by banks rose from $27.7 billion in 1922 to a peak of $41.5 in 1929. Banks' own direct investments, in addition to loans, rose from $12.2 billion in 1922 to $16.9 billion in 1929. That's a combined total increase of about 50 percent over the period.

Table 6.2 summarizes the volume of bank loans and direct investments from June 1922 through June 1929.

Table 6.2 Bank Loans and Investments, 1922–31 ($ millions)

	Loans	*Investments*	*Total Deposits*
1922	27,732	12,224	37,615
1923	30,378	13,360	40,688
1924	31,523	13,657	43,405
1925	33,865	14,965	47,612
1926	36,157	15,404	49,733
1927	37,360	16,391	51,662
1928	39,464	17,801	53,398
1929	41,512	16,962	53,852
1930*	40,612	17,490	54,954
1931*	35,384	19,637	51,782

*The years 1930 and 1931 are included for the purposes of contrast and for the discussion to follow.
Source: Fisher, *Booms and Depressions*, Table 9, p. 179.

The above data still do not include lending and investments by the shadow banking system. Nor do they explain how commercial bank loans and investments may be connected with the shadow banking system. Part of banks' loans and investments include loans to the brokerage and investment bank subsidiaries of the banks. The commercial banks' shadow subsidiaries (brokerages, investment banks (I-banks), investment trusts, etc.) then engage more aggressively in speculative investing.

Like the trusts before World War I, brokerage houses and I-banks were among the leading shadow bank institutions during the 1920s. Brokerages and I-banks each doubled their respective share of total financial system assets from 1900 to 1925. Investment banks set up hundreds of investment trusts as subsidiaries. In 1928 alone, more than 200 such trusts were created, and in 1929, in the nine months leading up to the October 1929 stock market crash, a trust a day was established. In 1929 alone, their combined assets increased from $2 billion to $3 billion. The I-banks and their trusts were primarily vehicles for what was called 'stock pooling' at the time, a virtually pure speculative stock activity.

The favorite speculative vehicle of the brokerages and their shadow banking satellites was issuing 'brokers loans.' These were 'buying on margin' financial vehicles. The brokerages borrowed from banks, corporations, and wealthy investor groups, and then loaned in turn to stock buyers purchasing common shares with leveraging. In the twelve months leading up to the October stock market crash, brokers loans rose by 50 percent. In 1928 the Fed attempted to dampen the stock speculative fever by forcing its member commercial banks not to loan to brokerages. But the brokerages simply did an end run on the Fed and borrowed "from corporations and individuals who preferred to get 10 per cent on call loans rather than to invest in enterprises which were paying only 4 to 6 percent."[22] The banks also circumvented the Fed by creating a new balance sheet category of 'loans by others,' which provided funds to their largest customers for stock speculation. Brokers' loans peaked at $9.4 billion in October 1929.

Other financial intermediaries, or shadow banks, that grew rapidly during the decade were life insurance companies acting in part as investors, mutual savings banks, and Savings and Loans (thrifts). As the first wave of land speculation ebbed around mid decade, stock speculation became the leading speculative activity, riding a new wave of corporate securities issues, growing M&A activity, the formation of utility holding companies, stock pooling, and margin buying.

It has been estimated that the total debt accumulated during the 1920s from all the above categories—corporations, banks, urban mortgages, farm mortgages, etc.—was in excess of $200 billion.[23] Public and foreign debt constituted another $44 billion. Total debt from all sources was therefore $244 billion.[24]

These totals include consumer installment debt, a major element of which was auto debt. At the start of the decade only 5 percent of auto purchases were on credit. By 1929 it was more than 50 percent; despite restrictive one-year financing, down-payments of 33 percent, interest rates of up to 30 percent, and aggressive repossession in the event of just a one-month late payment. Consumer installment debt in general, as well as all forms of non-mortgage consumer debt, more than doubled between 1922 and 1929.[25]

As a percentage of GNP, the $244 billion total debt was roughly two and a half times GNP in 1929, which was about $103 billion.[26] In 2009, that $244 billion total debt would have been equivalent to around $35 trillion!

In absolute terms, the $35 trillion in 1929 was less than the $51 trillion total debt in the U.S. in 2009.

The point of the preceding is to show that a massive accumulation of debt occurred at virtually all levels and sectors of the economy during the period 1922–29. While it is not possible due to lack of specific data to identify what proportion of the $200 billion private sector debt was due specifically to speculation, and what was non-speculative debt, it is nonetheless very probable that speculation-driven debt rose significantly relative to the total debt, especially in the second half of the 1920s.

Both financial and consumption fragility undoubtedly deteriorated significantly during the decade, at least from the 'debt' side of the equation of fragility. Deflation was already becoming a problem, as will be shown shortly, during the decade. Defaults were also beginning to appear—in farm mortgages, residential housing, and interior banks. And debt, as noted, was rising sharply on several fronts. Financial and consumption fragility had not yet 'fractured.' The cash flow side for business financial fragility was growing toward the decade's end. Meanwhile, real disposable income on the consumption side was stagnant at best.

All that was needed was the 'match' of a precipitating event to set off a financial crisis and in turn commence the 'unwinding' of debt and asset price deflation. There is debt from real asset investing and debt from speculative investing. The latter is particularly volatile. And if the financial system has become fragile, with an extraordinary proportion of speculative debt, it is significantly more unstable. Speculative debt is more highly leveraged and even 'layered.' So when the unwinding begins, it occurs faster, spreads more rapidly, and thus more deeply throughout the financial system. For example, common stock purchased on margin with call loans derived from brokers loans, provided in turn by corporations who issued stock with funds borrowed from investment banks, who were loaned the funds in the first place by a parent commercial bank—all that is infinitely more unstable than, say, debt incurred as a result of the purchase of a radio on installment credit.

With speculative debt, asset prices have the potential to collapse across a long chain from financial institution to institution, leading to a contraction of credit for financial and non-financial businesses alike. If the credit contraction continues for an extended period, non-financial business deflation and default take place. Before proceeding to default, non-financial businesses first attempt to cut costs and increase revenue. Product price deflation and wage deflation follow. Deflation in assets provokes deflation in product prices and eventually wage deflation as well. The three price systems become mutually reinforcing. In instances where leveraging and layering of debt has occurred, the unwinding of debt is even more rapid and has an even greater effect on the deflation–default process.

Deflation

The economy approached 1929 with product prices—both consumer and wholesale—already weakening. Consumer prices fell in each year between

1926 and 1930. Farm and real estate prices led the fall. An index created by the National Bureau of Economic Research (NBER) in 1929 measuring the prices of consumption goods for urban employees, farmers, and families spending $5,000 and $25,000 annually shows the percentage declines in consumer goods prices after 1926, as depicted in Table 6.3.

Table 6.3   Change in Prices of Consumption Goods (%) (1913 = 100)

	Families Spending $5,000 Annually	Families Spending $25,000 Annually	Farmers	Urban Employees
January 1927	–1.5	–1.6	–5.0	–1.3
January 1928	–1.8	–0.7	–3.7	–2.0
January 1929	–0.9	–1.2	–1.7	–0.1

Source: NBER, "Recent Changes in the Cost of Living," *News Bulletin no. 32*, January 10, 1929, p. 3.

Wholesale prices in July 1929 were roughly at the same level of late 1921—i.e. after collapsing during the 1920–21 severe recession.[27] In other words, both consumer and wholesale product price deflation was already well underway for several years before the 1929 stock crash. Despite record productivity and profit gains during the decade, wages earnings—the price for labor—were stagnant in real terms. Wages defined as weekly earnings, which measures hourly wages times hours worked, were actually lower in 1929 than at the beginning of the decade in 1920, as Table 6.4 indicates.

Table 6.4   Weekly Earnings in Manufacturing, 1920–29

Year	Earnings
1920	$29.48
1921	$23.97
1922	$23.23
1929	$27.36

Source: Leo Wolman, "Wages During the Depression," NBER, *News Bulletin no. 46*, May 1, 1933, p. 2.

In an effort to offset declining real earnings, working-class households turned to consumer debt to make purchases in the absence of real wage and disposable income gains. For example, one study of the period shows that household debt rose 12 percent in the year preceding the stock market crash, even though the value of household financial assets continued to fall in 1928. In other words, net household wealth was declining even before the recession and crash of 1929.[28] The decline was likely not just a one-year occurrence, but a trend developing during at least the last three years of the decade. In terms of both debt and income, consumer fragility was clearly increasing over the decade, along with financial fragility.

Deflation in product prices and labor prices was therefore a chronic, though not yet severe, problem in the second half of the decade. Only asset prices were rising in the years immediately prior to the 1929 crash. The index of common stock prices rose 77 percent from September 1927 to September 1929, i.e. the two years preceding the October crash.[29] But product prices and wages as weekly earnings were falling. Fragility was thus 'primed' for a potential collapse in asset prices. Already weakening, asset price collapse could easily push product and wage deflation into a more severe decline.

Defaults

Defaults were also a low-grade but chronic problem during the 1920s. There were the aforementioned growing farm mortgage defaults. And after the real estate bust of 1926, housing defaults started to spread to that sector as well, and housing unit production began to decline rapidly during 1927–29. The combined farm–housing stress and falling farm–real estate asset values translated into a moderate rise in bank suspensions and business failures. In the four years from 1925 to 1929 the number of banks that suspended business averaged about 900 each year—from a total of 27,638 in 1925 to 24,026 in 1929. General business failures rose sharply in 1926 and then remained at the relatively high 20,000 per year level through 1929.[30] Defaults, like deflation, were a chronic but not yet severe problem. Levels were nothing like that which would take place after the 1929 market crash and the subsequent banking crises that followed the crash from 1930 to 1933.

Signs of a growing instability began to appear by 1928. Two critical events occurred. In 1928–29 the Federal Reserve nearly doubled its discount interest rate at which banks borrowed from it, thereby further reducing available liquidity and credit to the real economy. Bankers began to raise their bankers' loans and call (margin) loan rates. The rate hikes cooled the already softening real economy, but had little effect on speculative stock investing, which continued to rise. A second development was a major outflow of gold from the U.S. in late summer 1929, which further reduced liquidity and credit. In an attempt to pop the speculative bubble in the economy, the Fed was about to stick a pin in the financial balloon.

Industrial production began to fall noticeably thereafter, in the second quarter of 1929. The U.S. economy crossed into recession at the latest sometime in late spring 1929 and in some sectors of the economy before that. The real economy thus approached the October 1929 financial bust already beginning to decline.

The stock market crash of October 1929 did not yet precipitate depression. After October 1929 the economy was facing neither recession nor yet a depression. As the economist, Irving Fisher, described it at the time, the stock market crash "helped to force the rest of our debt structure into liquidation, and it was the hopeless magnitude of the debt burden which made it so difficult...."[31]

At this point it is now possible to move to the central theme of this chapter, which maintains that the period roughly from the summer of 1929 to spring

1931 represents a 'Type II' form of Epic Recession. Two key questions immediately arise: first, in terms of what criteria does the period June 1929 to April–June 1931 qualify as Epic Recession?; and, second, what happened in spring–summer 1931 that caused the economy to evolve from an Epic Recession to a much worse bona fide depression?

Before proceeding to each of these key questions, however, it is necessary to provide a picture of the overall first 'phase' of the depression, that in which the economy contracted rapidly 1929–33 and then stagnated in 1933–34. Given the overall picture, it is then possible to discuss the important two 'stages' within that 1929–34 phase—the Epic Recession phase, the roughly two-year period from the summer of 1929 to late summer 1931; and the subsequent transition stage to depression that occurred during the late summer–fall of 1931.

THE GREAT DEPRESSION PHASE I: 1929–34

Debt unwinding

Debt unwinding is best represented by the collapse of asset values on balance sheets. For the commercial banks that were members of the Federal Reserve system (i.e. a subset of total banks which also does not include shadow banks), total assets and deposits fell, as indicated in Table 6.5.

Table 6.5   Member Banks' Total Assets ($ millions)

	Total Assets	Total Deposits
1922	31,414	40,814
1929	47,553	59,832
1930	47,164	58,092
1931	43,991	49,509
1932	37,042	45,886
1933	34,367	42,125

Source: Elmus Wicker, *The Banking Panics of the Great Depression*, Cambridge University Press, 2000, Tables 1.1 and 1.3, pp. 2, 8.

What Table 6.5 clearly shows is that, in 1930, assets had not yet collapsed, nor had deposit withdrawals from banks occurred as yet in particularly great volume. There was not as yet a general lack of confidence in the banking system itself. The collapse in confidence in the banking system came with a vengeance in 1931.

Deflation

Following the October 1929 stock market crash, stock asset prices plummeted by 89 percent from October 1929 to 1935. But the fall was not a straight-line collapse. There were a series of weak, partial recoveries within the longer 89 percent decline, or what are sometimes called 'bear market bounces' that are typical to Epic Recessions and depressions. There was a brief November election 1932 stock market bounce, which collapsed again after the election, followed thereafter by a partial recovery once again after Roosevelt stabilized the banks in the spring of 1933. At its low point in June 1933 the stock market was still 66 percent below its 1929 peak. Stock asset prices remained stable, neither rising nor recovering significantly, for an extended period from June 1933 to as late as June 1935.[32] Housing asset prices fell in similar fashion as the number of new housing units collapsed from 509,000 in 1929 to 74,000 in 1932 and then leveled off at only 55,000 new units in both 1933 and 1934. A modest recovery in housing did not begin until prices fully stabilized in late 1934, nearly five years after the depression began.[33] Other asset prices followed a similar path of collapse followed by stagnation.

The stabilization, then stagnation, of stock asset prices between 1933 and 1935 occurred while Roosevelt's unsuccessful NIRA was being implemented and despite the stabilization of the banking system during that two-year period. This point perhaps deserves particular emphasis. The banking system was stabilized in 1933–34, but there was no recovery in those years. There was stagnation. The evidence therefore suggests that stabilizing the banks was perhaps necessary but not sufficient for generating sustained economic recovery. It suggests that stabilizing the banking system may put a floor under the collapse of prices and the real economy, but bank stabilizing does not necessarily ensure recovery—a lesson of history that current policymakers have not as yet absorbed as of late summer 2009.

In contrast to the chronic low-grade deflation of the 1920s, rapid decline in product price deflation was the rule after 1929. Wholesale prices fell 38 percent from July 1929 to March 1933, prices received by farmers fell by 65 percent, retail food prices by 42 percent, and consumer non-food prices by 41 percent. An important determinant of future business investment, prices for capital equipment, also fell by 27 percent.

In terms of wage deflation, average hourly wages of manufacturing labor declined by 21 percent.[34] Average weekly earnings declined 32 percent between 1929 and 1932, as shown in Table 6.6.

Table 6.6   Weekly Earnings in Manufacturing, 1923–33

Year	Earnings
1923	$29.48
1924	$23.97
1925	$23.23
1929	$27.36
1930	$25.39
1931	$22.51
1932	$18.18
1933	$17.60

Sources: Leo Wolman, "The Recovery in Wages and Employment," NBER, *News Bulletin no. 63*, December 21, 1936, p. 6. Figures for pre-1929 are from Wolman, "Wages During the Depression," NBER, *News Bulletin no. 46*, p. 2.

The highest month for weekly earnings was April 1929 at $28.21. The very low point in weekly earnings occurred in August 1932, at $16.93. Wages and earnings therefore began to decline before the October 1929 crash, reflecting the decline in production and the real economy that began earlier in 1929.

To sum up, deflationary pressures over the 1929–34 period, all three prices systems—asset, product, and wages—fell from 1929 well into 1933. Only after mid 1933 did the three price systems begin to stabilize.

Defaults

Following the stock market crash in October 1929, asset prices began to unwind and collapse and at an increasing rate. Defaults followed closely thereafter. Already a chronic problem in the previous decade, farm foreclosures escalated after 1929, from 16.7 per thousand in 1926 to 1930 to a peak of 38.8 per thousand in 1933. Residential housing and small business mortgages defaults also began to rise in number. The result of the real estate and farm collapse was an increase in bank suspensions in 1930. These were focused largely outside New York and affected state banks, non-Fed member banks, and other non-bank financial institutions exposed to real estate and farming. There was not yet in 1930 a New York money center bank panic or collapse.

The stock market crash of October 1929 did not result in a banking panic or bank crisis. The number of suspended banks in October–December 1929 was no greater on average than had been occurring in the first nine months of the year or in 1928. The same holds true for the first ten months of 1930. There was no bank crisis or escalation of the number of bank suspensions throughout most of 1930 either. The first clear evidence of an increase in bank suspensions only occurred in November–December 1930. This was called the 'first banking crisis' of the depression. But this 'first bank crisis' could hardly be called a banking panic or crisis. In terms of number of suspensions, its center was St. Louis. In New York, only one bank, the Bank of the United States, failed. A large regional investment bank in the south, Caldwell and Company, was also suspended.[35] A more accurate description of November–December 1930 might be a 'dress rehearsal' for what was to come more generally throughout the economy in 1931. Bank suspensions quickly abated in a few months, by February 1931, and the stability of the financial system appeared restored.

The first true banking crisis of the depression did not occur until April–June 1931 and was quickly followed by another in September–October 1931. The two bank crises in 1931 were essentially one event. It was after April 1931 that bank suspensions began to escalate, bank losses rose, and depositors' confidence in the banking system deteriorated. April–October 1931 is the bank crisis bridge that represents the fracturing of financial fragility that produced a deep and widespread credit contraction that drove the economy past the threshold of Epic Recession and toward depression.

The record on bank suspensions from 1929 through 1932 is summarized in Table 6.7. These numbers, however, still do not include most shadow financial institutions like insurance companies, thrifts, and so on, which would raise the total number of suspensions.

Table 6.7   Bank Suspensions, 1928–33

Year	No. of Suspensions
1928	498
1929	659
1930	1,350
1931	2,290
1932	1,453
1933	4,000

Source: NBER Macrohistory Database IX: Financial Status of Business, *U.S. Number of Suspended Banks, 1921–1933*.

Failures of non-bank businesses rose dramatically in number in 1930, rising by 22 percent over 1929. Business failures continued rising thereafter in 1931 and 1932. More than 100,000 businesses failed in the course of the above four-year period, as summarized in Table 6.8.

Table 6.8   U.S. Number of Business Failures, 1928–32

Year	No. of Failures
1928	20,373
1929	19,073
1930	24,107
1931	26,381
1932	28,773

Source: NBER Macrohistory Database IX: Financial Status of Business, *U.S. Number of Business Failures, 1893–1933*.

As Tables 6.7 and 6.8 show, general business failures preceded the 1931 banking crisis. This suggests that business failures contributed significantly to bank losses and asset value deflation, in addition to falling farm and real estate values. Banks were undoubtedly faced with writing off collapsing mortgages, and falling land and real estate prices, plus losses from the growing number of non-financial business failures in 1930 and after. It was defaults and failures in the real economy in 1930–31 that fed back into the financial system in 1931, and contributed heavily to bank suspensions in turn.

The feedbacks also worked in the opposite direction. As banks' assets collapsed their balance sheets deteriorated, requiring a further contraction of credit to general businesses. Bank credit to non-financial business dried up fast in 1930–31. Businesses that could not obtain necessary loans failed—or else sold off other real assets to stay afloat.

But deflation was a cause as well as an effect in the process. Debt servicing requirements (interest and principal payments on debt) undertaken at the time of initial borrowing do not change. Terms of lending remain the same, despite economic collapse. So a business must pay for the credit taken with less revenue and income. Its debt in real terms therefore rises as its prices and revenue fall. That results in greater financial fragility. The point is that both rising real debt and deflation exacerbate defaults and business failures, just as those failures result in subsequent bank losses, write-downs, and restriction of credit, and further deflation and rising real debt.

Other quantitative characteristics

If the banking system does not appear to have collapsed as yet in 1930, what then was driving the decline in the real economy in 1930? It is not likely that the stock market crash in October 1929, nor even the continuing sharp decline in stock prices in 1930, was responsible for the real economy's decline in 1930 and beyond. Falling stock values do have some impact on consumption, from what is called the 'wealth effect.' But it is not significant in the overall impact on output of the economy. Out of a U.S. total population of 121.4 million in 1929, there were no more than 5 million who owned stock, and about 0.5 million owned 80 percent of all stock. The 1929 labor force totaled about 46 million, 9.7 million of whom were self-employed. That left about 36 million wage and salary workers. It is extremely unlikely that falling stock values had any direct effect on this latter group's consumption, which declined notably.

Consumption as a share of gross domestic product (GDP) in 1929 was roughly 75 percent.[36] The U.S. economy, measured in GDP, declined by 45 percent between 1929 and 1933. Even adjusting for deflation, the fall was 23 percent. As a component of GDP, investment fell most dramatically and consistently from 1929 through 1932, only leveling off in 1933. On the other hand, consumption behaved somewhat differently. While consumption of durable goods fell sharply in 1930, consumers minimally reduced their purchases of non-durable goods and services in 1930. A deep contraction of consumption—i.e. durables, non-durables, services—did not come until 1931, and then mostly after mid year. In fact, it appeared between January and March 1931 that the economic decline of the preceding year, 1930, in which GDP fell by –8.6 percent, might be leveling out. But this changed in the second quarter, April–June 1931, when the banking crisis began. After April 1931, consumption was no longer focused primarily on durables, but began to fall across the board as well, more or less in tandem with the still continuing decline in investment.

The point is that something important changed around mid 1931, and not just on the financial front with the onset of the first serious general banking crisis.[37] The real economy also crossed a kind of economic 'Rubicon' in the spring–summer 1931. The fracturing of financial fragility that occurred congruent with the banking crisis between April–October 1931 appears to have had a further profound effect on consumption around that same time. Consumption fragility similarly fractured in mid to late 1931, or very soon thereafter.

Household balance sheets were steadily deteriorating in 1930. With rising layoffs and wage cuts, disposable income was no doubt falling and households' real debt servicing requirements were rising in turn. In addition, households' real debt was rising as well, causing a further deterioration of consumption fragility. As recent studies show, consumers purchased homes, cars, and other durables in record numbers in 1928–29, thus incurring significant additional debt and debt servicing load. But those studies suggest that consumers cut back consumption elsewhere in order to hold onto their homes and autos as long as possible. In short, both falling disposable income and rising real debt levels must have resulted in a steady deterioration in consumption fragility from late 1929 through the spring of 1931. The onset of the banking crisis of 1931 may have caused a major shift in consumer confidence that was sufficient to 'fracture' consumption fragility in its wake as well. Sometime around mid to late 1931, consumption in general fell off a cliff.

The general point to be made is twofold: first, the contraction of the real economy during the two years from early summer 1929 to summer 1931 was no normal recession. In terms of quantitative characteristics, 1929–31 was clearly of Epic Recession dimensions. Similarly, qualitative criteria and dynamic processes associated with Epic Recessions appear to have been at work as well, whether associated with processes of debt and debt unwinding, deepening deflation across all three price systems, and emerging defaults, or related to evidence of financial and consumption fragility. Already worsening in the late 1920s, both forms of fragility appear to have been deteriorating as processes of debt–deflation–default gained momentum.

Quantitatively, while unemployment did not rise in 1930 to depression levels, the unemployment rate did rise from just under 4 percent in 1929 to 8.9 percent in 1930—a not insignificant increase. But layoffs had not yet spread in any great number to other sectors of the economy, apart from manufacturing and construction. The 8.9 percent was an Epic Recession level of joblessness, but not yet depression level. The real employment collapse would come later, once again after mid 1931. Between 1929 and 1933, industrial production fell by most accounts between 45 percent and 50 percent. The index for total production only stopped declining in mid 1933 and then stabilized over the next two years, 1933–34.[38] For 1930, however, most of the production decline centered on durables, and only a relatively small decline occurred in the production of non-durables or services.[39] That, too, would change after mid 1931. And similarly for other quantitative indicators considered in this analysis—i.e. stock prices, exports, etc.

The second point is that the first major, system-wide banking crisis of April–October 1931 resulted in a qualitative shift in financial fragility, a 'fracturing' as it is referred to in this analysis. This fracturing of financial fragility produced a decline in the general state of confidence so that it likely fractured consumption fragility as well. Certainly the banking crisis resulted in an intensification of the contraction of bank lending, a more rapid rise in unemployment and fall in production, and a worsening of other indicators. That precipitated more deflation and defaults. Consumption was no doubt negatively impacted by all that. But the collapse in the general state of confidence that seems to have been associated with the banking crisis of 1931 also undoubtedly had a negative impact on consumption and consumption fragility. By late 1931 the real economy was making the transition from Epic Recession to a classic depression.

EPIC RECESSION TYPE II: 1929–APRIL 1931

There are two distinct 'stages' within the longer economic contraction 'phase' of 1929–33. The first is 1929–31; the second, 1931–34. The first extends from June–July 1929 through around August 1931. It is this stage that is referred to as Epic Recession.

Chapters 1 and 2 of this book described the quantitative and qualitative characteristics that differentiate an Epic Recession from both normal recessions and depressions. These Epic Recession characteristics are summarized in the second column of the Table 6.9 as 'benchmark minima.' How the 1929–31 period compares to these benchmarks is indicated in the third column of the table. What the two columns reveal is that the 1929–31 period satisfies more than 90 percent of the benchmark characteristics for Epic Recession.

The period July 1929 to summer 1931 was not a normal contraction. Many accounts by participants and observers at the time in fact did not see the period as a depression. Many thought 1929–30 was just a more severe version of the normal recessions that occurred in 1923 and 1926. But 1929–31 was far worse than either 1923 or 1926, and not as bad as 1931–34 would soon reveal.

The economic decline following October 1929 was centered primarily in the housing construction and durables manufacturing sectors of the economy. It was not generalized throughout the entire economy. Already declining earlier in 1929, construction activity plummeted by nearly 40 percent in 1930.[40] Manufacturing was also contracting well before October 1929 and accelerated thereafter. But the manufacturing decline in 1930 was limited largely to the durable goods sector of manufacturing—i.e. 'big ticket' items like autos, furniture, appliances, and so forth. Construction and durables manufacturing were thus the leading edge of the contraction in 1930. In contrast, non-durable goods manufacturing declined only modestly in 1930 and services essentially not at all, according to U.S. Bureau of Economic Analysis data. It would not be until 1931 that non-durables and services joined durable goods in a general economic contraction after mid 1931. Given the concentration of the economic decline in housing and durables manufacturing, consumption for these goods fell sharply in 1930, but consumption overall fell by only 6.2 percent—not an insignificant fall, but by no means yet of depression dimensions.

In terms of business spending, in 1930 neither the general state of business confidence nor confidence in the banking system had yet collapsed. Business was quickly shelving new investment plans, but existing production (with the exception of construction and durables manufacturing) was slowing but not collapsing. The index for industrial production fell 15.7 percent immediately following the stock market crash in the last quarter of 1929. The rate of decline of industrial production thereafter actually slowed during 1930 from that initial pace. The total decline in industrial production from October

1929 to the end of 1930 in real terms was around 23 percent, or about 8 percent more in 1930. Compared to the initial 15.7 percent, that represents a significant slowdown in all of 1930 equal to about half the initial rate of 15.7 percent.

Table 6.9   Characteristics of Epic Recession, Benchmarks versus 1929–31

Characteristic	Benchmark Minima	1929–31 as Epic
GNP/GDP	5–15% two quarters	11.8% in 1930
Unemployment Rate	10% Increase	9% 1930 + 2% 1931: I
Industrial Production	10–20% Decline	23.9% in 1930
Exports	10% Decline	17.4% in 1930
Stock Prices	40% or more Decline	47% first 15 months
Duration	18–24 months	24 months (7/29–7/31)
Debt	100% Increase prior decade	From $95 (est.) to $244 billion
	Financial Institutions	+60% (banks loans only)
	Non-Financial	+242% (corp. security issues)
	Consumer	+162% (non-mortgage debt)
	Government	No change over decade
Deflation	Asset (10–40%) Decline	Stocks –47%
		Household financial assets –4%
		Land prices decline
	Product (2–10%) Decline	
	Consumer	–6.4% in 1930
	Wholesale	–30.2% (7/29–10/31)
	Commodities	–15.7% (7/29–10/30)
	Retail Food	–24.6% (7/29–10/31)
	Wage/Earnings(emerging decline)	
	Ave. Hourly Wages	n/a (but –27% from 8/30–12/32)
	Weekly Earnings	–7.2% (manufacturing 1930)
	Total Compensation	n/a
Defaults	Financial (Commercial & Shadow)	
	Suspensions	1,350 in 1930 (vs. 659 in 1929)
	Failures	Unknown
	Non-Financial Business	
	Failures	24,107 in 1930 (vs. 19,073 in 1929)
	Restructurings	Unknown
	Consumer	
	Foreclosures	Farm and housing rise sharply
	Consumer Credit	Defaults minimal
Qualitative	Financial Instability	
Characteristics	Bank Runs & Withdrawals	Yes (deposits –4% in 1930)
	Capital & Insolvency	Yes (stocks/deposits/assets)
	Credit Crunch & Crash	Yes (both 1930 & 1931)
	Shadow Banking Growth	Yes (brokerages/trust/I-banks)
	Consumption Fragility	Yes (earnings + debt to income)
	Speculative Investment Shift	Yes
	Global Synchronization	Yes (esp. before Sept. 1931)
	Rate of Propagation & Spread	Accelerates in 2H 1931

The October stock market crash undoubtedly created a more uncertain business investment environment, causing businesses already postponing new investment to continue to do so. In 1930 cost-cutting was spreading but was not yet generalized across the economy. Production cutbacks were occurring, unemployment was rising, but was once again heavily concentrated in construction and durables manufacturing and not throughout the entire economy. Those sectors of the economy represented the lion's share of unemployment, which rose to 8.9 percent by the end of 1930. But the floor had not yet totally fallen out of the job markets. What many businesses were doing in lieu of layoffs in early 1930 was cutting hours of work, renegotiating orders with suppliers, and generally reducing operational costs.

Labor cost-cutting first began to deepen around mid 1930. In addition to reductions in working hours and selective layoffs in construction and durables manufacturing, now direct wage-cutting began to spread as well. Table 6.5 showed that workers' weekly earnings were falling in 1930. About mid 1930, wage-cutting began to show up more frequently as a method of labor cost-cutting preferred by employers. Government surveys at the time show that more than 90 percent of companies polled in June 1930 were now cutting wages. Another survey conducted shortly thereafter, in July 1930, showed that all firms in the survey sample—100 percent—were cutting wages and that 86 percent of the workforce in the surveyed firms were experiencing wage cuts.[41] It appears, therefore, that business first reduced unnecessary labor via layoffs, then reduced the hours of those still working, and thereafter focused on cutting wages. A further step of engaging in mass layoffs was yet to take place. That would come in 1931.

Despite rising mortgage defaults, farm and housing foreclosures, and losses from the stock market crash, bank suspensions were no greater in 1930 than they had been in 1929 or even 1928. The stock market crash of October 1929 did not immediately precipitate a banking panic or even a banking crisis. It was not until November–December 1930 that bank suspensions began to rise noticeably. However, as previously noted, the rise in suspensions at year end reflected a regional crisis, localized in the Midwest and just one mismanaged bank in New York. As one chronicler described the November–December banking problems, "it was not a national crisis, if by that phrase we mean a fairly uniform distribution of bank suspensions and hoarding across the twelve Federal Reserve Districts."[42] This largely localized crisis quickly receded by January 1931. By February 1931, the rate of bank suspensions returned to pre-November 1930 levels. The problem did not spill over to the rest of the banking system. Bank runs and depositor withdrawals did not rise significantly for the overall banking system. Bank assets fell only slightly in 1930 compared to 1929. Bank credit was tightening in 1930. Credit was progressively contracting but not yet disappearing. A general hoarding of money by banks was not yet occurring.

On the other hand, exports were more seriously impacted in the summer of 1930 with passage of the Smoot–Hawley tariff by the U.S. But production for exports was a smaller part of total U.S. GNP in 1930 than today. Moreover, as others have argued, tariffs often result in a switching of production from foreign to U.S. markets. So the net effects of the 1930 tariff on overall production did not drive the economic contraction in 1930 either.

This does not mean that 1929–31 was a mild economic event. This was an extraordinarily serious recession, an Epic Recession. In 1930 alone, there was nearly 9 percent unemployment, GDP declines in excess of 10 percent, industrial production falling by more than 20 percent (and in freefall in durables manufacturing and housing), exports declining, foreclosures and business failures steadily rising—i.e. a major economic contraction quite unlike anything that occurred in the 'normal' recessions of 1923 and 1926.

But deeper underlying forces in 1930 were building toward an even more severe crisis in 1931. As noted, financial and consumer fragility had already deteriorated by late 1929 and were becoming even more unstable in 1929–30 as real debt rose and cash flow and disposable income declined. Over-extended stock and bond markets at the decade's end—driven by new forms of speculative investing, new financial instruments, and fast-growing new shadow banking institutions—had stalled by 1929 and had begun to contract. Common stocks were the first of the financial asset markets to explode and begin to unwind. The decline in investor and business wealth caused by the stock market crash was more than sufficient to halt further new investment—whether in the form of speculative or real assets. But the stock crash and initial asset price declines were not sufficient for generating a generalized collapse of current production and depression-level unemployment. For that to happen, asset price deflation would have to deepen further and spread beyond stocks, real estate and farm land values, and into the general business sector, which was beginning to happen in 1930. Asset price deflation would need to generalize beyond just stock prices and to spill over to products, provoking product price and wage deflation—both already softening even before October 1929. Asset price deflation would first need to eat away at business balance sheets and general business revenues before product deflation accelerated further. Real debt levels would need to continue to rise. Defaults in greater number and volume would have to occur. This process would take time. That time was 1929–30.

Businesses that had over-extended in terms of borrowing in the prior decade, in 1930 were in need of credit for refinancing debt more than ever. Not only to service rising real debt but to simply continue to finance daily operations. But credit availability was steadily declining. And business defaults do not occur overnight. There is a process that takes time to develop. That process was underway for 1930–31. In this process, facing a growing unavailability of credit, the first response is to cut costs. The second is to resort to cutting prices on inventory and products.[43] Cutting costs usually means renegotiating prices with suppliers and/or reducing labor costs. The latter can take several forms: reducing hours of work, reducing hourly wages, implementing layoffs, and other means to raise productivity per worker remaining to reduce unit labor costs. If not sufficient to raise needed cash flow, businesses then sell off physical assets and parts of the business. As a near-final option, they seek a merger with another company or try to sell the company itself. When all the foregoing prove insufficient, default and then bankruptcy is inevitable—the latter involving either reorganization in bankruptcy court in which deep asset firesales occur, or as liquidation of assets at firesale prices. To put off the inevitable, the business in question might be able to renegotiate or delay debt payments in whole or part and buy additional time. But lenders, themselves facing economic problems, may be reluctant to allow that time. The essential point, however, is that this general process does not 'mature' overnight. It requires a certain period in which to develop. In a sense, Epic Recession is the stage during which the processes of debt–deflation–default continue to grow worse and deepen their feedback effects upon each other, until they eventually erupt in a more serious collapse (i.e. fracturing) of financial fragility and its reflection in a generalized banking crisis. The processes just described also represent a concurrent deterioration of financial fragility, which deepened throughout 1930–31. But accompanying growing financial fragility at the time was a no less significant deterioration in consumption fragility—defined in part as a rise in debt (or debt servicing) to disposable income ratio. Like banks and businesses, households also loaded up on debt during the 1920s, for durables like cars and housing in particular. Out of a workforce of 46 million in 1929, 26.6 million had a car or truck, or one vehicle per 1.29 households. More importantly, 4.5 million were purchased in 1929 by one out of every four households—and half of those 4.5 million were bought on credit.[44] Similar credit buying for housing and durable goods was also the case by decade's end. At the same time, real earnings for 36 million workers in the labor force had essentially stagnated or were drifting lower in 1929, which meant that real debt servicing costs were rising. Like banks and businesses, households' consumption fragility grows as their incomes fall and/or their real debt rises. After 1929, real weekly earnings began to fall even further—as businesses began cutting back first on hours worked in early 1930 and then on hourly wages as well around mid 1930. As Table 6.6 indicates, earnings fell in 1930 by 7.2 percent and at an even faster rate in 1931. What this general picture represents, in other words, is the already weakening of consumption fragility before October 1929 began to further deteriorate in 1930–31.

Farmers' consumption fragility probably deteriorated even more dramatically. They had also loaded up on debt in the early to mid 1920s, mortgaging their land assets in order to expand and mechanize in anticipation of a continuing acceleration in food for exports, which never materialized. Their product prices fell after mid decade and now, in 1930–31, were in virtual freefall. Their incomes fell in turn, but their debt servicing burden did not. In fact, it rose in real terms. Their land values fell. Unable to make debt payments or to refinance due to collapsing land values, they foreclosed in growing numbers in 1930 and in record numbers after mid 1931. Local banks now held nearly worthless mortgages and repossessed the farms. Repossession meant that banks were then required to write off the values of those collapsed mortgages, resulting in growing losses on their own balance sheets. They, too, were thus caught in the downward spiral. As housing and farm mortgages, commercial mortgages, and loans and investments to now bankrupt businesses collapsed in value, bank losses deepened. And as they deepened, banks reduced credit even further. When they themselves failed (i.e. bank suspensions) bank credit reduced absolutely. In this manner, bank defaults followed business failures, farm mortgage and land price declines, and housing–construction mortgage defaults. But it didn't happen overnight. It took nearly a year, from October 1929 to October 1930, for the spiral to even begin to impact on some banks at the close of 1930. It then took another six months, to mid 1931, before losses at banks became generalized throughout the economy.

The fundamental deep causes at work in 1929–31 were the debt unwinding, the spreading deflationary pressures from and within the three price systems exacerbating the debt problem, and the defaults that followed. At an advanced stage of debt–deflation–default, feedback effects between the three begin to occur, further exacerbating each. Feedbacks between deflation in the three price systems—asset, product, and wage—start to occur as well. Debt stress drives deflation, which in turn contributes to defaults. But defaults feed back on debt and debt accelerates defaults. And so on.

When debt loads and debt servicing are heavy and businesses and banks are thus 'financially fragile,' or when households' debt loads and servicing are likewise high and households are thus 'consumption fragile,' then the downward debt–deflation–default spiral propagates at a faster rate. The process grows worse as cash flow and disposable income also decline. Already serious before 1930, financial and consumption fragility deteriorated progressively during 1930 to early 1931, became even more unstable, and then finally 'fractured.' The break in both financial and consumption fragility occurred in mid 1931, financially with the banking crisis and soon after for households and consumers. Debt–deflation–default processes thereafter worsened, with feedbacks, driving the economic contraction to new lows and toward depression conditions.

A BRIEF DIGRESSION ON POLICY

If government institutions are not able to aggressively intervene and contain the downward spiral of short-run momentum effects between debt–deflation–default, the process will continue to worsen and the economy will decline further. Policy must either halt deflation, and prevent its spread across the three price systems and thus contain the feedback effects, or policy must target debt or defaults. Roosevelt's NIRA policies in 1933–34 targeted product deflation but failed due to an inability to stop asset and wage deflation—suggesting that a policy response targeting deflation must address all three price systems simultaneously or fail. Government bailouts target the default process but do nothing about bad debt remaining on balance sheets and continuing to grow. Federal Reserve liquidity injections target debt but merely offset bad debt and don't remove it or reduce it. What this all suggests is that targeting just one of the three processes will prove insufficient. A containment strategy to prevent the maturation of Epic Recession must include programs targeting all three—debt, deflation, defaults—more or less at the same time.

But even a comprehensive strategy for addressing debt–deflation–default processes in the short run will likely prove ineffective over the longer run. If excess debt and debt servicing is a key determinant setting off the process, it is still only half of the picture of financial and consumption fragility. The other half of fragility is income—i.e. cash flow for the business sector (financial fragility) and disposable income for the household and consumer sector (consumption fragility). Income thus plays a strategic role in both forms of fragility. If households' earnings and incomes are falling due to job loss, working hours reductions, and wage rate cuts, they reduce consumption. This reduces demand for products, leading businesses to reduce product prices further, introduce wage-cutting, and so on, in a vicious cycle resulting in yet a further decline in incomes. Similarly, when cash flow and liquid assets decline due to rising debt servicing requirements and/or declining consumer demand, the response is further price-cutting and deflation that result in rising real debt, falling revenues, and reduced cash flow.

Government policies must therefore also target income enhancement over the long run, not just debt–deflation–default in the shorter run, to ensure Epic Recession is checked and contained more than temporarily. On the consumer and household side this means various programs that raise household disposable incomes, whether tax restructuring, wage supports, reducing benefits costs, promotion of re-unionization, and so forth. On the business side, it means policies that prohibit speculative investing, leveraging, and debt accumulation, and instead promote and substitute debt financing with equity and other non-debt forms of financing, and otherwise redistribute income from speculators and the institutional vehicles of the global money parade.

Multiple explanations are offered by economists for declining consumption spending in 1930 and its subsequent collapse thereafter in 1931. Some focus on the deterioration of household balance sheets as the cause of consumption collapse. Others cite as a primary cause the decline in perceptions of wealth produced by the stock market crash, which result in consumption declines thereafter. Others talk about growing 'consumer uncertainty' causing households to cut back spending. Others say it was a fall in consumer spending autonomous of financial forces. Others argue that households cut spending in order to continue to pay for existing installment debt first. But all these views represent a derivative, secondary explanation behind which resides the debt–deflation–default process described above. The more fundamental force is the unwinding of debt, and its consequences in terms of deflation (all three price systems), defaults (business, banking and households), and the feedback effects between debt–deflation–default that lead to even greater pressure to contract on an already declining real economy. And the virulence of the debt–deflation–default process is conditioned to a great extent by the degree of financial and consumption fragility in the system at the time of crisis, as well as how fast fragility deteriorates once Epic Recession commences.

One further observation: if 1929 was the year in which emerging recession and financial fragility erupted in one sector of financial markets, the stock market, then 1930 is the year in which fundamentals in the real economy continued to deteriorate below the surface. In 1931 those fundamentals would provoke another financial crisis—this time a true banking crisis. If the stock market crash was the first financial crisis, then the banking crisis of April–August 1931 was the true second crisis. A third financial crisis was yet to come, i.e. the banking crisis of November 1932–March 1933. But by then the economy had clearly transitioned from the Epic Recession stage of 1929–31 into a bona fide depression. Throughout Phase I of the Great Depression, from 1929 to 1934, the general scenario is one of a series or sequence of financial crises and successively deeper real economic decline, with the two cycles—financial and real—beginning to interact and feed back upon each other. A scenario of ever-deepening real economic contraction (1930) followed by renewed financial crisis (1931), followed by real contraction (1932), and again by financial crisis (1932–33) in a mutually reinforcing downward spiral.

To sum up: epic recessions are set in motion when an economy entering a recession encounters a major financial crisis that is the result of growing financial fragility created by years of debt accumulation driven by excessive speculative investment. The financial crisis event represented by the stock market crash of October 1929 propelled the economy toward an Epic Recession. But the crash itself was insufficient to trigger a depression. For that to happen, the economic decline had to continue to deepen over the ensuing 18–24 months of 1930–31. Deflation had to develop and extend across the three price systems. Processes of debt–deflation–default had to deepen and begin to feed back—provoking an already weakened state of financial and consumption fragility in 1929 to deteriorate further. Type II Epic Recessions consequently require a prior base and degree of both financial and consumption fragility. This dual fragility magnifies the contractionary effects of the debt–deflation–default processes. Consumption fragility accelerates the decline in the real economy while financial fragility plays a similar role on the financial crisis side, and the two interact and reinforce each other. Financial and consumption fragility are the 'triggers,' while the general process of debt–deflation–default are the 'hammers' that propel the projectile of economic contraction once the triggers set it off or cause it to deepen.

TRANSITION TO DEPRESSION: APRIL–AUGUST 1931

The transition of Epic Recession to depression occurs when debt–deflation–default processes have generalized and deepened to a point such that financial and consumption fragility 'fracture'; i.e. shift abruptly instead of slowly and steadily. The precipitating event representing financial fracture is typically a generalized banking crisis. The corresponding event representing the fracturing of consumption is typically a sharp acceleration in the decline of production and the emergence of mass layoffs. Both 'fracturings' thereafter feed back upon each other by intensifying the processes of debt–deflation–default and their mutually reinforcing interactions. Real investment, production and output, and consumption then shift to a lower level than previously (i.e. a 'lower equilibrium,' as economists would say). In a Type I Epic Recession, the economy stagnates for an extended period at that new, lower, equilibrium which may include periodic short and shallow recoveries followed by similar declines over years—or what is sometimes described as a 'W'-shaped recovery trajectory. In a Type II Epic Recession, the stagnation stage does not last as long and subsequent abrupt shifts in fragility drive the economic contraction to an even lower level—i.e. a depression.

Since 1929–31 qualifies as an Epic Recession, the subsequent question is how and why did it make the transition toward depression over the summer of 1931? The summer of 1931 marks the spread and deepening of decline in current levels of production outside construction and manufacturing. It also marks a general collapse of consumption. Consumption averaged $70 billion a year over the 1925–29 period. In 1930 it hardly declined, by less than $1 billion (to $69.1 billion) below the 1925–29 average of $70 billion. In 1931, however, it fell $13.7 billion below that $70 billion average.[45] No longer primarily housing and durables, consumption began to fall sharply for non-durables and services as well. Why, then, did both production and consumption decline far more rapidly at that particular point in time?

The onset of the first banking crisis is part of the answer. Emerging in April–May 1931, it ebbed, flowed, and then deepened in September–October. As the banking crisis dragged on and deepened it created a crisis of confidence in the banking system itself. Credit contraction in 1930 became a de facto credit crash in 1931. Businesses now denied credit began to default at a faster pace. So did banks themselves, as more than a year of falling asset values on their balance sheets—farm mortgages, real estate mortgages, mortgage bonds, bankers' loans and call loans' losses, commercial loans, etc.—finally took their toll. Those that did not default cut back operations aggressively. Bank cutbacks mean fewer loans issued to non-bank businesses, as well as interbank loans to other banks in need or trouble. Both bank suspensions and general business failures accelerated. Nearly 2,300 banks were suspended in 1931. This time the suspensions were general and widespread geographically. Bank runs and deposit withdrawals surged, the latter by 15.7 percent. Money hoarding was becoming general, by banks, businesses, and households. Bank assets, having barely declined in 1930, now fell in 1931 by 7 percent. With the collapse of confidence in the banking system came a general collapse of confidence in the economy in general.

With the banking crisis, business access to credit—difficult in 1930—now became a severe problem. Credit for new investment wasn't the only problem. Credit for funding general operations, credit for financing debt, credit for making payrolls, were increasingly the concern. Lacking that, businesses had little recourse but to attempt to cut costs even more aggressively than before, to reduce product prices even further, and sell assets at firesale prices. Cutting costs meant reducing payments or arrangements with suppliers, which spread the contraction. It also meant aggressively cutting labor costs: unemployment rose appreciably in 1931 over 1930, nearly doubling from 8.9 percent to 16.5 percent. The cutting of hours of work and wages was increasingly harsh. Weekly earnings fell dramatically in 1931, reducing another 11.3 percent on top of 1930's 7.2 percent decline. Both wholesale and consumer prices plummeted even further and more rapidly, consumer prices falling now by more than 9 percent in 1931 and wholesale prices by 18 percent. With product price deflation came rising real debt levels.

The banking crisis sealed the case for business spending, as operations and production cuts grew. The accelerating layoffs, working hours and wage cuts pushed households over the edge in terms of consumption. Consumption fragility, built upon an edifice of stagnating weekly earnings, mortgage debt, auto and installment debt, worsened in 1930 as layoffs, working hours, and later wages were reduced. But just as financial fragility finally shattered with the banking crisis in 1931, so too did consumption fragility finally fracture in 1931. Consumption fell off a cliff in 1931. The dual breakdown of financial and consumption fragility is what pushed the economy to the edge of depression in the summer of 1931, then over the precipice. These two developments converged with global economic events in September 1931, as Britain left the gold standard. That 'synchronization' event added to the financial and consumption collapse. With Britain leaving the gold standard, gold and thus liquidity flowed out of the U.S. economy even faster. Attempting to prevent the outflow, the Fed raised its discount rate in the midst of the crisis, a move which did not cause but certainly exacerbated the crisis. The economic Rubicon had been crossed. By all magnitudes and measures, it was no longer an Epic Recession by fourth quarter 1931. It was depression.

So why did Epic Recession make the transition to depression in 1931 and not after 1908? The long speculative build-up in the 1920s certainly played a key role. Moreover, the speculative trends were widespread by 1929, involving not only the stock market but also bond markets, farm mortgages and land, urban and suburban housing and commercial properties, gold and currency markets. In contrast, speculative investing in the run-up to 1907 focused more narrowly on stocks from mergers and consolidations of companies and to some extent commodities speculation. The sheer volume of creation of new companies and industries in the 1920s, and resort to speculative devices like holding companies, drove stock speculation in the latter period to greater excesses, as did the greater recourse to the use of bank loans and call loans. Gold flows to the U.S. and the U.S. central bank, the Fed, a new factor, together provided even more liquidity, credit, and debt for speculative purposes in the 1920s. The number and relative weight of shadow banks had also expanded greatly by 1929 compared to the earlier period. In addition to a more serious debt situation, deflation and defaults were already rising for the years prior to 1929 compared to 1907. Consumer debt was now also a totally new factor. In short, debt levels and debt servicing were more severe, and deflation and defaults were already serious problems in select sectors of the economy like farming and construction. Conditions of financial and consumption fragility were already more fragile in 1929 than in 1907. There was also the important new factor of economies elsewhere that had already entered depression, including Britain and most of Europe. 'Synchronization' was thus a force not at work in 1907. Finally, there is the question of policy response.

A theme of this book is that monetary policy designed to bail out the banks and provide massive liquidity injections may result in a temporary stabilization of the banking system in crisis, but it cannot provide a permanent stabilization so long as bad assets remain on financial institutions' balance sheets in significant quantity. Injecting liquidity to prevent a general banking collapse can put a floor under the collapse. But it cannot ensure a vigorous long-run return to bank lending and sustained economic recovery, especially if bad loans and assets remain on bank balance sheets and if banks are permitted to lend first to speculative ventures while reducing lending to real investment. The banking crisis of 1907 was stabilized by 'lender of last resort' action, but the real economy remained insufficiently stimulated thereafter to ensure sustained recovery. Thus, the extended stagnation period from 1908 to 1914. In contrast, in 1931, monetary policy failed even to stabilize the banking system. In fact, Fed policy exacerbated the banking crisis. Subsequent banking crises followed, until the stabilization was finally achieved in 1933–34. However, even that late bank stabilization in 1933–34 did not result in sustained recovery either. A major difference between the two periods, therefore, was bank stabilization in 1907 versus the failure to attain bank stabilization in 1931 and 1932. But in both cases, the lack of substantial fiscal stimulus accompanying the monetary policy (or lack thereof) failed to generate a sustained recovery.

Extended stagnation results when monetary policy stabilizes the financial system but cannot generate fuller recovery—as in 1907. Descent to depression occurs when monetary policy even fails to stabilize the banking system—as in 1931. What remained in 1931 was both financial fragility and consumption fragility that continued to deteriorate further—i.e. a precondition for a subsequent descent toward depression. In 1907 at least financial fragility was stabilized, whereas in 1931 neither financial nor consumption fragility was adequately addressed.

The critical questions concerning the current crisis that commenced in 2007 can now be asked: Is the recent financial crisis and real economic contraction an Epic Recession? If so, is it best categorized as a Type I or a Type II? That is, will it result in an extended stagnation or an eventual descent into depression? Have policymakers been able to intervene successfully so far to disrupt the debt–deflation–default processes at one or more critical junctures? What is the record for debt, deflation, and default during the recent crisis to date? What are the prognoses for debt, deflation, and default for the immediate future? Have the Fed and the U.S. Treasury 'succeeded' so far in stabilizing the banking system and putting a floor under the financial collapse? If so, what are the future consequences of the methods employed to do so? Will financial stabilization prove temporary? Are the several trillion dollars of liquidity injections by the Fed and the Treasury sufficient to generate a sustained general economic recovery? Have accompanying fiscal policy measures—i.e. tax and stimulus spending—adequately supplemented monetary polices enough to ensure sustained recovery in 2010 and beyond? If not, what policies are necessary? Where and how might the current crisis evolve in 2010 and beyond? These are questions to which we now turn for consideration and analysis in Part Three, the remaining three chapters of the book.

Part Three

Epic Recession, 2007–10

7
The Epic Recession of 2007–10

The financial crisis and Epic Recession of 2007–10 did not begin with the bust of the subprime mortgage market in August 2007. Nor did it begin with the Federal Reserve (Fed) lowering interest rates in 2003–04 to 1 percent. According to this view, the subprime explosion was the result of an overheated housing market and housing price inflation. Everybody wanted to buy a home at a 1 percent mortgage rate, or a second or a third. Some to hold as a long-term investment. Others to 'flip' within months for a quick capital gain. By lowering mortgage rates to a record low 1 percent and keeping them there over an extended period, the Fed, it is argued, created the subprime problem. Thereafter, the subprime bust of August 2007 set off the financial crisis that followed.

But the housing boom was not driven by the Fed's low interest rates. It was driven fundamentally by rising speculation in the housing market over the longer term. Speculation in housing markets preceded the Fed's 1 percent rates of 2003 by at least five years. And the escalation of housing prices started as early as 1997. According to the Case-Shiller Home Price Index, home prices rose 12 percent a year between January 1998 and March 2000 after rising only an average 3 percent per year over the entire preceding decade.[1] Housing prices continued to accelerate right through the recession of 2001, while other prices were slowing or even beginning to fall. Between March 2000 and March 2006, home prices accelerated further, rising at a clip of 20 percent per year—almost double that of 1998–99. In short, home prices were accelerating at double-digit rates for more than five years *before* the Fed had lowered interest rates to 1 percent.

So if the housing boom and escalating housing price inflation began well before the Fed lowered rates, how, then, was the Fed the cause of the housing boom? And if the Fed wasn't the cause, what was? To answer that question requires understanding some basics about financial asset speculation, the role of leverage and securitization in speculative investing, and how speculative investing creates fragility in the banking and financial system.

HISTORICAL BACKGROUND TO THE CURRENT CRISIS

Financial fragility has grown steadily in the financial system since at least the 1980s. It was around that time that the shadow banking system began to expand once again—as it had historically several times before in U.S. history—in size and influence within the overall financial system.[2] The shadow banking system enables wealthy investors—individual, corporate, and institutional—

to move into more speculative and profitable forms of investment activity otherwise denied to the rest of the more regulated traditional banking system. A speculative investment shift is not new, however. Similar shifts occurred in the 1920s, and before that at the turn of the twentieth century. Earlier experiences in 1898–1907 and 1919–29 led to greater financial fragility, financial instability, and eventual financial crises in 1907 and again in 1929. These events were described in Chapters 5 and 6.

The experiences of 1907, 1929, and now 2007, show that a rise in financial speculation, shadow banking institutions, and financial fragility go hand in hand. Together they produce a financial crisis of major dimensions that can lead to an extraordinary near-shutdown of the financial system. That shutdown results in a contraction of credit and lending by banks, which in turn produces a contraction of the real economy of equally epic dimensions. Normal recessions are not precipitated by extraordinary financial crises and system-wide credit crashes. Epic Recessions are.

But time is required for the necessary financial fragility and instability to mature, to develop, deepen and reach the financial implosion stage. The run-up period was a decade at least in the earlier cases of 1907 and 1929. The gestation was a bit longer for the financial implosion that occurred in 2007–08, for reasons that will be explained later. The financial crisis of 2007–08, in other words, has been developing for at least two decades.

Early signs of instability in the U.S. financial system began to emerge in the 1980s, when the Savings and Loan (S&L) industry, the then primary source lender for residential mortgages, was allowed to detour from its original, regulated, and less profitable home financing business into more speculative markets and investing.[3] The Reagan administration's policy of pushing interest rates to record levels between 1980–82 devastated the home mortgage industry and the S&Ls in turn. Nearly 20 percent of S&Ls disappeared between 1980 and 1982, the industry lost $45.7 billion, and revenues collapsed by 40 percent as a direct result of the Reagan and Fed policies raising mortgage interest rates to 18 percent at the time.[4] Reagan believed that the way to rescue the industry that his policies devastated was to deregulate it. The view at the time, becoming increasingly dominant, was that the market corrected all ills and never caused them. Markets were always and everywhere more 'efficient' than government regulation. Therefore, let the free, unregulated marketplace correct the S&L crisis of the early 1980s. That strategic error proved disastrous then, as it would again later.

Reagan-era legislation produced the Garn–St. Germain Act that allowed and encouraged S&Ls to venture into unregulated, speculative investments. The Act allowed S&Ls for the first time to enter markets for commercial real estate, consumer loans, land loans, and junk bonds—i.e. where S&L managers had virtually no previous experience doing business and the competition was intense. Garn–St. Germain permitted the S&Ls to reduce their reserves on hand to less than 3 percent of total loans and investments and thus to leverage themselves to the hilt—a formula for inevitable failure and collapse of the industry.[5] Garn–St. Germain meant hundreds, perhaps thousands, of newly created S&Ls now entered an ever-crowding market, which depressed profits further in the industry at a time when leveraging and therefore debt servicing levels were rising. The consequence was a temporary boom in mid decade and then a second and even larger housing bust by the late 1980s. Widespread S&L failures required a major government bailout of the industry at a cost of at least $250 billion to the taxpayer.[6]

But the S&L financial implosion did not spill over to other credit markets. That would come later in 2007 when another housing boom based on speculative investing collapsed and dragged other financial markets down with it in a matter of just a few months. In the 1980s the collapse was limited to the industry itself. That also made it relatively easier to contain through bailouts by the Fed and the Treasury, despite significant costs to the taxpayer.

A second parallel speculative bubble in the 1980s involved the corporate junk bond market. It too escalated, over-extended, and then imploded around 1990, requiring a rescue. Speculation in the junk bond market was driven by the corporate takeover (sometimes called the mergers and acquisitions (M&A)) movement. This was essentially a stock speculative play. Investors and corporate raiders raised funds in the junk bond market to buy stocks of targeted takeover companies. The threat of a raid and takeover drove up the stock price of the company. Once having taken over the company, the new raider-owners immediately slashed costs in a draconian fashion, sold off assets, broke contracts with suppliers and unions, reduced wages and increased layoffs—all in order to make the company appear more profitable in the short run in order to boost its stock price. Once that price rose, the stock was quickly sold at a substantial profit.

Speculators would borrow money with which to buy up the stock of the targeted company, or raise cash by issuing junk bonds to buy the stock. Sometimes management of the company would resist the takeover by raising cash itself via the junk bond market, to pay off existing stockholders and 'take the company private'—sometimes called a management or 'leveraged' buyout. Paying stockholders for their shares in order to prevent a takeover also raised the stock price. Prices for junk bonds surged as well. Junk bond mutual funds were also created, and their shares rose as the practice spread. Banks and insurance companies also got in on the game, as they loaned money to buy the junk bonds. S&Ls also speculated in the junk bond market, one of the main reasons for their losses.[7]

The shadow banking institutions, the investment banks (I-banks), were at the center of the speculative activity, in particular the I-bank Drexel Burnham, which was the Bear Stearns of its day. Like the I-bank, Bear Stearns went bankrupt as the junk bond market collapsed. The precipitating event involved a leading department store conglomerate company, Campeau Corp., that had taken on excessive debt via junk bond financing to purchase major competitors. When it couldn't service its debt, and as retail sales and revenues fell, Campeau became insolvent and went bankrupt. Its collapse caused a chain reaction among other investors. The junk bond market in general took a dive. Drexel Burnham attempted to get a bailout from other banks, but they refused (much as occurred later in 2008 when Bear Stearns was denied emergency funding by J.P. Morgan Chase bank, ensuring its demise). Drexel requested government and Fed bailout assistance, but, unlike Bear Stearns, was refused by both. Speculators in the Campeau affair and junk bonds, like Ivan Boesky and Michael Milken, went to jail. None would do so after the Bear Stearns collapse 18 years later.

Stock speculation was tightly integrated with the S&Ls and junk bond market implosions. After 1983 common stocks had a major run-up until they crashed in October 1987. On October 19, 1987, the market fell 508 points, the biggest decline since the depression of the 1930s. The speculative run on stocks came to an end in 1987 when it became clear that the junk bond and S&L industries were in trouble, had peaked, and that their asset prices could only head downward. Technical trading factors precipitated the 1987 stocks reversal. But computerized trading was not the cause, only the precipitating factor. The true causes of the 1987 stock market crash were the escalating speculative frenzy in S&Ls, leveraged buyouts and takeovers, and junk bond debt financing of it all.

But the stock market crash of 1987 did not provoke a consequent Epic Recession. Epic Recessions require a major financial bust, in stocks or banking failures, but that alone does not ensure that Epic Recession will follow. What is required is a generalized collapse in asset prices that spreads throughout credit markets and provokes deflation in all three price systems—assets, product prices, and wages.

These three interrelated events—the S&L bust, the junk bond collapse, and the stock market retreat and consolidation—were warning signs, dress rehearsals, for a more generalized financial crisis yet to come. The generalizing of the financial crisis in the late 1980s was averted. The contagion was caught in time and did not spread beyond housing and junk bond markets. It was containable. In comparison, the even more serious financial crisis of 2007–09 would prove much larger in magnitude, thus more difficult to contain or prevent from spreading.

The government was able to bail out the S&Ls and junk bond markets in the late 1980s, albeit at a significant cost. Jointly engineered by the Fed and the U.S. Treasury, liquidity was pumped into the system by the Fed and Congressional authorized bailouts from Congress's general budget funds. However, the bailouts had the consequent effect of injecting significant additional liquidity into the general financial system between 1987 and1992, i.e. liquidity that would ultimately help fuel the next excessive round of speculative activity later in the 1990s.

Liquidity is what enables the issuing of credit, and excess liquidity generates excess credit. Credit is what banks and financial institutions extend to borrowers. Those who borrow credit then assume a debt. Consequently, excess liquidity means excess credit, borrowing, and excessive debt accumulation. Debt must be 'serviced'; i.e. regular payments of principal and interest must be made to the creditor. Too much debt means payments grow so large that the borrower-debtor (which may be a company or household or even another bank) must cut back on real investment activity that might otherwise have expanded their business; or reduce purchases of goods (if households); or decrease lending (if banks or shadow banks). Excess debt may even lead to more borrowing and debt in an effort to make the payments on the original debt.

When banks load up on unserviceable debt and implode, the government (Fed and Treasury) must engineer a bailout. If not, bank failures can drag down major parts of the real, non-financial economy. Large non-bank corporations may also get bailed out. But smaller companies, small businesses in general, households, and in particular working-class households, rarely get bailed out. Those who were most severely impacted during the Great Depression of the 1930s, for example, were the latter—small businesses, median- and below-median-income households, farmers, small banks. The large banks and large corporations weathered the depression fairly well.

In the initial years of the 1990s, speculative investing slowed in the wake of the S&L and junk bond busts of the late 1980s and the 1990–92 recession that followed. A kind of 'clean up' was in order. Hundreds of billions were spent by the government in mopping up the S&L and junk bond industries in the early 1990s. By 1990 the parallel system of shadow banks had become a major force, and a source of ready liquid assets for speculative investing. By the mid 1990s speculative activity led by shadow banking institutions began to grow rapidly once again. A comparison of assets in the shadow versus traditional banking systems at the start of the decade of the 1990s is shown in Table 7.1.

Table 7.1   Traditional versus Shadow Bank Assets, 1990 ($ billions)

Traditional Banks		*Shadow Banks*	
Commercial Banks	4,231	Life Insurance	1,268
Savings & Loans	1,233	Private Pensions	1,163
		Mutual Funds	555
		Finance Companies	519
		Other Insurance	491
		Money Market Funds	428
		Mutual Savings Banks	283
		Credit Unions 199	
Total	4,464		4,906

Source: Robert Litan, *The Revolution in U.S. Finance*, Brookings Institution, 1991, p. 7. Note that Litan's estimate in terms of assets does not include investment banks and broker-dealers. If included, that would raise the shadow banks' share of assets even further.

The two sectors of finance were roughly the same size. This dual banking phenomenon was largely the result of changes in the overall structure of finance in the 1980s. The approximately equivalent size of the two sectors would continue. By 2007 both sectors grew substantially larger in absolute terms, at about $10 trillion in assets each. That's a more than doubling of total assets for both sectors in barely a decade and a half. This equivalent weight in terms of assets obscures the even greater relative weight of the shadow sector in terms of speculative investing. The main reason for the shadow sector's even greater relative weight is due to the increasing use of securitization and massive leveraging which became common practices in the shadow banking sector, which is explained shortly.

In the 1980s the shadow banking institutions and markets that grew fastest in size and influence were the mutual funds, commercial paper, and finance companies. All had been around before 1980, but their growth in assets after 1980 accelerated almost exponentially. Money market mutual funds first appeared in the late 1970s, but from 1980 to 1990 their total assets rose from about $80 billion to just under $500 billion.

Non-bank corporations also entered the shadow bank ranks by issuing commercial paper (CP). CP is like a short-term private corporate bond, backed by the assets of the issuing company. Large multinational companies are typically big issuers of CP. Like money market mutual funds, CP also expanded rapidly throughout the 1980s. By 1990, $130 billion in CP had been issued. By the end of the 1980s about as much CP was being issued as bank commercial and industrial loans.[8] Smaller companies in need of credit, but without sufficient assets to issue CP, turned to finance companies for credit. Finance companies are the 'bank-like' arms of big corporations like General Electric, General Motors, Ford, Chrysler, Sears, as well as specialty giants like CIT, Household Financial, and Transamerica. They actually issued more credit by the end of the decade than did the CP market. They also provided increasingly large amounts of credit to consumers, "lending $140 billion of the $728 billion in consumer installment credit outstanding at year end 1989."[9] By 1995 an important new entrant to the shadow bank sector emerged and began to grow rapidly. Like the 'trusts' before in 1907 and the 'I-banks'/'broker-dealers' in the 1920s, in the 1990s the shadow sector's new institutional stars leading the new speculative wave were called 'hedge funds.'

One of the earliest and most successful hedge funds was a company called Long Term Capital Management (LTCM). Based upon complex mathematical models, LTMC pioneered new speculative financial instruments and methods of investing that resulted in super-profits for a time. It also over-extended itself, went bust in 1997, and was bailed out by the Fed and the Treasury—much like the S&Ls and junk bonds less than a decade earlier. Not only were billions of dollars required to bail out LTCM, but the Fed also pumped additional liquidity into the economy to avoid what it feared would be a spread of the collapse of LTCM to other sectors of the financial system. Liquidity—the fuel for further excess credit expansion and debt—once again surged after the middle of the decade.

Earlier in the decade the Fed had injected liquidity into the economy to deal with the S&L and junk bond market collapses, to prevent the spread of those localized financial implosions spreading to the rest of the credit markets. The Fed additionally injected liquidity into the system to assist recovery from the 1990–92 recession. The U.S. Treasury under Clinton in 1993–94 further engineered liquidity expansion by introducing a policy to reduce long-term bond rates. Then came LTCM and further liquidity. But that would not exhaust the successive bouts of liquidity injections. In fact, the practice was just beginning.

At the end of the decade the big commercial banks were intent on getting into the game of speculative investing with both feet instead of playing at the periphery by loaning to the shadow banks and hedge funds. The excess profits that accompany speculative investing (until busts occur) were too inviting to leave to the new institutions like the hedge funds. Robert Rubin, the recent head of the giant Citigroup bank, had become Treasury Secretary in the Clinton administration. Rubin led the charge within the Clinton administration to allow the traditional banking system to engage in more speculative ventures, buying shadow institutions, or setting up their own 'in-house' shadow banks off their main balance sheet. This was achieved by a series of Clinton administration decisions, capped at the end of the decade by the repeal of the last vestige of banking regulation that once prevented banks with consumer deposits from engaging in risky speculative investing. This was the 1930s legislation, the Glass–Steagall Act. It was replaced with a new law, the Gramm–Bliley Act, that actually provided incentives to banks to enter speculative markets. At the same time, what remained of controls on capital flows was also eliminated and additional legislation was passed expanding global futures trading in oil and other commodities. This also allowed investors reaping the super-profits, individuals and institutions alike, to park their 'winnings' in offshore tax shelters without the concern of Internal Revenue Service (IRS) or government scrutiny.

All this deregulation contributed, but did not cause, the speculative excesses and growing financial fragility that was already building up within the system. The financial deregulation expanded the shadow banking sector and allowed the traditional banking sector to compete more directly with the shadow banks. It thus exacerbated the shift to more speculative forms and activity. But that shift itself was already well underway before the legislation was passed. It only served to accelerate the process. The new laws only served to formally legalize and accelerate a process that had already begun.

In the concluding years of the 1990s three U.S.-related developments occurred that further revealed the continuing growing weight and mix of speculative investing in the system. One was the 'dot.com' boom that began gaining momentum around 1997. The other was the beginning of the housing boom. A third speculative event of particular import also occurred in 1997. It was the 'Asian meltdown' of 1997–98, in which U.S. banks and the Fed were also centrally involved. The Asian crisis represented global speculation in national currencies, especially currencies of south Asian countries like Thailand, the Philippines, Korea, and others. At the center of the currency speculation were hedge funds and other shadow bank institutions, which borrowed heavily from U.S. commercial banks to enable the speculation in currency movements.[10]

The new speculative triad of tech stock boom, housing boom, and currency speculation now displaced the 'old' 1980s speculative plays in S&Ls, junk bonds, and stocks of corporate takeovers. The new would make the former pale in comparison, both in terms of magnitude and their overall negative impact on the economy. And marching together with them, in lock step, were the big U.S. commercial banks, hedge funds, and their wealthy investor clients.

The first of the three great speculative bubbles of the 1990s—dot.com stocks, housing, and foreign currency speculation—to go bust was the speculation in Asian currencies. It 'popped' in 1997, dragging down the hedge fund, LTCM. The Fed quickly bailed out LTCM. Then it also pumped up liquidity to the U.S. banks to ensure they could weather the storm from the Asian meltdown and the spreading of that crisis to loans extended by the banks to sovereign borrowers in Latin America, Asia, Russia and elsewhere. Banks and shadow banks alike were now being 'rescued' by the Fed, not only for speculative activity in the U.S. but for the same banks' speculative activity offshore.

What was also different by the late 1990s was that both financial and consumption fragility had matured to a much greater extent over the course of the intervening 15 years. Also different, the world of speculative investing was now more integrated institutionally and globally than ever before. Consequently, financial instability also had the potential to become more synchronized than ever before.

SPECULATION AND SECURITIZATION

It is no coincidence that the beginning of the home price escalation around 1997–98 corresponded almost exactly with the banks' escalating use of securitization in housing and other credit markets. Extending the initial discussion of speculation in Chapters 2 and 3 is perhaps appropriate at this point.

Investing short term in anticipation of a price rise and quick, price-driven profit has always been the essence of speculation. But in the twenty-first century that essence has been enhanced by the introduction of securitization, which takes speculative investing to an entirely new level. Securitized financial assets create an enormous new channel for generating even greater speculative profits.

Securitization is about taking a financial asset (in this case a home mortgage), creating a bond (i.e. a 'security') out of it, repackaging that bond with other types of financial assets, and creating an altogether new financial instrument (i.e. a security derived from a security) that is then sold on secondary markets. It may also mean creating an even further derived third form of speculative financial asset—i.e. credit insurance for the first and second derivative securities.

Here's an example of how it works: a home building company constructs a house, the original physical asset. The financial institution issuing the original mortgage for that house then sells the mortgage at a profit to another institution. That institution then combines a group of mortgages into a mortgage bond or residential mortgage-based security (RMBS), marks up the price for the RMBS and sells it to another financial institution. That mortgage bond is then combined with other kinds of financial assets. These other assets may be commercial paper or junk bonds, or other bonds created by combining credit card, student loan, or auto loan debts. Sometimes the mortgage bond and other bonds are each chopped up into a dozen or more parts in order to create an even larger number of financial assets to mark up and sell. Together the mortgage bonds and other assets are combined into yet another financial asset called a collateralized debt obligation (CDO)—i.e. what is called a 'derivative' financial asset. The price of the new financial instrument, the CDO, is also 'marked up' and resold. A group of CDOs may be packaged into a super-CDO, called a 'synthetic CDO.' At each step in the process, multiple layers of paper assets and profits, typical double-digit, are created. Brokers then take the CDO, charge a fee, and again sell it to still other investors. The investors then sell them off for yet another profit to government agencies, like Fannie Mae and Freddie Mac, which in turn sell them to offshore governments, central banks, other investors, and so on. Profits are made along every step of the process. Thus securitization, which starts with a real asset like a house, eventually piles paper financial assets upon paper assets, each time generating further profits. In the end, the total profits from the layers of paper assets created are many times the market price of the original physical asset of the house itself. The real asset gets the process going, but the creation of the layers of paper financial assets soon take on a dynamic of their own, driven only by the demand and price for the financial asset, increasingly divorced from the original asset itself.

A key characteristic long associated with speculative investing is 'leveraging.' Leveraging means putting up, say, 10 percent of one's own money and borrowing the other 90 percent from a bank, hedge fund, or other shadow banking institution. Since borrowing and debt are one and the same thing, leveraging is the super-highway to debt accumulation. In the 1920s the most prominent form of leveraging was stockbrokers and dealers offering 'call loans' (sometimes called margin loans) to clients purchasing stocks. Call loans enabled a stock investor to borrow to buy more stock. Securitization is similar in role in the twenty-first century to what call loans and margin buying were in the 1920s, except with far greater widespread impact on credit markets. Securitization and leveraging therefore accelerate the accumulation of debt at an even faster pace than otherwise.

Securitization first began to gain momentum in the 1980s. Of the $1 trillion in outstanding residential mortgages in 1990, approximately 35 percent had been securitized, with most sold off to the government agencies, Fannie Mae and Freddie Mac. 50 percent of new net mortgages between 1984 and 1989 were securitized. Securitization had come of age, enabling a major increase in liquidity and credit, and therefore the potential for debt.[11] Securitization also spread to other consumer markets; autos and revolving credit in particular. The Federal Reserve did not start keeping records on securitized auto and revolving credit until 1989, but in less than two years, from the start of 1989 to November 1990, 10 percent of all consumer installment debt was securitized.[12]

Profits from securitized financial instruments are exceptionally lucrative, since prices for such financial assets tend to keep rising as more investors pile into the market for quick capital gains. As investors rush in, demand for the assets accelerates and drives prices up still further, which brings more investors into the market and more demand, driving the price still further. Since these 'financial instruments' or products are made only of paper, there is no problem of running out of a supply of materials to create them, unlike other normal products like, say, cell phones which may run short of parts at some point. Only demand is a factor driving the price of these derivative financial assets. But the demand–price upward spiral cannot continue indefinitely. For example, should the price of the original physical asset, in this case the house, fall for some reason, prices for the financial assets built upon that house will collapse in turn like a house of cards. Other shifts in speculative psychology of investors, unrelated to underlying real asset values, may also cause a sharp price reversal.

Because of this possibility of severe price collapse, financial assets are 'risky.' Because of their great potential to collapse and unwind, yet another layer of financial instruments were created in the late 1990s on top of it all. These higher-level derivatives were called credit default swaps (CDSs). They were essentially insurance contracts on the mortgage bonds, CDOs, etc. If the original house price or the mortgage bonds and CDOs derived from the house collapsed, then the CDS pays off investors for their loss. But CDSs soon diverged from serving as a mere insurance instrument. Betting on collapsing or non-collapsing outcomes soon took over the CDS market and contracts were written on assets many times the value of those assets themselves. By 2007 the value of the securitized financial instruments was just under $2 trillion. The value of the derivatives, the CDSs, insuring those securitized instruments was $60 trillion.

THE TWO FACES OF SPECULATIVE INVESTING

There are two kinds of 'speculation' that need to be distinguished. There is the initial investment in a physical asset; for example, a house. Owners, real estate brokers, or buildings may 'speculate' on that original asset by taking ownership of it, waiting for the market price to rise, and in a relatively short period reselling it at a higher price. Holding an asset short term in expectation of a price rise and then selling that asset at the higher price is the 'essence' of all forms of speculation, whether in real or financial assets. Selling a real asset, the house, at a higher price is the form of speculation that might be termed 'physical asset speculation.' This is different from speculation based on the creation of financial instruments derived from that real asset, the house—i.e. mortgage bonds, bundles of mortgage bonds, bundles of bonds combined with other financial assets like commercial paper, etc. This is 'financial asset speculation' and is fundamentally different from 'physical asset speculation.'

Super-profits are possible from speculative investing. With returns on investment obtained in a short period, why invest in old-fashioned real physical assets, one might ask? Indeed, bankers and shadow banks asked that very question over the past decade, and then proceeded to shift to speculative profits. Banks and shadow banks and institutions have turned to speculative investing increasingly over the past two decades. So too have large corporations. And wealthy individual investors. Especially if the financial asset can initially be bought with borrowed money (leveraged), and if it can be quickly repackaged and sold on secondary markets around the globe (i.e. securitized) in a matter of weeks, and sometimes even days, after the initial purchase and sale of the asset.

However, to realize super-profits the entire process requires prices to continually rise all along the supply chain of financial instrument creation. And the faster the creation and greater the price escalation, the greater the profits. But should prices stop rising, and, even more dangerous, start falling on the original asset, the home, then the deflation reverberates back from the product (house) to all the financial assets built upon it. Product price deflation translates into (financial) asset price deflation. Those financial institutions and investors still holding the now deflating housing financial assets then must start recording massive losses and write-downs on those securities.

So long as prices continue to rise, it's a golden goose for banks and investors. So banks, and shadow banks in particular, found ways from 1997 to 2007 to ensure that an ever greater quantity of mortgages and the financial assets based upon them were created and made available. On the housing end that meant lowering loan requirements, eliminating down-payments, and resorting to what were called 'liar' loans to enable borrowers unqualified to buy homes to purchase them nonetheless. So what if their credit was bad, or income was insufficient to pay for the mortgage on the home? The bank was going to 'sell off' the mortgage in a new financial package and make a killing on the latter, not the original loan on the home. Banks actually sent representatives out to the field to work with brokers and real estate agents to teach them how to produce large quantities of mortgages, regardless of the quality of the mortgage or the affordability of the buyer. Thus the 'subprime' mortgage was born.

Between 2002 and 2006 in the U.S., about $4 trillion in new mortgages was issued.[13] Nearly half of that, by some estimates, were subprime mortgages—i.e. loans undertaken by those who couldn't afford them. To further stimulate mortgage creation, the banks created jumbo, option ARMs[14] (adjustable rate mortgages), no interest, reverse mortgage and other innovations to originate even more new mortgages. Again, quality of borrower was of no concern to the banks and mortgage lenders. The quantity of borrowing was. But to be absolutely clear, the initiators and instigators of the general process were the banks and shadow banks themselves.

THE FED, LIQUIDITY, AND CREDIT

The Fed enables the expansion of credit in the commercial banking system by means of buying government bonds back from the banks, changing banks minimum reserve requirements, loaning money to individual banks directly through the Fed's discount window, and by handing out 'free money' at 0 percent interest from special Fed-run auctions since December 2008.[15] By these methods the Fed helps to determine the level of credit and liquidity available in the commercial banks for lending. But it is the banks themselves that in the final analysis create the credit.

Since the 1980s, the Fed certainly has contributed significantly to injecting excess liquidity and thus credit availability in the overall financial system. Every time there's been a recession, the Fed injected liquidity. That means 1981–82, 1990–92, and 2001–03. And every time there's a financial crisis, the Fed also injects liquidity to offset banks' anticipated losses. That means 1987–88 for the stock market, 1989–92 for S&Ls and junk bonds, 1997–98 for the LTCM hedge fund and the Asian meltdown, and 2001–02 for the tech stock bust. So the Fed is no doubt a contributor. But the housing boom and bubble begins in 1997, and Fed liquidity injections did not target the housing market in particular at that time.

Yet something was fueling the housing bubble for six long years before the Fed dropped its rates to 1 percent in 2003. Credit was coming from somewhere. So where did the excess 'credit fuel' come from between 1997 and 2002? How much was the Fed responsible for the widespread and available credit between 1997 and 2007 and how much were other credit sources responsible? What were those other sources of liquidity and credit that apparently were the main driving forces for the escalating housing debt and bubble?

The Fed is not the only source determining the level of credit. There are non-Fed sources of liquidity and credit creation at work in the shadow banking system. And they have been growing over the last three decades, and since the late 1990s in particular.

The shadow banks by 2007 had grown as large as the commercial banking sector. Yet the Fed had no direct control over the process of credit creation by the shadow banks. Even in the case of the commercial banking system, over which the Fed had some degree of influence, credit creation independent of the Fed was also rising. Since the 1990s the commercial banks had begun setting up their own in-house shadow banking institutions—i.e. hedge funds, structured investment vehicles (SIVs), conduits, I-bank operations, private asset banks, and so forth. Establishing these in-house meant commercial banks did not have to report profits or losses from speculative investing activities of these bank-owned shadow institutions on their own bank balance sheets. In other words, both independent and bank-owned shadow banks proliferated in number and in terms of total assets. But it wasn't just a question of a larger number of unregulated institutions creating credit at will, i.e. outside the Fed's influence. It was also a question of the new ways in which credit was being created.

SECURITIZATION AND CREDIT

Since 1997 the shadow banking system has been the main driver of securitization. Sometimes referred to as 'financial intermediaries,' their ranks include I-banks, insurance companies, hedge funds, private pension funds, money market mutual funds, real estate investment trusts, primary dealers, broker-dealers, private banks, asset management companies, private equity firms, finance arms of big companies like GE, Ford, GM, SIVs, conduits, and others.[16]

Shadow banks aren't required to keep minimum reserves—as in the case of commercial banks. Shadow banks therefore could, and often did, lend out virtually all liquidity available to them, and in addition borrowed from traditional banks and in various short-term markets to make loans or invest directly in speculative markets. So too did commercial banks that set up their special conduits and SIVs off their regular books. The banks' shadow subsidiaries also kept virtually no reserves. By shifting loans to their off-balance sheet structures, commercial banks did not have to count loans made to their in-house hedge funds against their regular bank reserves. In this manner, they could simply keep issuing credit and dumping it into the new SIVs and conduits in order to maintain reserve levels.

An even greater boost to credit, however, was made possible by the process of securitization itself. Securitization meant that the credit extended was quickly bundled into new securities and then sold off in the secondary market. Selling off the security freed up reserves once again for additional lending. Leveraging and selling off into secondary markets enabled a level of credit to be issued many times what was previously possible without securitization. Finally, leveraging also became 'layered.' As more levels of securities from other securities were created (i.e. derivatives), additional leveraged loans were issued. Thus debt was created upon debt. An important element of speculative investing, leveraging was thus greatly expanded as a result of securitization and secondary markets for securitized assets. And with that expansion, debt was thus also greatly expanded.

In short, securitization enabled banks/shadow banks to create credit on their own, apart from and in addition to whatever the Fed created. Liquidity was expanded almost at will by the unregulated banking sector. Securitization plus layered leveraging plus secondary markets led to excessive credit creation and debt accumulation.

THE 'GLOBAL SAVINGS GLUT' AND GLOBAL LIQUIDITY

Besides the Federal Reserve and shadow banks creating credit, a third source of credit is what is sometimes referred to as the 'global savings glut.' This term, however, is a euphemism for the vast increase of wealth and investible liquid assets that has accumulated globally among the world's wealthiest investors—individual, institutional, and corporate. 'Glut' is a term that means an 'extreme, over-supply' of something. In this case, the over-supply is income and wealth concentrated among the wealthiest 1 percent of investors, financial institutions, and corporations.

Perhaps a third or more of this wealth and income resides in the U.S. Another sizeable percentage is in Europe and Asia. A good part of the so-called 'savings' is held in offshore tax havens, i.e. island nations like the Caymans, the Seychelles, Vanuatu in the Pacific, Bermuda, the Isle of Man off the west coast of England, small countries like Lichtenstein in the European Alps, the island of Cyprus in the eastern Mediterranean Sea, and private banks in countries like Luxembourg and Switzerland. Governments from the U.S. to the European Union and Japan have virtually no idea of how much is hidden in these 'global savings glut' depositories. Only in the past year or so have they even tried to find out, though with marginal or little success thus far. This part of the global savings glut represents anywhere from $6 trillion to $11 trillion in assets stuffed away in what the IRS calls 27 'special jurisdictions' where it has little or no access. That part of the 'glut' shielded from government tax collectors is not the entire stock of liquid assets. There is also the part that resides in banks and other financial institutions that is publicly reported. That part is likely larger than the tax-shielded portion held offshore. A good percentage of shadow banks' reported $10.5 trillion is probably highly liquid and available for speculative purposes.[17] Assuming that roughly half of the $10.5 trillion in shadow banks is liquid, and $5 trillion of the $11 trillion in offshore havens represents U.S. investors' share, the total amounts to at least $10 trillion in readily available liquid assets. With the U.S. share of global assets standing at around 40 percent, and conservatively doubling the $10 trillion to include other investors around the world, the grand total is well over $20 trillion. That's a $20 trillion massive pool available for borrowing and lending.

The term 'savings glut' should therefore be redefined. It's not about 'savings.' It's about the concentration of income, wealth, and investible liquid assets that has accumulated in the accounts of the wealthiest individuals, institutions and corporations worldwide. It is highly liquid financial assets that are near perfectly mobile on a global scale. And 'glut' here really means the overaccumulation and concentration of that liquidity. Speculative investors shift typically their assets between investments on short notice as opportunities arise. Their liquidity is moved around globally totally unhindered by government rules and tax collectors, unregulated, unmonitored, and largely unknown. Cash and liquid assets are injected on short notice by speculative investors into markets experiencing rapid price rise, where quick profits are taken, and then extracted from those markets on just as short a notice and invested in other projects elsewhere. Rather than call this a 'global savings glut,' it should be rightly termed the 'global money parade.'

The assets of the 'global money parade' flow back and forth around the globe taking advantage of speculative opportunities and boomlets as they rise and fall. Commodities one day. Gold the next. Oil futures. Emerging markets. Currencies. Derivatives of all kinds. Emerging markets and stocks in China and India. Copper, silver, and other minerals…and of course housing, land, and real estate in general. This global savings glut was a major force behind the speculative housing boom in many countries, not only in the U.S., during 1997–07. So what caused the housing boom in those countries, one might ask? The Fed lowering U.S. rates to 1 percent? But the Fed's contribution to liquidity and credit in 2002–06 in the U.S. pales in comparison to the global savings glut.

INEQUALITY AND LIQUIDITY

According to a McKinsey & Co. study done in 2006, the value of financial assets worldwide in 2005 was $140 trillion. The U.S. share of this was $47.6 trillion, or 33.5 percent. The euro-area was the next largest at $26.5 trillion, and emerging Asian markets at only $9.5 trillion. That $140 trillion is about three times all the real goods and services produced globally that year. The U.S. share of $47.6 trillion was about four times the U.S. GDP in that year. The U.S. was also the epicenter of global financial investment flows emanating from that total stock of $140 trillion, receiving 85 percent of global capital flows from the rest of the world; 90 percent of all global capital flows were between the U.S., the U.K. and European countries.[18] Note once again that $47.6 trillion and 85 percent represents *financial* assets, not physical assets, or output and trade of goods and services.

An approximation of this wealth of financial assets, the income of just individual wealthy investors, i.e. excluding corporations and institutions, has been estimated in the previously referenced work by economists Emmanuel Saez and Thomas Picketty.[19] They trace the wealthiest 1 percent of households since World War I using IRS data and show how the wealthiest 1 percent of households' share of after-tax income rose rapidly and dramatically during the 1920s up to the 1929 stock market crash, to about 22 percent of total income in 1929. It thereafter fell and leveled out over the next four and half decades to a low of around 8 percent, and remained at 8 percent from the 1950s to the late 1970s. It thereafter rose rapidly once again from 1980 up to 2007. It is no mere coincidence that the periods (1919–29 and 1980–2007) that witnessed the greatest income inequality trends favoring wealthy investors and corporations were also the periods experiencing growing financial and consumption fragility. Nor is it coincidental that each of the two periods culminated in major financial crises, followed by extraordinary sharp declines in the real economy.

Speculative run-ups to financial crises create exceptional income growth and wealth expansion for both wealthy individual investors and corporate institutional investors. The extraordinary income concentration provides in turn further available liquidity for investing in speculative ventures. It thus becomes a source of 'internal' liquidity expansion. The Fed and the shadow banking sector both create excess credit and liquidity that feeds ever-growing speculative investing over the course of the upswing of the financial cycle. But the global savings glut and growing income and wealth concentration and inequality in the U.S. represent huge pools of available pre-existing liquidity that serve the same function as well. All four sources have been growing since the 1980s and feeding the speculative boom and financial fragility over the past three decades.

To conclude, there are at least four major sources of liquidity expansion that occur during the run-up period to a financial crisis. These four sources in recent decades have been: (1) the Fed responding to recessions, financial instability events, and other conditions with repeated, significant liquidity injections; (2) the multiple ways by which the shadow banking sector creates internal credit on its own apart from the Fed; (3) the global savings glut/ global money parade as a source of liquidity and credit; and (4) the massive accumulation of income and near-liquid wealth by speculative investors since the early 1980s. The major sustained surge in liquidity has enabled a corresponding historic expansion of credit—and in turn borrowing and debt by consumers and businesses alike.

THE SHADOW BANKING SYSTEM POST-2000

The global money parade consists of that segment of wealthy individual investors, institutions, and corporations that commit their short-term liquid assets to speculative investing around the world, chasing and even creating financial bubbles in the process. At their disposal is perhaps as much as $20 trillion, a global pool of cash and liquid assets that shift back and forth and between various opportunities on a short-term basis, seeking projects where price escalation can deliver quick and above-historic-average investment returns. The money moves out as fast as it moves in, which serves to further magnify instability.

Wealthy investors and corporations may directly invest in the speculative opportunities, but more often deposit their investible assets with hedge funds, I-banks, private banks, etc., that carry out the investment on their behalf. The financial institutions also invest on their own organizational behalf. And since they retain few reserves, the shadow institutions regularly obtain additional funding from commercial banks. Investors and corporations leverage their investing by borrowing from shadow institutions; in turn, the shadow institutions, which keep little or no reserves themselves, borrow heavily from the commercial banks. When the borrowing is for investing in derivatives, the leveraging becomes layered. Debt rises accordingly by multiples.

A complex network of financial institutions has grown up around the expansion of global liquidity and a global money parade seeking, as a rule, more and more speculative returns instead of investment in real assets that might deliver an income stream over a longer period but not the possibility of such quick 'turns' on investing of potentially much greater return. This institutional network is largely composed of the various shadow banking institutions, but not totally. It includes central banks and, as explained, commercial banks that have become increasingly integrated with shadow banks and thus have begun orienting themselves more toward speculative investing as well.

Together, these forces, institutions, and investors are responsible for what is called a 'speculative investment shift' that has been growing in recent decades. However, that shift could not occur without the expansion of forms of credit and in turn liquidity that make borrowing, leveraging, short-term price pursuit, quick returns on investing, and other elements of speculative investing possible.

In the theory sections of this book, in Chapter 2 specifically, the evolution of the shadow banking institutional heart of the speculative shift was described, beginning with 1900. In Table 7.1 in this chapter an estimate of the growth of shadow banks was provided as a further update. But those estimates, from 1900 to 1990, are still only partially complete. As was noted, it is not only the shadow banking sector that is driving the speculative shift. A good part of the regulated, commercial banking sector had joined the global money parade as well since 1990. They provide significant amounts of loan capital to the shadow sector and speculative ventures. They also now participate directly, by setting up their own hedge funds and, until recently, diverting massive amounts of capital to their 'off-book' subsidiaries, the SIVs and conduits. Some estimates are that $5.2 trillion in commercial bank assets were thus 'offloaded' to their SIVs and conduits in the last decade. There is no longer any clear distinction between shadow and commercial banks, and both now increasingly participate in speculative investing. As will be discussed later in this chapter, the commercial and investment banks (now fully blended) have been able to increase their cash on hand in 2009 by about $1 trillion. They have done this by lending heavily to the new speculative ventures that have emerged since spring 2009, not by lending to normal job-producing businesses in the U.S. Lending to the latter has fallen for nine consecutive months, while lending to offshore speculative markets is where bank funds have gone. Banks' profits in the U.S. consequently recovered. But that recovery is due to lending to speculative markets like exchange-traded funds, emerging market funds, Asian properties, commodities, gold and currencies, and the like.

In June 2008, Treasury Secretary Tim Geithner publicly estimated the size of the shadow banking sector (see Table 7.2). This was summarized and reported subsequently by one of the more reputable sources tracking the evolution of the current crisis, the *RGE Monitor*.[20] Geithner's and the *RGE Monitor*'s, summary estimated only part of the shadow and commercial banking sectors', total respective assets. The summary showed that the shadow banking sector in late 2007 was even larger than the commercial sector (disregarding the latter's participation in the shadow sector). Shadow banking assets were worth $10.5 trillion compared to commercial banking's $10.0 trillion. That compares with Table 7.1 above, also a partial representation of the two sectors, with the shadow sector's assets at $4.9 trillion and the commercial sector's at $4.4 trillion. And that's just for the U.S.-based institutions. Table 2.6 from Chapter 2 is reproduced below as Table 7.2 for the purposes of immediate comparison.

But Tables 7.1 and 7.2 are only partial representations of the scope and magnitude of the shadow sector and the speculative investing shift it has been driving (though once again not the sole driver). A more complete compilation of all the shadow banking institutions and their total asset base has yet to be undertaken. But it is more than $10 trillion, and far more when considered on a global basis. How much of that has been funneling into speculative investments has also not been accurately determined to date. That would require a matching up of shadow (and commercial shadow) assets with those markets that are clearly speculative-investing focused. Table 7.3 is a more comprehensive list of shadow sector financial institutions and the corresponding financial markets that have been the favored loci of speculative investing.

Table 7.2   Shadow versus Traditional Banking System, 2007

Banking Sector	Assets ($ trillions)
Traditional Banking	10.0
Top 5 Bank Holding Companies	6.0
Other Banks and Savings Institutions	4.5
Shadow Banking	10.5
Asset Backed Commercial Paper Conduits	
Structured Investment Vehicles	2.2
Auction Rate Preferred Securities	
Variable Rate Notes	
Triparty Repos	2.5
Hedge Funds	1.8
Top 5 Investment Banks	4.0

Source: *RGE Monitor*, May 26, 2009.

Table 7.3   Shadow Institutions and Speculative Markets (partial list)

Shadow Banking Institutions	Preferred Speculative Markets
Investment banks	Securitized Subprime Mortgages
Brokerages & Dealers	Securitized Commercial Mortgages
Hedge Funds	Asset-Backed Commercial Paper
SIVs and Conduits	Securitized auto, student, credit cards
Finance Companies	Leveraged Loans
Private Equity firms	Auction Backed Securities
Mutual Funds & Money Market Funds	Sovereign CDS
Monolines (bond insurer companies)	Reverse Repo markets
Real Estate Investment Trusts	Over-the-Counter Derivatives Markets
Pension Funds	Exchange Traded Funds (currencies)
Private Asset Banks	Dark Pools (stocks)
Insurance Companies	Emerging Markets Funds
Government-Sponsored Enterprises	Global Commodities Markets
(Fannie Mae, Freddie Mac)	China Real Estate

There are three main global markets that encompass some of the above and yet extend beyond. Not all the investments that occur in these markets are necessarily speculative, but a growing proportion are becoming so. These 'big three' are global stock markets, global real estate, and global derivatives. The total value of stock markets globally is approximately $100 trillion, real estate about $75 trillion, and total derivatives markets (opaque and still unregulated) $683 trillion (in 'notional' terms or total trades) and $21 trillion (in potential real losses). The latter, global markets for derivatives, are all virtually speculative in nature. They have grown from a 'mere' $100 trillion in 2002 to $516 trillion in 2007 and still surged through the first year of the financial crisis, to $683 trillion by June 2008.

A panoply of specialized instruments has also been created in recent decades by which the institutions invest in the speculative markets. They are too numerous to list, but the most noted are: residential mortgage-backed securities (RMBS), commercial mortgage-backed securities (CMBS), asset-backed securities (ABSs), collateralized debt obligations (CDOs,) synthetic CDOs, leveraged buyouts (LBOs), collateralized loan obligations (CLOs), credit default swaps (CDSs), over-the-counter interest rate swaps and currency swaps, repos, and so on.

A PARTIAL SUMMARY

A partial summary is perhaps appropriate at this point. What has been described thus far are the fundamental, enabling causes of the financial implosion of 2007 and the Epic Recession that has followed. It started with the explosion in available global liquidity driven by various sources. That liquidity is a necessary requisite for the historic expansion of credit. The excess liquidity and credit must be invested somewhere. Real asset investment—i.e. investing in real physical assets like structures, factories, equipment, products, and services, etc.—is unable to fully absorb the more rapid expansion of liquid assets. And if it could, it still does not yield the rate of returns possible from investing speculatively in financial and other non-real assets. Financial institutions expand and arise to channel this excess liquidity from and to investors becoming increasingly oriented to speculative ventures. A global money parade of investors and institutions arises to pursue speculative opportunities. Various new financial instruments and markets, primary and secondary, are created to absorb the investing. Since speculative investing is short term and more risky, an increase in leveraging and borrowing occurs in the wake of the new instruments' and markets' creation. The consequence is a corresponding acceleration in debt accumulation. A progressive relative shift to more profitable and 'quick' speculative investing grows over time, creating financial fragility and instability with it.

Excess liquidity, excess credit, financial institutions increasingly focused on speculative markets, the growth of those markets, and a shift toward a greater weight and mix of speculative investing, together produce a significant rise in debt accumulation. And in that debt accumulation lie the seeds for the inevitable volatility that leads to financial busts, and in turn the extraordinary credit contractions that produce Epic Recessions.

FROM EXCESS CREDIT TO EXCESSIVE DEBT

Excessive debt is a reflection of excessive credit creation and liquidity availability. The massive and historic volume of the debt accumulated since 1980—financial, business, consumer, and government—is represented by the Fed's *Flow of Funds* dataset. Presented in Chapter 1 as Table 1.3, it is reproduced below as Table 7.4.

Table 7.4   Total Debt, U.S. 1978–2008 ($ billions, seasonally adjusted)

Year	Total Domestic	Total Households	Mortgage	Consumer	Non-Financial Business	Financial Business	Government (Fed/state/local)
1978	3,623	1,105	708	311	1,188	412	1,079
1988	11,596	3,043	2,054	745	3,410	2,145	2,997
1998	22,554	5,920	4,057	1,441	5,410	6,328	4,895
2008	50,666	11,434*	8,063*	2,595	11,153	19,486*	8,593

*$2.4 trillion of mortgage debt is adjusted from the Federal Reserve's data, reducing household mortgage debt by that amount and adding the same to financial business debt, based on Moody Inc.'s prediction of 8 million foreclosures in the current recession cycle. That debt must, upon foreclosure, revert back to the financial institution or else be written off as a loss. The $2.4 trillion is estimated based on 8 million foreclosures on mortgage loans averaging $300,000 that were incurred by homeowners during the residential mortgage boom of 2002–07. Total household debt includes elements other than mortgage and consumer debt not indicated by an additional column.

Source: U.S. Federal Reserve, *Flow of Funds Accounts of the United States*, First Quarter 2009, Washington D.C., June 11, 2009, Table D.3, "Debt Outstanding by Sector," p. 8.

The above data show the largest contributing column to total domestic debt accumulation over the preceding three decades is 'financial business,' contrary to the conventional wisdom that it has been the federal government as the big debt accumulator. Between 1978 and 1988, and then again between 1998 and 2008, the financial sector multiplied its debt load many times that of the government, consumer, and even non-financial business sectors. Moreover, it is impossible to argue that this volume and rate of increase in financial institution debt reflects loans and credit extended only to invest in real, physical structures, equipment, and other categories of physical assets. It is likely that a very large proportion of the debt reflects speculative investments—i.e. investment in financial assets, securities, instruments, and derivatives of various kinds for speculative purposes.

The total 2008 U.S. debt of $50.6 trillion from all sources represents approximately 3.6 times GDP in 2008. That compares to a debt to GNP ratio in 1929 of 2.9 times. In other words, the debt load today is greater, when measured in terms of output, than it was on the eve of the Great Depression of the 1930s.[21] Today's $50 trillion U.S. debt is also roughly equal to the total net worth of all the approximate 114 million households in the U.S.

Not only is the magnitude of the debt in 2008 greater than in 1929, but its quality is also more fragile and potentially volatile. First, it is probably more highly leveraged. Second, as of late 2009 the total debt has not really been 'worked off,' as in the 1930s, but only 'moved around,' from bank and shadow bank balance sheets to government balance sheets. That will mean eventual further build-up of debt on bank balance sheets while the 'old' debt still remains on government balance sheets. It is not likely that the government will be able to afford a 'rescue' of recent dimensions (2008–09) again should another financial crisis event occur.

Prior to 2007, the government share of total debt has been the consequence of massive income transfers from general taxpayers to wealthy households (mostly investors) and corporations since 1980, as well as bailouts, again at taxpayer expense, for the same when they over-extend and financial crises ensue. For example, in the early 1980s Ronald Reagan's tax cuts amounted to a then unheard of $752 billion, 80 percent of which went to the top 20 percent and corporations. He was outdone by George W. Bush who, in his first term alone, pushed through $3.7 trillion in tax cuts, once again to the wealthiest 20 percent and corporations. Repeated bailouts of financial and other non-financial businesses at taxpayers' expense since the early 1980s ran up the government's share of total debt still further. In 2008–09 the totals for bailouts of banks, car companies, insurance companies, credit card companies, mortgage lenders, and a host of others amounted to between $3 trillion and $4 trillion at minimum, $2.7 trillion from the Fed and another $1 trillion from the Treasury and Congress. As hundreds of regional banks continue to fail, the tab will no doubt grow even larger.

Consumers' share of the $50 trillion debt totals represents a distinctly different set of causal factors. Contrary to media spin, the lion's share of their debt is not due to consumers' overly conspicuous consumption. It is due to stagnating real weekly earnings over three decades and consumers, out of necessity, resorting to greater installment, credit card, and home refinancing debt in order to offset stagnating real earnings and income. As one financial analyst admitted, "capitalism's dirty little secret" was that "excessive [consumer] lending was the only way to maintain the living standards of the vast bulk of the population at a time when wealth was being concentrated in the hands of an elite."[22]

Those who blame the consumer for their rising debt conveniently ignore the rapidly escalating costs of necessities such as higher education, insurance and medical bills running wild, and the rising costs of basic transportation (autos, gasoline, etc.) over the past three decades. Prior to 2000, consumers offset rising costs by working longer hours, putting spouses to work, drawing down savings, and using installment credit and credit cards. But by 2007 most spouses had been put to work, savings had been decimated and the savings rate turned negative, and refinancing of homes was no longer an option. Only credit card debt remained, but after 2007, terms for card usage rapidly tightened and monthly credit card rates, penalties, and fees were steadily raised. According to the American Bankers Association, household debt as a proportion of disposable income was only 60 percent in 1980. It had risen to 90 percent by 2000, then accelerated to 133 percent by year end 2007.[23] This amazing increase in 'consumer fragility,' it is important to note, was not due simply to raising debt levels. It was due to falling real income levels as well.

As the Fed's *Flow of Funds* data show, the overwhelmingly greatest share of total debt is financial institutions' debt. More than $19 trillion in debt held by financial businesses in 2008 represents about 140 percent of GDP in 2008. In contrast, total government debt was only about 60 percent of GDP— about the same percentage it was 50 years earlier in 1958. And consumers' installment debt was only 18 percent of GDP (70 percent if home mortgages are included). So it is something of a myth that consumers are the main source of the excessive debt accumulation, or that profligate government is the cause of the massive debt accumulation of recent years.

The primary source of the massive debt run-up is business—financial business in particular. And within financial business, the majority of that debt accumulation is attributable to the shadow banking sector, the main funding sector of speculative investing in financial assets. As one well-known *New York Times* financial columnist put it, "In 1958, 75 percent of financial sector debt was on the books of traditional financial institutions—banks, savings and loans, finance companies. Now the proportion is 18 percent."[24]

Whereas financial institution debt more than tripled in the course of just a decade after 1998, non-financial business debt also doubled. A good part of this was debt incurred to pay investors. For example, with profits in general at a 100-year high, the S&P 500 companies between 2004 and 2008 paid out about $2.6 trillion to buy back stock and pay dividends to investors.[25] And that is just for the Fortune 500 companies. Thousands, and perhaps tens of thousands of other large and medium-sized corporations no doubt did the same. Much of that $2.6 trillion delivered to investors by the Fortune 500 likely found its way into hedge funds, private equity, and other shadow bank institutions committed heavily to financial asset and other forms of speculative investing. Part of that $2.6 trillion payout was borrowed. Thus corporations took on debt to pay the dividends and stock buybacks in addition to financing it from the record internal profits.[26]

THE DOT.COM BUST

The dot.com market surged after 1997, along with the take-off of the housing bubble, the collapse of the speculative bubble in Asian currencies, and the implosion of LTCM, the hedge fund. All these speculative bubbles began circa 1997–98. To date, there has been very little attempt by economists or finance analysts to explain the linkages between these four events. Together, they represent a harbinger, a warning, of the even more synchronized global financial bubble that would burst in 2007–08.

Between 1996 and 2000, tech stock prices surged to record levels. Many tech stocks represented companies that existed only on paper, with no product or revenues. Stock prices of these revenue-less companies often escalated to more than $100 per share. Rising prices drove demand for the stocks, which pushed prices still higher. Investment was not based on what kind of long-run income or profits the tech companies might generate, only on how fast or high their stock prices might go. It was a classic speculative play, with short-term price gains as the primary objective. Investors from around the world piled into the U.S. tech stock goldmine. Insider trading and stock manipulation was rife. But while it lasted, it was a profits bonanza for many.

By 2000, several events signaled investors that the speculative run in tech stock prices was about to finish. Tech stock prices plummeted, taking much of the technologies-heavy stock index, the NASDAQ, with them. That led to a collapse in levels of real technology investment, equipment, and products.

The souring mood soon spilled over to more traditional manufacturing and construction stocks, and thereafter to service sector stocks. The recession of 2001 was underway.

The dot.com stock bubble and collapse was forecasted by one of the few prescient economists at the time, Robert Shiller of Yale. Shiller asked what the connections were between the stock collapse, the housing boom, LTCM, the Asian currency crises, and the sovereign debt crises in Russia and Mexico circa 1997–2000. His answer: price changes—inflationary and deflationary—were amplifying the bubbles, on both the upswing and the downswing. Fundamentally, as Shiller observed, "speculative instability appears to be increasingly important."[27] The absolute number of speculative investors had grown significantly since the 1980s, the scope of speculative markets had expanded and the kinds of risks taken were broadening over a wide range of trading. Shiller argued that 1996–2000 witnessed the biggest 'speculative upsurge' in stock market history, with the Dow Jones rising from 3,600 in 1994 to 11,722 by January 2000. Moreover, it was a truly synchronized 'world stock market boom,' a 'millennium boom.' Shiller added that there was no way that fundamentals in the real economy justified the extent of the stock price highs. Nor was the collapse caused by the 'Fed Model'—falling interest rates engineered by the Fed. Neither fundamentals nor the Fed was capable of provoking the magnitude of the more than 8,000-point stock price run-up or the bubble's eventual price collapse.[28] The prime cause was speculative activity feeding the stock price escalation. To Shiller, the Asian currency crisis, the dot.com boom, and the housing bubble were "three separate crises [that] fed on each other."[29]

Shiller saw a similar process at work with regard to the parallel development simultaneously occurring in the housing bubble. Like the tech stock bubble, the emerging housing bubble was not primarily due to the Fed lowering interest rates, nor due to housing materials cost increases. As he observed, "there is no hope of explaining home price increases in the U.S. solely in terms of building costs, population, or interest rates."[30] And, furthermore, "the interest rate cuts cannot explain the general nine year upward trend that we have seen in the housing market. The housing boom period was three times as long as the period of low interest rates, and the housing boom was accelerating when the Fed was increasing interest rates in 1999."[31] He further noted a clear relationship between rapidly concentrating wealth and income, on the one hand, and the growing tendency toward speculative bubbles, on the other. Each speculative bubble in turn tended to create a further uneven distribution of wealth, resulting in an ever larger pool of liquidity feeding subsequent speculative bubbles, and so on.

Billionaire hedge fund investor George Soros noted a similar long-term speculative trend, wherein a decades-long, general 'super' bubble was being fed by a series of more market-specific speculative bubbles—i.e. "not just a one boom-bust process or bubble," but a "longer-term super bubble."[32]

But neither Soros or Shiller provide an adequate institutional explanation of the greater speculative trend or the increasing frequency of discrete speculative bubbles—whether in housing, stocks, commodities trading, national currencies, or whatever. The 'speculator' appears as the individual common stock buyer, homebuyer, or lender. The role of the shadow banking sector is left largely undeveloped in their analyses. Consequently, their solutions are limited to the belief either that the Fed can reflate the economy to resolve the crisis, or in the necessity of implementing technical, incremental measures to dampen the growing speculative social psychology.

THE JOBLESS RECESSION OF 2001–04

Epic recession is not just about financial fragility, financial instability, and financial crises, but also about consumption fragility and how both forms of fragility—financial and consumption—overlap and feed back upon each other, causing a further decline than what otherwise might occur in a normal recession. Financial fragility grows for businesses, bank and non-bank alike, as their cash flow declines while their costs of debt servicing rises. Similar, consumption fragility occurs for households and consumers as their disposal income declines as their debt servicing costs rise. These are two concepts different from what economists ordinarily consider 'investment' and 'consumption.' These are deeper, broader concepts that take 'investment' and 'consumption' and expand them to consider the impact of credit, debt, and speculation. They are, furthermore, concepts whose development and evolution is also contingent upon the interactions of debt, deflation, and default within the process of economic contraction.

The dot.com bust was clearly a financial instability event. But it did not precipitate an Epic Recession. This financial instability event was more like that which occurred in 1884, 1890, or even 1987. Its impact was contained to markets for common stocks. It was not of sufficient magnitude and it did not spread to other credit markets. But the recession it provoked had the effect of causing both financial and consumption fragility to deteriorate further. So when the next financial instability event occurred, the 2007 subprime implosion, the economy was more unstable than in 2000. In other words, it was generally 'more fragile.' Moreover, the 2007 financial crisis was far more serious than the tech stock crash of 2000–01. The greater financial fragility, combined with the more serious financial event of 2007, created a far more serious financial implosion in 2007. The failure to check and contain that financial implosion in 2007–08 led to yet further financial fragility and, ultimately, to the banking panic of 2008. That more serious financial fragility reacted with the greater consumption fragility, and together drove the economy into Epic Recession.

Measured in terms of GDP, the 2001 recession was a relatively short affair. The recession officially began in March 2001 and ended November 2001, lasting a brief eight months.[33] The economy thereafter declined from early 2001 through September, with only residential housing showing any signs of moderate growth. The decline only slowed at the end of September, with the terrorist attack on the World Trade Center in New York and the subsequent surge in U.S. government spending for both domestic security and the war in Afghanistan. Accelerated spending on national defense stopped the fall, rising 12.5 percent in the fourth quarter of 2001 compared to the previous third quarter (which grew only 2.4 percent from the second quarter).[34] At the same time, the Fed cut interest rates dramatically from 3.5 percent to 1.75 percent from September through December 2001. The trough of the recession occurred in November.

The decline in GDP terms may have been checked after eight months, but the collapse of production and jobs continued for years thereafter. The most defining characteristic of the 2001 recession, therefore, was not its relatively short duration nor the quick fiscal-monetary stimulus and GDP turnaround. What characterized it most was the very weak recovery that followed, despite the extraordinary stimulus and the very long time—nearly four years—it would take the economy to generate jobs. For the first ten months, jobs were lost just as fast, or faster, as during eight of the ten postwar recessions, including the first ten months of the 2007 recession. While the pace of job losses slowed after ten months, the number of job losses nevertheless continued to grow for a full 30 months after the recession began in March 2001.[35] And it would take 46 months for jobs lost to recover to pre-2001 recession levels—in other words, a 'jobless recession.' According to the U.S. Department of Labor, there were 132,527,000 jobs in the economy in March 2001. It wasn't until January 2005—46 months later—that 132,573,000 workers were employed once again.[36]

The jobless recession of 2001–05 is a reflection of a growing trend in the U.S. in the postwar period. Since the 1945 period that trend is for jobless recoveries to stretch out longer and longer. In the 1948 recession it took only 20 months to regain total lost jobs; in 1973, 25 months; 1981, 28 months; and July 1990, 31 months. A summary of the job recovery data is given in Table 7.5.

Table 7.5   Job Recoveries in the U.S. Economy, 1948–2005

No. of Months to Recover Lost Jobs	
November 1948	20 months
November 1973	25 months
July 1981	28 months
July 1990	31 months
March 2000	46 months

Job Growth After Three Years (%)	
1948–52	9.5
1973–77	5.4
1981–85	3.9
1990–94	0.5
2001–03	−0.25

Source: Economic Policy Institute, *Jobs Picture*, February 4, 2005.

An important question is, what is the relationship between growing consumption fragility and ever larger jobless recoveries? There is clearly a relationship between increasing financial fragility and the growing frequency and magnitudes of financial crises over the last several decades. What about consumption fragility and the rate of collapse of consumption spending during the downturn of the real economy following a financial crisis? Financial fragility may exacerbate the magnitude of the financial crisis, thereby producing an extraordinary credit crunch and collapse of investment. But consumption fragility may simultaneously result in an extraordinary collapse of consumer spending at the same time following the more severe financial instability event.

The jobless recovery of 2001–05 certainly played a key role in exacerbating the already growing consumption fragility in the U.S. economy. For example, the average annual growth rates for wages and salaries in the five years following the end of a recession has deteriorated since 1982. The growth of wages in the five-year period following the 1982 recession averaged 4.4 percent. Following 1991, that average wage growth had fallen to only 2.4 percent. From 2001 to 2006 it had declined to only 1.9 percent, the lowest on record. The postwar average for the ten official recessions in the U.S. was 3.8 percent average annual wage growth for five years; 2001–06 experienced only half that normal postwar average.[37] The increasingly weak recoveries in jobs and wages following recessions are a clear indication of growing consumption fragility. They also explain in part why middle- and working-class households have had to turn to a greater use of debt to maintain consumption and living standards. Ironically, however, turning to debt means a further deterioration of consumption fragility—since that fragility is a function of both income and debt. As wage income falls or as debt rises, consumption fragility grows. And both have been occurring since the 1980s. By 2007 the condition was particularly 'fragile.'

The 2001 recession further raises the question of whether traditional fiscal-monetary policy measures are becoming relatively less effective in stimulating job recovery and income growth for the majority of the labor force. Those traditional policies may boost other economic indicators and GDP. But perhaps those indicators, GDP in particular, provide a poor reflection of what's really going on in the real economy.[38]

And if traditional fiscal-monetary measures are proving increasingly ineffective in ensuring jobs and wage recovery from a 'normal' recession like 2001, what does that portend for recovery from an obviously more severe Epic Recession like 2007–10? Finally, to pursue the logic one further step, if job and wage recovery proves even more difficult post-2010, what will this mean for consumption fragility and the next financial crisis event?

In terms of jobs and wages, the 2001 'normal' recession was not really as brief or mild as many claim. The vast majority of wage-earners were left in a very weak—i.e. 'fragile'—position when the next economic crisis erupted in 2007. Their debt had risen and their disposable income had fallen. At the same time, financial fragility was worsening within the system as well. How the two forms of fragility—consumption and financial—interacted and fed back upon each other between 2007 and 2008 has important consequences.

THE $27 TRILLION NON-RECOVERY

The 2001-2006 period was not only one of the weakest economic recoveries in the postwar period, but was astoundingly weak when considered in relationship to the massive government stimulus effort introduced into the U.S. economy between 2001-2006. A mountain of stimulus was injected, but produced a 'molehill' economic recovery nonetheless.

Starting in 2001 for each of the next four years major income tax cuts were passed favoring wealthy investors in particular by reducing capital gains, dividends, and inheritance taxes to record post-1945 lows and culminating in a series of industry-specific corporate tax cuts in 2004–05. Without those capital incomes tax cuts, or the reductions in corporate income tax rates and acceleration of capital depreciation, the record corporate profits, dividend payouts, and stock buybacks that followed would not have been possible. The total amount of the tax cuts, 80 percent of which accrued to the top 20 percent of households and corporations, was around $3.7 trillion, give or take a trillion. Targeting investors and corporations, the cuts should have resulted in huge increases in fixed investment, equipment and inventories—but didn't. So where did the money from the tax cuts—i.e. the $3.7 trillion-plus in liquidity injected into the system—go, one might therefore ask?

In addition to tax cuts, starting in the fourth quarter of 2001 defense spending grew by more than 10 percent per quarter on average for the next three years. The Fed, we have seen, added to the stimulus by dropping interest rates from 6 percent in early 2001 to 1.75 percent at the end of the year, and then in steps to 1 percent by 2003, where rates were kept until summer 2004. That kind of combined major fiscal and monetary stimulus should have accelerated investment in real assets and GDP at least two to three times greater than it had between 2002–06. However, except for residential housing, which grew moderately in 2002, real asset investment actually fell throughout all of 2002. GDP growth in 2002 was an anemic 1.8 percent. 2003 was also below the historic long run. In the best year, 2004, the economy grew only 3.6 percent, and in 2005–06 began to slow once again. By the third quarter of 2006, the U.S. economy was already headed for recession with a growth rate of only 0.8 percent.[39]

In other words, $3.7 trillion in tax stimulus, an estimated $1–2 trillion in additional Iraq–Afghanistan–Homeland Security war spending, and the record low 1 percent interest rates, were together only able to generate a recovery that was the weakest of all postwar recessions. Prior post-recession recoveries were significantly greater and with nowhere near the fiscal-monetary stimulus of 2001–06.[40] The question is, why so little for so much? And if so little after so much, what does this mean for recovery from the much worse downturn of 2007–10?

In 2002 it looked quite possible that the economy would fall back in a 'double-dip' recession. Especially worrisome to business and policymakers alike was the slow drift toward deflation at the time. In 2002, wholesale prices had turned negative and prices of manufactured goods fell 1.5 percent. Only prices for services, led by rapidly rising medical services costs, and escalating oil and energy prices due to global commodities speculation, kept the consumer price index (CPI) barely in positive territory. In comments to the November 2002 Federal Reserve's Open Market Committee, the then Fed chairman, Alan Greenspan, was reported to have said: "we are dealing with what basically is a latent deflationary type of economy, and we are all acutely aware of the implications of that kind of economy."[41] Ben Bernanke, then a Fed governor, a Greenspan protégé, and the future Fed chairman, followed Greenspan with a paper presented before the National Economists Club in Washington D.C. entitled: "Deflation: Making Sure 'It' Doesn't Happen Here." In it Bernanke outlined possible measures the Fed could take to prepare to prevent further deflationary pressures.

Greenspan's and Bernanke's concern is not surprising. With no major growth in real asset investment after 2001, with unemployment and industrial production still declining, and the economy barely responding to massive investor tax cuts in 2002, and with ballooning defense spending—the only game left in town was housing. The Fed was apparently willing to risk a housing bubble by over-stimulating the housing sector if it meant staving off a double-dip recession. So, too, was the Bush administration, with its plans to launch its Gulf War now well underway.

$27 trillion represents the amount by which total debt increased from 2000 to 2007, from roughly $22 trillion to $49 trillion. Only a small percentage of that represents government debt due to fiscal policies (tax and spending) to stimulate the economy. Or Fed monetary stimulus to generate the same. And as just argued, it had little impact except for housing. The lion's share of the debt accumulation was business-driven, accrued by investors and corporations. So did the investors-stockholders borrow to invest in real assets—i.e. structures, equipment, inventories, etc. that create jobs? Not much. Business investment in equipment, software, and buildings rose by only 21.7 percent over the five-year period from 2001 through 2006, or about 3.6 percent per year on average.[42] And most of that was construction of residential and commercial properties. With that kind of weak private sector investment growth, it is not surprising that the recovery of the real economy from the 2001 recession was "the worst since World War II."[43] So what did the massive borrowing spree of $27 trillion produce?

The answer is not all that complex. The credit and stimulus flowed largely *out* of the U.S. economy or, alternatively, *into* speculative investment in financial instruments—or both. A significant part was diverted to foreign markets in the form of foreign direct investment, to finance the boom in emerging market economies like China and elsewhere in Asia and Latin America. It flowed offshore into the 27 offshore tax havens identified by the IRS as 'special jurisdictions' to which it had no access. From those convenient locations and the hedge fund and shadow bank institutions domiciled in them, tens of trillions of dollars and currencies are electronically available in an instant to slosh around the world in search of speculative bubbles and super-profits—from stock market to stock market; from commodities bubble to commodities bubble in oil, metals, grain, and gold; from currency of country A to currency of country B; from derivatives to derivatives, futures trading to CDSs, and, of course, between residential and commercial property markets around the world, leveraged and securitized all the way. That is, the 'global money parade'—sometimes misnamed the 'global savings glut.'

THE FINANCIAL CRISIS OF 2007

The tip of the speculative iceberg in the U.S. during this period, 2002–06, was the subprime mortgage market of the residential housing sector. As noted previously, the housing boom in the U.S. began around 1997–98. It continued through the 2001 recession, a factor that accounts in part for the relatively moderate character of that normal recession. But by 2002 this segment of the market was approaching saturation. Most of the qualified homebuyers had bought homes in this cycle at that point. The lowering of Fed rates to 1 percent coincided with a relative shift by banks and lenders toward mortgage loans to less-qualified buyers. In 2003 the securitization of mortgages also accelerated. Mortgage originators deepened the practice of 'originate and distribute' and the reselling of packaged securities on secondary markets. Mortgage lenders therefore turned increasingly to selling homes to non-qualified buyers. With securitization and secondary markets, quality of borrower was unimportant. The mortgages would soon be repackaged and sold off before the new buyers ran into debt servicing problems. Anyway, that wouldn't happen so long as interest rates remained at 1 percent. Like speculators always and everywhere, a slowdown, cessation, or decline of rising prices was not thought possible. Or at least, the thinking went, when it does turn down, we can always time the market and get out before the collapse.

It all held together with financial 'chewing gum.' So long as housing asset prices continued to rise, so too could speculative financial instruments based upon those real assets continue to rise—and even continue to accelerate even faster than the price of the original assets. Financial securities based upon the real asset price inflation were able to springboard off the real assets, creating their own internal price momentum based on speculative demand for the securitized assets. But the wider the eventual spread, or gap, between real asset price inflation for real houses, and financial asset price inflation based on financial instruments, the greater the financial fragility and potentially more serious the eventual financial bust.

At some point, the over-building and over-supply of real housing assets was destined to catch up with the real housing demand. Real assets are subject to both supply and demand forces. Not so for speculative financial assets, that are driven largely by demand only. By mid year 2006 it was becoming clear that a growing percentage of subprime buyers could no longer make payments on their mortgage debt. Having taken on mortgage debt at temporary 1 percent rates, with no down-payments, no income qualification, and often 100 percent financing—all designed by lenders to generate a high volume of loans to 'originate and distribute,' securitize, and resell—subprime homebuyers began to default on their debt servicing terms by 2005–06 once the Fed began raising interest rates from the 1 percent floor in 2003 to 6.25 percent, and their 1 percent rates began to reset. In classical terms, their debt servicing costs were now rising faster than their real disposable income. Defaults were inevitable.

Noticing the early trend in 2006, the more savvy investors in mortgages and securitized instruments began abandoning the market. The artificial excess demand driving mortgage asset prices was simultaneously being undermined by the over-production of real housing assets, on the one hand, and by a basic shift in the speculative psychology of investors on the other. Housing prices, as well as prices of financial securities derived from that housing—i.e. mortgage bonds, RMBSs, asset-backed commercial paper, etc.—therefore both began to decline. By mid 2006 the U.S. housing bubble was fundamentally finished. Yet the boom in housing speculation would drag on for another year while the bubble only slowly deflated and less savvy investors and speculators convinced themselves it would go on forever. As is typical among speculative investors in the early phase of reversal of the market, the remaining majority of investors continued to anticipate that the 'average opinion of average opinion' was that subprimes, subprime securities, and housing in general was still a profitable play—to paraphrase the economist, Keynes.[44] That the price run had only slowed temporarily or was 'gathering its breath' before another leg up, was often the wishful thinking of 'late' speculators.

Essentially a gambler, the average professional investor is generally an overly-optimistic person who likes to believe the immediate and long-run future is always the same as the immediate recent past. To him/her, time is constant, not variable. His/her horizon is never too far back or too far forward. He/she is thus repeatedly the victim of his/her own short-term myopia. Thus, the 'average opinion' continued to believe and to gamble that the golden goose that was the residential mortgage market would continue to lay its golden eggs, despite all the evidence that the goose was clearly in the late stages of menopause by mid 2006. After all, the goose had been laying since 1997, hadn't it? Why should it simply stop now, a decade later? So the speculator 'herd' mentality believed.

Shadow banking financial institutions, like Bear Stearns and Lehman Brothers, continued to invest in a major way in the housing and commercial property sectors despite its declining phase, buying up companies with a heavy position in mortgages and the securitized assets based on them. So too did traditional banks like Citigroup, Bank of America, and others as they tried to get a larger share of the super-profits from speculation in the mortgage markets.

Lehman Brothers, for example, embarked upon a major debt-financed binge well past 2006, acquiring multiple companies in both the residential and commercial mortgage property markets in the U.S. and offshore as late as May 2007. Lehman significantly expanded its leverage and debt in the process, buying companies with financial assets based on housing that had already peaked and in some cases were coming down. Lehman was also an early and major investor in subprimes, leveraged buyouts, and apartment buildings commercial property from the early 2000s on. "Between 2003 and 2007, Lehman securitized more than $700 billion in assets, according to its annual filings. About 85 percent of these, or about $600 billion, were residential mortgages."[45] Acquisitions, debt, leverage, securitization, subprimes, commercial property, derivatives, CDSs, etc.—the story was the same for many shadow bank institutions, and increasingly as well for commercial banks like Citigroup and Bank of America who were diving deeply into speculative markets. It was all becoming the norm for investing by mid decade. And as the speculative pricing and euphoria grew, so did leveraged debt rise in magnitude and decline in quality, and with it the costs of servicing that debt and general financial fragility.

The surge in speculative investing was not limited to subprime mortgages, however. More and more financial assets were bundled into bonds and then repackaged into various derivative financial instruments, CDOs, in the run-up to the August 2007 financial bust. Other favorites included taking auto loans and securitizing them. Or student loans and credit cards. Other commercial property mortgages (apartments, resorts, hotels, offices, etc.). Loans for LBOs, M&As. Business loans by banks to non-financial companies (CLOs). Bonds were created out of anything that remotely resembled some future income, including certain rock star music performers' future concert sales. Or beer pub chains future revenue. Combinations of the above were mixed, and often 'salted' with slices of commercial paper issued by non-financial corporations, school district bonds, and municipal bonds of cities and water districts.

And the riskier it all became, the more insurance could be created and sold against it, which resulted in the booming CDS market. Another form of derivatives that exploded after 2002, CDSs attained a global total dollar value of $60 trillion by 2007. That was far more than the value of the assets they 'insured,' which proves that CDSs were essentially just gambling bets. With CDSs, speculation had left behind any pretense of being based on real assets. Starting with a real asset, a house, now a pyramid of paper-based, speculative financial instruments were being created: first RMBS, then CDOs, then synthetic CDOs, then CDSs. And along the chain, more debt and leveraging was piling upon debt and leveraging. And all the borrowing and debt carried debt servicing costs. The costs could be ignored so long as asset prices rose and assets were sold and resold on secondary markets. Asset price inflation thus meant there were no effective costs of debt. But once the price escalation slowed, stopped, or reversed, then the assets could not be sold so easily, or even at all. At that point debt servicing became a requirement. In fact, not only would debt payments now have to be made, but the borrowed money would also have to be paid to the lender in part, equal to the amount borrowed and the now collapsed price of the asset. Asset price unwinding was now on the agenda. Emergency 'sales' of assets now falling meant asset price deflation. And asset deflation in turn tended to provoke still more asset deflation.

Real investment in residential housing began falling rapidly in the second half of 2006. By early 2007, homebuilders and major mortgage lenders were already collapsing. Companies like HSBC, D.R. Horton, and Accredited Home Lenders all announced they were in trouble. Then on April 2, 2007 the second largest mortgage company in the U.S., New Century Financial, filed for bankruptcy. The stock market shuddered, then temporarily recovered, as stock investors still denied the party could ever end.

In mid June another shock emerged when the I-bank Bear Stearns announced that two of its big in-house hedge funds, that were created to speculate in subprimes, had lost much of their value and had to sell off $8 billion in mortgages at below market value to raise cash. Other big bank investors in the funds, Merrill Lynch and Citigroup, Barclays, and J.P. Morgan Chase, Deutsche Bank, and Credit Suisse, that had provided $9 billion in start-up capital to the funds, began seizing the funds' remaining collateral. In a matter of a few weeks, by June 2007 Bear Stearns' two hedge funds had lost $20 billion. Both funds would be liquidated in less than six weeks.

By the time of the Bear Stearns funds event, the securitization of subprime mortgages had created more than $1.8 trillion in financial securities, according to the industry newsletter, *Inside Mortgage Finance*; $500 billion in CDOs in 2006 alone.[46] The unraveling of that $1.8 trillion was about to begin and with it a protracted period of asset firesales in subprimes and mortgage bonds in general.[47]

A year after the housing market began a real decline in mid 2006 and foreclosures began to emerge in late summer 2006, investors now began to take a closer look at the financial institutions—shadow and traditional—that were holding securitized assets in mortgages. According to the business research firm, Thompson Reuters, between 2000 and 2007, more than $17 trillion in mortgages were bought by the shadow banks, half of which were sold off to foreign buyers.

By mid July 2007, investors finally came to the conclusion that the two Bear Stearns funds "were virtually worthless because of bad subprime bets."[48] Concern now grew that the subprime problem was general and could drag down other assets like LBOs, foreign exchange trades, CDOs, CLOs, and other securitized financial assets. In the final weeks of July 2007 a flurry of announcements by housing industry and finance firms in trouble, both in the U.S. and abroad, drove the New York stock market down from its peak of 14,000 by nearly 800 points. But that was only the beginning.

Financial fragility growing over decades finally shattered with the general implosion of the subprime mortgage market in early August 2007. Events thereafter began to move more quickly as the financial crisis spread and deepened from subprime mortgages to other credit markets, and from the U.S. to Europe and elsewhere in a matter of weeks. Price deflation in stocks and other financial assets quickly followed. The fall in asset prices at banks and financial institutions meant major losses on their balance sheets. As liquidity at financial institutions began to disappear and bank losses mounted, a general contraction of credit began. Initial efforts to repair liquidity and offset losses between August and December 2007 generally failed. The Fed and other central banks at first acted too slowly in lowering interest rates. Congress and the Treasury remained silent in terms of any stimulus. The banks were encouraged to solve their problem voluntarily. They attempted to patch together several voluntary funds and bring off balance sheet loans and speculative investments onto their formal balance sheets. But this was not 1907. The voluntary effort by banks to bail themselves out by setting up collective emergency funds quickly failed. Bank efforts to get foreign government sovereign wealth funds to bail them out by providing capital also failed. Abu Dhabi, Singapore, and Chinese sovereign wealth funds bought stakes in several banks. But the losses were now accelerating faster than capital could be added. 'Black holes' in banks' balance sheets were opening up faster than injections of liquidity by the Fed or other foreign investors like the sovereign wealth funds could offset. By December, banks globally were beginning to refuse to lend to each other in overnight markets. The banking system itself was beginning to freeze up by December 2007. It was now a rapidly generalizing financial crisis, beyond merely subprime markets and beyond the U.S. By the year end it was also clear that the financial crisis had provoked a recession. A general credit contraction had quickly emerged after August 2007.

THE RECESSION BEGINS

The U.S. economy officially entered a recession in December 2007. At year end 2007, unemployment was still only an official 5 percent and numbered 7.1 million. But declines in manufacturing and construction, retail sales, mortgage defaults at a 21-year high, and other indicators strongly indicated that the future direction of the economy was clearly headed downward. The deepening financial crisis was beginning to bite into the real economy through the medium of credit contraction impacting non-financial business. Falling asset prices were causing banks and shadow banks to tighten and refuse loans; liquidity and credit was becoming slowly but progressively unavailable. The debt unwind was beginning.

By January 2008, unemployment began to noticeably rise. Thereafter, employment declined every month in 2008. At first it was relatively moderate. Monthly job losses averaged about 50,000 through July 2008. Industrial production declined through April only moderately as well, and then actually leveled off and remained steady from May through July. Production for exports even rose from January through July as global trade remained relatively unaffected as yet and as the bubble in commodities, especially in oil, continued to grow. Credit was contracting but had not yet crashed. Businesses were laying off but still selectively. Hours of work were being cut to avoid more general layoffs. Full-time workers were being converted to part-time workers in record numbers. Seven million involuntary part-time employed were added to the new jobless totals, though they were not counted as unemployed due to questionable government methods used for counting unemployment totals. As a group, workers' total earnings were falling, but direct wage cuts were not yet occurring.

A qualitative shift for the worse began to occur in both the financial and real sectors of the economy around July–August 2008. On the financial side, speculators called 'short sellers' entered the stock market aggressively and began betting on the imminent collapse of those banks that had over-expanded in terms of debt and were over-exposed to housing and property mortgages. They also attacked the quasi-government agencies that were required by law to buy up bad mortgages—Fannie Mae and Freddie Mac. The latter had used up virtually all their reserves purchasing bad mortgages from the banks and were ordered by Congress to buy more. Despite their status as government agencies, they were also public corporations with common stock outstanding. Short sellers began betting in huge amounts that their stock prices would fall; in so betting, they drove down the stock prices in the process faster. Congress did nothing to halt the speculative practice, which had been growing in volume during the past decade in general. Speculators also began attacking the banks most exposed to mortgages and securitized financial instruments as well. Lehman Brothers was a favorite target, as were all the remaining shadow I-banks—Morgan Stanley, Goldman Sachs, Merrill Lynch—as well as traditional commercial banks and insurance companies that had invested heavily in mortgages and securitized assets, like Citigroup, AIG, and Bank of America.

As this author wrote in mid 2008: "the worst of the financial crisis in the U.S. may be yet to come. And odds that the U.S. economy will transition to an 'Epic' recession in 2009 have risen further at mid-year 2008."[49] In other words, there was strong evidence that "the current recession is transitioning to an epic recession."[50]

THE EPIC RECESSION EMERGES

By July 2008 the temporary factors that had slowed the decline of the real economy in the second quarter had run out of steam. Exports now leveled off, the tax rebate from the fiscal 2008 stimulus bill had been spent, saved, or used to pay down debt by consumers, and business investment had once again begun to decline. Industrial production and unemployment were about to begin falling sharply once more.

July was also the month during which financial instability shifted to a more serious phase. The quasi-government agencies, Fannie Mae and Freddie Mac, which were tasked with buying mortgage debt from private lenders, were running out of money. Holding more than $5.3 trillion in mortgages, their combined reserves had declined to $81 billion—a ratio of reserves to liabilities of only 1.6 percent. If the agencies collapsed, it would mean losses on $1.7 trillion of their bonds bought by foreign banks and investors. Projections were that those investors would lose a minimum of $300 billion over the coming year. That amounted to potential losses ten times the cost of the bailout of Bear Stearns just months before. Short sellers and speculators targeted Fannie and Freddie stock in June and their stock price went into freefall in July, collapsing 50 percent in just one day on July 11. On July 14 the Fed and the Treasury announced a bailout, including a $300 billion line of credit to Fannie and Freddie to prevent their imminent collapse.

What the Fannie/Freddie bailouts in July 2008 represented was that a strategic threshold and shift in financial instability had been reached for the system. It was now clear—despite declarations to the contrary by Fed chairman Ben Bernanke and then Treasury Secretary Henry Paulson—that the bailout of Bear Stearns the previous March was not a 'one-off' affair. Also clear was that the Bush administration was going to do nothing about speculators and short sellers driving down stock prices of financial institutions holding excessive subprimes and other bad assets. The speculators were being eaten by speculators. The crocodiles were now cannibalizing their own. Following Fannie/Freddie, the short sellers went to work. The stock prices of the agencies were driven down even further, to a few dollars per share. Treasury Secretary Paulson reluctantly implemented the $300 billion line of credit for Fannie/Freddie passed by Congress in July and took over the agencies in August. Stock speculators now shifted into high gear, targeting every bank and financial institution over-exposed to subprimes, mortgages, and securitized assets in general.

By August, bank losses on subprimes alone amounted to $500 billion. But that was only what the banks reported and was thus a low-end estimate.[51] Other respected independent sources at the time estimated bank mortgage losses and write-downs at $1 trillion, and potentially as high as $2 trillion.[52] And if housing foreclosures continued to rise beyond the estimated 2 million at the time, and housing prices dropped further, these numbers were only a floor. Considering all potential bank losses and write-downs, not just mortgage-related, the International Monetary Fund (IMF) estimated losses of $3.1 trillion in the U.S. alone, and another $.9 trillion in Europe and Asia.

As short sellers in late August began attacking even more aggressively the stock prices of banks and shadow banks, the real economy that same month began to renew its decline after the brief spring 2008 pause. In August the unemployment rate rose from 5.5 percent to 6.1 percent and the jobless number increased by 84,000 as industrial production renewed its decline, exports stalled, and the decline in durable goods consumption doubled. The financial crisis and the real economy were now feeding back upon one another, each exacerbating the other. Financial fragility had reached a 'fracturing' point and financial instability was intensifying, causing banks to sharply reduce credit as their balance sheets melted away. Anticipating the further credit contraction, non-financial companies accelerated layoffs and reduced production further. Consumption fragility was also now deteriorating. Households and consumers were rapidly reducing spending on 'big ticket' consumer durable items.

THE BANKING PANIC OF 2008

From the beginning of September 2008 to the government seizure of Fannie Mae and Freddie Mac on September 8, 2008, and the collapse of Lehman Brothers I-bank a week later, intensive short selling of financial stocks was the norm. Stock prices of all the major banks, I-banks in particular, were the targets, and their stock prices fell precipitously. On September 15, Lehman Brothers was allowed to collapse, Bank of America absorbed Merrill Lynch for $50 billion, and the government seized the insurance giant, AIG, at an initial cost of $123 billion. Washington Mutual and Wachovia were forced into mergers at firesale prices. Not only were banks' stock asset prices falling precipitously, but bank real assets were selling at firesale prices as well. The collapse of bank stocks spilled over to stocks in general by early October. Having fallen only 350 points throughout September, the Dow Jones fell by 20 percent in a one-week period in early October alone, concluding the worst week in its entire history.

The deepening financial crisis led to an attempt to bailout the banks by the Treasury purchasing their bad assets. To enable the purchases, Treasury Secretary Paulson demanded, and was granted by Congress, a fund of $700 billion, the Troubled Asset Relief Program (TARP). Justified as necessary to buy up the banks' bad assets, TARP proved a total failure in that regard. No assets were bought by the Treasury in the end. The financial crisis thereafter spread from credit market to credit market, causing a freeze-up of the commercial paper market, the market for money market funds, municipal bonds, commercial property, commercial and industrial loans, and other short-term credit markets. Financial fragility had clearly 'fractured.' The credit contraction had become a credit crash.

Additional hundreds of billions of dollars for bailouts and rescues were quickly arranged in November–December by the Fed and the Treasury. In a matter of a few months, the Treasury and the Fed together had put up $300 billion for the two mortgage agencies, $180 billion for AIG, $320 billion for Citigroup, $700 billion in TARP for banks, additional tens of billions for auto companies, $800 billion for the credit markets, $600 billion to buy-up mortgage debt, and $200 billion to boost consumer lending. The $700 billion for TARP received the most public attention, but several times that was committed by the Federal Reserve. In all, between $3 trillion and $4 trillion was put up to bail out the financial system itself, not just individual banks.

Debt was unwinding at an accelerating rate and market values of assets collapsed, were written down or written off. With that debt unwind followed asset price deflation on several fronts. With bank asset price collapse and losses came a credit crash as bank lending began to freeze up. An even more serious further decline in the real economic than had occurred in August 2007 followed.

In October 2008, consumption fell off a cliff. Consumption spending fell by 3.1 percent—the first such absolute decline in 17 years. Asset price deflation began to spill over to product price deflation, as the CPI also fell in October at a rate not seen since the 1930s. On the investment side, disappearing credit now meant businesses not only continued to shelve new planned investment but now sharply reduced existing production levels as well. Industrial production fell by 10 percent in a matter of a few months. The monthly increase in the new jobless numbers tripled and then doubled again, from 84,000 in August to 240,000 in October and 553,000 in November. New jobless claims would continue rising more than 500,000 for six months, tracking unemployment almost exactly the same as had occurred in 1930–31. GDP fell by more than 5 percent in two consecutive quarters: the fourth quarter 2008 and following first quarter 2009.

EPIC RECESSION WINTER–SPRING 2009

Through at least the first half of 2009, economic conditions deteriorated further. Most notable was the continuing loss of jobs well in excess of 500,000 a month on average, and a rise in the more accurate 'U-6' unemployment rate to 17.5 percent. More than 24 million were effectively unemployed by October 2009. Residential housing foreclosures were also doubling and quadrupling, and reached the 6 million mark by fall 2009. Millions more delinquencies were occurring, filling the foreclosure pipeline, and about a third of all mortgages were considered 'under water'—i.e. the mortgage debt remaining was worth more than the market value of the home (negative equity).

Industrial production and exports were flat at best in early 2009. Deflation was serious on the asset side and just beginning to penetrate the product side, with consumer prices down –1.5 percent, but wholesale prices fell much further and the wholesale 'pipeline' showing even worse deflation ahead. In terms of wage deflation, official government data appeared to indicate that it was not yet a serious problem. Weekly earnings were down only a mild –2.4 percent. But the government data are misleading with regard to wage deflation. They do not pick up alternative forms of wage deflation that were deepening throughout 2009. Wage deflation in 2008 focused on cutting hours of work, not the hourly wage rate. The result was that 4–5 million full-time jobs were converted to part-time status throughout 2008. That isn't a classic hourly wage cut, but it is a wage reduction in weekly terms, nonetheless. In 2009 the wage-cutting also assumed additional forms. Those forms included reducing paid leaves, initiating non-paid forced time off several days each month (called furloughs), eliminating or cutting employer contributions to pensions, reducing the employer's share of health benefit costs, shutting down operations for a week or more at a time without pay (unpaid vacations), requiring those on salary to work longer hours in addition to taking pay cuts, and numerous similar methods. To view wage-cutting and wage deflation only in terms of reducing the hourly wage rate is to miss these other forms of wage deflation that were underway in 2009. Accelerating job losses and these approaches to wage deflation were both further reducing consumption, and created even further consumption fragility for the 'bottom 60 percent' of the workforce, a not insignificant group of 90 million production and service non-supervisory workers.

In the first half of 2009, therefore, asset deflation was deepening, product price deflation was impacting the wholesale side and beginning to penetrate the consumer side, and wage deflation quietly assuming new forms. The debt–deflation process, in other words, was continuing below the surface in 2009. The trio relationship of debt–deflation–default was beginning to emerge, but had not yet reached an intense, depression-like level of development.

Bank defaults involving the 'big 19' banks, with two-thirds of all the bank assets in the U.S., were prevented from happening by the Fed's massive, multi-trillion-dollar bailout of the 'big 19,' 'too big to fail,' institutions. They were essentially propped up by the Fed and the U.S. government and not allowed to fail, although many of the 'big 19,' perhaps half, were technically bankrupt and insolvent—government bank 'stress tests' notwithstanding. Not candidates for bailout, however, were the remaining 8,400 smaller community and regional banks in the U.S. They began to fail in ever larger numbers in 2009, estimated to exceed 200 in 2009 by the Federal Deposit Insurance Corporation (FDIC), with twice that number to occur in 2010 as the commercial property market was expected to continue to decline and as new layers of 'prime' home mortgages began defaulting at accelerating rates as well.

On the non-bank side, corporate defaults were also quietly rising in the first half of 2009, with forecasts of rates of default to come in the high teens by the rating agencies, Moody's and Standard & Poor's. But just as the big banks were being kept from failing, many non-bank corporations were also able temporarily to prevent default and bankruptcy in early 2009 by rolling over their debt with new junk bond issues, although at dangerously high interest rates approaching 20 percent; or by activating terms on their prior debt, called 'covenants' and payments in kind (PIKs), which prevented banks from seizing their assets. But both methods—reissuing junk bonds at extreme rates and activating covenants—only delay a flood of eventual defaults to come in 2011. Larger companies also were not as stressed, having access to high-grade corporate bond markets, which surged in 2009. Smaller companies, on the other hand, faced increasing stress as bank lending to them continued to decline throughout all of 2009.

Consumer defaults were also building in momentum in 2009, including in particular credit card defaults, student loan defaults, and auto loans—while, equally serious, new 'waves' were building in home mortgage defaults in the 'Alt-A', prime, ARMs, and jumbo segments of that market. Major subprime-like credit bombs also loomed on the horizon, in particular the commercial property mortgage market, as well as with credit cards, student loans, and auto loans. The multi-trillion-dollar securitization credit sector, and its many shadow banking institutions, had essentially collapsed and showed no signs of revival.

Given the above scenarios for debt, deflation, and default through the first half of 2009, it is evident that financial fragility continued to deteriorate in some sectors while improve in others. The debt servicing needs of the big banks were eased by free government Fed loans and direct liquidity injections. Smaller and regional banks more exposed to continuing residential mortgage foreclosures and falling prices, or continuing deflation in commercial properties and rising defaults, were clearly experiencing further financial fragility. The $2 trillion market for securitized consumer loans—auto, student, credit card, mortgage—remained moribund by the end of 2009. Small banks and credit unions were thus still unable to recover. For non-bank businesses, once again small businesses were no doubt growing more fragile as bank lending continued to dry up. Companies lending to small businesses, like CIT Group, went bankrupt at year end, further drying up access to credit for smaller businesses. In terms of cash flow, certain industries continued to discount and lower product prices, in particular consumer retail goods, entertainment and lodging, and some services. In other words, financial fragility improved for larger banks and companies but continued to decline for smaller banks and companies.

On the consumption fragility side, given the massive layoffs and forms of wage and benefit cuts, given general credit unavailability to consumers and households, except for bankers and traders who once again received big bonuses the majority of households continued to experience consumption fragility decline in 2009. Contrary to impressions, their debt levels and servicing did not decline appreciably. In other words, it is a misconception that households and consumers were vigorously 'paying down debt.' Households' debt to disposable income ratios did not decline significantly in either 2008 or 2009. A ratio of 140 percent in late 2007 had improved only marginally by late 2009, to just under 130 percent.

In other words, both financial fragility and consumption fragility remained at serious problem levels by the end of 2009—despite the apparent stabilization and partial recovery of the big banks and large non-financial corporations.

In February and March 2009 a new strategy of fiscal and monetary bailouts was put together by the new Obama administration. An analysis of those policies in some detail, and their impact on the Epic Recession and financial crisis, is the subject of the chapter to follow. That chapter will show how the Obama program was sufficient only to slow the freefall in the real economy and to temporarily stabilize the continuing erosion of bank balance sheets. The economy's freefall was slowed, but the policies were not sufficient to generate a sustained economic recovery. The fundamental problems in the financial sector were painted over and not resolved. The trillions of dollars of bad assets still remained on the balance sheets of the 'big 19' banks. In fact, the problem was in some ways worse. Those bad assets were now also mirrored on the public balance sheets of the Fed, the FDIC, and the Treasury, resulting in projected multi-year trillion-dollar U.S. budget deficits and rising public debt levels for a decade to come.

Concern was growing in the U.S. among policymakers, as well as globally, about what the impact of the public balance sheet debt would mean for the future economy and the value of the dollar in global markets. Projected annual deficits of more than $1 trillion for the next eight years meant that the problem of 'public debt' and its economic consequences was not going away soon. Of no less concern was what would happen to the economy once the massive liquidity support by the Fed and the $787 billion fiscal spending package passed in early 2009 by Congress was withdrawn and had been spent. Additional major fiscal stimulus appeared unaffordable, given deficits. Many credit markets had not yet recovered at all, and some, like commercial property and prime mortgages, and credit cards, were projecting even more serious problems in the immediate future. Although at a declining rate, jobs were still being lost. Consumers were showing no sign of sustained recovery in retail sales. Bank lending was still falling, except for speculative offshore markets. Forecasts were for foreclosures to continue to rise, home net worth to fall, and home prices to renew declines in 2010. And, of course, as noted, financial and consumption fragility still remained serious problems. It was not a scenario for a robust, sustained 'V'-shaped recovery in the immediate future.

A TYPE I EPIC RECESSION?

The preceding sections of this chapter have described how the various key qualitative and dynamic characteristics of Epic Recession have been evident in the current economic crisis. As in prior cases in the history of similar Epic Recessions (1907–14, and 1929–31), the enabling fundamental forces of exploding liquidity and credit in the run-up boom period, the growing number of shadow banking institutions, the growing weight and influence of speculative investing, and the global money parade, have all contributed to the emergence of the current Epic Recession. Important dynamic processes involving historic levels of debt accumulation in the boom phase, followed by debt unwinding, deflation across all three price systems, and defaults, have also been at work in the contraction phase of the crisis. A deterioration of financial and consumption fragility despite the boom phase, both of which thereafter deteriorate even faster and deeper in the contraction phase, is also a characteristic of Epic Recession. Unlike normal recessions, it is the presence and increasing interaction between these variables and forces that determine the unique nature of Epic Recessions: liquidity, credit and speculative investing shift; debt accumulation and debt unwinding; debt–deflation–default processes; financial and consumption fragility.

In the preceding chapter, Table 6.9, a comparison was made between benchmark criteria for Epic Recession and the Epic Recession of 1929–31. Table 7.6 replicates the same benchmark criteria and compares it with the period 2007–09. The table shows how the period 2007–09 also fulfills the criteria for an Epic Recession in terms of both quantitative and qualitative characteristics.

Table 7.6   Characteristics of Epic Recession, Benchmarks versus 2007–09

Characteristic	Benchmark Minima	2007–09 as Epic
GNP/GDP	5–15% two quarters	–6.3% and –5.5%
Unemployment Rate	10% Increase	9.7% (U-6 jobless rate: 16.8%)
Industrial Production	10–20% Decline	–16% (June 08–June 09)
Exports	10% Decline	–22% in 9 months
Stock Prices	40% Decline	–53% (Dow average)
Duration	18–24 months	22 months (continuing)
Debt	100% Increase prior decade	
	Financial	204%
	Non-Financial	106%
	Consumer	80% (consumer credit)
	Government	76% (non-agency only)
Deflation	Asset (10–40%) Decline	Stocks –53%
		securitized assets –85%
		Bank mortgage loans –35%
		Home prices –27%
		Commercial property –39%
		Hedge funds –14% (buyouts)
		Art prices –35%
	Product (2–10%) Decline	
	Consumer	–1.5% (CPI June 08–09)
	Wholesale	–4–6% (PPI June 08–09)
		–12.5% (PPI intermediate)
		–40.0% (PPI crude)
	Retail Food	2.2% (June 08–09)
	Exports	–6.4%
	Imports	–17.4%
	Wage/Earnings(emerging decline)	
	Ave. Hourly Wages	2.6% (full-time only)
	Weekly Earnings	–2.4% (hourly × hours work)
	Wage Income	–5.0% (share of personal income)
	Benefits Cuts	major trends occurring
Defaults	Financial (Commercial & Shadow)	
	Suspensions	630 hedge fund liquidations
	Failures	102 (banks only, July 09)
	Non-Financial Business	140 large corps (June 09)*
		54% rise in bankruptcies (08)
		45% rise in bankruptcies (09)
		15% junk bond default rate
		14% leveraged loan default
		2.45% commercial mortgages
	Consumer	
	Foreclosures	8 out of 55 million (S&P forecast)
	Consumer bankruptcy	1.4 million 33% rise (2009 vs. 2008)
	Student loans	50% default rate rise (to 6.9%)
	Credit Card defaults	12% credit card charge off rate

continued

Table 7.6   continued

Characteristic	Benchmark Minima	2007–09 as Epic
Qualitative Characteristics	Financial Instability	
	Bank Runs & Withdrawals	Institutional runs on I-banks, Hedge funds, Money Market Funds, and Private Equity > $1 trillion fund withdrawals
	Capital & Insolvency	8 of 'big 19' banks insolvent 702 'regionals' on FDIC list
	Credit Crunch & Crash	Credit crash after 10/08 Banks still not lending, 9/09
	Shadow Banking Growth	Hedge funds, private equity, private banks, corporate finance companies, SIVs, bank conduits
	Consumption Fragility	Yes, especially bottom 60% households' debt to income ratios > 125% Consumption crash after October 08
	Speculative Investment Shift	Securitization & derivatives revolutions, CDSs, global short selling, flash trading, hedging, dark pools
	Global Synchronization and	Yes, Eurozone, Japan, Korea and South Asia
	Rate of Propagation & Spread	

* With assets worth more than $250 million.

THE 'RECOVERY' OF 2009

Although many were proclaiming the recession was over by the third quarter 2009 based solely on the limited characteristic of GDP, by a broader set of criteria that was not the case. The economy by the third quarter 2009 is more accurately described as 'moving sideways.' The collapse of economic indicators in select areas was stabilized. But stopping freefall does not constitute recovery.

A year earlier, in the summer of 2008, it became increasingly clear that the dynamic processes of debt–deflation–default had been set in motion. Financial and consumption fragility deteriorated over the course of the preceding year, 2007–08. By July–August 2008, rising debt levels were causing businesses to cut wages—by layoffs, reduced hours, and direct measures—and businesses were once again cutting production further. This was all before the banking panic of September 2008 occurred. Following the panic, businesses began to accelerate production cuts, and sell assets and products at below market prices. When asset and product deflation as a means to raise cash proved insufficient, mass layoffs, reduced working hours, and wage-cutting escalated. default occurred, resulting in further asset price declines. Wage deflation led to more consumer defaults, in home mortgages, auto and student loans, and credit cards. Reduced consumption meant less demand for business services and products, and further price discounting. Debt–deflation–default began to feed back on each other. Rising business debt, asset and product deflation, and defaults caused a further deterioration of financial fragility. Rising household debt, wage deflation, and defaults led to a further deterioration of consumption fragility. The fracturing of both financial and consumption fragility more or less simultaneously—i.e. the hallmark of an Epic Recession—was driving the real economy to a qualitatively new, lower level.

But these processes had not yet fully spun out of control. In 2009, the Fed and the Treasury pumped increasing amounts of liquidity into the banks, shadow and commercial alike, to prevent the need to sell assets at below market prices. Major non-financial businesses were also bailed out with TARP money. Shadow banks were arbitrarily declared to be commercial banks so they could receive government funds. Wholesale prices fell but did not collapse. Consumer prices declined but fell slowly. Banks were prevented from defaulting by access to trillions in zero cost (0 percent interest) loans from the Fed. Banks were permitted to falsify their balance sheets with new accounting rules, and thereby obviate technical default and insolvency. Banks held off activating bankruptcy proceedings against companies that could not meet debt payments. Fortunate non-bank companies activated provisions in their loans (PIKs and covenants) that allowed them to put off payments to creditors. Larger companies went into the junk bond market to raise record levels of cash as a cushion against debt payments and default. Continuing mass layoffs after April were slowed by the first disbursements of the $787 billion fiscal stimulus in early 2009. State and local governments and school districts were 'bailed out' by hundreds of billions of direct injection of funds by the federal government. A further rapid deterioration of consumption fragility was slowed by increases in unemployment insurance, food stamps, and government-paid medical insurance premiums.

In short, debt was offset by massive liquidity injections—to banks, businesses, and consumers. And with rising debt pressures offset to some extent, deflation pressures abated and stabilized. Defaults slowed or were postponed. Further deterioration in financial fragility and consumption fragility slowed. But while a further collapse to a deeper level in the real economy was temporarily averted, policies were not yet in place that would generate a sustained recovery. Fed policies stabilized the banking collapse, but bank lending to non-financial businesses nonetheless continued to decline throughout 2009, according to both Fed and independent sources.[53] Commercial and industrial loans and lending to smaller companies continued to decline in particular. As another business source reported, "bank lending is contracting faster than the Fed is buying assets…No matter how much the Fed seems to do, banks are not extending loans."[54] Lending to consumers was also contracting rapidly. Like lending and credit to non-financial businesses, credit to consumers also fell for nine consecutive months in 2009, through October. Credit card lending contracted at the fastest rate, while auto loans experienced a brief recovery due to the 'cash for clunkers' program. On a total basis over a two-year period, from November 2007 through November 2009, total credit in the U.S. economy contracted by $1.5 trillion.[55]

The 'recovery' of 2009 depends on how recovery is defined. Certainly, some areas of the economy have stabilized. But none can be said to have robustly recovered as yet. There is no firm indication of sustained recovery in progress, or even about to occur. Like the condition of financial and consumption fragility, the picture is mixed and tentative. The most likely scenario is, given the still serious problems remaining in both the financial system and the real economy, that the economy for the next one to two years will show a pattern of unsustainable growth and recovery; recoveries that are short and shallow, and perhaps even followed by renewed declines, also short and shallow. In other words, a picture similar to 1909–14, following the crash of 1907–08 and brief recovery of 1908–09. It could be 'U'-shaped or even 'W'-shaped, but not likely a 'V'-shaped trajectory of recovery. That is, a Type I Epic Recession.

The potential remains, however, for a more serious Type II Epic Recession, more similar to 1929–31. But that will require another major financial collapse similar to 2008. That renewed, subsequent financial crisis need not occur in the U.S., however. It can, and will likely, come from an unanticipated direction. A renewed shift to a decline might also be precipitated by the timing or character of the removal of Fed and government stimulus supports: too soon, too abruptly, or too deeply. There is no doubt that the only force keeping the economy from descent into depression at the moment is recent massive government liquidity injections and not so massive, but nonetheless somewhat offsetting, government spending stimulus. It is noteworthy that the massive monetary and fiscal stimulus has only been able to generate a stabilization in part, and not a recovery in whole. But that dual stimulus has put a floor under what was an evolving financial and consumption collapse. But what happens when that floor is removed is anyone's guess. Will bank lending and business autonomous investment pick up the slack? That remains to be seen. The lure of speculation and the global money parade may prove too great for the big banks, which will likely defeat any meaningful financial regulator reform and thus return to their 'old ways.' And large corporations will most likely continue their current orientation toward production and sales in offshore emerging markets. Thus one thing is certain: the future after Fed–government support will not include a return to the status quo ante of 2006 and before. Finally, there is yet a third possible outcome that may precipitate transition to a Type II Epic Recession in lieu of the current most likely Type I. Capitalist sources in and out of government may in fact decide consciously to choose to protect the dollar, foreign markets, and economic relationships with foreign partners over that of a sustained domestic recovery of the U.S. economy. Not an 'error' in strategy or tactic in withdrawing recent government economic supports, but a conscious plan to emphasize global economic returns over domestic.

8
The Bush–Obama Recovery Programs

One of the central arguments of this book is that *Epic Recessions are unlike normal recessions*. The fundamental causes, enabling forces, and precipitating events of Epic Recessions are not the same. The defining characteristics— quantitative, qualitative, and dynamic—are different as well. If origins and characteristics differ, can policies and programs that succeed in generating recovery from normal recessions also succeed in generating sustained recovery from Epic Recessions? Or is it more likely that they will fail?

The ten normal recessions that have occurred in the U.S. since 1945 have been resolved ultimately by some combination of 'traditional' monetary and fiscal policy.[1] However, recoveries from Epic Recessions are not achieved by traditional fiscal or monetary policies. Epic Recessions—like their larger cousins, depressions—require a massive dose of government spending in the short run and major structural changes in the economy in the longer run that restore a more equitable distribution of income. Without a recovery program that encompasses extraordinary fiscal stimulus and structural redistribution of income, a sustainable economic recovery is not possible and measures that fall short result in extended economic stagnation in one or several forms. The stagnation may be virtually flat; or it may take the form of short, weak recoveries followed by moderate and also short downturns, in a pattern that averages out over the long run as a virtually flat recovery nonetheless.

TRADITIONAL POLICIES AND EPIC RECESSIONS

The two prior experiences of Epic Recession in the U.S. in the twentieth century occurred in 1907–14 and in 1929–31. They were only resolved by massive injections of government spending, structural change, and income rebalancing. In the former 'Type I' Epic Recession of 1907–14, that change and spending injection took the form of the war economy of 1915–18. In the latter case, the Epic Recession of 1929–31 was initially not resolved by such change. In the absence of such structural change and spending, the Epic Recession consequently transformed into a classic depression following the first national banking crisis of April–September 1931, a 'Type II' Epic Recession.

Like the Epic Recession phase of 1929–31, normal fiscal-monetary measures were also not able to generate sustained recovery during the classic depression phase of 1931–40 that followed. It was once again, as in 1915–18, only the onset of the war economy of 1941–42 that finally ended it. (This does not mean, however, that war is the only solution to Epic Recessions or depressions, as will be clarified shortly.)

Contrary to popular belief, the stabilization of the banking system in 1933–34 was not sufficient to end the depression. Nor was the fiscal policy shift of the New Deal in mid decade, 1935–37, able to generate a sustained recovery. Roosevelt's 1935–37 New Deal lacked both sufficient magnitude and duration. And both that magnitude and duration were cut short in 1937 with the beginning of the dismantling of the New Deal after only a few short years. Moreover, as the dismantling process began, other fiscal and monetary policies of 1935–37 that accompanied the New Deal were reversed as well. The result was that the U.S. economy quickly slid back into depression in 1938.

In the face of the imminent 're-depression' in 1938, Congress and the President abruptly reversed policies once again. Government spending picked up and the Federal Reserve (Fed) shifted from restrictive to expansionary monetary policy. The Fed's policy was aided by the flow of gold into the U.S. in 1938, further increasing the money supply. But the return to fiscal-monetary stimulus in late 1938 did not end the depression. The renewed stimulus of 1938 again, as previously in 1935–37, only stabilized the downturn, preventing it from collapsing further. More than two years later, in late 1940, the unemployment rate was still a significant 14–15 percent.

Sustained recovery from depression only began in 1941–42 when the level of government spending more than doubled. A major point of this book, therefore, is that monetary policy can at best only succeed in stabilizing the banking system. It cannot generate a sustained recovery in the wake of either Epic Recession or depression. Nor can 'normal' fiscal policy generate sustainable recovery. Both financial and consumption fragility must be simultaneously addressed. Containing financial fragility only results, at best, in an extended stagnation.

In 1929 the combined federal and state and local government spending amounted to only 10 percent of gross national product (GNP), with the federal proportion only 2.6 percent. In 1933, in the depths of the great depression, the combined spending was only a meager 10.2 percent. In 1939—after the New Deal and the re-stimulating of the economy in 1938—the combined spending of all sectors of government was still only 17.2 percent, with the federal share having risen to only 8.9 percent.[2] That 17.2 percent was less than 'normal' government spending in the late twentieth century, at around 20.0 percent. It was not until 1942 that federal spending as a percent of GNP had risen to 38.7 percent.[3] It was only then that the depression clearly ended.

To achieve and implement that 38.7 percent spending level in 1942 required major structural changes in the economy. From an economic point of view, what matters is not that the spending was for war goods. That spending could just as well have been for public infrastructure as for bullets and guns. And in fact much of government wartime spending was just that—renovating and upgrading much of the industrial base of the economy, creating state-of-the-art efficient production facilities by the government, and a redistribution of income in favor of the working classes that, together, resulted in a long-term positive impact on the post-1945 economy and a sustained recovery after 1945.[4]

OVERVIEW OF POLICIES AND PROGRAMS, 2007–09

The Fed's initial response to the financial crisis in August 2007 was too little, too late. And there was no fiscal policy response to speak of for nearly nine months after August. During that nine-month period, the Bush's Treasury Secretary, Henry Paulson, did virtually nothing besides watching the Fed lower interest rates cautiously and slowly as it implemented traditional monetary policy measures.

It wasn't until December 2007 that the Fed chairman, Ben Bernanke, began to take the crisis more seriously and initiate measures besides simply reducing interest rates. But the emphasis was still on getting the banks to voluntarily bail themselves out by encouraging joint, bank-financed rescue funds, all of which quickly collapsed. Economic conditions thereafter deteriorated quickly from January to March 2008, rendering the Fed's December efforts and banks' voluntary measures ineffective. Nonetheless, the Fed continued in early 2008 to rely on traditional monetary measures, as it fell even further behind the rapidly developing crisis curve.

By March 2008 it was becoming increasingly clear that the economy was on the brink of a new kind of economic crisis—not a normal recession. The Fed was finally forced to take new, emergency measures to try to get ahead of the crisis curve. Those measures included the bailout of the investment bank, or I-bank, Bear Stearns. But even with the bailout, the Fed was still lagging events. In arranging the bailout the Fed also exhausted much of its roughly $850 billion of reserves. It temporarily retired to the sidelines after Bear Stearns, turning subsequent bailouts over to Paulson and the Treasury.

On the fiscal side, it was similarly a case of 'too little, too late' during the first nine months following the August 2007 financial explosion. Bush and Paulson mostly sat on the sidelines, avoiding all fiscal stimulus and advocating that the banks adopt and implement voluntary measures to bail themselves out, even as the real economy quickly slipped into recession after only three months, in December 2007. It wasn't until March 2008 that Bush even proposed, and Congress passed, a fiscal stimulus bill. That bill provided only $168 billion in stimulus in a combination of business tax cuts and spending. The tax cuts were ineffective, however, in a rapidly declining real economy just entering recession. No business will invest in expansion while cutting current production as consumption is rapidly declining. The consumption measures in Bush's 2008 stimulus bill were also mostly ineffective. In a few months the stimulus had run its course. Notwithstanding all that, the mild 'recovery' of spring 2008 was hailed as the 'end of the recession.' The bailout of Bear Stearns was equally trumpeted by politicians and bankers alike as the end of the financial crisis. All the heads of the big banks held press conferences in April in an orchestrated, coordinated effort, declaring that the banking system was now stabilized. Most would be gone before the end of the year as their banks collapsed later in 2008.

The March 2008 bailout of Bear Stearns was only the tip of the financial iceberg that was rapidly melting. Bank losses were escalating far faster than private capital injections or the Fed could offset them. The black hole in banks' balance sheets was opening up faster than the Fed could fill it. And the real, non-financial economy was rapidly deteriorating as well below the policy radar.[5]

Financial fragility then 'fractured' in the events of July–September 2008, beginning with the collapse and bailouts of Fannie Mae and Freddie Mac through the banking panic of September–October 2008. It was only then that the Fed and the Treasury, Bernanke and Paulson, turned to more aggressive measures—i.e. well over a year after the crisis first erupted in August 2007. Paulson and the Treasury introduced the 'doomed to fail' $700 billion TARP (Troubled Asset Relief Program); and the Fed a proliferation of new liquidity auctions and new policies of zero interest rates and 'quantitative easing' (which will be explained shortly). These measures were followed in early 2009 by a second fiscal stimulus package of $787 billion by the new Obama administration, and a series of additional bank rescue proposals. The fiscal measures would have only a moderate short-term effect on the economy, while the bank rescue measures would prove dead on arrival.

THE GREENSPAN LEGACY IN MONETARY POLICY

Fed chairman Paul Volcker, who succeeded in the early 1980s in squeezing double-digit inflation out of the economy, was dumped by then President Reagan and replaced by Alan Greenspan in the mid 1980s. Some sources conjecture that Volcker was dumped because Reagan's then Treasury Secretary, Donald Regan, and Reagan's key advisor, James Baker, both wanted faster financial industry deregulation. Reportedly, Volcker was not so certain. In contrast, Greenspan was a true believer in deregulation in all forms and convinced that unregulated markets always and everywhere were more efficient and "can do no wrong." Greenspan had chaired a special commission on reforming social security during Reagan's first term. The outcome of that commission was the implementation of payroll tax increases on social security that, over the next quarter of a century, would create a social security surplus of between $2 trillion and $4 trillion. That entire surplus was subsequently 'borrowed' by the federal government to partly reduce annual U.S. budget deficits over the following 20 years, much of which was due to repeated rounds of tax cuts for wealthy investors and corporations.

It is not so coincidental that on Greenspan's watch for the next two decades financial bubbles and crises began to occur with increasing virulence and frequency—starting with the trio of speculative bubbles in the 1980s (i.e. the Savings and Loans (S&L) crisis, the junk bond market blow-up, and leveraged buyouts (LBOs) and stock speculation discussed in the preceding chapter), and continuing through the 1990s with Fed bailouts of hedge funds, Asian banks, Russian debt, the dot.com booms of the 1990s, and the speculative bubble in housing after 1997. While Greenspan and the Fed were not the fundamental cause of these bubbles, it cannot be said Greenspan did much to stop them. Indeed, at the slightest excuse Greenspan and the Fed pumped up liquidity in the system in response to all these above events, even when it was highly unlikely that it was ever necessary.

Greenspan's predilection to expand liquidity at the slightest excuse was perhaps best represented by the Russian debt crisis, which erupted in 1998 in the wake of the Asian currency meltdown and hedge fund implosion of the preceding year. Rescuing the U.S. hedge fund Long Term Capital Management (LTCM), and providing funds to U.S. banks to deal with the Asian meltdown, was one thing. Even pumping money into tech stock and housing bubbles. But using the Russian debt crisis, which had no connection to the U.S. economy? As Greenspan admitted years later in 2003, "following the Russian debt default in the fall of 1998, the Federal Open Market Committee (FOMC) eased policy despite our perception that the economy was expanding at a satisfactory pace...We eased policy because we were concerned about the low-probability risk that the default might severely disrupt domestic and international financial markets."[6] A 'low probability risk' in an expanding economy? Not likely. Assisting banks in international financial markets? Quite likely.

Greenspan's bias toward injecting liquidity into the system at the slightest excuse was taken to ridiculous extremes with the so-called 'Y2K' crisis of late 1999. This was the hyped claim, largely pushed by tech companies, that on January 1, 2000, computers would stop running throughout the economy due to a programming glitch in their operating systems. Computers and networks thus had to be upgraded. Concerned that it would stop the boom in the tech industry, and in turn the then escalating tech stocks boom that was carrying the entire stock market to new record price levels, the Fed again pumped liquidity into the system. In other words, the Greenspan policy was 'when in the slightest doubt, throw liquidity at it.' Liquidity was the solution to all ills, even if slight or imagined. Of course, it was also great for the speculative boom in securitized financial instruments that was then gaining momentum, which required significant leveraging (i.e. borrowing and debt) to keep it escalating and growing.

Greenspan vigorously denied for a quarter of a century that his liquidity boosting policies had anything to do with the financial busts that followed the speculative booms launched on his watch in the 1980s (S&L, junk bonds, corporate takeover bubble, stock market crash of 1987) or in the 1990s (tech stock boom, general equities bubble, commodities' booms, housing bubble, securitized assets super-bubble). According to Greenspan, speculation in assets might well create bubbles, but there was nothing that could (or should) be done to prevent asset booms and busts. All the Fed could do was to clean up the mess in the end. Greenspan protégé Bernanke would adopt a similar attitude. As Bernanke, echoing his mentor, Greenspan, said: "First, the Fed cannot reliably identify bubbles in asset prices. Second, even if it could identify bubbles, monetary policy is far too blunt a tool for effective use against them."[7]

But was it really a question of the Fed not being able to stop speculative bubbles—or not wanting to? And why would monetary policy necessarily prove more effective in cleaning up a much larger mess after a financial bust, than it would in preventing a much smaller asset bubble as it emerged?

Even after subprime mortgages imploded in August 2007, Greenspan was still arguing that the subprime bust couldn't have been caused by the Fed since it occurred in other countries at the same time and the Fed's policies had no influence outside the U.S. Furthermore, Greenspan argued government regulators cannot know the future because of its extreme uncertainty any better than the market itself can know. Therefore the market should be left to regulate itself. If it messes up, only then should the Fed go in and correct it. "The core of the problem lies with the investment community. It is not credible that regulators [read: the Fed] could have prevented it."[8] Like Greenspan, in 2007–08 Bernanke would also wait for months for the market to correct itself, believing it was not the role of the Fed to intervene aggressively to deal with financial asset busts. In short, let the speculators run free.

For Greenspan, the housing asset bubble was due to foreign investors. The crux of the problem lay in excess savings in the developing world, meaning primarily Asia. The excess savings in China and elsewhere caused global interest rates to fall everywhere. That excess savings in Asia then flowed into the housing market in the U.S., causing housing asset prices to escalate. Thus it was the 'global savings glut' that was ultimately the cause behind the U.S. housing bubble.

Greenspan was only in part correct. Global speculators have and do contribute to asset bubbles, in housing, real estate, currencies, stocks, or whatever. But so too has the Fed. And the shadow banks with their new forms of money and credit creation. And the U.S. government for half a century maintaining its economic and military empire. None are the sole cause. All have contributed. That's why global liquidity has escalated so rapidly in recent decades. It's escalation has produced a 'perfect storm' of credit. More than necessary to finance real asset investment. So the growing residual is diverted and directed toward speculative ventures.

That growing pool of excess liquidity is what Greenspan and others call the 'global savings glut.' But that glut is not some mysterious depersonalized market phenomenon, as they would have us believe. The 'glut' is really the combined income and liquid assets of that network of wealthy individual investors, corporations, and institutions that commit, on short notice, vast sums to the speculative bubbles of the day on behalf of their clients, shareholders, and themselves. And when those speculative opportunities have been sufficiently 'farmed,' they move on to the next speculative opportunity. At times their ability to commit super-large blocs of capital even creates those opportunities. Greenspan is correct, in so far as it is global. But Greenspan and others like to refer to it as some mysterious depersonalized force, which it is not. For Greenspan, the crisis was simply an accident waiting to happen. "If it had not been triggered by the mis-pricing of securitized subprime mortgages, it would have been produced by eruptions in some other markets."[9] But the housing bubble was no 'accident.' No mystery of the global market. It was created by individuals, wealthy investors, and their financial institutions.

BERNANKE THE PROTÉGÉ

Greenspan's two-decades-long monetary policy did not change in 2006 with Bernanke's transition to Chairman of the Fed. Bernanke reflected Greenspan's views—i.e. don't intervene to prevent or stop asset bubbles; the basic cause of financial crisis is the global savings glut (i.e. them, not us), and if and when a crisis arises, throw mountains of liquidity at it to bail out those investors and institutions left holding the remaining bad financial assets. As Stephen Roach, vice-president of the investment bank Morgan Stanley, summarized:

> Mr. Bernanke is cut from the same market libertarian cloth that got the Fed into this mess. Steeped in the Greenspan credo that markets know better than regulators, Mr. Bernanke was aligned with the prevailing Fed mindset that abrogated its regulatory authority in the era of excess. The derivatives explosion, extreme leverage of regulated and shadow banks and excesses of mortgage lending were all flagrant abuses that both Mr. Bernanke and Mr. Greenspan could have said no to. But they did not. As a result, a complex and unstable system veered dangerously out of control.[10]

Bernanke has always been what is called a 'monetarist' in policy. Since his early days as an academic, he has taken the typical monetarist view that the Fed caused the depression of the 1930s with bad monetary policy. And it was the expansion of the money supply after 1938—due in part to Fed policy and in part to gold inflows to the U.S.—that finally resulted in the depression's end. Quoting his intellectual mentor, conservative monetarist economist Milton Friedman, Bernanke declared that, if necessary, the Fed would drop money from the air to prevent banks from becoming insolvent. From this came the oft-quoted reference to 'Bernanke's helicopter.' As a good 'Friedmanist,' Bernanke also subscribed to the view that the Fed caused the Great Depression of the 1930s by not providing enough liquidity. As he said directly to Friedman in a conference in November 2002: "Regarding the Great Depression. You're right, we [the Fed] did it. We're very sorry. But thanks to you, we won't do it again."[11]

Bernanke elaborated upon the classic Monetarist view by arguing that the Fed failed in the 1930s because of problems of 'intermediation,' which means the banks were unable to lend due to difficulty identifying and getting loans to businesses at a local level that were in need of credit for Bernanke. It wasn't that the banks didn't want to lend. It was a mere coordination problem. The solution to the depression therefore was simply to help lenders and borrowers link up better.[12] The Fed and the markets finally got it right at the close of the 1930s. The gold standard was the other major 'monetary' cause of the depression. But once the gold standard stabilized and gold flowed to the U.S. at the end of the 1930s, the depression ended.[13] Thus monetary forces—the Fed policy, coordination problems at the local level, and gold flows—both caused and ended the depression, respectively. As in all monetarist views, however, there is little or no account given to finance or consumption, or their degree of fragility. The economy is a 'black box': just plug in the money supply (read: pump liquidity into the system gold or by making the credit delivery system from banks to borrowers more efficient) and the crisis is over. Like Greenspan, Bernanke also maintained that speculation-driven asset price bubbles like the housing crisis, tech stocks, commodities, or whatever, cannot be prevented; like Greenspan, the cause of the housing bubble was the global savings glut.[14]

The global savings glut theory is a convenient device for deflecting attention from the real speculative forces behind all the bubbles, most of which originate with Anglo-American investors. It is a way to blame China and other economies for accumulating too much foreign currency and reserves, the dollar in particular. It assumes erroneously that those excess reserves then get funneled back into the U.S. stock and housing markets, precipitating the price inflation and causing the boom and bust. There is no hard evidence, however, that excess currency reserves in emerging markets, in China, Asia and elsewhere, were recycled into U.S. housing and other speculative opportunities in sufficient magnitude to alone have caused the bubbles. As even Stephen Roach argued recently,

> it is absurd to blame overseas lenders for reckless behavior by Americans that a US central bank should have contained. Asia's surplus savers had nothing to do with America's irresponsible penchant for leveraging a housing bubble...Mr. Bernanke's saving glut argument was at the core of a deep-seated US denial that failed to look in the mirror and pinned blame on others.[15]

This view of the global savings glut is almost uniquely an American explanation. Other major economies do not subscribe to it, including the euro-region. The 'glut' theory as the cause of bubbles arose in practical policy form once again in late September 2009 at the G20 nations meeting in the U.S. The U.S. position at the gathering was that 'global imbalances' are what caused the global financial crisis of 2008–09. The idea once again is that China and other emerging market countries have been pursuing policies that maximize their foreign currency and other assets, especially U.S. Treasury bonds. That 'imbalance' (read: glut) then flows back and destabilizes the U.S economy and financial system.

Reviewing both Greenspan's and Bernanke's earlier views is not a simple historical exercise. These perspectives and conservative biases conditioned Bernanke's initial slow response to the subprime crisis and consequent recession once it began to unfold after August 2007. For example, Bernanke's initial response to August 2007 was to wait an entire month before lowering rates, and thereafter to reduce rates by token increments of only 0.25 percent on only two occasions during the entire remainder of 2007, as the economy rapidly slid into recession. As late as October 31, 2007, after cutting rates a meager 0.25 percent, the Fed still believed that inflation was a "greater threat than recession."[16] A month later, in December, the U.S. economy entered recession territory, according to the official recession dating authority, the National Bureau of Economic Research (NBER).

By December it was clear that the banking system, in the U.S. and globally, was in rapid decline. Banks were not lending even to each other, out of concern as to whether they were solvent or not. They were even less inclined to lend to business in general. Since 2001 more than $2.6 trillion in subprime mortgages had been originated and they were souring at a rapid rate, causing massive losses on bank balance sheets. With insufficient reserves to cover their losses, bank credit rapidly began to dry up.

It has been argued that Bernanke's cautious reduction of interest rates was motivated by his concern that lowering rates would cause a sharp decline in the U.S. dollar in world markets. Protecting the dollar was apparently the more important Fed policy at the time (as it would be once again after mid 2009). Instead of more aggressive rate cuts, the Fed decided instead to provide $20 billion in direct loans to banks in trouble, the Term Auction Facility (TAF), with bids for the loans starting at a rate of 4.17 percent, just barely below the Fed's official 4.25 percent federal funds interest target rate. It was yet another measure that proved insufficient to stabilize the banks or get the economy moving again, both of which continued to deteriorate. At the end of 2007, Bernanke and Fed policy were well behind the crisis curve, which was accelerating.

In the opening months of 2008 the economic crisis—financial and real—deteriorated further and at an accelerating pace. Bernanke and the Fed turned to more aggressive interest rate cuts. In January, two rate reductions lowered the federal funds rate by 1.25 percent, to 3.00 percent, including an emergency reduction of 0.75 percent on January 22. But the moves now had little impact on bank balance sheets. Losses from subprimes were exacerbated by losses from other assets. Securitization of subprimes and other mortgages had tied those assets' decline to others, including commercial paper and other credit market instruments. Losses were multiplying and bank balance sheets were turning negative faster than capital could be borrowed from the Fed or other sources to shore them up. At this point, speculation began to feed off of itself. The speculative excesses in subprimes and securitized assets, now collapsing, were bringing into the market increasing numbers of speculators called 'short sellers' who began betting on the fall in the stock prices of those banks and institutions facing the greatest losses from the subprimes and securitized assets. Short selling speculation drove bank stock prices down further. This meant additional capital losses on balance sheets, bringing still more short sellers into the market, in a downward spiral of the stock prices of the banks in trouble.

The group of shadow banks called 'investment banks' or I-banks were particularly hard hit in this process during the opening months of 2008. The investment banks that had aggressively speculated in subprimes, and securitized collateralized debt obligations (CDOs), or the credit instruments insuring CDOs, called credit default swaps (CDSs), were particularly impacted by the short selling. The most vulnerable of the I-bank/shadow banks at the time were Bear Stearns and Lehman Brothers. Both had extended deep into subprimes and other securitized assets. Both companies bought residential and commercial mortgage companies and assets as late as 2007 when prices of these companies' mortgage portfolios had peaked and could only decline. Short sellers would soon attack them both aggressively.

Bear Stearns was especially dependent on day-to-day funding from the big commercial banks like J.P. Morgan Chase and others. As Bear Stearns' stock plummeted it had to use up virtually all its capital. As it did so, other commercial banks began to refuse to loan it overnight funds in order to keep operating. Other shadow bank investors like hedge funds with money in Bear Stearns began pulling out their funds. What this represented was a kind of 'wholesale' or institutional run on the bank in the case of Bear Stearns. It was about to go bankrupt. Were Bear Stearns a commercial bank and thus a member of the Federal Reserve system, the Fed could have provided funds to it through its recent TAF auction or by other direct means. But at this time the shadow investment banks like Bear Stearns were not members of the Fed system and could not join even if they wanted. Bear Stearns also 'owed' other banks and financial institutions. Had it simply gone bankrupt, that would have resulted in additional major losses of those other institutions at a time during which their losses were growing rapidly for other reasons. The chain reaction of losses and bank defaults might have been serious.

The Fed at this point, in mid March 2008, intervened unilaterally, redefining its own charter to cover the investment bank segment of the shadow banking sector. It 'arranged' for the sale of Bear Stearns to J.P. Morgan Chase at firesale $2 per share prices, or about $236 million, a total value more than $1 billion less than Bear Stearns' Manhattan, New York, office building. The Fed gave J.P. Morgan $29 billion to ensure the deal. Morgan would not even have to put up its own collateral, the Fed allowing it to use Bear Stearns' assets instead. In short, J.P. Morgan Chase was given Bear Stearns virtually free, hand-delivered by the Fed. In arranging the firesale of Bear Stearns to J.P. Morgan Chase, the Fed entered new territory as 'lender of last resort.' It gave the signal that banks, even shadow banks, henceforth would not be allowed to fail. Moral hazard was no longer a factor to the Fed.

The bankruptcy of Bear Stearns set off instability in other areas, including globally. In addition to the $29 billion Bear Stearns bailout, the Fed instituted new emergency lending facilities for primary dealers/investment banks/brokers and put up another $300 billion in funding. It also arranged $36 billion in swap loans to European central banks.

With the Bear Stearns bailout, the Fed had used up half of its available $850 billion of resources on hand. Having 'shot off its big gun,' it retreated temporarily to the sidelines. Bernanke's public position at this point was that banks and shadow banks still experiencing growing losses should now raise private capital on their own and not expect a bailout. But failing banks tend to have trouble raising capital, to say the least. And the new Fed policy of mass liquidity injection and bailout had now been set in motion. Market speculators were not fooled by talk of banks' raising capital on their own. and would soon test the limits of the Fed's new liquidity policy.

For a few months, in April–May 2008, it appeared the financial crisis had somewhat stabilized. The temporary effects from the fiscal stimulus bill passed in February were also entering the economy. That stimulus and continuing expansion in world trade, and thus exports, together appeared to prop up the real economy, which recorded a moderate rise in gross domestic product (GDP). But it was the weakest of recoveries, and sustaining it was never a question. It had dissipated in three months. The real economy continued to deteriorate below the surface throughout the spring of 2008 and into the summer. Nearly a year of credit tightening, slowing industrial production, and steadily rising jobless for seven straight months was taking a deeper toll on the real economy.

By June 2008 the decline of the real economy began to reappear. Debt loads were rising for banks, consumers and businesses alike. Prices were beginning to slow and level off. The exports and commodities boom was over. Unemployment was rising faster. Signs were growing the fiscal stimulus package passed in February was beginning to run out of steam. Oil, commodity, and export prices were starting to unwind. Bank lending to non-financial businesses was falling at a 9.1 percent annual rate—the fastest since 1973. Yields on corporate loans, investment grade bonds, and residential mortgages were falling—a reflection of the growing financial fragility of borrowers. Financial fragility and consumption fragility were both continuing to deteriorate. Meanwhile, short sellers and speculators were sharpening their knives, preparing to go after the next subprime burdened financial institution. By late June 2008 their next target was clear: the quasi-government agencies, Fannie Mae and Freddie Mac, that were required by law to buy up bad mortgages, and were now becoming overloaded as private sector lenders in effect transferred their debt and falling financial assets to Fannie and Freddie.

In July 2008, the renewed financial instability focused on Fannie/Freddie. A new phase in the financial crisis was about to emerge. In July the lead role as 'lender of last resort' shifted from the Fed—now on the sidelines trying to absorb the Bear Stearns bailout and the other emergency auctions initiated in March—to the U.S. Treasury and its Secretary, Henry Paulson.

THE PERILS OF PAULSON

Former CEO and Chairman of the largest I-bank, Goldman Sachs, and billionaire banker, Henry Paulson, was brought into the Bush administration at the end of June 2006. His prime task was to complete the deregulation of the financial sector. Initiated under Reagan, financial deregulation accelerated into high gear under Clinton in 1999–2000 with the repeal of the 1930s Glass–Steagall Act and its replacement with the Gramm–Bliley Act in 1999 and the passage of the Commodities Modernization Act soon after. The federal regulatory structure for banks and shadow banks was largely eviscerated by 1999–2000. I-banks like Goldman Sachs were removed altogether from the Securities and Exchange Commission's (SEC's) regulation. But state-level regulators were still an obstacle and an annoyance.

Paulson's first task was to clear the decks of this remaining obstacle on the road to total and complete financial deregulation. One of his first efforts in office was to form a Committee on Capital Markets Regulation (CCMR) along with other big financial institution players. The CCMR issued its 148-page report in November 2006. At the same time Paulson addressed the Economic Club of New York explaining the objectives of the report was to put in place curbs on state regulators, like New York's Eliot Spitzer and others. The report came up with 32 specific recommendations for legislation, and called for a basic change in financial regulatory policy that would focus on "the soundness of the financial system" instead of an individual institution's acts of wrongdoing. Regulators at the SEC and elsewhere would henceforth have to do cost-benefit analyses for every rule, economists would replace lawyers on the staff, and the federal government would be given power to block indictments by state regulators. Paulson and the Treasury held a conference in early 2007 to push the proposals further toward legislative enactment.[17] It was followed by a recommendation by the Paulson-headed President's Working Group on Financial Markets that the hedge fund industry, now with nearly $2 trillion in assets, should not be regulated. Nor should the government levy taxes on hedge funds and private equity firms, another new form of shadow banking. Such was the mindset of the man who the Bush administration would call on to bring discipline and regulation to the banking system once it began to collapse.

A final *coup de grâce* for financial regulation, the Supreme Court added its weight to efforts to silence state regulators who were now increasingly warning of growing financial irregularities and pending crisis. The Court ruled in April 2007 that mortgage subsidiaries of national banks were no longer subject to state regulators. States were thus stripped of the authority they had exercised for 35 years.

Once the subprime mortgage bust occurred in early August 2007, Paulson had little to say and did even less, leaving action to the Fed. In October 2007 in another speech he called for better monitoring of mortgage brokers, but added that a new 'regulatory blueprint' would take years to develop and implement.

Paulson, like Bernanke at the time, was deeply committed to voluntary solutions to the crisis, advocating that banks pool their remaining assets as a defense to the crisis. Some of the larger banks attempted to do so, forming a 'super-conduit fund' called the Master Liquidity Enhancement Conduit (MLEC). As for homeowners, now beginning to default in increasing numbers and foreclose, Paulson's answer was voluntary action by lenders in which they would renegotiate loans. When Sheila Bair, head of the Federal Deposit Insurance Corporation (FDIC), proposed to freeze interest rates temporarily on 2 million mortgages, Paulson opposed vigorously. Instead, he led Bush efforts to launch what was called the 'HOPE NOW Alliance Plan' for voluntary mortgage relief. The *New York Times* called the Paulson plan "too little, too late, too voluntary," designed to create the appearance of action to undercut more aggressive proposals pending U.S. House of Representatives bills introduced in November–December 2007. Outside experts, like Harvard

University bankruptcy expert Elizabeth Warren, called the Paulson proposal "the bank lobby's dream."[18]

Paulson continued to sit on the sidelines in early 2008 as the Fed struggled to get ahead of the crisis curve in the weeks leading up to the Bear Stearns collapse in mid March 2008. In March the Fed originally requested that Paulson and the Treasury bail out Bear Stearns, but Paulson refused, putting forward the excuse that the Treasury could do nothing without an Act of Congress.[19]

In a U.S. Chamber of Commerce speech in March after the Fed's bailout, Paulson continued to argue that I-banks should not be regulated like commercial banks, adding that "recent market conditions are an exception to the norm" and it was premature to attempt a system-wide bank stabilization effort.[20] Instead, he referred to his blueprint for a new deregulated system and proposed that oversight of state banks should be reassigned from the FDIC to the Fed and Bernanke.[21] That blueprint also proposed replacing the SEC, tasked with bank regulation since the 1930s, with a "self regulating organization, an industry group that develops and enforces rules of conduct and business standards...."[22]

In other words, even after the collapse of Bear Stearns—an event which clearly signaled that other I-banks, and many hedge funds and mortgage lenders, were in deep trouble and were already technically insolvent—Paulson kept pushing the Bush party line of financial deregulation as he had from first entering office as Treasury Secretary a year earlier. He pushed for voluntary self-rescue by the banks and voluntary renegotiation of mortgages—neither of which happened. Paulson's main proposal for dealing with the growing financial crisis was for the banks to 'raise capital' on their own to offset the deepening losses on their balance sheets.

Paulson, the champion of financial deregulation, of hands-off and voluntary solutions, and of the view banks should rescue themselves, was, in a matter of days, thrust into the opposite role, in which he would perform even more questionably. It all began with the crisis of the quasi-government mortgage agencies, Fannie Mae and Freddie Mac, in early July 2008. That date marks the beginning of the road to the banking panic of 2008 in September–October and to a subsequent virtual shutdown of the financial system.

By law, Fannie and Freddie were required to buy up mortgages. Before the crisis erupted, they were limited to buying no more than 40 percent of mortgages issued. By June 2008 that had risen to more than 80 percent. Like private mortgage lenders and financial institutions, Fannie/Freddie resold $1.7 trillion worth of bundled mortgages, but in their case directly as U.S. securities to investors, banks, and central banks around the world. Thus bad subprimes bought by the agencies were recycled globally, tying financial institutions worldwide into the web of bad mortgage debt. By summer 2008 the two agencies found themselves with a total of $5.3 trillion in liabilities, but with only $81 billion in reserves. That meant reserves equal to only 1.6 percent of the mortgage liabilities they owned or guaranteed. It was a classic case of severe and sharply deteriorating financial fragility.

As it became increasingly apparent Fannie/Freddie were taking on more and more bad debt, investors became more concerned that the two agencies could not cover their multi-trillion-dollar liabilities with their miniscule liquid funds on hand. With housing prices continuing to fall and foreclosures rising, in early July analysts estimated losses by Fannie/Freddie over the coming year ranging from $100 to $300 billion. It was a perfect scenario for speculators and short sellers to jump in and repeat the process that drove Bear Stearns into financial oblivion, and which was now eating away at other I-banks like Lehman Brothers, Morgan Stanley, and others. The big attack came the week of July 7–11 as speculators began aggressively short selling their stock. The commodities speculation boom was now over; there was even more available liquidity now with which to speculate by short selling. Fannie/Freddie was the target.

In the days immediately leading up to July 11, Paulson repeatedly proclaimed that the two agencies had sufficient capital, were voluntarily raising more, and that no rescue of the agencies was necessary. Of course, Paulson never bothered to explain how companies with such a collapse in stock prices might be able to raise capital. By the end of the week of July 7–11, Fannie Mae's stock price was down 76 percent over the previous year, and Freddie's had fallen 83 percent. Nevertheless, as late as July 10 Paulson was publicly stating that there was no anticipation of the need for a bailout. As he publicly declared, "For market discipline to effectively constrain risk financial institutions must be allowed to fail."[23]

Over the weekend of July 12–13, Paulson did an about-face. When markets opened on Monday, July 14, Paulson and Bernanke together announced a plan that guaranteed that the government would not allow Fannie/Freddie to fail. The plan required that Congress provide $300 billion of bailout funding. Paulson graphically explained that he wouldn't need to use the $300 billion. It was just his 'bazooka,' he said, the threat of which would prove sufficient to deter collapse of the agencies. Until Congress passed the funding, the Fed provided interim emergency loans to the two agencies from its 'discount' window and the newly established Fed special auction. Paulson also proposed that the U.S. Treasury buy the two agencies' public stock, thus propping up their stock prices, if necessary.

Congress passed an emergency housing industry law in late July. In it were provisions for $100 billion immediately and up to $300 billion later to bail out Fannie/Freddie if needed. Paulson said he wouldn't need to use it; that the mere option of its availability would prove sufficient to calm the speculators, markets, and investors. He was wrong again. Throughout August, short sellers were driving the agencies' stock prices down to record lows. Sometime in August Paulson shifted to bailout. At the end of the first week of September, he shot off his bazooka and bailed out Fannie/Freddie. The shot was heard around the financial world. Now it was crystal clear that the Fed's and the Treasury's policy was to bail out whatever financial institution was in trouble. Bear Stearns was not an aberration, a one-time event. It was now all about helicopters and bazookas.

What explains the 180-degree shift by Paulson? One plausible interpretation is that foreign investors, banks, and central banks that had accumulated $1.7 trillion in Fannie/Freddie agency debt began to panic and demand that Paulson take action to ensure Fannie/Freddie wouldn't collapse. As the two agencies' stock prices fell to single digits, Paulson stepped in to protect foreign bondholders. Failure to placate foreign bondholders could well mean a sharp decline in their purchase of U.S. bonds needed to finance the continually rising U.S. budget deficit, which was about to accelerate by trillions in the next year. But by protecting bondholders in the Fannie/Freddie bailout and allowing preferred and common stockholders to lose everything, Paulson doomed the rest of the investment banks to the short seller wolves. With stockholders seeing the writing on the wall, they were now more than ever willing to sell their stock, creating the perfect situation for short sellers. It also made it virtually impossible for Fannie/Freddie or any I-bank to voluntarily raise equity capital. The manner in which Paulson handled the Fannie/Freddie bailout exacerbated the pressures on the investment banks. Then bailing out just the bondholders worsened the situation. In short, Paulson bungled the process.

By the Fed bailing out Bear Stearns and the Treasury Fannie and Freddie, Bernanke and Paulson thought it would restore confidence in the institutions and the financial system in general. All it did was encourage speculators to go after the remaining I-banks more aggressively. It was now the end of the first week of September, and the worst was yet to come.

Between the first and second weeks of September the stock prices of all the remaining investment banks went into freefall. The 'raise capital voluntarily' strategy of the preceding three months thus collapsed with the collapse of banks' stock. In other words, financial fragility was rapidly worsening as a consequence of the bailouts of Bear Stearns and Fannie/Freddie. The remaining large I-banks—Merrill Lynch, Morgan Stanley, Goldman Sachs, Lehman Brothers, and others—were also in big trouble by September. The most serious was Lehman Brothers, an I-bank with $639 billion in assets but with leveraged debt of 30 to 1, and most of that in subprimes, commercial property, and LBOs. Of all the I-banks, Lehman was also the most exposed to securitized assets in general. Between 2003 and 2007, Lehman had securitized $700 billion in assets—85 percent of which ($600 billion) were residential; 40 percent of its subprimes were delinquent. And by September Lehman had less than $20 billion in liquid resources on hand and couldn't raise capital despite multiple attempts to do so. Lehman sought desperately to sell its best assets at firesale prices to raise capital, even seeking buyers in Korea, Japan, and China. But all walked away from deals. It then tried to get the Fed to extend its status as a bank holding company (as the Fed did for Bear Stearns) to allow it access to emergency Fed auctions and funding. But the Fed refused.

One might reasonably ask, why were short sellers and other speculators intent on driving down stock prices of I-banks like Lehman when it might result in the latter's collapse? The answer is yet another example of speculation in financial assets running rampant. Investors after 2000 were able to purchase

CDS derivatives. CDSs were originally conceived as insurance against the collapse of a company. If the collapse occurred, those who bought CDS contracts as insurance would be paid off. But CDSs soon evolved into more than insurance contracts. They became a form of investment gambling. CDS contracts had zoomed in worth to $60 trillion worldwide in less than a decade. Speculators were increasingly buying CDS contracts as a 'bet' that a company would in fact fail and they'd receive a payoff. CDS purchases typically totaled even more than a company was worth. CDS betting thus presented an incentive for speculators to drive a company into bankruptcy by short selling. Speculators could make money as the stock price fell, and then again when the company collapsed Short sellers made money on driving down stock prices. But as stock prices fell, CDS prices escalated in value. Speculative profits were thus possible in both directions simultaneously—on stock asset price collapse and CDS asset price inflation—in a dual kind of betting. All this amounted to speculating on speculation—i.e. 'casino investing.'

The Bush administration for years resisted any effort to regulate CDS trades. There was no public market for CDSs and thus no regulation possible. Trades were conducted privately and no one knew for certain, least so the government, where the trades were made and for how much or how many parties there were to a trade. Nor was the Bush administration willing to do much about the growing number, weight, and influence of short sellers. Once the commodities boom ended in the spring of 2008, more short sellers entered the market attacking the I-banks' stock prices. The Bush SEC had placed token limits on short selling earlier in the year. The SEC then allowed those limits to expire in mid August, which resulted in even more intensified short selling of Fannie/Freddie, Lehman Brothers, and other banks' stock. Lehman stock in particular came under massive short selling pressure between September 8 and 12.[24]

On September 15 the Treasury held an emergency meeting to which 30 top banks globally were invited to try to arrange a buyer for Lehman Brothers. At first, Bank of America appeared interested. But Merrill Lynch quickly offered itself to Bank of America on terms the latter could not refuse, and Bank of America bought Merrill Lynch instead. There were potential buyers for Lehman and it could have been bought. The lynchpin of the problem was the Treasury's refusal to 'insure' the deal for any of the buyers—just the opposite of the insured deal J.P. Morgan Chase got from the Fed with the Bear Stearns bailout. Lehman, in contrast, was allowed to go bankrupt. But before it was announced the following Monday, the banks were allowed a special four-hour trading session to hedge their possible losses with CDSs and other derivatives. Lehman Brothers was history that following Monday. Within days the fall of Lehman set off a collapse of a string of financial institutions. The biggest was the insurance giant AIG, which the government then bailed out quickly for $123 billion (later extended to more than $180 billion).

A key, still unanswered, question is, why did Paulson support the Fed bailout of Bear Stearns prior to Lehman Brothers' collapse and AIG immediately after, but allow Lehman itself to collapse? One possible answer is that Bear

Stearns and AIG were both heavily involved with CDSs, while Lehman was overexposed to subprime and commercial mortgages and leveraged loans but not particularly exposed to CDSs. Could it be, then, that the problem wasn't that AIG and Bear Stearns were 'too big to fail,' but that the CDS derivatives market was 'too big'? Another, perhaps more conspiratorial explanation is that Goldman Sachs, Paulson's old company where he was previously chairman, had heavily invested in Bear Stearns and stood to lose billions if it went under, whereas Lehman was Goldman Sachs' main competitor. But estimates of a Lehman bailout were no more than $85 billion, less than half that spent on AIG a few days later. Then again, AIG was one of the biggest players in CDSs. Arguments by Paulson that bailing out Lehman would have created a 'bailout culture' are simply not convincing; that culture had already been created with Bear Stearns and Fannie/Freddie.

The decision to let Lehman Brothers collapse was, in the last analysis, Paulson's. To his bungled handling of the Fannie/Freddie bailouts was thus added his even greater misstep with Lehman. But it would not be his last. Lehman's mid September failure set off the banking panic of 2008. Unlike Fannie/Freddie, where stockholders lost everything but bondholders were protected, Lehman bondholders also lost everything, months later only recovering 8 cents on the dollar. Only those who held derivatives on Lehman were first in line to claim whatever assets were left—i.e. to recall, the 'big 30' banks that Paulson brought together on the eve of the Lehman collapse and which Paulson allowed four hours to buy CDS claims to hedge their losses before the Lehman bankruptcy was announced. They lost little, if anything. In contrast to bonds and stocks, CDS claims delivered 91 cents on the dollar.[25] But of course that's not 'insider trading.'

The Lehman Brothers collapse and how it was allowed to unwind exacerbated an already deteriorating state of confidence in the banking system's future. Now no one knew for certain what the government's policy was—bailout if 'too big,' or let them fail if 'too big.' Paulson's handling of it in effect created the worst of both worlds.

In quick succession a series of other banks either folded or were absorbed into others. Washington Mutual, Wachovia, Merrill Lynch, AIG—all quickly imploded. The case of AIG is of particular interest. This time Paulson didn't call in the CEOs of the leading banks to his office to mutually decide. He brought in only his old alma mater, Goldman Sachs. To recall, AIG was deeply exposed to CDSs. And Goldman Sachs was deeply exposed to AIG. Paulson not only bailed out AIG—he bought them out! AIG was bought by the government, the U.S. Treasury, for 100 cents on the dollar. Full price. No negotiations and no 'haircuts' for those exposed to AIG—one of which was Goldman Sachs, the only bank allowed in the decision with Paulson the weekend before the AIG announcement. Initially the cost to the taxpayer of the AIG bailout was $123 billion. Shortly thereafter the terms were adjusted more favorably to AIG and even more money was doled out to them. Still another dose followed. The sharp contrasts between the way Lehman was handled and the way Paulson 'resolved' the much larger AIG crisis raise interesting questions—especially given the presence of Goldman Sachs as the only bank present in the decision to take over and bail out AIG.

Following the collapse of AIG and the big banks, the run by institutions and 'wholesalers' on shadow banks spread rapidly to other financial institutions and markets. Hedge funds were hard hit by the Lehman failure. They held 32 percent of the entire $60 trillion CDS market. Withdrawals of investors from the funds accelerated, forcing the funds to freeze withdrawals. They would quickly lose $600 billion in withdrawals. Almost immediately hedge funds therefore began selling their assets. The prices for loans for leveraged buyouts also began to collapse. Money market funds with their $4 trillion in assets began experiencing withdrawals, and one of the largest funds, Primary Reserve, nearly went bust. The commercial paper market shut down. Nearly all securitized consumer credit markets collapsed. The stock market plummeted with the Dow Jones experiencing a series of its worst days on record.

In other words, asset price deflation was rapidly spreading to other sectors of the shadow banking system. In contrast, prices of CDSs soared, delivering super-profits to gamblers and speculators. Foreign banks began withdrawing funds from the U.S. banking system as well, as the banking crisis spread rapidly in Europe with failures of British, Belgian, and Icelandic banks. Registering massive losses, U.S. banks, traditional and shadow, began freezing credit. No longer a credit crunch, the system entered a phase of virtual credit crash after September 19, 2008. The credit crash accelerated the transmission of the financial crisis to the real economy. Mass layoffs quickly followed in November and December, continuing through the first half of 2009.[26] Financial fragility had 'fractured' seriously with the events of September–October 2008. Mass layoffs meant that consumption fragility was now about to deteriorate further as well, as credit to households collapsed while disposable income fell.

On September 19 Paulson proposed to Congress that it give the Treasury $700 billion to buy-up bad assets of the banks in order to resolve the crisis. At first Congress balked and rejected the bill. Paulson's proposal was a simple one-page request, saying nothing about how or where the $700 billion was to be spent. It was essentially a blank check for him to sign and spend as he alone determined. After the 'no' vote, it was revised. Between the first and second votes a massive business lobbying campaign descended on Capitol Hill. Legislators were threatened with a financial Armageddon, for which they would be solely responsible should the bill not pass. The $700 billion was all necessary, Paulson argued, in order to buy the bad assets on the balance sheets of banks. Cleaning up the bad assets was necessary, he argued, in order to get the banks to begin lending again—both to homeowners and the mortgage markets and to general business. The government relented and gave him his $700 billion check, with the understanding that he would buy the bad assets on banks' books and thereby end the credit crash.

With the money in hand he set out to purchase the assets. He soon found that $700 billion was far too little. The value of the assets on the balance sheets of banks that had collapsed were worth at least $4 trillion, as was later revealed by the International Monetary Fund (IMF) and other independent estimates.[27] Worse, the banks themselves didn't want to sell them; that is, unless Paulson and the government were interested in buying them at the prior, full purchase market value. The banks were keeping the assets on their books at inflated, above market price. They had no incentive to sell them at market prices and register even greater losses in doing so. They wanted Paulson to buy them at above market price.

This, of course, posed a serious problem for Paulson. If he purchased assets worth 50 cents or even 10 cents on the dollar, he would be charged with providing a windfall profit to the banks purchasing the assets well above what they were worth. Besides, the $700 billion would hardly dent the $4 trillion, and the problem would remain. But the banks wouldn't sell at the true market value of the assets. If they did, then they would have to write down trillions of dollars more on their balance sheets, which were already deep in the red. There would be no doubt that they were insolvent in that case. So it was a stand-off. Banks wouldn't sell at true market value; Paulson couldn't buy at their inflated initial purchase value. The bad assets remained on the books—and continued to grow. Bank balance sheets continued to deteriorate as the value of housing prices, mortgage bonds, and other securities continued to collapse in value as housing, stock market, and various securitized asset prices continued to fall.

Congress repeatedly requested information on what he was doing with the $700 billion in the weeks following the passage of the $700 billion bill, now called the Troubled Asset Relief Program (TARP). Unable to buy the assets and clean up the banks' balance sheets—which all agreed was the necessary first step to get 'credit flowing again,' as the bankers' favorite phrase goes—Paulson instead threw $125 billion at the nine biggest banks. He called their CEOs to his office and told them they had to take the money whether they wanted to or not. He followed the disbursement by another roughly $125 billion to scores of regional and smaller banks. None of the $250 billion was used to purchase bad assets. Another $80 billion or so went to AIG in several installments. Tens of billions of dollars more to Citigroup and Bank of America in November. Nearly $20 billion to auto companies. By February 2009, less than $190 billion of the $700 remained. Once again, none of it had been expended to purchase bad assets.

To sum up his performance, Paulson's term in office amounted to a series of actions that did nothing to address or correct the crisis, and actually served to exacerbate it. His errors were both strategic and tactical. Right up to August 2007 he continued to push financial deregulation, when it was clear that deregulation was contributing to the problem of financial fragility and instability. He then did virtually nothing for nine months after the crisis evolved, deferring to Bernanke and the Fed. His one weak foray into the crisis in 2007 was to push Bush's plan to get banks and mortgage lenders to voluntarily renegotiate mortgages, announced in December 2007. Reportedly, no more than 50 such mortgages were ever reset under this plan. He stood by and played cheerleader to Bernanke as the Fed bailed out Bear Stearns, and distributed $400 billion to banks, including those offshore, in March 2008.

After March he pushed once again for banks to voluntarily raise capital on their own, even as speculators were hammering their stock prices throughout the summer of 2008. He did nothing to limit short sellers, and in fact opposed measures that would have reduced their impact. When thrust to the fore in the case of Fannie Mae and Freddie Mac in July, he repeatedly denied that they needed government bailout, and said publicly that he would not use the $300 billion allocated by Congress if it were given to him, and signaled that if he did bail them out, he would protect bondholders only, which accelerated the dumping of their stock and the short selling. He then totally reversed himself and bailed out the agencies in early September. The flip-flopping and dragging out of the bailout decision fueled the speculation in their stock that doomed Fannie/Freddie. It also fueled speculation in the stocks of investment banks like Lehman Brothers and others, pushing them past the point of no return in September.

Bailing out Fannie/Freddie after insisting that no more bailouts would occur, then switching 180 degrees and refusing to bail out Lehman Brothers, destroyed whatever confidence might have been restored by consistent Fed–Treasury policy action. After letting Lehman collapse he then reversed a second time and bailed out AIG, in a process that was highly suspect given the presence of only one bank, Goldman Sachs, participating in the decision. Paulson thereafter panicked Congress into providing the $700 billion TARP, which he never put to the authorized use, but instead partially dissipated on a string of piecemeal rescue efforts. As former IMF economist Simon Johnson commented in January 2009, "How could a person with so much market experience be repeatedly at the center of such major misunderstandings regarding the markets...?"[28] Following the TARP fiasco, Paulson steadily slipped into policy oblivion, as Bernanke and the Fed assumed center stage once again.

As Paulson was about to leave office, he gave an interview to the British financial daily, the *Financial Times*, in early January 2009. In it he admitted, in ex-college football lineman terms, "we are dealing here with something that is really historic and we have not had a playbook."[29] A problem, indeed, when the quarterback does not know what plays to call, has no strategy, and doesn't even want to be on the field in the first place.

BERNANKE'S B-52

True to his philosophical 'monetarist' roots, Bernanke's solution to a deep financial crisis was simply to throw money at it—i.e. a liquidity solution to an insolvency crisis. As Bernanke publicly told the famous monetarist economist Milton Friedman, at a Fed conference in 2002, thanks to him (Friedman) the Fed now knew how to prevent a depression: just drop money from a helicopter.

But to ask a rhetorical question: isn't excess liquidity one of the root sources of the increasing shift to speculative investing, that in turn has been driving excess credit, debt, and financial fragility and instability? Won't pumping more liquidity into the system now result in more fragility and instability later, one might ask? Is there no correlation between Greenspan's doing just that since the 1980s and the growing frequency and virulence of financial crises worldwide the last quarter of a century? Isn't the so-called global savings glut an example of excess liquidity, feeding the global money parade, sloshing around the world seeking and provoking speculative bubble after bubble?

After the banking panic of October 2008, an even more massive injection of Fed provided liquidity occurred. Bernanke traded in his helicopter for a B-52. With all the attention on Paulson's $700 billion TARP package, the real action was at the Fed. Between mid September and early January 2009, the Fed injected or guaranteed more than $4 trillion of liquidity by means of the following various programs and actions:[30]

Table 8.1   Federal Reserve Liquidity Provisions and Guarantees, September 2008–January 2009

Fed Action	Date
$85 billion credit line extension to AIG	September 16
$240 billion credit swap lines to central banks (U.S. and foreign)	September 18
$50 billion credit line to money market funds	September 19
New asset-backed mutual fund liquidity facility (AMLF)	September 19
$300 billion increase in TAF auctions liquidity	September 29
$330 billion additional increase in central bank swap lines	September 29
$450 billion increase in TAF auction cash to banks	October 6
Fed begins paying interest on reserves of banks	October 6
New commercial paper funding facility (CPFF)	October 7
Coordinated interest rate cuts with other central banks	October 8
Unlimited commitment to swap facilities with central banks	October 13
$600 billion for new money market funding facility (MMFF)	October 21
$30 billion swap lines set up with emerging markets	October 29
$326 billion to Citigroup ($20 billion loan; $306 guarantee)	November 24
$200 billion for term asset-back securities lending facility (TALF)	November 25
$600 billion to purchase mortgage bonds and mortgage-based securities (MBSs)	November 25
$300 billion to purchase long-term Treasury bonds	December 1
$100 billion to purchase Agency (Fannie/Freddie) mortgage debt	December 1
$90 billion for Bank of America ($20 billion capital; $70 billion loans)	January 16

The above amounts are in addition to the Bear Stearns bailout and related measures that totaled more than $400 billion earlier in the year, the $300 billion authorized for Fannie/Freddie bailouts passed by Congress, the Treasury's $700 billion TARP, and hundreds of billions needed by the FDIC to pay off depositors as smaller banks began to collapse by the hundreds. And in addition to the Fed's direct 'auctions' noted above, there are the Fed policies of lowering interest rates to 0.25 percent; Fed decisions to pay banks interests on their reserves; the Fed's policy of 'quantitative easing,' the commitment to buy more than $1 trillion in mortgages, and to buy $300 billion in long-term Treasury bonds.

The Fed's balance sheet as of June 2009 was officially in the red by more than $2.1 trillion.[31] And the Fed was still prepared to write more checks to the banks if necessary. Beyond the publicly reported $2.1 trillion it has spent to date, *Bloomberg News* reported "the U.S. government is prepared to provide more than $7.76 trillion on behalf of American taxpayers."[32] The true, full amount of all the deals, and what has actually been spent and committed, is as yet unknown. In fact, to date, Congress itself has demanded but cannot get a full report from the Fed.

THE LIMITS OF LIQUIDITY SOLUTIONS IN EPIC RECESSIONS

The fundamental policy pursued by both the Fed and the Treasury has been to throw whatever liquidity was necessary at the problem to prevent the 'big 19' banks from going bust. The 8,400 smaller and regional banks could go under. It was the job of the FDIC to bail out, close, restructure, and reimburse to them. It was likely that more than 200 smaller community and regional banks would go under by the end of 2009, and at least another 300–500 in 2010. Countless other shadow banks will have gone bust as well. The Fed–Treasury strategy is to save the 'big 19' at whatever cost. But 'saving' here means offsetting their collapsing balance sheets with liquidity injections, not resolving the banks' problem of insolvency and removing the huge volume of bad assets still remaining on their books.

Throwing liquidity in massive amounts at bank and financial institution balance sheets doesn't resolve the fundamental problems with those balance sheets. The bad assets on their books haven't even come close to being 'recapitalized' by bank stock price appreciation. To date, only about 40 percent of total losses have been recapitalized. Throwing liquidity into those balance sheets only temporarily offsets those bad assets; it doesn't get rid of them. And what remains on their books serves as a serious drag on bank lending recovery, which evidence today confirms. As reported previously, bank lending to businesses fell consecutively every month throughout 2009. It has been falling similarly in Europe and elsewhere. Similarly, credit card and other lending to consumers has fallen as well. Only bank loans to speculative ventures, much of it offshore, has risen appreciably and has, in fact, been the main source of recent bank profits.

And there's the important question: is liquidity the solution when it is also part of the problem? And the equally important related questions: can resurrecting the securitized consumer and property markets—another Bernanke objective—be part of the solution when it has been a central part of the problem? If liquidity is all that is required by the Fed, what happens when central banks withdraw that excess liquidity? Will there be even less bank lending? Can anything be fundamentally resolved so long as the global money parade and global capital can flow freely, anywhere, anytime, and in any amount, without concern as to its financial and economically destabilizing consequences? Then there's the even more fundamental question: are banks and shadow banks becoming so addicted to the excess returns from speculative investing that they have become relatively less interested in lending to real asset investment that produces only a 10 percent income stream over 20 years, when they might realize returns equivalent to that in one year or less from speculation in derivatives, currencies, real estate, stocks and the like?

It is not possible to fully resolve a financial crisis of the dimensions witnessed since 2007 by a strategy of liquidity injection—no matter how large the amount of that liquidity injected. That strategy only succeeds, at best, in offsetting losses temporarily and fails to eliminate the bad assets that remain on balance sheets. And according to the IMF and other reputable sources, those bad debts are projected to continue to rise in 2010–11, while massive new refinancing of debts is also coming due thereafter in 2012–14.

Financial fragility is not eliminated, just temporarily checked, by liquidity injection. Throwing liquidity at the problem can relieve the problem of cash flow insufficiency and reduce financial fragility from the income side of the debt to cash flow ratio; but in doing so it only worsens the debt side of the ratio in the longer run. And when the liquidity support is withdrawn by the Fed, what then? Do both sides of the ratio collapse again? With liquidity injection only, the fundamental debt servicing problem remains, and may even have got worse. Furthermore, injecting liquidity into the financial system does nothing for consumption fragility in the real economy. Fiscal stimulus policies, in a sense, may be thought of as supplying 'liquidity' by providing a floor under the income side of consumption fragility. But what about the debt side of consumption fragility? Where are the policies that address that? Can the U.S. household and consumer keep the economy going without access to ever larger amounts of debt? Can debt not rise, so long as disposable income for tens of millions or more remains stagnant? And what if the fiscal policies are composed of temporary 'aid' injections and do not create ongoing income from job creation? The easing of consumption fragility in such case is thus also only temporary, just as recent liquidity injections by the Fed that ease financial fragility are temporary. What happens when 'temporary' is ended, and fragility in both forms is no longer 'offset' by Fed and fiscal liquidity injections? Can temporary solutions generate a sustained long run economic recovery?

Both forms of fragility, financial and consumption, must be addressed in the long run—on both the debt side and the income side. In the shorter run, deflation and defaults must also be contained. And in the most fundamental sense, the originating causes of excess liquidity, credit, and the shift toward speculative forms of investment require resolution, since they underlie much of the long-run problems with financial and consumption fragility.

The Greenspan–Bernanke monetary strategy relying primarily on liquidity injections addresses only a small isolated part of this picture. It provides only short-run, temporary assistance, only to offset financial fragility, not to resolve it long run. Their strategy addresses none of the problem with consumption fragility. And the strategy provides nothing to resolve consumption fragility. That's why the strategy to date can at best only stabilize the financial system and may only achieve a kind of flat or stagnant recovery. It can put a floor under financial fragility and prevent a further banking collapse, but alone cannot generate a sustained recovery of the economy.

The U.S. financial system has also come to a point of near-dependency on securitized markets. The implosion of those markets have contributed significantly to the depth, spread, and speed of propagation of the current financial collapse. Despite Bernanke's trillions of liquidity injected into the U.S. financial system, the securitized markets, once amounting to more than $2 trillion, have not revived. The U.S. economy had become dependent on securitized markets to finance commercial property, residential mortgages, auto, student, and credit cards, corporate loans of various kinds, and other assets. Those securitized markets were still, as of October 2009, largely frozen. Bernanke's goal is to try to resurrect them by providing liquidity. Bernanke believes the economy needs the revival of securitization. But the system may not be able to afford the debt, excess leveraging and instability that it also produces over time.

With banks still not lending, with the securitized markets still moribund, the only major source of financing for non-financial companies in 2009 has been the corporate bond markets. Corporate bond issuance has experienced a mini-bubble as a result. Speculation based on the junk bond markets yielded a 43 percent return in 2009 alone. But bond financing is still debt financing. And a good deal of that bond debt is of the poorest quality; i.e. refinancing using junk bond-grade debt results in companies paying up to 20 percent to refinance that debt. But it in essence amounts to adding debt in order to pay for debt. The bubble of sorts that has been created in the bond markets, junk bonds in particular, has enabled businesses to buy time to deal with their financial fragility. But should Fed interest rates rise sharply in 2011, the bond markets bubble could very well explode with greater force than the housing bubble did. Failures of companies that have become highly dependent on junk bonds are projected to rise to 15 percent, according to Standard & Poor's and Moody, Inc. the rating agencies. There are also signs that small- and medium-sized companies are also beginning to feel the increasing pressure. These are companies that have been unable to obtain finance via the corporate bond markets, or even junk bonds markets, unlike larger companies. They rely on loans from finance companies and banks, which have been drying up. An indicator perhaps of their growing debt stress, and likely future rise in defaults, is the pending bankruptcy of a company called CIT Inc. that has served as a primary source of credit for small businesses in the U.S.

Non-financial companies have been able to avoid a rise in defaults thus far also by the use of what are called 'covenants' and 'PIKs' (payments in kind) that allow them temporarily to postpone debt payments and bankruptcy. By mid 2009, the spreading use of covenants and PIKs appears to have been increasing once again. But like bond financing, these measures do not reduce financial fragility; they only postpone its effects.

OBAMA'S $787 BILLION FISCAL STIMULUS

In January 2009 Obama proposed an economic recovery bill called the American Recovery and Reinvestment Act (ARRA).

By February 2009, the real economy's decline was accelerating. GDP for the fourth quarter 2008 showed the US economy had contracted by more than 6.2 percent. Jobless levels from November 2008 through February 2009 rose nearly 2 million, according to official US government data. When properly adjusted to include the 6 million new underemployed since the recession began, plus discouraged and other workers not recorded in the official data, the increase in jobs lost was nearly 3 million in just three months.

At the same time the financial side of the economy continued to deteriorate. In January–February 2009 the balance sheets of banking and finance giants like Citigroup, Bank of America, AIG, Fannie Mae, and more than 250 regional banks then on the FDIC's official danger list, deteriorated further. A growing number of once financially sound banks and financial institutions became 'zombies' (i.e. banks in name only and not performing the functions of banks in fact), while previous zombies became virtual cadavers.

In an attempt to check and stabilize the growing real and financial decline, the new Obama administration proposed a four-part recovery program. The first part was the $787 billion fiscal stimulus bill passed in February targeting the real economy. On the banking side, there were three proposals to try to stabilize the financial system. These included the so-called public–private investment plan (PPIP), the term asset-backed securities lending facility (TALF), and the homeowner affordability and stability plan (HASP).

The Obama $787 billion fiscal stimulus bill called for only $180 billion in total spending in 2009 and only $26 billion of that allotted for jobs creation spending, according to the U.S. Congressional Budget Office. Less than $200 billion of the total $787 billion was designated for actual new jobs over the package's three-year term. Moreover, the majority of the jobs were associated with longer-term, capital-intensive infrastructure investment in alternative energy and public works, which produce relatively fewer jobs that take longer to create. The magic number thrown around by the administration was that the package would create 3 million new jobs. A few months after its passage, the claim of 3 million net *new* jobs changed to 3 million jobs created *or saved*. 'Saved' is unverifiable and whatever the government wanted to claim. But nearly 3 million real jobs had already been lost in just the preceding three months. That was verifiable. By the end of 2009 it would become clear that the ARRA and the Obama recovery plan did not come close to creating the jobs predicted. Debate intensified once again on how to amend the $787 bill to make it begin to appear as a jobs program.

Job losses approaching nearly 1 million a month, the collapse of consumer credit, rapidly rising home foreclosures, spreading wage-cutting, and falling house values were now causing a further deterioration of consumption fragility. In addition, the falling values of 401k pensions, the freefall in stock and homeowner equity, and a reduction in hours of work as the normal working week fell to only 33 hours, also meant that consumption continued to weaken. Even if all the $787 billion were targeted for restoring consumption, the $787 represented barely 4 percent of total GDP. Contrast that with China's stimulus spending launched in 2008, which represented nearly 20 percent of China's GDP.

Constituting about 71 percent of the US economy's GDP, consumption fell off a cliff from October 2008 through March 2009. For the first time ever in data-collecting history, consumption declined absolutely in the U.S. in 2008, while the index for future consumer spending hit a postwar low of 35 out of 100. Business spending after October 2008 fared no better. Business plans for capital expenditures in early 2009 showed a decline of more than one-third. At the same time, exports and world trade were now beginning to contract at the fastest rate in decades.

The $787 billion was comprised of both government spending and tax cuts. The tax cuts portion of the package was 38 percent, or roughly $300 billion. So just under $500 billion represented spending stimulus. However, only $180 billion total spending was earmarked for the first year, and only $27 billion of that was purportedly targeted for jobs creation. The remaining $320 billion in spending was allocated for the second and third years. Much of that $500 billion total spending was thus conveniently 'back loaded' by Congress—i.e. to take effect mostly in the second year, 2010, not in 2009. Not surprisingly, 2010 is a Congressional election year.

The composition of spending in the first year, 2009, focused on aid to the states, unemployment insurance, assistance for the unemployed to continue their health insurance payments, food stamps, Medicaid, $250 one-time rebates to social security recipients, and similar 'one-shot' spending injections. These kind of measures are not designed to generate jobs which translate into longer-term income growth and thus a more sustained recovery. While all these 'aid' measures were necessary and would have some limited impact on GDP recovery in 2009, they were essentially short term in nature and designed only to offset temporarily the anticipated longer-term collapse in spending occurring for other reasons noted previously. Once again, not resolving the problem of consumption fragility but only temporarily offsetting it.

The spending provisions of the stimulus show the true focus of Obama's grand recovery strategy: Obama's bank rescue measures were designed to put a floor under the collapse of the big banks. The fiscal measures were similarly designed to put a floor under the consumption collapse in the short run. Neither the financial bailout measures nor the stimulus measures were designed to regenerate the economy in sustained fashion over the longer run. Both the financial and spending plans were thus 'stop-gap' in nature, i.e. to put a floor under the economic collapse until the economy could recovery on its own. The Obama stimulus, in other words, reflected the dominant view and belief since the 1980s that the market system was 'efficient,' that it could regenerate itself. But the theory of efficient markets is fundamentally incorrect. Natural, self-recovery of the economy does not occur in cases of Epic Recessions or depressions. Recovery must be engineered. Merely holding the line on the collapse will, at best, result in long-term stagnation.

Obama's estimated $300 billion tax cut share of the $787 billion would prove as ineffective as Bush's in generating sustained recovery. In the early stages of deep business cycle declines, such as that which was occurring from October 2008 through early 2009, cutting taxes has very little effect on recovery. Conservatives make a fetish out of proposing business tax cuts, arguing that any kind of business-investor tax cuts create jobs no matter what stage of the business cycle, regardless of the magnitude or rate of the economic decline, regardless of whether that decline is globally synchronized, and whether the downturn was precipitated by financial instability. All these qualifications to the impact of a tax cut are considered irrelevant to those claiming that business tax cuts create jobs, no matter the conditions or causes.

On the consumer side, reducing taxes in a situation of a deep contraction precipitated by a financial crisis and extreme consumption fragility is also ineffective when incomes are collapsing, joblessness is rising sharply, and consumer debt levels were exceptionally high entering the downturn. Like business tax cuts, consumer tax reductions under these conditions are barely spent. They result in consumers saving the tax cuts or else paying-down debt levels.

Apart from spending and tax cut provisions, the third element of the $787 billion package amounted to various direct 'aid' measures. Fully 38 percent of the stimulus included measures like extending unemployment benefits, expanding costs of food stamps, medical costs assistance, and direct grants to state and local governments and school districts. While worthy and necessary, none of these measures are designed to create jobs. To sum up, 76 percent in combined tax cuts and aid promised little job creation. Of the remaining 24 percent, or $188 billion, only $27 billion was earmarked for projects that could create jobs in 2009. And all that at a time in which job losses were running at nearly 1 million a month! In terms of jobs, consumption, and general economic recovery, one may conclude that the $787 billion Obama recovery package, passed by Congress in early 2009, was too little, too late.

PIPP: SON OF TARP

In October 2008 when Henry Paulson was given $700 billion to buy up the banks' bad assets, the main argument made in its favor, by Paulson, the banks, Obama and his advisors, was that the $700 billion was necessary in order to 'get credit flowing again.' Congress gave Paulson the $700 billion based on the understanding that he would buy up the banks' bad assets and also use it to directly assist recovery in the housing industry. But, as explained earlier, Paulson never bought the bad assets, because the banks wouldn't sell them to him—at least not at the assets' true market value. So the banks continued to keep the bad assets on their books at inflated, above market price. The inflated prices were typically as high as 98 cents on the dollar, on average, whereas the real market prices were 10–50 cents on the dollar. In the final analysis, none of the $700 billion was used to purchase bad assets. Instead, the money was simply 'given' to the banks and other non-bank companies like AIG, GM, GE Credit, and of course tens of additional billions of dollars to Bank of America and Citigroup. By February 2009 less than $190 billion of the $700 remained. But none of it was expended as Congress intended: to purchase bad assets necessary to get credit moving again.

In February 2009 the new Treasury Secretary, Tim Geithner, faced the same dilemma as Paulson. Geithner's solution was to continue Paulson's TARP, but now with a twist. Geithner's 'son of TARP,' or TARP II, was called the private–public investment program, or PIPP for short. Geithner announced an initial version of PIPP in February 2009 as the $787 billion fiscal stimulus bill was being debated and passed in Congress. PIPP–TARP II would throw the banks and investors a big bone to get them to sell and buy the bad assets. The government, the Treasury, would do this by providing a subsidy both to the banks (the sellers of the bad assets) and to the investors (the prospective buyers of the bad assets). The banks were only willing to sell the bad assets at prices way above what those assets were worth on the market; the investors were only willing to buy them at the then market valuation prices. The idea of PIPP was for the government to close the price gap between them by making payments to both. To begin the process a public auction was held. A market price would be reached, undoubtedly unacceptable to both banks and investors. But the government then would make payments to each, in effect subsidizing that market price for each; i.e. it would make up the losses for the seller selling below top price, and guarantee any future losses for the investor if the market price should thereafter fall. Incredible as it seems, this first Geithner plan was attacked vigorously by bankers, investors, and the general business press. The details were not specific enough, they argued. The stock market plunged following the announcement of the outlines of the plan. Geithner thereafter went back to the drawing table to revise and clarify the plan, making sure it was more palatable to bankers and investors alike.

On March 23, 2009, Geithner released his revised formula for PIPP. The bad assets were divided into two basic types: bad bank mortgages and loans called 'legacy loans,' on the one hand, and bad securitized assets, on the other—i.e. the latter based on subprime mortgages, asset-backed commercial paper-based CDOs, securitized auto, credit card, and student loans, etc., bundled into the new derivatives based securities. What was new with the revised PIPP is that Geithner clarified that interest-free government loans would be provided up front to investor (buyers) with which to buy both types of the bad assets. If the auction at which the price of the assets was determined was too low, the investors could keep the government loans to make up the difference. Most importantly, the loans were now what was called 'non-recourse loans.' If the bad assets that were purchased later fell in value after the purchase, the borrower (investor) did not have to pay the government back. Nor was the borrower required to put up any collateral of his own for the government 'free money' loan.

To 'finance' this arrangement Geithner proposed using $100 billion from the original TARP funds held by the Treasury. The government was prepared either through the Treasury or the Fed to provide another $1 trillion as necessary to finance the proposal. The FDIC would administer the legacy loan part of the program, and the Fed the securitized bad assets part.

There were two fundamental problems with the PIPP, however. First, the banks were still reluctant to sell at anything below the 98 cents and original purchase price of the assets. If they did sell below, it would require write-downs and further losses when many of them were already technically insolvent. Recording losses also meant no annual bonuses for the senior managers in many cases. The other problem was the volume of the bad assets, which was much larger than government had imagined (how much larger the government would not know for certain until it performed 'stress tests' on the banks later in the coming months). To recall, one of Paulson's great errors was to fail to do 'due diligence' before he asked for the $700 billion. He estimated that $700 billion was enough, but soon discovered that the total volume of bad assets on the banks' books was many times greater.

So how much bad assets were there at the time that PIPP was supposed to 'clean up'? A total of $3.6 trillion, according to New York University professor Nouriel Roubini, who had been accurately predicting the magnitude of the crisis and bank losses for more than a year. A total of $4 trillion, according to *Fortune* magazine. Others ranged from $3 trillion to as much as $6 trillion. The PIPP was to fund initially at $1 trillion, which would prove grossly inadequate, especially if housing and other asset prices continued to fall and the losses consequently continued to rise. And they did. Housing and other asset values continued to plummet throughout the first quarter of 2009. As prices and the value of the assets to be sold continued to fall, it was even more difficult to determine even a subsidized market price per PIPP. Not surprising, nothing got sold. Six months later, in 2009, the PIPP program was essentially dismantled.

As public criticism continued to grow concerning the unlikely prospect of the PIPP's success, academics and the business press began to raise the idea of 'bank nationalizations' as a solution. What this meant to most was the government should simply take over the banks and expunge their bad assets. A version of this was undertaken by the Swedish government in the early 1990s. A 'bad bank' was set up by the government, into which the bad assets were dumped, thereby cleaning up the banks' balance sheets and theoretically clearing the way to allow them to lend once again. But the banks and the Obama administration pushed hard against this alternative, no doubt due to the extreme opposition to the idea by the banks themselves. The idea faded by the spring of 2009.

Government taking over insolvent banks and subsequently liquidating their remaining bad assets is essentially what happened in the 1930s. Housing prices did not stop falling for more than five years into the depression, until 1935, when the Roosevelt administration revitalized the Reconstruction Finance Corp. (RFC) and created the Home Owners Loan Corp. (HOLC). Together, both agencies determined a market price for the bad assets and enforced it. Bad banks were dissolved and their worthless assets written off. Those banks that could be saved were forced into mergers. Those that couldn't be saved were liquidated. The HOLC also directly renegotiated with homeowners, resetting their interest and principal to keep people in their homes. No voluntary lender programs then. No begging the banks to modify mortgages. No extended negotiations that produced no results, as the banks refused to rid themselves of the bad assets. That approach finally stabilized the housing market.

As PIPP failed to take off, the banks essentially boycotting the solution once again as they did with Paulson, an alternative was adopted by Congress quietly a few months later. That alternative was simply to change bank accounting rules to allow banks to value the bad assets on their books at above market prices. By so doing, the banks could make it appear they were in sounder financial shape than in fact they were. The banks liked this solution. It meant they could keep the bad assets and report an increase in value on their balance sheets. This was followed quickly by a series of government 'stress tests' conducted on the big 19 banks, that showed indeed that the banks were now better off than thought. The stress tests were done in private, with all the necessary give and take negotiations between the government and the banks to ensure the appropriate positive results were the outcome. As a result, the banks now appeared to have recovered from their deep losses and were no longer technically insolvent.

It was hoped by the government this discovery, trumpeted to the public, would raise public confidence in the banks and enable them to raise capital once again as their stock prices rose. It worked. Bank stock prices began to rise. But not due to PIPP. The PIPP did not 'rescue' the banks. What temporarily staved off their further collapse, allowing them to raise further capital, was the permission granted by the Obama administration, endorsed by the House and Senate banking committees, allowing banks to value their bad assets at phony prices not supported by the markets. The means by which this was specifically done was the suspension of what was called 'mark to market' accounting rules that prevailed up to then, which Congress now suspended. Thus, phony accounting changes and phony stress tests were the real solutions. The beginning of the recovery of bank stocks is closely correlated with the abandoning of 'mark to market' accounting in the spring of 2009 permitted by the Congress, once it became apparent that the banks would still not sell their bad assets according to any formula developed by the government.

But this solution only addressed part of the 'bad assets' problem. PIPP addressed bad loans that were not securitized. The other part was what to do with the additional trillions of dollars of bad *securitized* assets on their balance sheets. This is where the Obama administration's second major element of the bank bailout program came in, TALF.

TALF: RESURRECTING SECURITIZATION

The term asset-backed securities lending facility, or TALF, was created by the Fed earlier at the close of 2008 with $200 billion originally earmarked for its operations. But it was not implemented until the Obama administration assumed office, and then was expanded to $1 trillion as part of the bank rescue package announced by Geithner in February 2009. Unlike PPIP, TALF was envisioned as a plan to resurrect the shadow banking system and thus the securitized asset markets that had collapsed after 2007. Approximately half of all U.S. lending in 2007 ($5.65 trillion) occurred in the securitized markets. The securitized credit markets had declined to $160 billion in 2008 and to a mere several tens of billions of dollars by early 2009. By the fall of 2009, TALF-supported lending of securitized assets was barely $100 billion.

TALF was specifically designed for the government to provide another $1 trillion or more to resurrect securitization markets. These were the RMBSs (bundled residential mortgage-backed securities), CMBSs (bundled commercial mortgage-backed securities), CDOs, (collateralized debt obligations bundling commercial paper with whatever), CLOs (collateralized business loans), and other myriad forms of derivatives securities. Major segments of the commercial paper credit market, auto loans, student loans, credit cards, commercial property loans, subprimes, and other similar securities, had come to depend deeply on the ability to resell such securitized assets. Shadow institutions like hedge funds, private equity firms, money market funds, pension funds, and others realized major profits from such transactions. But now this market had essentially collapsed. Getting it going again was particularly important, according to Bernanke and the Fed, given that a 'subprime-like' new bombshell of losses and write-downs was looming for the commercial property markets in 2010.

Unlike PIPP, TALF was fully funded by the Federal Reserve. The $787 billion stimulus package and other bank bailout programs had increased the U.S. budget deficit to more than $1.5 trillion in 2009, and unofficially to more than $2 trillion. For the U.S. Treasury to finance the $1 trillion TALF and the $1 trillion PIPP was exceedingly difficult given those rising deficits. Congress authorized all Treasury spending, and more funding granted by it was highly unlikely. But the Fed does not need to obtain funding from Congress. The Fed, by law, can finance its own spending. It has the power to essentially create and issue its own bonds—i.e. raise its own money. The Fed indicated that in order to fund TALF it was prepared to do so.

TALF meant that the Obama administration and the Fed was not counting on the traditional banking system to lead the way out of financial instability—i.e. to get credit moving again. The big unanswered question, however, was will investors and major players that had once participated heavily in these securitized markets—like the shadow banking hedge funds—again re-enter the securitized markets once again in enough volume to resurrect them? Hedge funds lost half their total asset value in the first 18 months from August 2007 due to losses and withdrawals. Total assets had fallen to well under $1 trillion, or about two-thirds from original levels. Similar declines have characterized the state of the private equity firms. It is hard to see how the securitized asset markets might be revived, given their 'toxic' reputation and the still virtual total collapse of these markets by the fall of 2009.

Nevertheless, a central element of the Fed's and the Obama administration's strategy remains to somehow resurrect the securitized markets and the shadow banking institutions—i.e. those same folks that were the cause of much of the speculation that led to the collapse of the credit markets in the first place.

HOUSING: BAILING OUT BUILDERS AND LENDERS

The third element of the Obama bank bailout plan announced in February–March 2009 addressed the housing market that was still continuing to decline. The Obama plan had two elements. The first was to set aside $200 billion in funding to keep Fannie Mae and Freddie Mac continuing to buy-up mortgages originated by lenders. Without their purchasing of mortgages, the real estate market in the U.S. would likely have totally collapsed after 2007.

Obama's proposed 'rescue' of the housing market was essentially an extension of prior arrangements introduced under the Bush–Paulson period. Despite Fannie/Freddie's key role in propping up the housing markets, they owned only 26 percent of the $12 trillion residential mortgage market. And most of the home foreclosures that were occurring involved mortgages that Fannie/Freddie's hadn't purchased, or couldn't. Furthermore, much of the foreclosures problem involved securitized residential mortgages, the owners of which might be many investors. Getting all to agree on a sale was extremely difficult. In many cases the owners weren't even identifiable, since the securitized mortgages were often chopped up and distributed into other types of assets (CDOs) and resold who knows where or to whom? Adding more funds to Fannie/Freddie to buy more mortgages was necessary, but it meant Fannie/Freddie could assist less than half of the growing foreclosures problem.

The second part of the Obama housing program proposed a new program funded by $75 billion. These funds were not designated to rescue homeowners in foreclosure, about to pass the 5 million mark at the time (and approaching 7 million at the year's end). The $75 billion was to subsidize mortgage lenders to get them to lower their interest rates on new mortgages. In other words, the government would use the $75 billion to buy down new mortgages. Once more the solution was to 'subsidize' those who had created the problem in the first place.

With the primary focus of the lending new first time homebuyers, this was not a program to help keep homeowners about to foreclose in their homes. It was a program to assist banks to get new buyers into the homes that were foreclosing. The banks naturally favored this approach, since it meant they now could screen new buyers' ability to pay more thoroughly than before and require tighter loan qualifying standards. Those clearly unable to continue to pay would be forced out of their homes. Focusing on first-time homebuyers also aided companies that built homes, whose inventory of unsold new homes had risen to unsustainable levels.

Strategically, the Obama housing rescue approach was to try to stimulate housing demand and in that way to slow the collapse of housing prices—not to focus on reducing excess housing supply steadily rising due to foreclosures. But the supply of houses coming onto the market was and still is greater than any new demand created by the Obama program. Foreclosures are projected to rise to 8 million by Moody's, Inc. and Standard & Poor's and, more likely per our forecasts, to exceed 10 million eventually. That is, nearly one-fifth of the 50 million or so mortgages in the U.S. But so long as foreclosures and supply continues to rise, the Obama 'rescue' of lenders and builders will not fundamentally succeed in resolving the housing market crisis. In turn, this will mean continuing downward pressure on housing prices, mortgage assets, and losses for financial institutions holding those assets on their books.

The subprime mortgage sector led the decline in the housing market in 2007–08. But a growing relative contributing role to the problem in residential housing is the now rising defaults and foreclosures in the next two tiers of mortgages: what are called 'Alt-A' and the prime mortgages. Prime mortgages, the most safe, in particular represent the fastest growing rate of foreclosures as of mid year 2009. Their numbers and rate will likely continue to rise as jobless levels continue to approach the 25 million mark, as the duration of unemployment as well as number of unemployed continues to grow, and as homeowners simply walk away from mortgages as the value of their homes fall well below what they still owe on their mortgages.

Following the passage of the $787 billion stimulus, the announcement of the bank bailout plans in March, and rising estimates of the costs of the bailouts, political sentiment shifted dramatically in Congress by early summer 2009 over concern with the U.S. budget and deficit. The deficit for 2009 was estimated at $1.8 trillion.[33] Another $1.4 trillion was estimated for 2010. Some academic studies forecast $1 trillion deficits in each year for the next decade.

As official jobless numbers continued to exceed 500,000 a month on average through the second quarter of 2009, calls were raised for passing yet another 'Stimulus 2' spending package. They were quickly silenced, however, by the Obama administration leading economic spokespersons, Bernanke, Geithner, and Larry Summers, to 'give the first stimulus a chance'. For six months more calls for a second stimulus remained muted. Only by the fourth quarter 2009 did debate renew about the need to focus more on jobs and foreclosures, no doubt reflecting politicians' nervousness with mid-term elections less than a year away in 2010.

A STRATEGIC SHIFT?

In June 2009, however, the Obama administration made a strategic turn. In testimony before the House Budget Committee on June 3, 2009, Bernanke revealed the new focus of the administration's economic recovery plans. When questioned about the ballooning federal debt due to the stimulus, bank bailouts, and the Fed's prior promise to purchase $1.2 trillion of mortgages and 30-year Treasury bonds, Bernanke made it clear those proposals were now all under review and might not continue. As he succinctly put it, "the Fed will not monetize the debt."[34] In his testimony he noted that some hard choices would have to be made and that the government could not afford deficits "of even 5 percent of GDP." Long-term strategy need to rely more on the banks raising capital. He admitted banks were still not lending to consumers and small business, and that the commercial property lending situation was particularly difficult. The House Committee members' questioning then turned to Treasury Secretary Geithner's meeting in Beijing that was occurring that same day with the Chinese on economic policies. One representative noted that when Geithner reportedly told them the U.S. was going to get control of its debt, the Chinese laughed at him (Geithner). Bernanke subsequently replied "We need to rethink the government role in the housing markets." Bernanke thereafter made clear to the Committee that the Fed was re-evaluating its previously announced intentions to buy $1.2 trillion in mortgage debt and to purchase $300 billion in long-term Treasury bonds. The Fed and U.S. government would hold the line on further spending to prevent greater budget deficits and rising debt levels that might in turn undermine the U.S. dollar. If the Chinese were to continue purchasing U.S. securities to help finance U.S. deficits, then the U.S. had to ensure the Chinese that the value of the dollar would not decline. Such a decline would wipe out hundreds of billions of the more than $1 trillion in U.S. denominated currency and securities held by the Chinese. This was the new emerging quid pro quo. To get the Chinese to buy more U.S. debt, the U.S. had to ensure that the value of the debt bought did not collapse due to the dollar's decline. But that meant in turn no more rise in U.S. deficits. And that meant no more stimulus, bailouts, or tax cuts; perhaps at best only token, 'one-off' programs here and there, like the 'cash for clunkers' and first-time homebuyers credits that Congress would subsequently pass, or the TARP-funded tax cuts for jobs debated at the year's end. But no new major stimulus to create jobs or stop foreclosures. In other words, as of June 2009, U.S. domestic economic recovery policy was becoming increasingly impacted by U.S. dollar and capital flows requirements.

OBAMA'S FAILED BANK RESCUE PLAN

In June 2009, the FDIC, as the administrator of PIPP, also announced it was indefinitely postponing the plan. The cover explanation was that banks were successfully now raising their own capital. But as the *New York Times* revealed in early June,

> Many banks have refused to sell their loans, in part because doing so would force them to mark down the value of those loans and book big losses. Even though the government was prepared to prop up prices...the prices that banks were demanding have remained far higher than the prices that investors were willing to pay.[35]

On the investor (and shadow bank) buyer side, the resistance was significant as well. Investors were concerned that the super-profits they would realize as a result of the deals might be limited by regulators or Congress as part of legislation pending to restrict bankers' (and shadow bankers') excess bonuses.[36] As a result, "the administration was forced to postpone indefinitely...the program to rid the banks of their bad home loans."[37] In other words, PIPP, or TARP II, as a plan to buy-up bad assets, had crashed before it even got off the ground, just as Paulson's original TARP, $700 billion proposal had. The banks simply did not want to play ball. Hedge fund managers wanted their super-bonuses. As of late summer 2009, the PIPP program was essentially defunct.

The official cover for the dismantling was that the banks now were sufficiently recapitalized (meaning they had voluntarily raised private capital themselves to offset the bad assets on their balance sheets). What the record facts regarding recapitalization show, however, is something different. For example, it is estimated that U.S. banks have experienced losses of approximately $1.8 trillion since the financial crisis erupted in 2007.[38] According to ratings agency Fitch, the total capital raised by all U.S. banks between October 2007 and September 2009 was approximately $500 billion.[39] That means the banks have raised only one-third the capital necessary to offset their losses, and about $1.3 trillion more is still required. And that does not count anticipated losses, write-offs and write-downs still to come, which, according to a recent report in September 2009 by the IMF, will amount to another $1.5 trillion worldwide by the end of 2010. As an editorial by the British business daily, the *Financial Times*, reported on October 1, 2009:

> the financial sector's dire state is essentially unchanged since the IMF's previous report a half a year ago...In the past six months, stock markets made record gains, growth returned to big economies, and even toxic assets began to trade again...but there is still a hole in the heart of the world's financial system almost as gaping as before...Notwithstanding a flurry of capital raisings, private markets cannot fill this gap...All this means the financial sector remains on extremely shaky ground.[40]

With only half the losses made up, it is not surprising that bank lending continued to decline throughout 2009. In July 2009 a senior loan officer survey conducted by the Federal Reserve showed that lending terms and standards continued to tighten on all major loans to businesses and households compared to a previous April survey. "Demand for loans continued to weaken across all major categories except for prime residential mortgage."[41] Particularly tight were commercial and industrial loans important to most small and medium businesses, home equity lines of credit, and commercial real estate. This survey was corroborated by the U.S. Treasury's monthly bank lending survey. According to this second view, consumer loans fell 1 percent in June, commercial and industrial loans 2 percent for the month, and commercial real estate by 1 percent.[42] Declines of 1–2 percent per month may not seem like much, until it is annualized. That means loans declining at annual double digit rates.

The TALF plan to resuscitate the securitized markets has produced only a few sales of bad assets thus far, in the amount of a few billions of dollars. Inducing shadow banking consortia to re-enter the markets in order to restart the securitized credit markets once again simply has not taken place to any substantial extent. The shadow banking system has not recovered, and there is little indication it will do so in the near future.

Like PIPP, the TALF program under Fed administration was scaled back within months of its passage. Administered by William Dudley, the head of the New York Fed, the program was quickly discontinued in June for collateralized loans and residential MBS securitized assets. And by mid August 2009 only $29 billion of the $1 trillion potential had been spent, and most of that for securitized consumer auto loans.[43]

In August the Fed announced it would extend the TALF, scheduled to expire at year end 2009, to June 2010 but only for commercial property securitized assets and other select asset-backed securities. No doubt the Fed recognized the looming crisis in commercial property assets. In a $6.7 trillion market, annually about 13 percent of total U.S. GDP, no less than $3.4 trillion in loans to commercial property had been made in the run-up to the financial bust of August 2007.

Paralleling the trajectory for subprimes earlier, prices for commercial properties had fallen by at least one-third from its peak in 2007 through June of 2009, according to a Moody's index. This meant major write-downs and losses for banks were already occurring. Neither bank lending nor bonds were widely available to developers in this market. As another indicator of this sector's current and continuing severe stress, commercial property sales in 2009 had fallen to just 10 percent of pre-2007 levels. Delinquency rates on securitized commercial property mortgages were doubling and tripling every three months after October 2008. Now hundreds of billions of loan renewals will soon come due, without a market to obtain finance. Meanwhile, delinquencies on loans had already risen from barely 10 percent in 2006 to 34 percent by July 2009 on average, and as much as 41 percent for medium-sized and larger banks.[44] This was, and remains, a potential 'subprime' bust in the making. But with TALF barely getting off the ground and being scaled back in other areas, it remains to be seen whether the Obama–Fed strategy for using TALF to prevent a subprime-like bust in commercial property in 2010 will succeed.

The third element of the Obama financial markets rescue plan addressing housing has had some minor success. But it appears it too is being phased out in those limited areas of some success. The housing market appears to have partly stabilized in terms of housing price declines, as measured by the Case-Shiller index. But this may be simply due to the short-term boost provided by the new first-time homebuyer subsidy of $8,000 per new homeowner passed by Congress. That subsidy was scheduled to terminate before year end 2009. It remains to be seen therefore whether the housing market can consequently stabilize on its own without the government subsidy. The key word here is 'stabilization,' of course, not recovery. For the Obama program may have temporarily achieved the former for a few months, but clearly has not laid the groundwork for a longer run, sustained recovery of the housing markets. Nor will it, so long as homeowners in foreclosure are allowed to lose their homes in their continuing millions. The key to continuing home foreclosures appears increasingly linked, moreover, to rising joblessness, restricted consumer credit,

and the various forces pressing on workers' incomes and cc
remain—in short, the continuing deterioration of consumpt
still plagues the U.S. economy.

AN HISTORICAL IRONY

In summary, the Obama recovery program has accomplished little, if anything,
to date after nearly nine months. The $787 stimulus package has been largely
a failure in terms of jobs creation. Efforts to loosen up credit availability to
consumers have been repeatedly thwarted by bank and credit card lobbyists
in Congress. Stock equity and retirement plan values have recovered less
than a third of their initial collapse after August 2007 and October 2008.
Consumption is still in decline, as are real earnings of the 110 million or
so working/middle class. Industrial production decline has leveled off and
select other indicators are no longer in freefall. But the absence of continued
decline does not constitute 'recovery,' despite media and government spin to
the contrary. By fall 2009 it appears the stock market recovery has in fact
stalled, and true jobless numbers record hundreds of thousands of new job
losses every month—notwithstanding the apparent slowing in jobs lost per
month. Well over 24 million will be unemployed and rising. The true jobless
rate is somewhere between 17 percent and 18 percent.

In terms of the real economy, the current situation at very best represents
a possible pause. What temporary recovery has occurred is due largely to
the $200 billion or so in extra payments to social security recipients and the
unemployed, neither of which will generate long-term jobs and sustained
recovery, and one-time special programs like 'cash for clunkers' and first-time
homebuyer credits, which were projected to expire. Even the original $787
stimulus is projected to have had its greatest effect by spring 2010. In short,
there is no longer-run, sustained economic recovery on the horizon.

The U.S economy at best, and only in select segments, is moving sideways.
What there is of recovery is slight and, given current programs and spending,
will not likely last beyond mid year 2010. The longer-term scenario is a
'double-dip' or 'W'-shaped decline that is typical of Type I Epic Recessions.

On the bank and financial side, financial fragility continues to be a very
real problem, just as consumption fragility continues to deteriorate as well.
The banks have not come close to fully recapitalizing. And they cannot
recapitalize their way out of this crisis. Allowing trillions of dollars of bad
assets to remain on bank balance sheets may prove the single, most serious
strategic error of the Obama administration in terms of financial instability. It
is furthermore highly likely that the volume of bad assets will continue to rise,
as commercial property and other losses multiply in the months immediately
ahead. Failure to do something soon enough to prevent the millions more
unemployed and underemployed in 2009, and the continuing millions more
foreclosures, is an equally significant second strategic error of the administration. Both errors have meant that financial and consumption fragility have

allowed to deteriorate further behind the facade of a temporary and
tenuous economic recovery.

The huge volume of the bad assets—at minimum $500 billion and likely
three times that—is a major problem for the administration. So is the refusal
in 2010 of the administration, the Fed, and Congress to significantly increase
spending to create more jobs out of concern for raising deficits further. The
rising deficits are increasingly threatening the stability of the U.S. currency,
the U.S. dollar, in global markets. Should deficits accelerate further, the U.S.
will not be able to continue to borrow from China, the petro-economies, or
elsewhere to finance its escalating budget deficit. The Obama administration
has therefore made the decision—as was clearly signaled by Bernanke and
Geithner in June and Obama and Bernanke again in November with the
President's visit to China—to protect its ability to borrow to cover deficits
and thus to protect its currency in international markets over ensuring a
more rapid domestic recovery. International considerations increasingly will
take precedence over domestic, although the two may more or less remain
in balance until the November 2010 elections. Following that, international
considerations will almost certainly prevail.

And that is truly ironic. This was the same dilemma that occurred in
1932, when the U.S. Federal Reserve decided to protect the currency by
raising interest rates, which in turn contributed in a major way to descent
and transition from Epic Recession in the summer of 1932 into a full-blown
depression in the fall of 1932. Ironic all the more, since this is precisely what
Fed chairman Bernanke, and many monetarists like him, maintains was the
primary cause of the depression—i.e. the Fed deciding to support the dollar
and the gold standard at the expense of the domestic economy. It is an historic
irony that Bernanke's policies have led to this precipice once more, despite his
having pledged in 2002 to Milton Friedman, the prince of monetarist theory,
that we now know how to prevent depression; we will not allow the Fed to
make the same error again, in other words. But it has. And it is.

ELEMENTS OF AN ALTERNATIVE PROGRAM FOR SUSTAINED RECOVERY

For another view of how to prevent the repeat of history, the concluding
chapter that follows offers a different perspective on how to avoid the descent
into depression. This perspective and the alternative program may be summed
up in the following statement, which provides an outline of the program
necessary for recovery.

Four broad measures are required for a sustained economic recovery. These
measures necessitate a restructuring of the U.S. economy in several critical
areas. The first measure is an immediate, additional injection of fiscal spending
equal to approximately 16 percent of GDP, or $2.5 trillion, with a primary
focus on job creation and fundamental labor markets reform. Only a major
injection of spending can break and reverse in the short run the process of debt–
deflation–default that ultimately exacerbates both financial and consumption
fragility. The second broad measure is a subsequent permanent increase of

the government's share of annual GDP, with the government assuming new roles in initiating necessary infrastructure and technology investment. That government share of annual GDP should rise from its post-1945 historical average of 20 percent of GDP to the 30–35 percent range. This in turn requires a fundamental restructuring of the tax system. The third broad measure is a nationalization of the residential mortgage and small business property markets, followed by consumer credit markets in general. Credit should be provided at cost to homeowners and consumers through a new network of government agencies at the state and local level. The nationalization of the consumer credit markets requires in turn a fundamental restructuring of the banking system into a for-profit sector and a consumer sector that is managed as a basic utility. It also includes a fundamental reform and restructuring of the Federal Reserve system. The fourth broad measure includes a necessary rebalancing of investment and consumption in the economy. Rebalancing consumption means implementing policies that establish a more equitable long-run distribution of income; rebalancing investment means policies that reduce the relative weight and mix of speculative forms of investment in the economy and restore the predominance of investment in real assets that create jobs over investment in speculative financial assets that result in financial instability. Rebalancing consumption and investment is the necessary step toward ensuring sustained long-term recovery.

9
An Alternative Program for Economic Recovery

Programs and policies that prove successful in generating sustained economic recovery address fundamental, root causes of economic crises. Programs that fail to generate recovery typically address causes that are only symptomatic or secondary. They consequently produce recoveries that fade or abort. They may even create preconditions for a re-emergence of crisis later in an even more virulent form. Successful programs, moreover, provide for both short-run and longer-run solutions.

Unlike normal recessions, Epic Recessions of the current type, 2007–10, are driven in the short run by processes of debt–deflation–default and the interaction of these processes with conditions of financial and consumption fragility. But the longer-run causes of Epic Recessions are rooted in the origins of financial and consumption fragility—i.e. the rising debt, debt repayment, and declining income. For businesses, both bank and non-bank, income means cash flow and liquid assets. For households and consumers, income means real disposable income. In the long run the major causes of rising debt and declining income derive from the growing relative shift toward speculative forms of investing, their negative consequences for investing in real assets, and the global money parade's access to ever increasing availability of liquidity and credit. From this basic scenario of the origins and processes associated with Epic Recession, it follows that programs to successfully contain Epic Recessions are not traditional and are not those employed to deal with 'normal,' not Epic, recessions. Conventional fiscal and monetary policies do not work well in conditions of Epic Recession. They do not succeed in generating sustained recoveries from Epic Recessions. At best, they may temporarily stabilize the economy and thereafter result in extended slow growth or even stagnation; at worst, they may precipitate a deeper downturn and even a transition to a classic depression. Successful policies must address the processes of debt–deflation–default in the short run, financial and consumption fragility in the intermediate term, and the global money parade and speculative investing in the longer run.

The Obama economic recovery program launched early in 2009 has failed to satisfy the above essential requirements for generating sustained recovery on nearly all counts. Consumption and financial fragility continue to weaken in the U.S. economy in late 2009. Nothing has been done to address the global money parade of speculators and speculative investing, which has once again, from mid 2009, begun to show signs of resurgence—in currency speculation, real estate, gold, select commodities, exchange traded and emerging market funds, dark pools and flash trading, and sovereign debt. Money flows in increasing amounts once again, not to businesses that need loans to generate jobs but to speculative ventures. The problem of excess liquidity in the global system may even have grown worse as the Fed, and other central banks, have pumped trillions of dollars more into the global economy. Despite their proclamations to the contrary, the Fed and others will have great difficulty retrieving that liquidity and, in so trying, are more likely than not to precipitate another financial crisis event in 2011 or beyond.

Obama's program, both in its financial banking elements as well as its attempts to resurrect the real economy by means of spending and tax cuts, has not addressed the fundamental causes of the crisis. It has addressed secondary causes and symptoms of the crisis. It additionally has been short-run focused, not long-run. It has been designed as a temporary 'holding action,' in both its banking rescue and economic stimulus dimensions. It is a program designed to address a normal recession, not an Epic Recession. As a result, in its present form it is doomed to fail to produce a sustained long-run economic recovery from the current economic and financial crisis.

The Obama program, and Bush policies preceding it, are based on the assumption that if the banking system's collapse can be checked and contained, then the market will over time eventually generate recovery. Obama's policies, like Bush's, have focused on restoring banks' deteriorating balance sheets with government-provided liquidity injections—i.e. fill the banks' ever widening black hole of losses and write-downs with taxpayer and/or printed money. The logical assumption has been that if banks' losses can be offset, then eventually they will start lending again. And that will drive financial recovery. As Obama himself has said on numerous occasions, the key is 'to get the banks lending again.' The problem is, after trillions of dollars of injections of liquidity by the Fed, the Treasury, and Congress, banks have continued to reduce their lending to businesses and consumers over the year following the eruption of the banking panic in September 2008. Banks have borrowed trillions of dollars from the Fed at no cost (0 percent interest) and have lent it out at higher rates, much of that lending going offshore and/or into speculative ventures.

A similar logic is contained in the Obama program for the real (non-financial) economy; i.e. offset the collapse in consumption with government safety net (unemployment insurance, Medicaid, Cobra, food stamps) and local government spending assistance. Thereafter the real economy will eventually heal itself as well and recovery—production, jobs, and the like—will naturally occur. But a program to temporarily offset part of the general consumption collapse underway does not equal a program for recovery of the real economy any more than putting a liquidity floor under the banking collapse constitutes a program for recovery in the financial sector of the economy.

Short-run solutions don't necessarily generate long-run recoveries. Addressing contributing causes don't resolve fundamental causes behind the crisis. Over-reliance on market-based solutions is more often part of the problem rather than the solution. A naïve and ideological belief in the eventual self-adjusting nature of markets has played a major role in creating the recent crisis; it is therefore absurd to believe that in the long run markets can eventually correct the very problems they've created, and the crisis will go away with just a little assistance by government fiscal and monetary policies. Nevertheless, that is the essence of the Obama program introduced in the first months of 2009.

Since the early 1980s, government has repeatedly intervened in the economy to deal with successive financial crises. Each time it intervened, however, it was able only temporarily to contain the financial instability, not fundamentally resolve it. Moreover, each intervention created conditions contributing to an even more serious subsequent financial bust. Each subsequent crisis was deeper and had wider sectoral and geographic impact. Initially it was a particular credit market or institution—the municipal securities market, the commercial paper market, real estate investment trusts, etc., in the 1970s. Then it was multiple markets—savings and loans, junk bonds, stock markets in the 1980s. Then it was more generalized globally—Japan, Scandinavia, multiple Asian nations, Russia, Latin America, in the 1990s. Then global tech and housing markets. The 2007 financial bust, however, has involved nearly all credit markets and institutions, synchronized across most major national economies, and has spread deeper and faster than ever before. Not only is something clearly wrong fundamentally with the internal workings of the system, but what is wrong is clearly producing more virulent and frequent bouts of financial instability and crises.

In terms of metaphor, with each outbreak the disease was only temporarily forced into remission with ever more massive injections of monetary antibiotics; but each time the disease returned more serious than before. The same antibiotics were thereafter injected once again, in increasingly larger doses. Larger injections of liquidity, bailouts, and fiscal stimulus were fed into the successive crises in order to contain them. But in so doing, only the symptoms were treated, not the more basic physiological illness. What is required is basic economic surgery—i.e. a more fundamental restructuring of the body economic itself.

FUNDAMENTAL CAUSES AND SUSTAINED RECOVERY

This book has repeatedly referred to conditions of financial fragility and consumption fragility as central to understanding how Epic Recessions, such as the present crisis, emerge and evolve. Neither forms of fragility are factors involved in normal recessions, but are essential to understanding how Epic Recessions emerge and evolve. Financial fragility applies to both bank and non-bank companies. Consumption fragility affects consumers and households, particularly those in the lower 80 percent income distribution earning less than $125,000 annually. Together, business spending and household consumption constitute 86 percent of the U.S. economy, 15 percent and 71 percent respectively.

Fragility in both its forms—financial and consumption—occurs due to two sets of causes: debt and income. Rising debt levels (plus deteriorating debt quality), on the one hand, and declining real income on the other. For businesses, the ratio of cash flow (and other forms of liquid assets) to debt signifies growing fragility. If cash flow declines and/or debt levels (and quality decline) rises, then financial fragility increases. Consumption fragility is similar, but applies to households/consumers. Consumption fragility rises when household real income declines and/or their debt levels (and quality) rises. Thus a rising ratio of disposable income to debt indicates worsening consumption fragility. The greater the degree of fragility in the system when a crisis breaks, the steeper and more rapid the decline—in bank lending, on the one hand, and in consumer spending, on the other.

Problems of fragility thus drive the recession toward epic dimensions and set in motion the dangerous processes of debt–deflation–default that, in turn, exacerbate both forms of fragility still further. If feedback between the factors is allowed to deepen, the system is pushed toward subsequent banking crises and may then slip into depression. If the feedback and processes are partially checked and contained, then the collapse may stabilize, but without a sustained long-term recovery.

It is relatively rare to have both financial and consumer fragility grow within an economy in parallel and to have both collapse more or less simultaneously. But when that occurs, the two forms of fragility reinforce each other and cause deeper contractions and instability in both the financial and real sectors of an economy. The 'dual' crises—financial system and real economy—become in effect increasingly congruent. That's precisely what happened in 2008: the banking crisis of 2008 represented the virtual collapse of finance and lending, which precipitated in turn a collapse of consumption quickly thereafter in the fourth quarter of 2008. But the collapse of both would not have occurred had the financial system become as fragile as it had beforehand, or the real economy become so consumption fragile in the months leading up to late 2008 due to a decades-long redistribution of income from workers to investors and corporations dating back to around 1980, which created the necessity of 90 million working- and middle-class households having to resort to debt to maintain living standards.

If underlying both forms of fragility are the twin forces of debt and income— the former rising and the latter declining over time—then an effective program of recovery must necessarily address both excessive debt and insufficient income; that is both forms of fragility at the same time in a program of recovery. Addressing one form, and not the other, is a formula for extended stagnation—i.e. a Type I Epic Recession. But the Obama program of 2009 has done just that. It has addressed financial fragility in part, and consumption fragility virtually not at all. It has pumped huge sums of money into the banks to offset lost income, but has not addressed the other side of fragility in the financial system—i.e. the debt side. It has done little to reduce debt for many non-financial companies that have approached the edge of default and who have been loading up recently on still more junk bond debt to postpone default. It has done nothing about removing 'bad assets' on banks' balance sheets. Instead it has placed its trust in the markets to eventually somehow remove those assets over time. It has ignored the debt side and provided a solution on the income side that will produce trillion-dollar deficits annually for a decade to come. Consequently, the Obama program represents only a half, or even a fourth, of a program addressing financial fragility.

In terms of consumption fragility, the Obama program has accomplished even less. It represents no program of recovery at all. If financial fragility has been addressed inadequately and only in part in the Obama program, consumption fragility has been addressed even less so. On the debt side, the program has only dabbled with reducing debt levels and debt quality problems for homeowners. Foreclosures in the Obama program have been permitted to rise to record levels and will continue to do so. Mortgage modifications proposals have been voluntary and ineffective. The program's strategy has been to permit foreclosures and subsidize lenders and new buyers to pick up the foreclosed housing stock over time. And virtually nothing in the Obama program addresses other forms of excessive consumer debt. Banks are still allowed to pile on credit card interest, fees, and penalties up to 40 percent. Attempts to adjust credit card and other forms of consumer debt via Congressional action have been repeatedly thwarted by bank and other financial lobbyists in Congress.

While little has been provided for in the Obama program to help reduce consumer debt, the program has provided for even less on the income side of consumption fragility. Income inequality has deteriorated in the U.S. for three decades, accelerating in the last decade. That has forced the lower 80 percent income households to work longer hours, access savings pools, and resort to debt in various forms to maintain living standards. Now that debt consumption is not available, consumption has and will continue to decline long term. The Obama stimulus package of February 2009 has not addressed this fundamental, structural problem in the economy at all. Moreover, the single most serious factor depressing consumption—i.e. the loss of close to 25 million jobs—has not been effectively addressed in the Obama stimulus package. Nor have other elements of the Obama $787 billion stimulus structurally addressed growing income inequality; i.e. declining wages, disappearing health benefits, fading retirement income, to name but the more serious elements of still-growing income inequality in America.

In contrast to the Obama program, the alternative program that follows specifically addresses the income side of consumption fragility, as well as the debt side of both consumption and financial fragility. It also proposes a better, alternative way for supporting the income side of financial fragility—a proposal that doesn't place the burden on taxpayers or create trillion-dollar budget deficits for a decade to come that will result in the scuttling of necessary reforms in health care, retirement, education, and climate policy reform.

If the current dual economic crisis has been quantitatively and qualitatively worse than prior post-1945 normal recessions in the U.S.—i.e. has been an Epic Recession in other words—it is because the conditions of both financial and consumption fragility deteriorated prior to the crises to levels not seen since the late 1920s. A successful program of sustained recovery must therefore address and resolve both forms of fragility, financial and consumption. That means that business debt and liquidity (bank and non-bank) must be addressed and resolved in a program, as well as consumer debt and consumer disposable income.

Failing adequate program provisions for the four forces—debt and income for business and debt and income for households and consumers—the recovery program will, at best, result in drawn-out economic stagnation, a period of weak and short recoveries followed by short and shallow declines; i.e. a 'W'-shaped or 'double-dip' recovery scenario. Or, at worst, will result in an eventual further collapse of the economy following a renewed financial crisis event. The former is what this book has termed a Type I Epic Recession; the latter a Type II Epic Recession.

But program provisions addressing the general problem of fragility in the economy are just the beginning of the task, not the end. As noted, lying deeper beneath financial and consumption fragility are problems of debt and income creating that fragility. There is also the factor of deflation. It is deflation in the form of the three price systems—i.e. asset prices, product prices, and wage or labor prices—that transmit debt deterioration and declining incomes into defaults—bank, non-bank business, and consumer alike. In the shorter run the debt–deflation–default process is thus critical as well to understanding fundamental causes of Epic Recession. It is the dynamic process by which financial and consumption fragility are caused to deteriorate further, feeding back upon each other, and in the process drive the economy still lower in a downward spiral, and accelerating in turn the process of debt–deflation–default as well.

Thus a successful program must also address the forces of deflation and default, while simultaneously confronting debt and income deterioration. The problem with the Obama program is that it has turned over the matter of deflation and default to the Federal Reserve (Fed), which has shown it is only interested in preventing default of the 'big 19' largest banks. Small to medium-sized businesses, smaller banks, homeowners, and consumers are on their own to fail as they might. Similarly, the Fed has clearly shown it will risk deflation far more readily than inflation.

What follows proposes an alternative economic recovery program. Unlike Obama's or Bush's, this program directly addresses the fundamental origins and causes of the recent financial crisis and Epic Recession. It is a program based on long-run as well as short-run requirements for recovery. It is a program that calls for long-run structural changes in the U.S. economy necessary for sustained recovery, as well as more immediate solutions. The proposals briefly outlined in the remainder of this chapter directly address the dual problems of excess debt and insufficient and declining incomes, the latter in particular for the bottom 80 percent of the household income distribution—i.e. the working- and middle-class households most heavily impacted by declining consumption fragility. The following alternative program also directly confronts the ultimate drivers underlying the current Epic Recession—the rise and growing economic power of the global money parade and increasingly serious consequences of the shift to speculative forms of investing.

THE ALTERNATIVE PROGRAM

PART I: HOMEOWNERS' STABILIZATION AND CONSUMPTION

The housing price collapse has been driven by rising housing supply, the largest cause of which has been rising foreclosures and defaults of subprime mortgages in the initial phase, followed thereafter by prime and Alt-A mortgages, jumbo-ARMs (adjustable rate mortgages), and HELOCs (home owner equity loans and lines of credit). Added to rising defaults and foreclosures have been trends in negative homeowner equity, meaning values of residential properties falling below less than the mortgage balance. It has been estimated that in this cycle more than half of the roughly 55 million mortgages in the U.S. will be 'under water'—i.e. in negative equity. One in seven homes with mortgages, roughly 8 million, will default or foreclose during the cycle.

Treasury–Fed programs have not addressed this root cause of supply driven housing price collapse, which is the continued rise in defaults, delinquencies, and foreclosures that continues to exceed new housing demand. Obama administration programs have instead focused on the symptom of the crisis—i.e. deteriorating bank balance sheets driven by the housing asset price collapse—and not the fundamental cause of rising housing supply due to foreclosures and defaults. Treating the symptoms has not resolved the fundamental problem. The following measures are thus designed to directly address the core problem of excess housing supply and consequent housing price collapse. The measures target reducing housing supply coming onto the market, not stimulating housing demand.

The following measures confront the problem of household debt, in other words, by reducing that debt. The measures also direct address the income side of consumption fragility, by raising income levels of households—both those in or approaching default and foreclosure as well as homeowners not in trouble. The measures are both short- and long-run proposals to reduce household debt and raise household income and consequently reduce consumption fragility. The concepts applied to residential housing are also extended, moreover, to small business property mortgages.

PROPOSAL 1: Reset mortgage rates for all loans originated in 2002–07

All forms of loan financing for the residential mortgage market (30-year fixed, conventional, jumbo, equity lines, ARMS, etc.) are reset to the Fed's 30-year bond rate plus 0.5 percent to cover administrative costs. That means effectively a 3.5 percent reset rate.

All loans issued between 2002 and 2007 are included in this provision, not just those facing foreclosure or default. Resetting all loans, not just those at risk of default and foreclosure, is designed not only to reduce excess housing supply coming onto the market that is driving down housing prices and causing further financial institution write-downs and losses, but to serve as a general economy-wide consumption enhancing measure as well. Boosting consumption in this manner provides a continued, long term consumption effect—unlike one-time government spending stimulus which, once spent, has no further effect. A ceiling of $729,000 on mortgages would apply for reset eligibility, which means the provision has the added effect of helping redistribute income to middle- and working-class homeowners. This measure also has the further beneficial economic effect of avoiding the necessity of additional deficit creation. If it affected just 25 million of the 55 million residential mortgages outstanding and reduced mortgage rates by 2 percent on average, the result is more than $200 billion in ongoing consumption every year. The resets also apply to small business property mortgages, where small business is defined as businesses with fewer than 50 employees and less than $1 million in annual net income.

PROPOSAL 2: Reset the mortgage principal for all loans originated in 2002–07

Principal balances for all loans originated in 2002–07 should similarly be reset according to the following formula: The rolling average for the property's market assessment for the six years prior to date of origination between 2002 and 2007. For example, a property sold in 2006, reflecting the inflated housing prices of 2003–06, would be reduced to the average price for the property from 2000 to 2005. The artificially inflated prices of 2003–06 were not the fault of the homeowner but of bank lending practices and speculation in the securitization markets, which artificially drove up house prices.

The rationale for principals resets is the same as for interest rate resets; i.e. to reduce the flow of supply of housing onto the market driving housing price decline and, equally important, to serve as a general stimulus to consumption demand, redistribute income, and reduce consumption fragility.

PROPOSAL 3: A new federal agency: FHBLC (Federal Homeowner-Business Loan Corporation), to administer nationalized residential mortgage and small business property markets

The Fed's current strategy of committing funds to the mortgage market through lenders, to provide incentives for them to lower interest rates, is not sufficient to revitalize the residential mortgage markets and prevent continued housing deflation. Nor is the Fed's focus on buying assets through Fannie Mae/Freddie Mac for a mere 20 percent of the market. Getting foreclosed homes resold to new buyers will not sufficiently stimulate housing demand to offset continued excess housing supply via foreclosures, defaults, and 'walkaways' due to homeowner equity collapse.

A new federal housing agency, a Home Owners–Small Business Loan Corp., or HSBLC, is proposed to provide direct lending to homeowners and small businesses. This is not simply a 'reconstruction trust corp.', as was created in the 1980s, designed to buy-up mortgage assets. The proposal for an HSBLC is similar, but incorporates elements of a 'homeowners loan corporation' concept that was introduced during the 1930s. The initial task of the HSBLC would be to purchase existing mortgages in foreclosure, resetting rates and principal according to the aforementioned formulas. Thereafter, it would extend mortgage financing to all potential home financing in the future, subject to the annual income limits set forth below. The HSBLC would be the primary agency administering a nationalized residential mortgage and small business property market.

To control initial costs, eligibility cutoffs for loan principle and mortgage rate resets might initially apply only to joint homeowners with annual incomes of $165,000 or less, indexed to future housing inflation rates. Mortgage limits of $729,000 would apply as well, indexed similarly. The proposal is intended to cover the approximately 80 percent of taxpaying households and thus the vast majority of homeowners facing foreclosure as well. More wealthy homeowners could continue to access private mortgage markets. Small business property mortgages eligibility is, once again, limited to 50 employees and $1 million annual revenues, the latter indexed to the annual rise in the price level for such properties.

The HSBLC would compensate current mortgage lenders not willing to participate in the interest rate and principal resets at a rate of 25 percent of their loan balance in the first year of the resets, and another 25 percent amortized over the remaining 30 years of the reset loans. Refusals to participate would result in the seizure of properties by the HSBLC (much as did the HOLC in the 1930s) and payment by the HSBLC on the above terms.

Financing for the takeovers would be made available by the immediate transfer of prior funding earmarked by the Fed for purchase of mortgages from lenders, approximately $700 billion, plus diversion of an additional $150 billion earmarked previously for Fed purchase of long-term Treasury bonds. Additional revenue for the HSBLC's staged expansion would be generated by packaging bonds and reselling to foreign and domestic investors as a special form of new US Treasury debt. Total funding would be managed through the restructured Federal Reserve Bank functioning as 'lender of first resort' to consumer credit markets. The total funding from the various sources would be used to purchase outstanding mortgages issued between 2002 and 2007 from lenders, as well as partially fund commencement of funding for new mortgages going forward. Income accumulation from payment of existing mortgages subsequently held by the HSBLC would also contribute to further financing new mortgage issuance by the HSBLC.

PROPOSAL 4: 15 percent homeowners investment tax credit

It is further proposed that all homeowners, with mortgages or having paid their mortgages in full, are eligible for a 15 percent homeowners investment tax credit on their annual tax returns. The credit would cover investment in items and categories such as home repair, home upgrades and expansion, and major maintenance and improvements, as well as purchases of major home consumer appliances like refrigerators, ovens, washer-dryers, etc. The purpose of the provision is to allow homeowners not participating in the resets, the HSBLC mortgage purchases, or new issues to benefit from housing related consumption measures. Like the proposals for resets and the HSBLC new low-cost mortgage issues, the 15 percent credit is designed to have the effect of shifting income to homeowners in the 80 percent or lower-income brackets, and thus relieving prevailing consumption fragility while stimulating the economy without expanding budget deficits.

PROPOSAL 5: Moratorium on residential foreclosures and small business property,
and commercial and industrial business loans

A one-year moratorium on residential and small business property foreclosures is proposed in order to prevent further consumption collapse estimated from 4–5 million new foreclosures projected to occur. The moratorium would allow necessary time for the organization of the HSBLC. The moratorium would apply to small businesses facing 'chapter 7' default, suspending default on commercial and industrial business loans incurred between 2002 and 2007 as well.

The preceding measures will serve to reduce households/consumers and small businesses' debt servicing load and simultaneously enhance both groups' income, thus reducing consumption fragility in the system that continues to build to unacceptable levels.

PART II: JOB CREATION AND RETENTION

A successful and effective jobs creation program requires proof of job creation and/or job retention prior to permanent funding. Monitoring and reporting of job creation-retention is a necessary element of the program. Failure to provide jobs following funding would carry a penalty fee by the institution, whether public or private, and returning of the funding via future tax levies on the institution. Priority of funding would go to institutions committing to job creation in the short term. Appropriate limits of annual income per job would accompany the program. Private and public employers receiving funds would provide matching contributions on an appropriate scale, reimbursed to the government through the medium of future tax returns.

The alternative jobs program carefully considers the composition of employment generation. The quickest way to retain and grow jobs is within existing industries and businesses, not primarily by creating new industries from scratch. Alternative industry infrastructure and energy jobs are part of the program but not its primary focus, due to long delay times in job creation for new emerging technologies and industries. A quick path to jobs creation is direct hiring by government, in particular state and local government and school districts. A third fast path is promoting hiring in those industries having shown in the past high job growth rates, and thus the potential for high job growth, such as health care. The alternative job creation-retention program also targets jobs in the $50–60,000 annual range on average, with workers receiving a pay level of $40,000 and benefits load of $10,000. A profits margin test accompanies the program. Employers receive a margin or profit per worker no larger than $10,000, or 20 percent. With these caveats in mind, the following job creation and retention program is proposed:

PROPOSAL 6: $300 billion for infrastructure jobs

Notwithstanding the limits of longer-term infrastructure projects for job creation, significant funding for infrastructure jobs is provided for by the alternative program. An amount of $100 billion would be allocated for projects already underway and in danger of postponement, so long as job retention and creation is proven. Another $100 billion would be given for intermediate civil construction for roads, bridges, ports, and other traditional projects, planned but not yet commenced. A final $100 billion would be dedicated to alternative energy infrastructure projects. Funding of long-run R&D (research and development) and capital intensive projects that provide minimal job growth are not included in the program. Labor-intensive projects are funded first. The alternative program sets a limit of no more than $50,000 per job created/retained. As with all elements of the jobs creation/retention program, proof of jobs would be required for sustained funding, and repayment with penalties would be a feature in the event that jobs are not created or retained.

PROPOSAL 7: $300 billion for public sector job creation and retention

Whereas proposal 6 above addresses infrastructure job creation in the private sector, proposal 7 provides for an additional $300 billion targeted for state and local governments. The Obama program funding for the state–local government sector in 2009 provides less than the projected decline in such government spending. With collapsing tax revenues and severe budget deficits in scores of states and hundreds of cities, mass layoffs in the public sector were projected for 2009–10. Job retention and job creation is possible relatively quickly in the public sector, absorbing many of the unemployed relatively easily. The alternative program provides for job funding of $200 billion earmarked for states and local governments. A third $100 billion grant in job program funding is targeted to school districts to retain staff and to reduce class sizes and hire new teachers in core areas of instruction; to provide additional employment for instruction for disadvantaged students in especially stressed geographic areas; and to restore projected cuts in state and local pension funds. Additional complimentary measures by the Fed would target the expansion of the municipal bond market, in order to facilitate bond sales by state, local, and school district governments.

PROPOSAL 8: $100 billion for further stimulating growth-sector jobs

This proposal targets and provides funding for job creation in industries like health care and related services where past rapid job growth has been the case, to ensure continued further expansion of employment. There is no quicker and easier way to increase the number of jobs than to focus on sectors where job growth is already robust. Funding of jobs for a network of thousands of local neighborhood medical clinics is an example of a possible jobs focus of this proposal. Such facilities would provide emergency medical care, thereby relieving private hospitals of costly walk-in use of emergency rooms by the uninsured. The proposal could work in conjunction with infrastructure spending to renovate existing buildings and facilities for such use. An ultimate objective is the rebuilding of the once ubiquitous public hospital system in the U.S., including the reconstruction of public medical facilities and clinics that have been dismantled over the past three decades. It could further include the construction of new doctor/nursing government training hospitals, to increase the supply of physicians and provide an economical medical services source for the low-paid and uninsured. What was once done for training via agriculture and mining colleges in the nineteenth and early twentieth centuries could just as well be done for health care and other essential medical services occupations in the twenty-first.

PROPOSAL 9: $100 billion for manufacturing job retention and creation

This element of the jobs program provides direct government subsidies, not investment tax credits or other business tax cuts such as in the past for which no proof of job creation has been required. The proposal is a one-time, lump-sum tax reimbursement for manufacturing companies that repatriate previously offshored jobs lost within the past three years. It is a three-year program, with a $25 billion repatriation subsidy in the first year and a similar amount disbursed in the remaining second and third years. A second major element of the proposal is the allocation of $25 billion to jump-start new manufacturing industries and companies. Agreement not to offshore any jobs for a period of ten years is a central condition of funding, as well as proof of job creation or job repatriation based on appropriate formulas and verification.

PROPOSAL 10: $200 billion for social safety net (unemployment insurance, medical coverage, food stamps), trade job loss assistance, and job retraining

In February 2009 the Congressional Budget Office estimated that $79 billion would be needed to fund unemployment benefits in 2009. This compared to $43 billion in 2008. That $79 billion was predicated, however, on the assumption of a 9.2 percent official unemployment rate. The official rate passed that level in mid 2009. The 'unofficial' unemployment rate (called the 'U-6' rate by the department of labor), was 17 percent by October. Every 1.3 percent added to the 9.2 percent means a projected need for an additional $20 billion in 2009 and for unemployment benefits alone. Given the massive increase of more than 3 million part-time workers, mostly converted from full time, in 2008, and the expectation many of these will convert to layoff status in 2009, it is imperative that unemployment benefits are extended to part-time workers and their families as well. That will require another $26 billion in unemployment benefits over the next two years. That brings the total unemployment insurance benefit costs to approximately $125 billion per year. Additional costs for COBRA medical insurance subsidies and food stamps will raise the total costs for 'social safety net' spending to $200 billion over the course of 2009–10.

PART III: FINANCING THE ALTERNATIVE PROGRAM

Parts I and II of the alternative program constitute short-run emergency measures designed to contain the two major forces of the downturn that, as of October 2009, still remain ineffectively addressed by the Obama program—housing deterioration and continuing rising joblessness. The two dominating forces continue to drive the economic crisis and Epic Recession. Without containing and reversing the massive job loss and the continuing problems of housing defaults, foreclosures, and falling prices, it is not possible to achieve a sustained long-run recovery of the economy. All the bank rescues cannot alone re-stimulate the economy. And voluntary recapitalization by the banks cannot eliminate financial fragility. Temporarily containing financial fragility can put a floor under the collapsing real economy for a time, but cannot generate long-term recovery so long as consumption fragility continues to deteriorate. Both financial and consumption fragility are responsible for the dynamic of Epic Recession; both must therefore be effectively addressed together before recovery from Epic Recession is possible. Solving the former problem at best results in a Type I Epic Recession; failing to resolve either results in a Type II Epic Recession and a high likelihood of descent into depression.

The cost of the two major short-run elements of the alternative program—the housing and jobless problems—requires funding of approximately $1 trillion each, or $2 trillion cumulatively over the subsequent two years from their initiation; i.e. about $1 trillion a year. That's one-third or less of that spent by the Bush–Obama administration programs on bailing out the 19 'too big to fail' banks.

The Fed has indicated it eventually plans to recover $1 trillion of the loans and grants issued to the banks between 2007 and 2009. The alternative program described proposes the transfer of that $1 trillion dollars to directly finance the two general proposals for housing and job creation outlined above; about $500 billion each in the first year of the program. An additional $1 trillion is thereafter needed to fund the second year of Parts I and II of the $2 trillion alternative program. That additional $1 trillion is raised by the following tax system restructuring measures, proposals 11–16, thereby providing for the second year of funding of Parts I and II of the program. Thereafter, commencing the third year of the alternative program, proposals 11–16 are employed in part to fund the longer-run income redistribution proposal—i.e. the 80 percent single-payer health care plan outlined under proposal 20 below.

Tax proposals 17 and 18 are designed from year one to provide funding for a second major restructuring—that of the retirement system. Proposal 17 introduces a value added tax (VAT). However, that tax is levied only on the sale of intermediate goods—i.e. a kind of producers' business VAT, not a retail, or final sale, VAT. This tax is dedicated to funding a new, national 401k retirement pool. Proposal 18 is dedicated to restoring a major surplus to the social security system after 2017, at which time the current annual surplus will reduce to zero. The alternative program proposes to create a new, integrated National Retirement System composed of the national 401k pool and the traditional social security system.

Both the 80 percent coverage single-payer health care plan and the consolidation of the national 401k pool and social security system represent major restructuring of the tax, health care, and retirement systems that, in effect, result in a fundamental re-redistribution of income that has been undergoing a redistribution since the early 1980s and which has been a major cause of growing consumption fragility. The health care and retirement restructuring are thus designed not simply to provide a new social safety net for the 80 percent of the households earning less than $165,000, but to have an income and consumption objective.

Just as the housing and jobs programs are designed to restore income and reduce consumption fragility in the short run, the health care, retirement, and other income redistribution proposals discussed in Part IV below are designed to restore the U.S. economy's currently fragile consumption base in the longer run. In short, the elimination of consumption fragility that now plays so central a role in the current crisis must be addressed in both the short and the long run. The short-run measures are proposals 1–10 above. The longer-run measures are described in Parts IV and V that follow. Part III describes how the alternative program finances Parts I and II in the short run and, thereafter, elements of Part IV after the first two years of the program.

Parts I and II address short-run financial and consumption fragility, whereas Parts IV and V address long-run consumption fragility (Part IV) and long-run financial fragility (Part V).

PROPOSAL 11: Offshore tax haven asset repatriation

The three-decades-long growing income inequality in the U.S. has provided an important basis for the diversion of trillions of dollars by wealthy investors and corporations to the 27 offshore tax havens, mostly island nations, which the Internal revenue Service (IRS) refers to as 'special jurisdictions.' A conservative estimate in 2005 by the investment bank, Morgan Stanley, found that total holdings in offshore shelters had risen from $250 billion in the mid 1980s to $6 trillion by 2005. Other more recent estimates place the amount up to $11 trillion. With U.S. investors' and corporations' share of total world assets estimated at approximately $47 trillion out of a world total of $140 trillion in 2006, according to the business consulting firm, McKinsey & Co., it may be safely assumed that U.S. investors' share of the $11 trillion held in the 27 offshore tax havens is likely to be around 34 percent. That translates into roughly $3.74 trillion at minimum.

Proposal 11 is that U.S. investors must repatriate no less than half that $3.74 trillion, or around $1.87 trillion, within the next 12–18 months. This is not a proposal for expropriation, but merely repatriation. That means investors must withdraw and redeposit the $1.87 in U.S. financial institutions located in the U.S. Assuming a long-run return on assets when repatriated to the U.S. of around 15 percent, the $1.87 trillion should yield annual revenue of around $280 billion, which thereafter would be taxed, per the proposal, at the new capital gains rate of 50 percent and yield the U.S. Treasury roughly $140 billion a year in new revenue.

This proposal would have the added benefit of providing liquidity to the U.S. banking system, thereby eliminating the need for Fed subsidization of the big 19 'too big to fail' banks in the U.S. The proposal would then free up the Fed to fund proposals 1–3 associated with residential housing and small business property noted above.

Tax haven repatriation thus provides an ongoing source of taxable revenue, a measure to reduce financial fragility in the larger banks, a reduction of pressure on the federal budget deficit, and/or an alternative source of reliable financing for the new role of the Fed in stimulating housing and consumer credit markets.

Following the lead of countries like Germany, the Obama administration launched several pilot initiatives in 2009 to repatriate some of these offshore sheltered funds. However, it focused primarily on UBS bank in Switzerland. After some token successes involving a small number of U.S. investors in UBS, it quietly unwound its efforts and struck a private deal with the bank and U.S. investors. To date little has been recovered. The alternative program would aggressively pursue this revenue source. The proposal calls for severe penalties levied on U.S. investors and corporations that refuse to cooperate, as well as measures to convince the 27 sovereign entities to fully cooperate (see proposal 19 below).

PROPOSAL 12: Foreign profits tax recovery

An area of chronic, and increasingly large, tax evasion by U.S. corporations has been the foreign profits tax. Hundreds, perhaps thousands, of U.S. corporations doing business offshore refuse to declare the full value of their offshore retained earnings and pay taxes due, despite being a provision of the U.S. tax code. In 2004 the estimated amount of shielded corporate funds in this area amounted to as much as $700 billion. In the late 2004 corporate tax bill, significant concessions were passed by Congress to entice the return of those earnings to the U.S. for taxation. The normal 35 percent tax rate was reduced to a mere 5.25 percent as a special, one-time incentive. The bill also required the companies in question to reinvest the returned earnings in job-producing investments. The companies return part of the total, and then mostly used the funds to buy back their stock, providing a massive capital gains windfall for their stockholders. Offshore corporate retained earnings are likely now in excess of $1 trillion. The return of those earnings reinvested in the U.S. economy would yield a tax revenue stream of at least $100 billion a year.

PROPOSAL 13: Capital income tax cut rollbacks

Candidate Obama during election year 2008 indicated that he would roll back tax cuts on capital incomes passed by the Bush administration between 2001 and 2005. Four consecutive years of annual tax cuts, of which between two-thirds and 80 percent were estimated to accrue to the wealthiest investor households, reduced tax revenues by approximately $3.4 trillion to $3.7

trillion from 2002 through 2010. But upon being elected, the Obama position softened and introduced a revised plan to rollback capital income tax cuts only to levels in effect during the Clinton administration.

There are approximately 114 million taxpaying households in the U.S., and the wealthiest 1 percent, some 1.1 million, have increased their share of IRS-reported income from 8 percent in 1978 to more than 24 percent in 2007. This 24 percent share is equivalent to that which existed for the wealthiest 1 percent in 1928. The severe shift in income distribution in the U.S. since Reagan has partly fueled the growing mix of speculative investment over the past three decades, a shift toward speculation that has contributed to the current financial crisis. No long-term recovery is therefore possible without a basic re-restructuring of the tax system in the U.S., starting with capital incomes taxation. Proposal 13 rolls back tax cuts on capital incomes—i.e. capital gains, dividends, interest, and rental incomes for business—to 1981 levels, not 1993. That is, back to that point at which the major tax restructuring began in the U.S., a restructuring which has contributed perhaps more than any factor to the growing income inequality that dates approximately from that point as well.

PROPOSAL 14: Excess speculative profits surtax

During the later years of the speculative boom of 2003–08, many owner-managers of shadow banking institutions like hedge funds earned $1 billion a year. For example, if a hedge fund manager (owner) made less than $1 billion at that time he was not considered even part 'of the club.' Some hedge fund managers earned as much as $2 billion. That's one person. And their top income tax rate was a specially discounted 15 percent of earnings; in other words, less than the tax rate paid by an average firefighter or factory worker. And that 15 percent, moreover, is before the hedge fund manager's stable of tax lawyers found additional loopholes and exemptions. In 2007 the hedge fund industry accounted for roughly $2 trillion and top owner-managers typically skimmed off 20 percent, or tens and perhaps several hundreds of billions of dollars as a group. The alternative program provides for a 70 percent excess profits surtax on returns from speculative investments that exceed a reasonable long-run average (10–15 percent).

Hedge funds and their managers are, of course, only one of many institutions and investors that reap super-profits from speculative investing in financial securities. Private equity firms, private banks, asset management funds, and even pension funds have all participated increasingly in recent decades in speculative forms of finance, and their participation has escalated rapidly in the last decade. The tax would extend to contracts on all forms of derivatives, including credit default swaps (CDSs) and other second- and third-tier financial derivatives products. This proposal would not only raise funding for other proposals of the alternative program designed to boost consumption, thereby alleviating consumption fragility, but would further discourage the most extreme forms of speculative investing and thus reduce financial as well as consumption fragility levels in the economy.

PROPOSAL 15: Financial transactions tax

Related, but separate, from the excess speculative profits tax is a 'financial sales tax' levied on both derivatives and non-derivative forms of financial transactions. This means financial transactions covering traditional financial assets such as sales of stocks and bonds, commodities, as well as all securitized asset sales and other forms of financial derivatives assets. The alternative program proposes a 10 percent tax on all such financial transactions. (The excess speculative profits tax is an additional measure that applies thereafter to profits that may exceed a defined threshold limit, apart from the 10 percent financial transactions tax.) To ensure a proper monitoring and accounting of derivatives' financial transactions, all derivatives sales would be limited to public clearing-house markets. Private derivatives sales would be henceforth illegal.

PROPOSAL 16: Retroactive windfall taxes

Until the onset of Epic Recession oil and energy companies have earned the highest profits in the history of corporate enterprise for four years running. As near-monopolies they have manipulated price levels by creating artificial shortages to reap what economists call 'rents', or excess profits unjustified by normal market conditions. Proposal 16 reaches back, retroactively, five years to 2004, and recaptures taxes the oil and energy companies should have paid on earnings above the companies' preceding ten-year average. The retroactive windfall provision applies to other companies that reaped 'rentier' profits (i.e. excess profits directly at the expense of profitability of other companies and consumers) during the period since 2001. These would include, at minimum, dominant companies in industries like banking, insurance, and pharmaceuticals.

There is a 'gang of four' industries in the U.S. that have evolved in recent decades into what economists call 'rentier' status. These include the oil and energy, health insurance, pharmaceutical, and banking and finance industries. By 'rentier' is meant a company that extracts excess profits at the expense of both consumers and other companies beyond what their normal market power would otherwise allow. Rentier companies charge excessive prices for their products as the means to achieve excess profits. Their excess profits are not determined by becoming more efficient, reducing their costs, or by improving their products so that consumer demand increases for their products. Their abnormal power is often the result of their attaining inordinate political influence. Clearly the banking and finance, oil, health insurers, and drug companies have attained such extraordinary political influence. This influence, combined with market power, has in recent decades allowed the dominant companies in these parasite industries to reap excess profits at the expense of both consumers and other industries and companies. Until the political and market power of these four parasite industries is broken, they will continue to economically destabilize the U.S. economy. They should therefore appropriately constitute the targets of retroactive windfall profits taxation such as provided for by this proposal.

The retroactive windfall tax provision extends, in addition, to excess compensation received by individuals in these companies and industries, in particular CEOs and their senior management teams who have typically received excess compensation as a consequence of their companies' excess rentier profits position.

PROPOSAL 17: Value added tax on intermediate goods

The alternative program's tax measures include VAT on all intermediate goods. Intermediate goods are products and services sold by companies to companies, before the final product is sold at retail to consumers. The proposal is therefore not a tax on final, retail sales. The entire proceeds from the tax are allocated to fund proposal 21 below—i.e. to provide financing for a 'national 401k retirement pool.' The level of the VAT on intermediate goods would vary by industry, as well as with the funding requirements of the national 401k retirement pool. An initial tax level of 2 percent is proposed.

PROPOSAL 18: Payroll tax on incomes of the wealthiest 1 percent of households

Proposal 18 is also a tax that addresses the emerging crisis in retirement in the U.S. In less than a decade the annual surplus generated by the payroll tax for social security will begin to turn negative. For a quarter of a century the social security trust fund has realized annual surpluses, due to revisions in the payroll tax for social security enacted in the mid 1980s. With the collapse of defined benefit pension plans and the total failure of private 401k pensions to adequately provide for retirement, more than 70 million retirees in the next decade will experience inadequate levels of income to sustain a reasonable standard of living. That condition will severely exacerbate consumption fragility within the general economy, already in a dire state. A solution to the funding crisis in social security retirement payments that will emerge after 2017 not only must provide for maintaining current social security payments for additional tens of millions new 'baby boom' generation retirees, but must compensate for the collapse in parallel of the traditional defined benefit and 401k pension systems. Social security must be not only stabilized but expanded. The alternative program proposes to increase the level of individual social security payments while extending it to the tens of millions more prospective baby-boomer retirees, estimated to be as many as 77 million. Tweaking benefit levels is insufficient. Thus, proposal 18 provides extending the current payroll tax rate for social security from earned incomes with a ceiling of $107,000 today by adding a new provision that taxes all capital incomes of the wealthiest 1 percent of households (with threshold earnings of $332,000 and above) at the current payroll tax rate.

PROPOSAL 19: 10 percent penalty tariffs and non-compliance fees

It is recognized that the foregoing restructuring of the tax system—at the expense of corporate earnings and investors' capital incomes and in favor of wages and salary incomes—amounts to a major redistribution of after tax incomes. However, this redistribution is in fact a 're-redistribution,' a reversal of a tax shift from wage and salary incomes to capital incomes and profits that commenced nearly three decades ago. Corporations, their management, and wealthy investors will therefore no doubt resist and refuse to comply. The alternative program consequently also includes penalty provisions as disincentives to resistance and non-compliance. For example, corporations that refuse to return foreign profits income to the U.S. for taxation will be levied a 10 percent tariff on all their goods sold in the U.S. until compliance occurs. Similarly, wealthy investors who refuse to repatriate their offshored sheltered earnings will have a non-reimbursable 10 percent penalty levied on their remaining earnings or property in the U.S. for the first 90 days of non-compliance. The penalty fee may be increased further with continued non-compliance.

Many of the preceding tax proposals have a dual objective of reducing both consumption and financial fragility. To the extent speculative investing, in particular in financial derivatives, is discouraged it reduces financial fragility. To the extent that income is redistributed from capital to wage incomes, it reduces both financial fragility (by reducing liquidity for speculative investing) and consumption fragility (by shifting income to consumers rendered more fragile by policies of recent decades as well as the current Epic Recession).

PART IV: LONG-TERM INCOME RESTRUCTURING

The key to recovery is to stabilize consumption demand, which has alternated in recent years between freefall and stagnation, due to massive job loss, cutbacks in hours worked, wage and benefits cuts for the 90 million-plus non-supervisory workers in the U.S, collapsing pensions and 401k plans, falling home equity, increasingly unavailable consumer credit, equity investments decline, multiple negative 'wealth effects,' and general economic uncertainty. In this kind of environment of continuing fragile consumption, and an environment in which banks still refuse to lend and are in the hundreds (and perhaps thousands) unprofitable, tax cuts for business have little effect as stimulus measures. Even consumption tax cuts provide little long-term stimulus when personal debt levels have risen, consumer credit is contracting, and consumers have shifted to saving from consumption.

The $2 trillion program for jobs and housing in proposals 1–10 is designed to restore consumption with a major demand stimulus shock to the system in the short run, over the course of just two years. But a more fundamental longer-term problem exists in the U.S. economy. That problem is the decline of consumption capability by the vast majority of the population, which has developed as a consequence of policies since the 1980s that have shifted relative income from the bottom 80 percent to the wealthiest households and corporations. The problem of consumption fragility has been building for decades in the economy, propped up temporarily only by a debt-driven consumer system introduced in place of regular wage and income growth for the bottom 80 percent of households. That debt-driven consumption system has abruptly ended and will not soon return, if at all. The other major temporary fix for stagnant real incomes for the bottom 80 percent has been the increase in working hours per family, as spouses have entered the workforce in record numbers since the 1970s and as many have turned to multiple part-time jobs to supplement stagnant incomes. A third fix has been the spending of savings and future assets. All three temporary solutions have, or are, disappearing, leaving an increasingly fragile consumption base in the U.S. economy.

Consequently, new longer term, structural reforms must occur to restore consumption demand in the US economy. Failing this, even the $2 trillion injection of spending will eventually dissipate over the longer term. Five specific measures, proposals 20–24, are suggested to re-redistribute income long term, thus reversing the negative trends of the past three decades and setting the US economy on a sustained longer-term recovery. These measures all involve restoring disposable income to families in the bottom 80 percent income distribution by means of fundamental health care spending reform, by the creation of a national 401k pool financed by matching contributions from a 2 percent business-to-business VAT, by de-privatizing the student loan market, by indexing minimum wages and contingent worker wages to inflation, and by eventually restoring unionization levels in the economy to the 20 percent of the workforce level at minimum. All aim at mitigating long term the trend toward consumption fragility.

PROPOSAL 20: 80 percent coverage single-payer health care

The U.S. has the highest rate of health care spending in the world for one of the lowest returns in health care quality and coverage. The U.S.'s current $2.3 trillion national tab for health care—double that of other single-payer national programs—includes $1.1 trillion in payments to non-health services providers such as health insurance companies and other 'middle men' in the system. There can be no long-term solution to the healthcare crisis in America (measured as deteriorating coverage, rising costs, and declining quality of care for the majority) so long as the insurance companies remain a primary player in the system. The U.S. simply cannot afford to spend $1 trillion or more on the administration of health care services delivery that is the health insurance company sector of the health care system. Health insurance company costs will continue to crowd out the consumer-patient's access and quality of health care services. It is a zero sum situation. Consequently, the insurance company sector must be fundamentally replaced eventually and inevitably with some form of single-payer universal health care delivery system. It is inevitable that in the long run this will entail an expansion and extension of the current Medicare system at some point. The longer the delay, the more financial resources will be wasted on profits to health insurance companies and, in addition, their Wall Street investors who have been demanding an ever greater share of the health care dollar for themselves at the expense of the consumer-patient. Therefore, as an interim step toward a universal single-payer system, proposal 20 is an interim single-payer system initially for the 91 million households earning less than $160,000 per year. Households earning above $160,000 (i.e. those within the top 20 percent income distribution) would be exempt, but could participate for a fee that would scale up with their income level.

PROPOSAL 21: National 401k pool and social security stabilization

The U.S. retirement system has been crumbling since the 1980s. Since the 1980s more than 100,000 defined benefit pensions have been dismantled and the remainder are under severe attack since the passage of the 2006 Pension Act. The 401k approach, introduced in the 1980s and rapidly expanded thereafter, and designed to provide an alternative retirement income as employers have phased out defined benefit pension plans, has proved an utterly failed social experiment. The average income balance in a typical 401k plan today is barely $18,000. For the tens of millions who had their defined plans displaced with 401ks, it is a crisis of immense dimensions, in particular for the 77 million baby-boomers about to retire starting in two years. The repeated collapse of equity markets in the past decade has further shown that employer-provided 401ks is a failed model for providing retirement benefits. In the past year alone, the value of employer-provided 401k pensions has fallen by more than $1 trillion.

Proposal 20 requires the US government to 'nationalize' the employer-provided and managed 401k plan system and create a single national 401k pool. This pool would function separate and apart from the 'pay as you go' social security system. Kept legally separate, the national 401k pool would thus provide a supplemental retirement system to the social security system.

The pool would work as follows: each participant in the pool would be able to make individual deposits to the pool and withdraw limited amounts from it annually, just as under present employer-managed 401ks. Each account within the pool would be 100 percent portable and immediately vested. Voluntary deposits by individuals into the pool in their own name would be matched by equivalent government contributions. Government matching contributions to the pool would be funded by means of the introduction of a 2 percent national VAT on the sale of intermediate goods (i.e. a business-to-business sales tax) that all businesses with annual sales revenues of more than $1 million would be required to make. Government investing of the pooled funds would be restricted to public ownership–public works projects, or government loans to publicly beneficial joint government–business projects such as alternative energy, green technology, and the like. Individuals would thus be able to invest in the growth and public welfare of the nation via deposits into the pool, even identifying projects of their choice. Returns on the public investments in the pool would result in the growth of individual accounts, above and in addition to, individual and government matching contributions funded by the 2 percent business-to-business VAT. Thus the individual's share of the pool could grow from three sources: personal contribution, government matching contribution, and returns on public investment projects by the government. Government provided insurance would guarantee no loss to the individual's account from public investment. Individuals' accounts would not fall to less than the value of their combined initial deposits plus matching government contributions funded by the 2 percent tax, and could grow significantly more depending on public investment returns.

The social security pay-as-you-go system would continue as an entirely separate system. Without having to make matching contributions to 401ks any longer, employers currently with defined benefit plans would be required to fully fund such plans if under-funded, as is currently the case for thousands of defined benefit pensions. In addition, to ensure the proper funding of social security going forward as well, the projected social security trust fund surplus of $1.1 trillion from 2008 to 2017 should remain within the trust fund and not be diverted to the general U.S. budget, as surpluses of more than $2 trillion have since 1987. Congressional resolutions to open the social security trust 'lock box' annually and transfer surpluses to the general U.S. budget should be considered a felony. The social security retirement system would be stabilized by proposal 18 above, extending the payroll tax to capital incomes of the wealthiest 1 percent of taxpaying households.

PROPOSAL 22: Deprivatizing the student loan market

Originally operated as a grant system, then as a government loans system, as the student loan market grew it was increasingly privatized. The result was various forms of profit taking that came to dominate this market, which should be run as a public good and non-profit program. Student loan lenders make money three ways: from charging market rates, from getting additional subsidies from the government, and by repacking and reselling student loans as collateralized debt obligations, or CDOs. Speculation in the latter financial securities market is largely responsible for the collapse of the student loan market in 2008–09. The alternative program therefore proposes to return the student loan market to a completely deprivatized program where it will function according to its original objective of providing financing to students at cost, in the form of either grants or subsidized loans. Rising costs of higher education also need to be brought under control. Government grants and low-cost loans to students might be increased proportionately to those education institutions that reduce or contain the cost of tuition and fees charged to students. Institutions of higher education that insist on raising tuition fees would receive a reduced allocation of student loans and grants as a means encouraging those institutions to maintain, or lower, tuition fees and costs to students.

PROPOSAL 23: Re-unionization of the private sector workforce

In 1980 the U.S. labor force was approximately 22 percent unionized. A vast archive of professional studies shows that union wage and benefits differentials, compared to non-union of the same industry and occupation, ranged at the time from 25 percent to 40 percent. By 2007 the unionized share of the workforce had declined to 12 percent, and in the private, non-government sector of the economy, to nearly 7 percent. Were today's workforce still unionized at the rate of 22 percent, it would mean that around 15 million more workers would enjoy the benefits and gains of unionization today. Because of the declining unionization rate, and other profound changes in U.S. labor markets, the union wage and benefits differential has fallen to about half of what it once was. Both the decline in the differential and the millions not eligible to receive it translates into a major factor in the stagnation, and even decline, of earned income for the bottom 80 percent of the income distribution. The median and below-median segments of the 90 million non-supervisory production and service workers in the U.S. have been especially negatively impacted by the decline of union wages and benefits. A long-term program for restoring income to the bottom 80 percent must therefore include policies and measures to restore the unionization rate to at least the 22 percent level of 1980. The first step toward re-unionization must include reforms to level the playing field between workers, their unions, and management at the level of legal rights. This alternative program therefore proposes the adoption and implementation of the Employee Free Choice Act, or EFCA, which permits a more fair process for union organizing.

The restoration of prior unionization levels will result in a restoration and shift of income from corporations and the wealthiest 1 percent investor households to a major part of the working population. It is not a redistribution of income, but more appropriately described as a 're-redistribution,' a reversal of a redistribution in favor of corporations and investors that began decades ago circa 1980. Like the leveling of health care costs to this group from single-payer health care and a restructuring of the retirement system, the re-unionization of the workforce will mean a re-stabilizing of long-run disposable income benefiting the 90 million in particular. Relieving the growing burden of credit and debt to this group—as has been described in Part I (housing proposals) and will be in Part V (consumer credit markets restructuring) of this alternative program—contributes to the same objective. Together, the restructuring of the health care system and retirement system, re-unionization, and restructuring of the housing and consumer credit markets amount to proposals that substantially reduce consumption fragility over the longer run.

PROPOSAL 24: Low and contingent wage indexation

An alternative program must also address those segments of the workforce that have historically been relegated to non-union status. This takes in particular two forms: the tens of millions of workers and their families earning minimum wage or just above minimum wage and the tens of millions more that have, in the last three decades, been converted in terms of work status by companies from permanent full-time job status to what is called 'contingent' job status. Contingent workers include those who are part-time, especially involuntary part-time, and the escalating numbers of workers transferred to various kinds of 'temporary work' status. Contingent workers receive on average only 70 percent of the wages of the permanent employed and 10 percent of the benefits. Part-time workers mostly receive no benefits and typically half-time pay. Nearly 4 million additional part-time workers were added to the workforce in 2008 alone. As these groups' numbers have risen beyond 40 million and closer to 50 million, approaching one-third of the workforce in the U.S., the aggregate annual wage and benefits of the workforce, in particular the 90 million private, non-supervisory workers, has fallen proportionately. This trend has also contributed significantly to the long-term growing consumption fragility in the U.S. economy. Wage income has atrophied in part by allowing the minimum wage to adjust only with a major lag of years and after falling purchasing power. Minimum wage adjustments require legislative approval. Despite periodic adjustments, the minimum wage adjusted for inflation still has only 30 percent of the purchasing power it once had decades ago before 1980. The alternative program proposals that the minimum wage be adjusted annually according to changes in inflation, much like social security payments to the retired are adjusted annually. The alternative program also proposes the introduction for the first time of legislated minima for wages and benefit levels for contingent labor. Without such a legal minimum pay and benefits floor, the incentive for companies will be to continue to convert even more full-time permanently employed to contingent status.

The consequence is a further decline in weekly earnings in aggregate for the wage and salaried workforce, and in turn a consequent continued deterioration of consumption fragility in the greater economy.

PART V: BANKING AND FINANCIAL RESTRUCTURING

Just as Part IV provided for economic restructuring that rebalanced incomes and thereby reduced consumption fragility, the following series of proposals provides for restructuring the financial and banking system in the U.S. in order to reduce financial fragility. These financial restructuring proposals focus on three areas of the financial system that require major changes: the consumer credit markets, the Federal Reserve, and what this book has called the 'global money parade' of speculators that have been increasingly, and repeatedly, destabilizing the economic system in recent decades and will continue to do so.

PROPOSAL 25: Nationalizing consumer credit markets

In all Epic Recessions and depressions it is the worker, the consumer, and the small and medium-sized businesses that are the most negatively impacted. Markets providing credit to these groups are often the most negatively affected. It has been no less the case in the recent Epic Recession. Markets that provide credit (loans) for consumer purchases of autos, for student loans, and for credit cards have been particularly reduced. This is in large part due to the penetration of speculative investing into these markets. Over the past decade, the practice of securitization of these markets has been widespread. Auto loans, student loans, and credit card debt have been combined, repackaged, and reissued as derivatives in the form of CDOs, collateralized loans, and other forms of derivatives. The dominant issuer of these assets has been the shadow banking sector, but the traditional banking sector as well. Because the critical consumer loan markets providing for autos, students, and credit cards have been integrated with the securitized derivatives and shadow banks, when these latter financial instruments and institutions imploded in 2007–08, these necessary consumer markets collapsed with them.

Consumer credit markets are too critical and necessary for the functioning of the consumption side of the economy, which constitutes 71 percent of the total U.S. economy, to allow these markets to remain exposed to speculative investing. They must be isolated from speculative excesses. Securitization must not be permitted on the loans and credit card debt that constitutes this sector.

The alternative program goes an additional step beyond disallowing securitization of these markets. It proposes to eliminate the profit motive from these markets altogether. As with student loans noted previously, auto loans should be financed at cost. And limits on credit card interest rates, penalties, and fees are necessary as well.

Residential mortgage, small business property mortgages, student, and auto loans markets should be nationalized, walled off from speculative and profit-seeking banking activity and administered through a new structure of 'utility banking,' as described in proposal 27 below. A new banking structure for mortgages was briefly outlined in prior proposals. A similar banking structure is necessary for other critical consumer credit markets. Consumer credit is much too essential for the economy to permit it to be subject to the regular, periodic, destabilizing effects of speculative investing in derivatives by banks—shadow or traditional—that engage in speculative investing. A new kind of Federal Reserve system should provide necessary liquidity directly to consumer credit markets, with the credit disbursed by a new network of local credit institutions administered through local government, regulated credit unions, or other non-profit institutional networks. This requires an entirely new concept of the Fed as 'lender of primary resort' to the consumer credit sector, and a more democratically structured and managed Federal Reserve system, as described in proposal 27 below.

While certain mortgage markets, student loans, and auto loans are less subject to destabilization if nationalized and administered on a non-profit basis through a new structure of utility banking institutions, backed by the Fed, the same is not necessarily true concerning credit cards. The credit card industry is not as amenable to nationalization. However, for decades now, that industry, run largely by the big banks themselves, has extracted increasing rentier profits at the expense of consumers. Banks now earn more income from credit card rates, penalties, and fees than many do from their traditional lending operations. This credit-based value extraction has played an important role in the growing consumption fragility in the economy. Extracting super-profits from consumers through credit cards was not always the case. There was a time, prior to 1980, when legal ceilings existed for credit card rates, penalties, and fees. It was called Regulation Q. Before its repeal (as a consequence of intensive bank lobbying), Regulation Q established maximum ceilings above which banks and other credit card lenders could not charge monthly interest. Thus, the alternative program calls for a more aggressive regulation of the credit card industry in general and, in particular, for the restoration of Regulation Q.

PROPOSAL 26: Democratizing the Federal Reserve

Restructuring the financial system by nationalizing residential and small business mortgage markets, and by establishing a utility banking system to administer key consumer credit markets shielded from the speculation driven for-profit sectors of banking and finance requires a corresponding major structural change in the Federal Reserve system. Not only would the mission of the Fed change, so too would its monetary tools and monetary targets.

The alternative program is not a proposal to increase Fed regulation of financial institutions in the consumer credit markets. Some parts of the economy are too important to try to regulate. Moreover, the history of regulation of banking has proven over the centuries to have been only partially effective at the best of times and in the best of conditions, and often grossly ineffective at other times. Financial crises produce pressure for more regulation, which occurs in token fashion. As the crisis ebbs and, over time, political pressures grow for deregulation, this occurs and leads to crises once again. In addition, no sooner have financial institutions been 're-regulated' once again than new financial institutions—i.e. new forms of shadow banks—are created outside the orbit of regulation, creating new forms of speculative instruments and new speculative investment bubbles. It is therefore necessary to permanently take critical consumer credit markets outside the private for-profit, sometimes regulated, banking system and run it based on a new concept of utility banking—i.e. banking conducted at cost on behalf of consumers and not for-profit on behalf of private financial institutions.

But if the Fed is to function as a 'lender of primary resort,' central to a new utility banking structure, it must be restructured in a fundamentally new way that in effect democratizes it and how it operates. When the Fed originated on the eve of World War I it was structured to allow private banks to control it even more directly than the private banking sector effectively dominating it today. The Fed was created in order to establish a permanent, institutionalized government body to provide the banks with emergency liquidity in the event of financial crisis. That was the central lesson of the 'financial panic' of 1907 that almost led to a depression, and did lead to the Epic Recession of 1907–14. In its first decade regionally dominant banks constituted the regional boards of directors of the Fed and unilaterally determined its monetary policies. There was little central, political control by Washington over these boards. From its inception, the Fed was, and has been, a conduit through which to funnel money to banks in trouble at taxpayers' expense. The Fed's deplorable handling of the Great Depression of the 1930s in the first five years of that crisis led to its marginalization by the Roosevelt administration and major reforms that increased central political power over the Fed's daily operations. But the reforms were only partial and did not break the power of the banks' control and influence over Fed policy and action. Moreover, in the 1950s the prior reforms were weakened and the Fed (and banks) reasserted their influence increasingly once again from the 1960s on. For the Fed to function as 'lender of primary resort' and in ways otherwise that are less concerned with the banks' balance sheets and more with the economic health of the nation at large, it must be fundamentally restructured and democratized. There is a need for a central bank function. The key question is not whether there is or isn't a central bank, but whether that institution functions on behalf of a private banking constituency or on behalf of the entire nation, the majority of which is neither banks or even businesses, but consumers and workers.

The alternative program proposes several measures by which the Fed might be more democratically structured. First, the twelve regional Fed banks' boards should represent diverse interests of the region, including consumers, workers, small business, and other segments of society. They might be elected in statewide referenda or appointed for terms by state legislatures. The national Board of Governors of the Fed, which establishes the general policy direction of the Fed, would expand in number and include no more than one-third banking industry representatives. Another six would include the chairman and vice-chairman—both appointed by Congress—the Treasury Secretary, and heads of the Federal Deposit Insurance Corporation (FDIC) and House and Senate banking committees. The remaining six additional governors would be elected directly in national elections in some manner. State utility commissions would add to their responsibilities oversight functions for the regional Fed district banks and its Board of Governors. All meetings and minutes of deliberations of the regional and central Fed Boards of Governors would be on public record for all citizens to access and review. Finally, no banking institution would be able to hire non-bank representatives who had served on the regional or central Fed Boards sooner than ten years after leaving those Boards. These are some initial measures to ensure democratic accountability of Fed operations, in particular with regard to its new lender of primary resort and new utility banking function.

PROPOSAL 27: Utility banking versus casino banking

With the recent financial crisis it is clear that the U.S. banking system, and in particular its shadow banking sector, has increasingly evolved toward what the economist, John Maynard Keynes, warned of in 1936 as 'casino banking.' To Keynes, the system was institutionally evolving toward more emphasis on speculative forms, creating more income inequality and more instability in the business cycle. But while noting the problem, Keynes did not take the analysis deeper. The later economist, Hyman Minsky, picked up Keynes' thread of analysis and took it a step further, discussing more in depth the idea of financial fragility and inherent financial instability within the banking system. What Keynes and Minsky both identified is what this book has attempted to further clarify: a financial system increasingly dependent upon speculative forms of investing, becoming more fragile and unstable over time, and a consumption base becoming fragile and unstable as well, in parallel and increasingly interdependent with growing financial fragility and instability.

Some contemporary observers have begun to recognize this development. They are calling therefore for a restructuring of the banking system such that it focuses more on banking's basic utility function for the rest of the economy and less on its profit motive. By 'utility function' is meant banks providing necessary lending and taking deposits from households and other sectors with which to provide that lending—i.e. the historically simple and basic function of banking for the economy which is distinct from speculative banking based not on deposits but on financial asset creation. There is a fundamental contradiction between the two principles of banking—banking as a utility and as a speculative profits center.

The alternative program offered here proposes also to create a utility banking sector. But its proposal differs from most other contemporary accounts of what utility banking is and how it would operate. Other proposals sometimes refer to the separation of functions as 'narrow banking' in which banks are required to maintain 100 percent reserves. In such cases, there is no need for a Federal Reserve as a 'lender of last resort.' There would be no 'fractional reserve' private banking system to 'rescue' in periods of financial crisis and bust. But this kind of 'narrow banking' solution would simply provoke investors to invent new forms of shadow banking outside that part of the banking system required to maintain 100 percent reserves. Speculation has the characteristic of water running downhill; it will always eventually find an outlet and path in some manner. New forms of institutions and new speculative instruments will find a way around regulation, no matter how stringent. Regulation is not a long-run answer to speculation, in other words. The idea of the original Glass–Steagall Act of the 1930s (repealed in 1999) was to shield consumers' deposits from the chronic and repeated excessive bouts of speculation by investors. But the 'walls' that Glass–Steagall put up were too thin and collapsed. No 'wall' will work in the long run. An entire new physical structure must be built to shield consumers from the vagaries of speculative investing, which will continue so long as capitalist investing continues. In the interim, a totally new structure of utility banking must be created outside the speculative, for profit, banking sector. It is necessary not only to shield depositors from the latter's inherent instability, but to place consumers beyond the potential instability. Glass–Steagall did so partially and temporarily, but only for consumers' deposits. It is necessary to separate not only deposits but credit availability to consumers as well.

The alternative program thus proposes, as described above, to create a totally separate utility banking sector. At the apex of that sector is a new, fundamentally restructured and democratized Federal Reserve, functioning now as a 'lender of first resort' to the new utility sector while continuing as a 'lender of last resort' for the remaining, speculative banking sector, but now democratized and accountable to the welfare of society in general rather than the 'too big to fail' private banking sector. The utility sector includes the now nationalized residential mortgage and small business property mortgage markets and consumer credit markets, especially for autos, student loans, and installment credit for 'big ticket' consumer durables products. It includes strict limits on consumer credit card charges and abuses. The securitization and resale of consumer-based loans of all kind are no longer permitted under a system of utility banking. Utility banking means credit extended at cost and without a profit mark-up in the key consumer credit markets. It means the creation of a new network of local financial institutions that take household deposits and issue interest payments equivalent to no more than the cost of credit. New local financial institutions in this system network function on a non-profit basis. Their purpose is to provide the essential service of credit provisioning for consumer markets. They may be local government-based, non-government local non-profit organizations, or community credit union-like financial institutions. The essential point, however, is that a separate institutional system of utility banking is established outside the for-profit system. Banking is a utility no less fundamental to the functioning of the economy than electricity, power generation, and water availability. Profit should therefore not be allowed on the provisioning of consumer credit any more than it should be on the provisioning of electricity or water. Not least, consumer credit provided at cost, as a utility, not only prevents severe financial fragility and instability, but alleviates growing consumption fragility as well.

PROPOSAL 28: Taming the global money parade

What some observers call a 'global savings glut' is really a concentration of income, wealth, and liquidity in the hands of a new cross-national global investor elite. That elite is composed of wealthy individuals, their various investing institutions like hedge funds, private equity firms, private banks, and the like, and the corporations that pass on profits to these investors and institutions while functioning as investors themselves. A massive concentration of liquidity in the hands of these sources has been one of the major hallmarks of the evolution of the global economy over the past three decades. Some call it a 'global savings glut,' but more accurately it represents a 'global money parade' of money capital that sloshes around the global economy in pursuit of the greatest short-term returns, which in recent years have become increasingly speculative in nature.

This historic concentration of liquidity over the past three decades is, in part, the result of a greater extraction of profits at the expense of working classes worldwide; of massive assistance and transfers by states in favor of business in general and finance in particular; of repeated and increasingly expensive bailouts of banks and the economy by central banks and legislatures with each consecutive financial crisis; and, not least, as a consequence of the relative shift globally toward more extensive and intensive financial speculative forms of investing relative to total investment.

By calling it a 'global savings glut,' the growing stock and increasing flow of money capital is in effect de-personified as well as stripped of any of its class content. But the global savings glut is essentially the same thing as the accumulated excess liquidity in the global economy concentrated in the hands of investors worldwide, whether individual, institutional, or corporate. Their liquid money capital is neither strictly financial nor non-financial. It can and does move in any direction or form, in and out of investment opportunities and bubbles as they emerge. In Asia in recent years the global money parade has taken more the form of physical asset investment, as this sector of the global economy has increasingly become the world manufacturing locus and as emerging economies like China, India, and others construct their infrastructure base. In the west, it has increasingly taken the form of investment in financial instruments and the multiple layering of financial instrument investment upon itself which is commonly referred to as derivatives. But the glut is nothing less than the global money parade that flows back and forth across borders, changing form chameleon-like at every opportunity, moving in and out of speculative bubbles with increasing frequency and ease.

How to tame this global money parade and prevent it from creating and feeding speculative bubbles of greater frequency and severity in the future is one of the greatest challenges of the current system. To date, however, those proposing how to reform it—i.e. to regulate it, as they say—have not come close to a workable solution. Nor are they likely to do so soon.

To effectively tame the global money parade requires getting control over its sources of money capital creation as well as its multiple, multi-directional flows. Not an easy task. A hallmark of recent decades has been the virtual dismantling of restrictions on capital flows—not simply between national boundaries, but between investment sectors and markets as well. Much of the global liquidity, moreover, is now held offshore, distributed across tax havens and multiple financial institutions. National central banks and national legislatures and their executives are unable to access most of it even in the tax haven locales for even the limited purposes of accurate accounting, let alone the control of its flows. Germany has attempted to penetrate the subterranean tax haven system, but with only minimal success. The Obama administration began to do so by targeting one of its location dens and banks, UBS in Switzerland. But then as political opposition swiftly rose, the administration quickly compromised and backed off.

The very concept of central banks creating and controlling 'money' is now meaningless. Historically traditional discreet forms of money (i.e. M1, M2, etc.) have been trumped by 'credit-money' in recent decades. Now credit creation is largely the purview of private non-central bank financial institutions. National institutions like central banks have lost the ability to control credit, let alone money and money supply, except for those local industries like residential construction, government services, and some local small businesses that have not yet been swept into the financial maw of the global money parade. But the sphere of central banks' influence continues to decline in a relative sense, and it finds that it must pump ever larger amounts of liquidity into the system in order to stabilize each consecutive financial crisis—thus in turn contributing even more excess liquidity to the next crisis.

Over the past year sovereign governments have barely penetrated the tax haven financial hideouts of the global money parade. Meanwhile, the trend continues away from bringing global capital flows to heel. And little appears will be done to bring runaway speculation in the form of financial securitization and derivatives under any control, except perhaps to have some of the most obvious derivatives trading directed through public clearing houses and exchanges in order to observe its level and flow. But until the global money parade is routed at minimum from its secretive tax haven dens; until capital flows are taxed, monitored, regulated and controlled; and until the ever rising edifice of speculation is prohibited in what is still becoming a growing 'house of cards' derivatives system, the financial instability and fragility in the global system will continue to grow. Subsequent financial crises of greater severity and frequency will continue to occur. Their destabilizing effects on the real economy will continue to deepen. Should corresponding consumption fragility further deteriorate in parallel to financial fragility as well, a potentially explosive mix of both forms of fragility and instability will certainly ensure repeated Epic Recessions until one is too large and severe to be successfully contained—at which point a classic global depression may well result.

As of the early fourth quarter 2009, the U.S. and global economy was not yet at that inflexion point. In some aspects the current Epic Recession has abated, though clearly not 'recovered' in any meaningful sense of the term. The end of freefall is not recovery. In other aspects the recession has continued to deteriorate. Much depends on the future direction of debt–deflation–default processes still at work within the U.S. and global economies. Should they deepen, so too will the potential for further deterioration of the financial and real economy. The banking and financial system is still very fragile. It has not recovered. Financial fragility may still deteriorate further given remaining serious problems in mortgages, commercial property, consumer credit, regional bank failures, sovereign defaults, and the like. More seriously still, consumption fragility continues to grow as jobless levels still rise, housing markets remain moribund, and available credit for consumers continues to contract. Stabilizing the banking system may stem the collapse on the financial side temporarily. Stimulus spending may place a floor under some elements of consumption collapse. But neither are capable of generating a long-run, sustained economic recovery. An alternative program such as that proposed is necessary for the latter. Failing implementation of a more aggressive alternative program for recovery, the outcome is a continuation of Epic Recession, Type I, in which recovery for years is shallow and short-lived, followed by similarly shallow and short downturns—in other words, a scenario over the longer run that represents an extended period of stagnation. On the other hand, not excludable as well is that financial and consumption fragility may collapse to a still lower level, with the consequence that the present Epic Recession makes the transition to another stage, propelling it in effect toward a more classical economic depression event.

Glossary of Key Terms

Listed in order of relative importance

Assets   An item with a store of value that is marketable or exchangeable. 'Real' assets are tangible and physical forms of property, like housing and business structures, buildings, equipment, machinery, software, inventory of products, productive land, etc. Real assets may also take intangible form, like patents, trademarks, copyrights. 'Financial' assets are cash or claims on income or the right to receive value from others, like stocks, bonds, options, certificates of deposit, commercial paper, money funds, foreign currency, precious metals, commodity futures, derivatives, redeemable insurance contracts, accounting receivables, etc. All assets represent forms of wealth that can be exchanged in the marketplace and interchanged with each other.

Liquidity   The characteristic of an asset that reflects its nearness to cash or ability to be quickly exchanged for cash, other assets, goods, or services. Cash is the most liquid asset and immediately exchangeable. Other assets are liquid the more easily or quickly they can be converted to, or exchanged for, cash. Cash earns no returns and represents the least risky form of asset. Non-cash, non-liquid assets earn returns but represent varying degrees of risk. Liquidity creation is facilitated by central banks influencing levels of reserves on hand by commercial banking institutions, but it is banks themselves that ultimately create money and liquidity. Banks and other financial institutions may create money and credit independently of central banks as well, a growing trend in recent decades. The pool of liquidity grows during economic boom phases and contracts in bust phases, but grows secularly over time as well.

Credit   Credit is exchangeable value created when a lender (creditor) extends a loan or other form of value to a borrower (debtor). Credit and debt are dual reflections of the same transaction. The extending of credit is referred to as 'financing.' Credit is provided when banks lend money to borrowers, creating a debt. Credit may be extended as well by non-bank financial institutions lending financial asset values to borrowers, also creating a debt. Credit is a form of money, and its issuance in new forms constitutes a way in which money has expanded in recent decades beyond the control of central banks. To the extent that forms of credit are exchangeable in markets, they represent near-liquid forms of money.

Speculative investing   Speculative investing is the investing in an asset with the expectation of a quick, short-term, significant profit realization based on an acceleration in the demand and price of that asset. It may involve investing in either real or financial assets. But it is the latter, i.e. financial assets, that produce the more frequent, faster, and greater rise in prices. Over the business cycle, speculation in financial assets diverges increasingly from the underlying real asset on which the financial asset is based. Speculative investing is also characterized by a high degree of leveraging—i.e. borrowing the greater proportion of funds for investing rather than non-borrowed funds. Speculation in derivative financial assets permits the 'super' leveraging—i.e. borrowing based on a prior investment that was already highly leveraged or based on borrowing.

Speculative investing shift   Speculative forms of investing, in financial assets in particular, tend to grow at a faster rate over the boom phase of a cycle than non-speculative forms of investing in real assets. This is due to the increasingly demand-driven price escalation character of speculative investing, which produces a greater rate of return, more quickly, at lower cost, and thus produces greater profits—so long as prices continue to rise. As secondary markets for financial assets proliferated globally, financial assets have become more liquid and expanded rapidly. Investor demand for faster and greater price-driven profits increasingly diverts investible assets from real asset to financial, speculative assets, thus produce a relative shift toward speculative investing forms, compared to total investing (speculative and non-speculative).

Derivatives   Financial securities or instruments whose price value is derived from another underlying asset. The originating asset may be 'real,' as in the sense of a mortgage bond representing one or more mortgage notes reflecting the value of the original physical asset, the house or other real estate property. Or the derivative may represent a financial asset that is derived from other purely financial assets. When a derivative is composed of other derivatives, it is referred to as a 'synthetic' derivative. For example, a derivative composed of other debt instruments is called a 'collateralized debt obligation,' or CDO. A derivative composed of loan notes is called a 'collateralized loan obligation,' or CLO. An insurance contract covering a possible loss of value of another financial asset is a 'credit default swap,' or CDS, a still higher (i.e. further derived) derivative. Purchases of derivatives are typically highly leveraged; i.e. purchased largely with borrowed funds, and thus represent a debt instrument. Interest rate swaps, currency swaps, and credit swaps are derivatives that are essentially speculative 'bets' on the price movement of another derivative or financial asset.

Securitization   Securitization is the creation of a marketable security from other financial assets, or combination of financial assets, including derivatives, for the purpose of sale in a secondary market. For example, the combining of subprime mortgage loans, or parts (i.e. tranches) thereof, into a bond and the further combining of mortgage bonds into a residential mortgage-backed security, or RMBS, that is sold on secondary markets after a further price mark-up, represents securitization. Student loans, credit card receivables, auto loans, commercial property loans, as well as mortgage loans, became highly securitized in the last decade. If derivatives served to integrate various financial securities, resulting in a chain reaction of collapse in values after financial crises, then securitization connected and synchronized markets globally in which securitized financial assets were sold and resold. Purchasers in secondary markets of securitized financial assets include government agencies, central banks, banks, funds, non-financial corporations, and individual investors. Securitization enables extreme leveraging, and debt accumulation, and represents a form of credit creation independent of bank reserves.

Shadow banking system   Financial institutions that do not take deposits from retail (general consumer) customers, were not part of the Federal Reserve system (prior to 2008), did not have to maintain defined levels of reserves, and were largely unregulated. Shadow banking system is comprised of various types of financial institutions, including investment banks, brokers and dealers, hedge funds, mutual funds, pension funds, private banks, private equity firms, insurance companies, finance companies, private asset banks, real estate investment trusts, foreign sovereign wealth funds, government agencies like Fannie Mae, issuers of commercial paper, off-balance sheet structured investment vehicles (SIVs) and conduits of commercial banks, and other forms of financial institutions that extend credit. In terms of assets, the shadow banking system had grown at least as large as the commercial banking system, worth approximately $10.5 trillion in 2007. It is a major source for providing finance for speculative investing, and increasingly integrated with the commercial banking system, which often provide financing to shadow banks, and which set up own 'in-house' shadow banking affiliates as well. With no firm reserve requirements, shadow banks engaged heavily in 'leveraged' debt. The collapse of the shadow banking system after 2007 dragged down much of the commercial banking system in turn.

Global money parade   The global network of shadow and commercial financial institutions, of corporate-institutional-individual investors, of proliferating forms of financial instruments, of speculative investing techniques, and of speculative investment markets, which together result in the manipulation of between $10 trillion and $20 trillion worldwide in relatively liquid assets. Driving the speculative investing shift, the global money parade seeks out, and/ or creates, short-term, price-driven speculative profits in commodities and currency volatility, derivatives of all degrees, stocks and stock funds, high-risk junk and other bonds, emerging market and exchange traded funds, landed property, leveraged buyouts, and other forms of financial instruments. The global money parade is a major factor driving the relative shift to speculative forms of investing, the growing trend toward global income inequality within countries, financial instability, financial bubbles and financial crises occurring in greater frequency and severity in the last several decades.

Debt   Debt is the incurring of a repayment obligation following the borrowing of funds and/or extension of credit. Debt carries repayment terms and conditions, or 'debt servicing.' A company's (or country's) inability to meet its debt servicing terms and obligations may result in a default on that debt, which may precipitate bankruptcy proceedings. Debt servicing typically requires cash or liquid payments; for example, interest payments on the debt principal. Debt may be sold or converted in markets, as in debt swaps for equity or for other debt. Leveraging in borrowing increases the level of debt. So long as prices for securities rise, debt may be 'financed' by additional debt or the security sold for profit before debt repayment comes due. When the price of securities fall, however, debt that was leveraged must be 'covered' with cash, in addition to debt repayments coming due. Securities are typically not easily sold to cover or make debt repayments when securities prices collapse.

Deflation   Deflation is the decline in the price level, a negative change in that price level, in contrast to a slowing of the rate of price level increase (disinflation). There are three distinct price levels: asset prices (real or financial securities), product prices (goods and services), and labor market prices (wages). Following financial crises, asset prices fall more rapidly and financial asset prices more rapidly than real asset prices. A sustained fall in asset prices produces a spillover to product price deflation, which in turn precipitates wage deflation. Deflation produces feedback effects between the three price systems when severe financial crises occur. Deflation in turn also exacerbates debt levels, as real debt and debt servicing costs rise when deflation occurs.

Default   Default in simplest terms occurs when a debtor fails to make scheduled debt servicing payments to a creditor; either interest or principal payments, or both. Bank and non-bank businesses may default, as may government entities and consumer-households. Business defaults in severest form result in bankruptcy and either reorganization of the company or liquidation of its assets. Defaults are avoided by taking on additional debt to pay existing debt; postponing payment of principal, interest or both; arranging deferment of debt with creditors; exchanging debt for other assets with creditors, or writing down the debt and taking a loss. If such measures prove insufficient, the consequence of default is deflation as companies sell off assets at firesale prices, courts order asset sales at collapsed prices, companies sell products at below market prices and reduce wage payments to workers. Default drives deflation, which in turn exacerbates pressures to default.

Debt–deflation–default nexus   This refers to the causal interdependencies and effects between debt, deflation, and default. Each intensifies the other. Debt causes deflation in assets that spill over to products and wages. Deflation in wages reduces demand for products and thus product deflation. Product deflation reduces revenue and in turn intensifies pressure to sell assets in weak markets, reducing asset prices. Deflation raises the level of real debt that must be serviced and paid. Debt payments do not decline but cash and liquidity to service debt declines, thus raising real debt levels. Debt and deflation lead to defaults which, when they occur, mean fewer jobs and income and thus less demand for products, and lead to losses on debt by creditors who in turn restrict credit to borrowers, causing less demand for products and more deflation. The debt–deflation–default nexus is a critical concept for understanding how the speculative investing shift results in greater financial and consumption fragility and how, in turn, that increasing fragility intensifies the debt–deflation–default nexus as well.

Financial fragility   The condition of financial fragility grows as debt levels and, more specifically, debt servicing requirements grow in relation to available cash flow and liquid assets available to make payments on debt. Speculative investing is highly dependent on leveraging and debt and thus intensifies debt servicing requirements, which grow as the business cycle (and cycle of cycles) grows. Thus debt and debt servicing rise over the cycle, causing a deterioration of financial fragility. But fragility is also a function of available cash flow/liquid assets as well as debt. And over the cycle, cash flow slows and declines while debt servicing rises. Thus both aspects of fragility grow worse over the cycle. When financial crisis breaks, debt servicing requirements rise sharply while cash flow declines sharply. Financial fragility therefore deteriorates even more rapidly after the financial crisis erupts than it did prior to the eruption. Financial fragility exacerbates debt–deflation–default processes. If these processes intensify, financial fragility deteriorates even further and faster. Financial fragility does not deteriorate in a linear, 'straight line,' but periodically fractures and ratchets downward.

Financial instability   Financial instability occurs when one or more financial markets collapses and multiple financial institutions fail or otherwise experience severe stress. Financial institution failure may take the form of formal bankruptcies, temporary bank suspensions that are subsequently reorganized, or forced mergers by government. Failures may be de facto and not just legal. Insolvencies may become public or kept opaque to the public by government and corporate management. Financial instability may also occur with widespread withdrawals and deep contraction of banks' capital and reserves. Runs on the bank are another indicator of financial instability, and may occur at a retail (general consumer) or wholesale (institutional investors) level. A severe and prolonged contraction and unavailability of credit are yet another representation of financial instability, as may be the collapse of one or more credit markets in which lending in the market virtually dries up. Financial instability is typically represented by a major financial institution or financial market undergoing a bust, followed by asset price collapse for the market or institution(s) in question.

Consumption fragility   Consumption fragility is a concept similar to financial fragility in role and function, except it applies to consumers-households whereas financial fragility applies to financial and non-financial businesses. Consumption fragility is a function of both consumer-household debt/debt servicing requirements and real disposable income (equivalent of consumer cash flow/ liquid assets on the business side). Should consumption fragility intensify over the boom phase of the cycle, due to increasing debt and declining real weekly earnings, when financial fragility fractures and lending by financial institutions worsens, layoffs and wage deflation cause in turn a corresponding 'fracturing' of consumption fragility. The fracturing of consumption fragility results in turn in a more severe collapse of general consumption and consumer demand. Consumption fragility also exacerbates debt–deflation–default processes. When both fracture, consumption and financial fragility cause a further deterioration in each other.

Normal recession   Refers to typical recessions that are represented by relative minor declines in various indicators such as gross domestic product, industrial production, employment, exports, and other measures of the performance of the economy. Normal recessions are typically caused by external supply and/or demand shocks, minor adjustment in inventories, policy over-reach and error by monetary and fiscal institutions, or natural events like weather, wars, or natural disasters. Normal recessions are due to causes that are relatively easily contained by traditional monetary and fiscal measures, tools, and responses. Both quantitatively and qualitatively, normal recessions are fundamentally different from depressions and Epic Recessions. Normal recessions are not precipitated or preceded by severe financial crises. Normal recessions do not 'evolve' into depressions and depressions do not dissipate into normal recessions.

Depression   Depressions are severe contractions of both the financial and real economy. Quantitatively, they are magnitudes worse than normal recessions in terms of depth, duration, deflation, default, employment, production, and other major measures. They are also qualitatively different. The internal processes of depressions are fundamentally different than that for normal recessions. Financial instability and crises are associated with depressions, both as precipitating and as contributing events once contraction has commenced. Depressions evolve in phases and stages and are not linear or straight-line economic collapses. Depressions are more resistant to traditional fiscal and monetary measures and require massive fiscal injections, as well as economic restructuring, to generate a sustained recovery of the economy. Depressions do not begin as recessions, nor fade into normal recessions at later stages.

Epic Recession   An Epic Recession is a hybrid contraction of the economy, with characteristics similar to both a normal recession and a depression. Like a depression, it is precipitated by financial instability. Quantitatively it is more severe than a normal recession but less severe than a depression, in terms of depth, duration, deflation, and other economic indicators. Unlike a normal recession, forces of consumption and financial fragility are present in an Epic Recession. Processes of debt–deflation–default begin to emerge in an Epic Recession, whereas they are absent in a normal recession. When the debt–deflation–default nexus and dual forms of fragility intensify and are allowed by policymakers to deteriorate, the containment of an Epic Recession by traditional fiscal and monetary measures becomes increasingly difficult. If debt–deflation–default, and consumption-financial fragility, are allowed to significantly deteriorate, Epic Recession may result in a second or subsequent financial banking crisis. At that stage in an Epic Recession the causal interdependencies may prove sufficient to push the economy into a classic depression-like condition. Thus, an Epic Recession may transition and evolve into a depression, unlike a normal recession, which never does. If the debt–deflation–default processes and fragility are stabilized— i.e. prevented from deteriorating further—but are not necessarily corrected and reversed, then Epic Recession may result in an extended period of economic stagnation in lieu of depression or sustained recovery.

Utility banking   Utility banking is a concept in which credit is extended at cost plus administrative mark-up to consumer credit markets, such as residential mortgages, small business loans, auto, student, and other typical consumer loans. It represents taking profits out of the lending business, in particular profits derived from speculative forms of investing. Financial institutions, commercial or shadow banks, pursuing other profit-seeking ventures are prevented from participating in utility banking. As defined in this book, utility banking requires a separate, parallel Federal Reserve System, which functions as a 'lender of first resort' to the consumer credit markets. Local non-profit financial institutions determine and disseminate the consumer credit to households and small businesses. A new, restructured banking system for such markets and customers is a requisite. The restructured system is democratically staffed and run, and directly accountable to the public. Banking functions similar to a regulated utility for consumer credit markets, leaving more risky and speculative forms of financing to a separate profit seeking banking system. Utility banking is an important means by which to alleviate both financial and consumption fragility, to ensure lending in periods of crises, and restore levels of income and effective demand.

Notes

INTRODUCTION

1. The word 'crisis' is generally overused when applied in relation to economic events. However, that is clearly not the case with the current economic event that erupted publicly in 2007 and continues to this day. The word 'crisis' refers, according to its dictionary definition, to a true 'turning point' and not merely a serious condition. Unlike a normal recession, the current economic event is indeed a turning point, a crisis, and in more ways than one. Some ways are already self-evident. There is clearly a turning point in monetary-fiscal policy, as will be described in Chapter 8. Another is the major upheaval now occurring in the world monetary system, and the likely transition from the U.S. dollar as the dominant world currency to something new as the 'Bretton Woods II' system of exchange rate regimes established in the early 1970s is replaced with another system. Other turning points are no doubt yet to be revealed in the wake of today's defining economic event of the early twenty-first century.
2. The National Bureau of Economic Research (NBER) identifies ten 'peak to trough' recession periods occurring in the U.S. between 1948 and 2001.This book will refer to nine recessions, however. It considers the two NBER recessions of 1980 and 1981–82 as the same single event, or what is sometimes called a 'double dip' or 'W-shaped' recession.
3. *New York Times*, March 1, 2009. Although Ferguson inaccurately reports that the average duration of recessions is 17 months, the NBER average in the post-1945 period is ten months.
4. Niall Ferguson, "A History Lesson for Economists in Thrall to Keynes," *Financial Times*, May 30, 2009, p. 7.
5. Bureau of Economic Analysis, *National Economic Accounts*, Table 1.1.1, May 29, 2009. More detail on the quantitative and qualitative differences between the current crisis and the 1973–75, 1981–82, and other recessions is provided in Chapters 2 and 3 of this book.
6. Bloomberg.com News, February 5, 2009.
7. Nouriel Roubini, "The Rising Risks of a Global L-Shaped Near Depression and Stag-Deflation," *RGE Monitor*, March 2, 2009. See also his contribution in the *New York Times*' Op-Ed debate, entitled "The L-Curve," *New York Times*, March 1, 2009.
8. Paul Krugman, "Fighting Off Depression," *New York Times*, January 5, 2009. Krugman later backed off his characterization of the crisis as a depression, reverting to the label of a 'Great Recession' in an exchange with economists Barry Eichengreen and Kevin O'Rourke ("A Tale of Two Depressions," *VoxEU*, April 6, 2009) who provided hard data and graphics showing at least two indicators, stock values and world trade volume, as falling even faster in 2008–09 than in 1929–30. Eichengreen and O'Rourke updated their findings in June 2009 to show 2008–09 world industrial production also tracking the 1930s. These declines, moreover, are despite action by central banks to lower discount rates far more aggressively than in the 1930s.
9. Ferguson, "A History Lesson."
10. Ferguson's charge that Krugman was 'in thrall to Keynes' is even more inaccurate since, to the extent Krugman maintains that Savings determines Investment, he is not really in the tradition—let alone 'thrall'—of Keynes. Krugman is rather in the tradition of what is called the 'Neo-Classical Synthesis,' or what some call postwar 'Harvard Keynesianism,' which differs from Keynes' original views in a number of fundamental propositions. Those who adhere to the 'Savings determines Investment' view include such decidedly non-Keynesians as Alan Greenspan.
11. Lawrence Mitchell, "Protect Industry From Predatory Speculators," *Financial Times*, July 9, 2009, p. 9.
12. Institute on Taxation and Economic Policy, Tax Model, June 3, 2003.

13. See the work of University of California, Berkeley, economists Emmanuel Saez and Thomas Picketty establishing overwhelming evidence of the massive concentration of incomes among the top 1 percent households, in the U.S. in particular. For the authors' earliest work see "Income Inequality in the United States, 1913–1998," *Quarterly Journal of Economics*, 118 (1), 2003, pp. 1–39. For most recent similar studies see "The Evolution of Top Incomes: A Historical and International Perspective," *American Economic Review*, 96 (2), 2006, pp. 200–5; and Emmanuel Saez, Wojciech Kopczuk, and Jae Song, "Earnings Inequality and Mobility in the United States: Evidence from Social Security Data since 1937," *Quarterly Journal of Economics*, March 2009.

14. Since Germany went after tax shelters for wealthy German investors in Lichtenstein in 2008, and hearings were commenced by Senator Max Baucus in the U.S. Senate, the scope of tax avoidance and fraud associated with 27 'special jurisdictions' (per the IRS) has become voluminous. An initial early source of value is Mark Hampton and Jason Abbot (eds.), *Offshore Finance Centers and Tax Havens*, Ichor Business Books, 1999. A good journalistic assessment can also be found in Vanessa Houlder and Michael Peel, "Harbours of Resentment," *Financial Times*, December 1, 2008, p. 11. See also David Crawford, "Tax Havens Pledge to Ease Secretary Laws," *Wall Street Journal*, March 13, 2009, p. 1.

15. See this author's work: Jack Rasmus, *The War At Home: The Corporate Offensive from Ronald Reagan to George W. Bush*, Kyklos Productions, 2006, and updates to the material in the book in three articles published in 'Z' Magazine in February, April, and May 2007 on the topic of 'The Trillion Dollar Income Shift.'

16. The debates on the origins, causes, evolution, and what ended the depression of the 1930s is voluminous and often contradictory. The most notable theories of the causes are Milton Friedman and Anna Schwartz's study of how the Federal Reserve and government policy in general provoked and lengthened the depression (*A Monetary History of the United States, 1867–1960*, Princeton University Press, 1963). Other perspectives focus on international forces and the gold standard as key. Others on general overproduction of industry or under-consumption. Still others on bank runs and crises, or the poor shape of household balance sheets in the early stages. There are many different positions and explanations for why the economy recovered briefly in the middle of the decade then collapsed again in 1937–38. And of course various interpretations of the 1938–40 period and whether that was a recovery or a stagnation, as well as sharp differences with regard to what actually ended the depression: monetary expansion or fiscal spending and the war. These themes will be taken up in more detail in Chapter 6.

17. NBER, "The NBER's Recession Dating Procedure," *NBER*, October 21, 2003.

18. An introductory history of this interesting first financial crisis of the twentieth century can be found in Robert Bruner and Sean Carr, *The Panic of 1907*, Wiley, 2007.

19. Arthur Burns, *Production Trends in the United States Since 1870*, NBER, 1934. There is a good deal of controversy over the data and statistics for the nineteenth century. It was not until the 1920s that more reliable data began to appear. For early studies on output, price, and the depressions of the 1870s and 1890s, there is O.M. Sprague's *History of Crises Under the National Banking System* (National Monetary Commission of the U.S. Senate report), Government Printing Office, 1910, reprinted by Augustus Kelley Publishers, 1977.

CHAPTER 1

1. By 'static' is simply meant characteristics at a given point in time and place, a kind of frozen-in-time 'snapshot photo' of a given condition describing an Epic Recession. This is in contrast to 'dynamic' characteristics, which change over time, are interdependent, determine and are in turn determined by other characteristics. By way of example, dynamic characteristics include transmission mechanisms and feedback effects by and between characteristics, both of which will be addressed in subsequent chapters.

2. The 2 percent average was estimated by economists in a study of international recessions. The recessions that recorded the greatest declines in real per capita GDP were Spain (1977),

Norway (1987), Sweden and Finland (1991), and Japan (1992). These latter five 'worst' cases of recessions experienced a 'peak to trough' fall of about 5 percent. See Ken Rogoff and Carmen Reinhart, "Is the 2007 U.S. Subprime Financial Crisis So Different? An International Comparison," *American Economic Review*, vol. 98, no. 2, pp. 339–44.

3. U.S. Department of Commerce, Bureau of Economic Analysis, *National Income Accounts*, Table 1.1.5, June 14, 2009.

4. NBER, *Business Cycle Expansions and Contractions*, website: www.nber.org/cycles/cyclesmain.html.

5. Federal Reserve Bank of Minneapolis, website, *The Recession in Perspective*, June 13, 2009: www.minneapolisfed.org/publications_papers/recession_perspective/.

6. U.S. Department of Labor, Bureau of Labor Statistics, *The Employment Situation*, May 2009, p. 1.

7. Federal Reserve Bank of Minneapolis, *The Recession in Perspective*.

8. Jack Rasmus, "From Global Financial Crisis to Global Recession," Parts 1 and 2, 'Z' Magazine, March 2008 and April 2008; Jack Rasmus, "2009: Twenty Million Jobless," *Against the Current*, January–February 2009, pp. 6–8.

9. For this author's earlier, evolving views predicting Epic Recession, see "An Emerging Epic Recession," 'Z' Magazine, June 2008, pp. 38–41, and "Epic Recession Revisited," 'Z' Magazine, January 2009, pp. 29–34.

10. U.S. Federal Reserve Statistical Release, *Industrial Production and Capacity Utilization*, June 16, 2009.

11. Barry Eichengreen and Kevin O'Rourke, "*A Tale of Two Depressions*," VoxEu column, April 6, 2009, updated June 4, 2009: www.voxeu.org/index.php?q=node/3421. For a quality graphic representation, see *Der Spiegel*, "Is 2009 the New 1929?" Spiegel Online, May 18, 2009: www.spiegel.de/international/world.

12. Eichengreen and O'Rourke, "A Tale of Two Depressions."

13. Martin Wolf, "How Today's Global Recession Tracks the Great Depression," *Financial Times*, June 17, 2009, p. 9.

14. Daniel Gros and Cinzia Alcidi, "What Lessons from the 1930s?" CEPS Working Document no. 312, Centre for European Policy Studies, May 2009, p. 5.

15. NBER, *Business Cycle Expansions and Contractions*.

16. Ibid.

17. Ibid.

18. Jean Strouse, "When the Economy Really Did 'Fall Off a Cliff'," *New York Times*, March 23, 2009, p. 19.

19. Joseph Stiglitz and Linda Bilmes, *The Three Trillion Dollar War*, New York: W. W. Norton, 2008.

20. U.S. Department of Labor, Bureau of Labor Statistics, *Usual and Weekly Earnings of Wage and Salary Workers*, Fourth Quarter, 2008. Readers should note that U.S. government data grossly overestimate wage and earnings growth. The preceding source, for example, includes management and financial traders' salaries; only full-time permanently employed workers (thus excluding 40 million part-time and temporary workers), reflects before tax earnings, and doesn't reflect benefit cuts. The average hourly wage rate since 1983 has only risen from $7.97 to $8.54 for the entire group, but the average of hours of work per week has fallen from 36.5 to 33.0, resulting in an actual decline in weekly pay today to levels below that of a quarter of a century ago. This book uses a broader definition of 'wage' or pay, to include hourly rate, hours worked, benefits and paid time off (vacation, holiday, sick leave, etc.) reductions, and reduced overtime pay. It also includes the 40 million or so part-time and temporary workers, the officially unemployed, and those forced to leave the labor force for various reasons. When calculated thus broadly and more accurately, the 100 million-plus non-supervisory workers in the U.S. have experienced significant pay cuts since the 1980s, and to a much greater degree than U.S. official data recognize.

21. For residential home asset prices, Standard & Poor's *Residential Real Estate Indicators*, May 26, 2009; for commercial property asset prices, Merrill-Lynch Research, *Economic Commentary*, April 17, 2009, and *RGE Monitor*, May 14, 2009. For consumer and producer

price indices, *RGE Monitor* reports from January through June 2009, as well as the Federal Reserve Board of San Francisco, *Economic Letter 2009–12*, March 27, 2009, p. 2.

22. *Financial Times*, April 17, 2009, p. 23, and August 7, 2009, p. 21.
23. *New York Times*, April 24, 2009, p. B1.
24. *Financial Times*, February 3, 2009, p. 23. Deutsche Bank similarly estimated that the much less risky investment grade bonds could also expect a five-year default rate of 25 percent. See also *RGE Monitor*, May 5, 2009, for additional default data projections.
25. *Financial Times*, August 11, 2009, p. 19.
26. *Wall Street Journal*, July 20, 2009, p. C1.
27. *Wall Street Journal*, October 31, 2009, p. 1.
28. *Financial Times*, July 2, 2009, p. 21; see also *Financial Times*, June 4, 2009, p. 16.
29. *Financial Times*, June 4, 2009, p. 16.
30. *RGE Monitor*, "Run on the $10 Trillion 'Shadow Banking System': Is Reflation or Debt Destruction the Solution?," May 26, 2009.
31. *Wall Street Journal*, June 18, 2009, p. C1.
32. *RGE Monitor*, October 23, 2009.
33. Jeremy Simon, "Big Credit Card Losses Continue to Dog U.S. Banks," Creditcards.com, June 5, 2009; and the data from the U.S. Federal Reserve for comparative recession period rates of credit card delinquency. Comparing student loan defaults over time is complicated by changes in the laws after 2000 which allow students to consolidate loans to avoid default, which was not the case in 1992 when records were first kept on student loan defaults. Also, the way the U.S. Department of Education maintains default records minimizes default rates by considering defaults only within the first few years of graduation. Most defaults do not occur within that short two- to three-year window, but after three years.
34. *Wall Street Journal*, December 6, 2007, p. 14.
35. For a more in-depth analysis of the reasons for the differences in auto defaults today and in the early 1930s, see Martha Olney, "Avoiding Default: The Role of Credit in the Consumption Collapse of 1930," *Quarterly Journal of Economics*, February 1999, p. 326.
36. *Wall Street Journal*, April 21, 2009, p. D1.

CHAPTER 2

1. *Financial Times*, August 19, 2009, p. 19.
2. Data from Thomas Reuters and Bank of International Settlements, as reported in *Financial Times*, September 15, 2009, p. 12.
3. Moody's Inc. report, November 10, 2009.
4. *RGE Monitor*, "Is Global Corporate Default Rate Near its Peak?" October 13, 2009.
5. 'Insolvency' means a bank or financial institution's total available assets, liquid or other, are insufficient to cover its debt obligations. This is in contrast to mere liquidity insufficiency, wherein assets may be sufficient to cover debt but are simply tied up in non-liquid, physical forms. This distinction is important. Different monetary authority strategies may be necessary to deal with a liquidity crisis than a solvency crisis. And major strategic errors may occur if a liquidity strategy solution is applied in an insolvency crisis situation.
6. Money market banks in 1966 bought large volumes of negotiable Certificates of Deposit, the price of which declined sharply after June, shutting down this money market. Banks were forced to sell off other assets, such as municipal bonds, to cover losses and this response spread the crisis to the muni market as well. By late summer the Fed had to step in, and it opened its 'discount window' to rescue the banks and quell growing fears of bank liquidity and solvency.
7. FDIC, *Failures and Assistance Transactions, 1970–2009*, Table BF02, July 2, 2009.
8. FDIC, *Changes in Numbers of Institutions*, Tables CB02 and S101.
9. Stephen Pizzo, Mary Fricker, and Paul Muolo, *Inside Job: The Looting of America's Savings and Loans*, McGraw-Hill, 1989.

10. *RGE Monitor*, "Run on the $10 Trillion 'Shadow Banking System': Is Reflation or Debt Destruction the Solution?" May 26, 2009.

11. Various sources: *Bloomberg News*, June 23, 2009; *Wall Street Journal*, June 18, 2009, p. C-1; *Financial Times*, March 19, 2009, for fourth quarter 2008, and June 18, 2009, p. 18.

12. *Bloomberg News*, January 8, 2009.

13. *Wall Street Journal*, May 19, 2008, p. B-1, from the Federal Reserve's "Senior Loan Officer Opinion Survey on Bank Lending Practices."

14. *New York Times*, June 19, 2009, p. B-1.

15. *Wall Street Journal*, July 11, 2009, p. 1.

16. *Wall Street Journal*, July 7, 2009, p. 10.

17. Creditcard.com, May 27, 2009.

18. An analysis of just this process during the 1930s was done by Ben Bernanke in his oft-quoted article, "Non-monetary Effects of the Financial Crisis in the Propagation of the Great Depression." See his *Essays on The Great Depression*, Princeton University Press, 2008, pp. 41–69.

19. Hugh Rockoff, "Banking and Finance 1789–1914," *Cambridge Economic History of the United States, Vol. II*, Cambridge University Press, 2000, pp. 643–84.

20. John Gurley and E.S. Shaw, "Financial Aspects of Economic Development," *American Economic Review*, September 1955, p. 533.

21. Raymond W. Goldsmith, *The Share of Financial Intermediaries in National Wealth and National Assets, 1900–1947*, NBER, 1954, p. 97.

22. Ibid., p. 27.

23. U.S. Federal Reserve, *Flow of Funds*, June 11, 2009, Table F.1.

24. Edward N. Wolff, *Recent Trends in Household Wealth in the United States: Rising Debt and the Middle-Class Squeeze*, Levy Economics Institute of Bard College, Working Paper no. 502, June 2007, p. 24.

25. Dirk Bezemer, "Lending Must Support the Real Economy," *Financial Times*, November 5, 2009, p. 11.

26. Thomas Picketty and Emmanuel Saez, "The Evolution of Top Incomes: A History and International Perspective," *American Economic Review*, 96 (2), 2006; "Striking It Richer: The Evolution of Top Incomes in the U.S., Update, March 2008.

27. A view of household balance sheet conditions on the eve of the depression is available in Frederic Mishkin, "The Household Balance Sheet and the Great Depression," *Journal of Economic History*, December 1978.

28. This is a term created by Hyman Minsky. A Ponzi financing unit (i.e. company) is one that has to take on additional debt in order to cover debt payments due, for both principal and interest, on previous debt incurred. Equity and net worth decline as it continues to service its debt. An example of a Ponzi financing act is when a company borrows money to pay dividends.

29. Hyman Minsky, *The Financial Instability Hypothesis*, Levy Institute of Bard College, Working Paper no. 74, May 1992. For Minsky's late articles on the topic, and securitization and financial instability, see the Levy Institute website, www.levy.org. For a consideration of his views applied to historical events of the 1960s through 1980s, see Minsky's collection of essays in *Stabilizing an Unstable Economy*, McGraw-Hill, 2008.

30. Korkuk Erturk, Macroeconomics of Speculation, Levy Institute, Working Paper no. 425, June 2005.

31. The research by several analysts in the 1950s to 1970s unfortunately focused primarily on the relationship between finance and economic growth, rather than on the role of finance in promoting endogenous economic instability and business cycle decline.

32. Phillip Carret, *The Art of Speculation*, 1930, republished by John Wiley, 1997, p. 6.

33. Ibid., p. 69.

34. John Maynard Keynes, *A General Theory of Employment, Interest and Money*, Macmillan, 1967; in particular, Chapter 12, pp. 153–63.

35. Bezemer, "Lending Must Support the Real Economy," p. 11.

36. U.S. Federal Reserve Release Z-1, *Flow of Funds Accounts of the United States*, Table F.1, June 11, 2009, and March 30, 2003. This compares with the traditional commercial banking sector in which net lending rose from $410 billion to $765.4 billion—for a total $2,776 trillion over the same period.

37. International Swaps and Derivatives Association, as reported by *Insurance Information Institute*, New York, January 2009.

38. Quoted in *Contrarian Profits*, "3 Reasons You Should Fear the $60trn Credit Default Swap Market," November 30, 2008.

CHAPTER 3

1. Other 'special auctions' were an additional means used by the Fed after November 2007.

2. See the following sequence of newspaper articles: Alan Greenspan, "The Fed is Blameless on the Property Bubble," *Financial Times*, April 7, 2008; "The Fed Didn't Cause the Housing Bubble," *Wall Street Journal*, March 11, 2009, p. 15.

3. Greenspan is partly wrong as well. The record low 1 percent short-term rates engineered by the Fed under his direction certainly affected mortgage adjustable rate loans and other teaser rates upon which much of the subprime mortgages were based. Thirty-year fixed mortgages may have been affected by long-term rates but fixed rates were not the problem with subprimes.

4. For this argument and extensive supporting data, see Robert Shiller, *Irrational Exuberance*, Doubleday, 2005, p. 13.

5. That cause, even more fundamental than Fed rates or the savings glut, lies in a proper understanding of the role of securitization in the housing markets —i.e. the important innovation in speculative investing that enabled an even greater 'leveraging' and reliance on debt to finance the housing boom.

6. *Financial Times*, October 22, 2008, p. 25.

7. *Financial Times*, July 17, 2008, p. 11.

8. *New York Times*, January 18, 2009.

9. John Maynard Keynes, *A Treatise on Money*, The Collected Writings of John Maynard Keynes, Vol. 5, Macmillan Press, 1971, p. 229.

10. Ibid., p. 272.

11. John Maynard Keynes, *The General Theory of Employment, Interest and Money*, Macmillan Press, 1967, pp. 155–8. Keynes' theory of investment, based on what he called the 'marginal efficiency of capital,' is thus a theory of the inducement to invest in non-financial, real assets, not financial assets. The latter was considered in his prior work, *The Treatise on Money*. But Keynes never integrated the two.

12. For a good summary of Keynes' different approaches in the *Treatise*, in contrast to the *General Theory*, see Korkut Erturk, *Macroeconomics of Speculation*, Levy Economics Institute, Working Paper no. 424, June 2005, pp. 17, 19.

13. Irving Fisher, "The Debt–Deflation Theory of Great Depressions," *Econometrica*, vol. 1, no. 1, 1933.

14. Hyman Minsky, "The Financial Instability Hypothesis," Levy Institute, 1992; also "Securitization," *Policy Note No. 2*, 2008.

15. Fisher, "The Debt–Deflation Theory of Great Depressions," p. 344. Also relevant and with numerous tables and data sources is Fisher's book *Boom and Depressions*, published in 1933, of which his article is a summary of major themes.

16. Minsky's three major published books include *John Maynard Keynes*, Columbia University Press, 1975, reissued in 2008 by McGraw-Hill; *Can 'It' Happen Again*, M.E. Sharpe, 1982; and *Stabilizing an Unstable Economy*, Yale University Press, 1986, reissued in 2008 by McGraw-Hill. A good summary of his proposed solutions are found in L. Wray and G. Papadimitriou, *Economic Contributions of Hyman Minsky*, Levy Institute, Working Paper no. 217, December 1997.

17. U.S. Federal Reserve, *Flow of Funds*, Z.1, June 11, 2009, Table D.3.

18. The source is Thomson Reuters Datastream, as reported in *Financial Times*, July 27, 2009, p. 5.
19. Wealthier households, especially the top 5 percent, hold most of the asset wealth in the U.S. economy. Measured in terms of 'net worth,' their consumption fragility ratio is not nearly as bad. For example, their net worth as a percentage of income has remained stable in the 500–550 percent range between 1993 and 2009.
20. See Frederic Mishkin, "The Household Balance Sheet and the Great Depression," *Journal of Economic History*, December 1978.
21. *RGE Monitor*, August 17, 2009.
22. Meredith Whitney, *Wall Street Journal*, March 10, 2009.

CHAPTER 4

1. This is the famous thesis of the forerunners of modern monetarist economic theory, Milton Friedman and Anna Schwartz, presented in their well known tome on U.S. monetary history: Milton Friedman and Anna Schwartz, *A Monetary History of the United States, 1867–1960*, NBER, 1963.
2. Their habit of extrapolating from the particular to the general is perhaps in part explained by the methodological error typical of many of the 'new classicalist' economics schools of thought—i.e. to assume that the whole is the sum of its parts; that micro-foundations of the economy may simply be 'rolled' up, or aggregated from individual firms, consumers, or markets to the broad macro-global economy. It also stems from their initial normative assumption that a capitalist economic system is inherently and internally stable, so that disturbances to that basic stability must be 'external' and temporary. Markets are always and everywhere more efficient than government intervention, so the latter should simply leave them alone and stability will naturally return. The most absurd variant is what is called 'Efficient Markets Theory' which has now virtually collapsed under the evidentiary weight of the recent global financial and economic crisis.
3. Some of the better known data sources written during the century include: Carroll Wright, *Industrial Depressions, The First Annual Report of the United States Commissioner of Labor, 1886*, reprinted by Augustus Kelley, 1968; O.M. Sprague, *History of Crises Under the National Banking System* (National Monetary Commission of the U.S. Senate report), Government Printing Office, 1910, reprinted by Augustus Kelley Publishers, 1977; Theodore Burton, *Financial Crises and Periods of Industrial and Commercial Depression*, D. Appleton & Co., 1902, reprinted by Cosimo Inc., 2005. Contemporary interpretations of data sources on the nineteenth century include: Joseph Davis, "An Annual Index of U.S. Industrial Production, 1790–1915," *Quarterly Journal of Economics*, November 2004, pp. 1177–215; Nathan S. Balke and Robert Gordon, "The Estimation of Prewar Gross National Product: Methodology and New Evidence," *Journal of Political Economy*, February 1989, pp. 38–92; and Christine Romer, "Spurious Volatility in Historical Unemployment Data," *Journal of Political Economy*, February 1986, pp. 1–27.
4. Burton, *Financial Crises*, pp. 282, 280.
5. Richard Sylla, "U.S. Securities Markets and the Banking System, 1790–1840," *Federal Reserve Bank of St. Louis Review*, May–June 1992, p. 90.
6. Richard Sylla, *Financial Disturbances and Depressions: The View from Economic History*, Jerome Levy Economics Institute, Working Paper no. 47, p. 6.
7. Jeremy Atack and Peter Passell, *A New Economic View of American History*, W.W. Norton, 1994, p. 100.
8. Peter Temin, *The Jacksonian Economy*, W.W. Norton, 1969, p. 71.
9. Sylla, *Financial Disturbances and Depressions*, p. 6.
10. Atack and Passel, *A New Economic View*, p. 97.
11. This compares to a general price level contraction of about 31 percent in 1929–33.
12. Sylla, "U.S. Securities Markets," p. 92.
13. Sylla, *Financial Disturbances and Depressions*, p. 7.

14. Wright, *Industrial Depressions*, p. 55.
15. Ibid., p. 56.
16. Burton, *Financial Crises*, p. 344.
17. Ibid., p. 286.
18. Tontine was a kind of speculative insurance scheme, which grew after the Civil War, in which a group of investors put money into the insurance policy. During the tontine period, if one investor died he didn't get any of the earnings of the insurance policy, only a flat amount put in. The last remaining policy holder earned all the surplus from the policy. It was a kind of betting on who'd die first. It was banned in the US later.
19. Elmus Wicker, *Banking Panics of the Gilded Age*, Cambridge University Press, 2000, p. 18.
20. Edward Chancellor, *Devil Take the Hindmost: A History of Financial Speculation*, Plume-Penguin Putnam Inc., 2000, p. 186.
21. Rendigs Fels, "American Business Cycles, 1865–1879," *American Economic Review*, p. 337.
22. Albert Fishlow, "Internal Transportation in the Nineteenth and Early Twentieth Centuries," in Stanley Engerman and Robert Gallman (eds.), *The Cambridge Economic History of the United States, Vol. 11*, Cambridge University Press, 2000, p. 585.
23. Burton, *Financial Crises*, p. 344.
24. Wright, *Industrial Depressions*, p. 61.
25. Fels, "American Business Cycles," pp. 336, 340.
26. Ibid., p. 327.
27. See the Balke and Gordon, and Romer, estimates in note 3 above. For the 20 percent, see Atack and Passell, *A New Economic View*, p. 537.
28. Clarence Long, *Wages and Earnings in the United States, 1860–1890*, Princeton University Press, 1960, Table A-10.
29. Atack and Passell, *A New Economic View*, p. 544.
30. See Fels, "American Business Cycles," p. 326, "Table I—Production and Monetary Statistics for the United states, 1865–1879," compiled from a dozen contemporary data sources at the time.
31. The only hard data available for unemployment were for one state, Massachusetts.
32. Wright, *Industrial Depressions*, p. 245. GDP, in contrast, does not appear to have fallen similarly, but this estimate is based on reconstructed data by economists in the 1980s. It is hard to see, however, why their highly conservative estimates would hold, given during the 1870s a contraction of bank lending of 40 percent, the widespread failures, the collapse of railroads and construction, the fall in investment, and other developments after 1873. Why would immigrant labor fall so dramatically if general unemployment only rose moderately, one needs to ask? Falling wages and prices are also generally associated with production and GDP declines. Contemporary economists' (Romer, Blake and Gordon) reconstructions of unemployment also ignore agricultural employment data in which most of the workforce was still employed, and agriculture was especially hard hit during the 1870s.
33. Sprague, *History of Crises*, p. 158.
34. Wicker, *Banking Panics*, pp. 55–7, Tables 4.1–4.4.
35. Sprague, *History of Crises*, p. 160.
36. Lawrence Mitchell, *The Speculation Economy*, Berrett-Koehler Publishers, 2007, p. 12.
37. Ibid., p. 71.
38. Sprague, *History of Crises*, p. 154.
39. Hugh Rockoff, "Banking and Finance, 1789–1914," in Stanley Engerman and Robert Gallman (eds.), *The Cambridge Economic History of the United States, Vol. II*, Cambridge University Press, 2000, p. 670.
40. Sylla, *Financial Disturbances*, p. 10.
41. Eugene White, *The Regulation and Reform of the American Banking System, 1900–1929*, Princeton University Press, 1983, pp. 12–13, 39; see also Atack and Passell, *A New Economic View*, p. 504.
42. Sprague, *History of Crises*, p. 169.
43. Burton, *Financial Crises*, p. 344.
44. Charles Hoffman, *The Depression of the Nineties*, Greenwood Publishers, 1970, p. 109.

45. Sprague, *History of Crises*, p. 208.
46. John H. Davis, "An Annual Index of U.S. Industrial Production, 1790–1915," *Quarterly Journal of Economics*, November 2004, Table III, p. 1189.
47. Sprague, *History of Crises*, p. 197.
48. *Commercial and Financial Chronicle*, September 16, 1893, p. 446, as reported in Sprague, *History of Crises*, p. 202.

CHAPTER 5

1. Our view here differs distinctly from many mainstream economists' view that the depression of the 1930s would not have occurred had proper monetary action by the Fed been undertaken during the early part of the decade, and that the depression finally ended only as a result of increases in the money supply after 1938. This is the traditional monetarist, or 'new classicalist,' view that sees monetary policy and other external 'shocks' as the cause of depressions and indeed all forms of recession as well. Nearly an entire generation of American economists suffer from this bias, preventing them from fully understanding the nature of depressions and Epic Recessions and leading them to confuse normal recessions with the former. Their economic myopia flows from their fundamental assumption that there is no 'endogenous' instability within the capital accumulation (investment) process in capitalist systems, but that instability is caused only and always by external factors—whether policy institution actions or unforeseen occasional and unpredictable supply or demand 'shocks.' It follows from their logic that, if crises are due to unpredictable, random, external shocks to an otherwise essentially stable system, then so must the solutions be necessarily external. Hence monetary authorities and proper monetary policies can always correct the crisis. But if it is true that random, unexpected shocks are the source of economic crises, it follows that Epic Recessions and depressions cannot be predicted. In that regard—and that regard only—one must agree that their view is accurate, since virtually none were able to predict the current 2007–10 Epic event.
2. Elmus Wicker, *Banking Panics of the Gilded Age*, Cambridge University Press, 2000, p. 83.
3. Jon Moen and Ellis Tallman, "The Bank Panic of 1907: The Role of Trust Companies," *Journal of Economic History*, vol. 52, 1992, pp. 612.
4. O.M. Sprague, *History of Crises Under the National Banking System* (National Monetary Commission of the U.S. Senate report), Government Printing Office, 1910, reprinted by Augustus Kelley Publishers, 1977, p. 227.
5. Ibid., p. 236.
6. Wicker, *Banking Panics of the Gilded Age*, p. 112.
7. A.P. Andrew, "Substitutes for Cash in the Panic of 1907," *Quarterly Journal of Economics*, August 1907, p. 559, as reported in Sprague, *History of Crises*, p. 231.
8. Lawrence Mitchell, *The Speculation Economy*, Berret-Koehler Publishers, 2007, p. 193. For further details see Robert Sobel, *The Big Board: A History of the New York Stock Market*, Free Press, 1965, p. 159.
9. Sprague, *History of Crises*, p. 240.
10. Sprague, *History of Crises*, p. 244.
11. Wicker, *Banking Panics of the Gilded Age*, p. 87.
12. Robert Bruner and Sean Carr, *The Panic of 1907*, John Wiley, 2007, p. 142.
13. Sprague, *History of Crises*, p. 314.
14. Wicker, *Banking Panics of the Gilded Age*, p. 99.
15. Sprague, *History of Crises*, p. 284. Wicker estimates the same period gold inflow at $208.4 million. The inflow was the result of then record export sales (paid in gold) from the U.S. This very large gold inflow to the U.S. (and outflow from Europe) in turn caused significant economic stress in Europe. Interest rates as a consequence rose in the latter, causing an economic slowdown. As would be the case again in the future, the U.S. was in effect exporting its economic crisis abroad.
16. Quoted in Wicker, *Banking Panics of the Gilded Age*, p. 96.

17. The premier business daily at the time, *Bradstreet's*, reported on January 4, 1908, that the impact of the financial crisis included significant layoffs and wage cuts "because of lack of money to meet payrolls" (p. 23; quoted in Wicker, *Banking Panics of the Gilded Age*, p. 109).

18. Sprague, *History of Crises*, p. 278.

19. In addition to the $125 billion disbursed to the nine largest banks, an additional $180 billion was allocated to AIG and another $125 billion, to start, to regional banks now also increasingly in trouble. Subsequently, further Fed money went to other segments of the shadow banking system: commercial paper, mutual funds, hedge funds, credit card companies, and even foreign banks holding U.S. currency.

20. 'Scrip' in the sense used here refers to the creation of non-legal tender currency by local governments, due to the lack of currency provided by New York and other big-city banks to smaller cities and towns. Cash was being hoarded by the big banks. To pay employees in small towns and cities, temporary currency (scrip) was created by local banks and companies.

21. Wicker, *Banking Panics of the Gilded Age*, p. 107.

22. These are the studies of Christine Romer, and Balke and Gordon, as reported in Wicker, *Banking Panics of the Gilded Age*, p. 108.

23. For example, Sprague referred to the crisis as "the most complete interruption of banking facilities that the country has experienced since the civil war." Even Milton Friedman and Anna Schwartz in 1963 would term the 1908 collapse as "extremely severe."

24. See Bruner and Carr, *The Panic of 1907*, pp. 236–7, for direct quote.

25. Arthur Burns, *Production Trends in the United States Since 1870*, New York, 1934, p. 249.

26. Nathan Balke and Robert Gordon, "The Estimation of Prewar Gross National Product: Methodology and New Evidence," *Journal of Political Economy*, February 1989, pp. 38–92.

27. The data for bank clearings is derived from *Bradstreet's* and presented in Wicker, *Banking Panics of the Gilded Age*, p. 109.

28. Joseph H. Davis, "An Annual Index of U.S. Industrial Production, 1790–1915," *Quarterly Journal of Economics*, November 2004, p. 1189.

29. Other estimates show the 1907–08 fall in industrial production exceeding that of the 1890s by as much as one-third. See Bruner and Carr, *The Panic of 1907*, p. 158.

30. NBER Macrohistory Database: XI: Securities Markets, *U.S. Index of all Common Stock Prices*, derived from Cowles Commission and Standard & Poor's Corporation data, 1871–1914 (1935–39 = 100).

31. NBER Macrohistory Database: VII: Foreign Trade, *U.S. Total Exports, 1866–1969*.

32. NBER, *Business Cycle Expansions and Contractions*, website: www.NBER.org/cycles.

33. Mitchell, *The Speculation Economy*, p. 169.

34. See note 28 above.

35. NBER Macrohistory Database: IV: Prices, *U.S. Price Index of Business Cycles, 1891–1914*.

36. The stagnant wages refers to average annual earnings of factory workers, railway workers, and agricultural laborers, which were virtually unchanged from 1909 to the end of 1914. NBER, *News Bulletin, no. 30*, February 10, 1929, p. 1. All earnings gains were recorded after 1914 and through mid 1920, after which average earnings for the three groups were again flat throughout the 1920s.

37. NBER Macrohistory Database, IX: Financial Status of Business, *U.S. Number of Suspended Banks, 1893–1921*.

38. NBER Macrohistory Database, IX: Financial Status of Business, *U.S. Number of Business Failures, 1893–1933*.

CHAPTER 6

1. 'Balance sheets' here may refer to financial corporations or other corporate business, or to consumers (households), or to government (federal, state, and local). 'Total debt' refers to all three sources: corporate, household, and government. 'Unwinding of debt' refers to removal and retirement of bad assets whose values have collapsed, not simply the transfer

of those bad assets from one group to another. A feature of the current Epic Recession has been the 'transfer' of bad assets from bank (and select non-bank) corporate balance sheets to the federal balance sheet, increasing the debt levels of the latter by more than $3 trillion initially, with projections to rise another $6–7 trillion over the next decade. This does not represent an unwinding of debt but rather a mere transfer from one set of balance sheets to another. Another way to look at the situation is that the original bad assets on corporate balance sheets have not even been transferred, but simply 'mirrored' on government balance sheets as the latter in effect 'insures' the former. The problem therefore may have been compounded, not even shifted from the private sector to the public. In policy terms, this may represent a desperate effort to resurrect monetary policy at the expense of future fiscal policy solutions to the crisis. However, as noted on several occasions previously, monetary policy is relatively ineffective in conditions of Epic Recession or depression (i.e. 'inelastic,' in economist terminology). So it may represent trading off potentially more effective policy responses (fiscal) for less relatively effective responses (monetary). Once again, monetary policy may under certain conditions 'stabilize' the crisis, but not prove sufficient to generate sustainable recovery.

2. John Maynard Keynes, *An Open Letter to President Roosevelt*, December 16, 1933, website: www.newdeal.feri.org.
3. Elmus Wicker, *The Banking Panics of the Great Depression*, Cambridge University Press, 2000.
4. U.S. Bureau of Economic Analysis, *National Income Accounts*, Table 1.1.1, revised May 29, 2009.
5. Much of the preceding data references may be found in Jeremy Atack and Peter Passell, *A New Economic View of American History*, W.W. Norton, 1994, Chapter 20, pp. 554–81.
6. Federal debt figures are from Irving Fisher, *Booms and Depressions*, Adelphi Publishers, 1932, Appendix III, Table 4, p. 170. Federal budget figures are from Atack and Passell, *A New Economic View*, p. 562. The latter estimated a federal budget surplus of $831 million in the first half of 1920.
7. Atack and Passell, *A New Economic View*, p. 565.
8. *Historical Statistics of the United States*, Table D-1, 1976: www.nber.org/databases/macrohistory/.
9. These data from NBER, November 20, 1930; and US Department of Labor's CPI index for All Urban (1982–1984 = 100).
10. Leo Wolman, "Wages During the Depression," NBER, *News Bulletin no. 46*, May 1, 1933, Table 3, p. 2.
11. From the *Commercial and Financial Chronicle*, as summarized in Fisher, *Booms and Depressions*, Appendix III, Table 7, p. 175.
12. Data from *Dun's Review*, reported in NBER Macrohistory Database IX: Financial Status of Business, *U.S. Number of Suspended Banks, 1893–1924*.
13. Data from *Bradstreet's*, reported in NBER Macrohistory Database IX: Financial Status of Business, *U.S. Number of Business Failures, 1893–1933*.
14. Thomas Piketty and Emmanuel Saez, "The Evolution of Top Incomes: A Historical and International Perspective," *American Economic Review, Papers and Proceedings*, vol. 96, no. 2, 2006, NBER Working Paper no. 11955, Figure 2.
15. Edward Chancellor, *Devil Take the Hindmost: A History of Financial Speculation*, Penguin Putnam, 1999, p. 197.
16. Atack and Passell, *A New Economic View*, p. 577.
17. Alexander Field, "Uncontrolled Land Development and the Duration of the Depression in the United States," *Journal of Economic History*, vol. 52, no. 4, December 1992, p. 792.
18. Atack and Passell, *A New Economic View*, pp. 574–6.
19. Fisher, *Booms and Depressions*, pp. 172–3.
20. Ibid., p. 173.
21. Field, "Uncontrolled Land Development and the Duration of the Depression," p. 792.
22. Fisher, *Booms and Depressions*, p. 181.
23. Ibid., pp. 184–5.

24. About $30 billion constituted all government debt—federal, state, and local. The remainder was 'foreign private debt,' or loans by U.S. institutions and investors to foreign borrowers, according to Fisher, *Booms and Depressions*, Tables 3 and 4, pp. 168, 170.

25. Martha Olney, "Avoiding Default: The Role of Credit in the Consumption Collapse of 1930," *Quarterly Journal of Economics*, February 1999, pp. 321–3.

26. U.S. Bureau of Economic Analysis, *National Economic Accounts*, Table 1.1.5, Gross Domestic Product, revised May 29, 2009.

27. Frederick Mills, "Aspects of Recent Price Movements," NBER, *News Bulletin no. 48*, October 31, 1933, Table 7, p. 8.

28. Frederic Mishkin, "The Household Balance Sheet and the Great Depression," *Journal of Economic History*, December 1978, p. 921.

29. NBER Macrohistory Database XI: Securities Markets, *U.S. Index of All Common Stock Prices* (Cowles Commission and Standard & Poor's sources), 1871–1939.

30. For the bank suspensions see Wicker, *Banking Panics of the Great Depression*, Table 1.1, p. 2. For general business suspensions, see *Bradstreet's*, as reported in NBER Macrohistory Database IX: Financial Status of Business, *U.S. Number of Business Failures, 1893–1933*.

31. Fisher, *Booms and Depressions*, p. 92.

32. NBER Macrohistory Database XI: *U.S. Index of All Common Stock Prices*.

33. David Wickens and Ray Foster, "Non-Farm Residential Construction, 1920–1936," NBER, *News Bulletin no. 65*, September 15, 1937, p. 2.

34. Mills, "Aspects of Recent Price Movements," Tables 5 and 6, p. 7.

35. Wicker, *Banking Panics of the Great Depression*, p. 29.

36. All the data references in this paragraph are from the Bureau of Economic Analysis, *National Income Accounts*, Table 1.1.5, Gross Domestic Product ($ billions), revised May 29, 2009.

37. This banking crisis is sometimes defined as the second and third banking crises. But they were really one crisis. It was also the first true bank crisis, since what is sometimes called the 'first crisis' in late 1930 was a limited regional affair, as discussed earlier.

38. Charles Bliss, "Production in Depression and Recovery," NBER, *News Bulletin no. 58*, November 15, 1935, Table 3, p. 4 (1927 = 100).

39. Ibid., Table 5, p. 7.

40. Barry Eichengreen, "The Origins and Nature of the Great Slump Revisited," *Economic History Review*, May 1992, Figure 6, p. 234.

41. Olney, "Avoiding Default," p. 325.

42. Wicker, *Banking Panics of the Great Depression*, p. 30.

43. Business inventories in fact declined particularly rapidly in 1930, to –0.2 percent after 1.5 percent growth in 1929, according to data from the U.S. Bureau of Economic Affairs, *National Economic Accounts*.

44. Atack and Passell, *A New Economic View*, p. 578.

45. See the table in Alvin Hansen, *Fiscal Policy and Business Cycles*, W.W. Norton, 1941, p. 88. 1932 would witness a doubling of the drop in consumption below 1925–29 averages, from the 1931 level of $13.7 billion to $25.5 billion in 1932.

CHAPTER 7

1. Case-Shiller Home Price Index, Standard & Poor's, May 26, 2009.

2. 'Shadow banking' is the more popular term given to this 'parallel' banking system. Others more formally refer to it as the 'security broker dealer sector' of the financial system. For the popular definition see Nouriel Roubini, "The Shadow Banking System is Unraveling," *Financial Times*, September 21, 2008. For a more formal approach, see Tobias Adrian and Hyun Song Shin, "The Shadow Banking System: Implications for Financial Regulation," *Federal Reserve Bank of New York Staff Report no. 382*, July 2009.

3. It is possible to argue that the financial instability began earlier in the 1980s, with the collapse of larger banks in Oklahoma and Illinois. Or even earlier in the 1970s. But these events were the consequence of recessions that preceded them, not the precipitating events of recessions,

normal or Epic, to follow. They were also isolated single institutional failures. This book is interested in financial market failures and, even more so, financial system failures.

4. Ned Eichler, *The Thrift Debacle*, University of California Press, 1989, p. 70. Other notable non-S&L banks that went under at around the same time were the Penn Square Bank in Oklahoma and Continental Illinois bank. The bank and S&L failures at this time were different from those that would come later in the decade. The 1980–82 failures were primarily the result of Reagan–Fed policies driving interest rates to 18–20 percent. In other words, the failures were due more to external policy shocks than to endogenous developments associated with excessive speculative ventures.

5. Ibid., p. 75. See also Stephen Pizzo, Mary Fricker, and Paul Muolo, *Inside Job: The Looting of America's Savings and Loans*, McGraw-Hill, 1989, for accounts of the losses and S&L implosion.

6. Robert Litan, *The Revolution in U.S. Finance*, Brookings Institution, 1991, p. 2. Approximately 250 S&Ls failed in 1982.

7. For a narrative of the junk bond boom and bust see Martin Wolfson, *Financial Crises: Understanding the Postwar Experience*, 2nd edition, M.E. Sharpe, 1994, pp. 111–12, 125–7.

8. Litan, *The Revolution in U.S. Finance*, p. 17.

9. Ibid., p. 18.

10. Leo Gough, *Asia Meltdown*, Capstone Publishing Ltd., 1998.

11. Litan, *The Revolution in U.S. Finance*, p. 14.

12. The amounts over this period rose from $29 billion to $70 billion (Litan, *The Revolution in U.S. Finance*, pp. 14–15).

13. U.S. Federal Reserve, *Flow of Funds Accounts of the United States*, First Quarter 2009, June 11, 2009, Table D.2.

14. Option ARMs are loans in which the borrower can choose to make a fully amortized payment (principal and interest), pay additional principal to accelerate the loan payoff, pay interest only each month, or even forgo paying interest due each month—in which case the interest is added to the principal.

15. Other 'special auctions' were an additional means used by the Fed after 2007.

16. See Chapter 2, Table 2.4, and related discussion for more detail.

17. "Run on the $10 Trillion 'Shadow Banking System': Who is the Shadow Lender of Last Resort?" *RGE Monitor*, July 29, 2009.

18. Joanna Slater, "World's Assets Hit Record Value of $140 Trillion," *Wall Street Journal*, January 10, 2007.

19. Thomas Picketty and Emmanuel Saez, "The Evolution of Top Incomes: A Historical and International Perspective," *American Economic Review, Papers and Proceedings*, vol. 96, no. 2, 2006, NBER Working Paper no. 11955.

20. *RGE Monitor*, May 26, 2009.

21. The debt data for 1929 are taken from estimates by Irving Fisher (*Booms and Depressions*, Adelphi Publishers, 1932) based on both public and private sources at the time. GNP data are from the U.S. Bureau of Economic Analysis. Debt today is from the Federal Reserve's *Flow of Funds*, and GDP from the Bureau of Economic Analysis's national income accounts as well. While GNP and GDP are not exactly comparable, the general point stands nonetheless—i.e. debt to output ratio was greater in 2008 than in 1929.

22. Ben Funnell, "Debt is Capitalism's Dirty Little Secret," *Financial Times*, July 1, 2009, p. 9.

23. *Wall Street Journal*, July 8, 2009, p. C14.

24. Floyd Norris, "Who's Most Indebted? Banks, Not Consumers," *New York Times*, April 4, 2009.

25. The times were certainly propitious for them to do so, since these years represent the implementation of the historic, and massive, Bush tax cuts on dividends and capital gains. It is estimated that about $3.7 trillion in such cuts were enacted in toto, 80 percent of which would accrue to the wealthiest 20 percent of households—i.e. the largely investing households.

26. Floyd Norris, "Easy Loans Financed Dividends," *New York Times*, January 9, 2009, p. B1.

27. Robert Shiller, *Irrational Exuberance,* 2nd edition, Random House, 2005, p. xvi.

28. Ibid., p. 9.
29. Ibid., p. 213.
30. Ibid., pp. 12, 14.
31. Robert Shiller, *The Subprime Solution*, Princeton University Press, 2008, p. 49.
32. George Soros, *The New Paradigm for Financial Markets*, Public Affairs, 2008, p. 82.
33. NBER, *Business Cycle Dating Committee*, July 17, 2003.
34. U.S. Bureau of Economic Affairs, *National Income Accounts*, "Percent Change from Preceding Period in Real Gross Domestic Product," Table 1.1.1, 2001–03.
35. Catherine Rampell, "Comparing This Recession to Previous Ones: Job Losses," *Economix*, May 8, 2009.
36. U.S. Bureau of Labor Statistics, *Current Establishment Survey*, March 2001 and January 2005.
37. This is U.S. Commerce Department data, where 'wages' include 65 percent of the business income (profits) of small proprietors. The 1.9 percent is thus boosted by their higher income. Were only production and service employees considered, the percentage would be significantly less.
38. As of late 2009 there is growing concern that this may in fact be the case, in particular with GDP as a leading or useful statistic of the state of the economy. See Ben Hall, "GDP Branded a Poor Gauge of Progress," *Financial Times*, September 15, 2009, p. 4, and other growing commentary.
39. These figures from U.S. Bureau of Economic Analysis, *National Income Accounts*, Tables 1.2.1 and 1.1.5, revised August 27, 2009.
40. For estimates of total war spending see Joseph Stiglitz, *The Three Trillion Dollar War*, W.W. Norton, 2008, pp. 30–1, for summary in Table 1.1.
41. "2008's Deflation Scare Echoes 2002," *Real Time Economics*, *Wall Street Journal*, November 19, 2008.
42. U.S. Bureau of Economic Analysis, *National Income Accounts*, Table 1.1.5, revised August 27, 2009.
43. Josh Bivens and John Irons, *A Feeble Recovery: The fundamental economic weaknesses of the 2001–07 Expansion*, EPI Briefing Paper, Economic Policy Institute, May 1, 2008 (updated December 9, 2008), p. 1.
44. John Maynard Keynes, *The General Theory of Employment, Interest and Money*, Macmillan, 1967, p. 157.
45. *Wall Street Journal*, June 17, 2008.
46. Kate Kelly, Serena Ng, and David Reilly, "Two Big Funds at Bear Stearns Face Shutdown," *Wall Street Journal*, June 20, 2007.
47. Justin Lahart and Aaron Lucchetti, "Wall St. Fears Bear Stearns is Tip of an Iceberg," *Wall Street Journal*, June 25, 2007.
48. Saskia Scholtes, "Bear Shock Waves Gain Fresh Force," *Financial Times*, July 19, 2007. See also Kate Kelly, Serena Ng, and Michael Hudson, "Subprime Uncertainty Fans Out," *Wall Street Journal*, July 18, 2007.
49. Jack Rasmus, "The Continuing Financial and Economic Crisis in America," *Amandla*, June 2008.
50. Jack Rasmus, "The Emerging Epic Recession," 'Z' *Magazine*, June 2008.
51. *Wall Street Journal*, August 13, 2008, p. C3, and Bloomberg News.
52. These are the estimates of PIMCO, the world's largest bond fund, and Nouriel Roubini's *RGE Monitor*, respectively.
53. Fed senior loan officer surveys from July to September 2009. See also Elisa Parisi-Capone, "Excess Bank Reserves and Slowing Credit Supply to the Private Sector: The Mechanics," *RGE Monitor*, September 8, 2009; and "Bank Lending Continues to Fall Amid Permanently Tighter lending Standards and Reawakening Demand," *RGE Monitor*, September 8, 2009.
54. *Financial Times*, September 25, 2009, p. 14.
55. *Wall Street Journal*, December 8, 2009, p. 1.

CHAPTER 8

1. By traditional monetary policy is meant the application of central bank (Fed) normal tools like open market operations, discount rate adjustments, and reserve requirement changes which are designed to increase the money supply in the economy and in turn lower short-term interest rates. Traditional monetary policy may also mean the Fed acting as 'lender of last resort' to banks in need of emergency injections of liquidity when those banks are faced with potential insolvency. By fiscal policy is meant Congressional or Presidential spending and tax cuts to stimulate the economy as well.
2. Hyman Minsky, *Can "It" Happen Again?*, M.E. Sharpe, 1982, p. 46-47.
3. U.S. Bureau of Economic Analysis, *National Income Accounts*, Table 1.1.10, Percentage Shares of Gross Domestic Product, revised May 29, 2009.
4. Robert Higgs, *Depression, War, and Cold War*, Oxford University Press, 2006; see in particular chapters 3 and 4.
5. Jack Rasmus, "A New Phase of the Economic Crisis: Is it Over—Or Just Begun?" *Against the Current*, no. 135, July 2008, pp. 5–7.
6. Alan Greenspan, "Monetary Policy Under Uncertainty," Federal Reserve Board, Remarks at a symposium at Jackson Hole, Wyoming, August 29, 2003.
7. Ben Bernanke, "Asset-Price 'Bubbles' and Monetary Policy," Federal Reserve Board, Remarks before the New York Chapter of the National Association for Business Economics, October 15, 2002.
8. Alan Greenspan, "The Fed is Blameless on the Property Bubble," *Financial Times*, April 7, 2008.
9. Alan Greenspan, "The Roots of the Mortgage Crisis," *Wall Street Journal*, December 12, 2007, p. 19. See also his later "The Fed Didn't Cause the Housing Bubble," *Wall Street Journal*, March 11, 2009, p. 15.
10. Stephen Roach, "The Case Against Ben Bernanke," *Financial Times*, August 26, 2009, p. 7.
11. Ben Bernanke, November 21, 2002.
12. Ben Bernanke, "Nonmonetary Effects of the Financial Crisis in the Propagation of the Great Depression," *Essays on the Great Depression*, Princeton University Press, 2000, pp. 41–69.
13. Ben Bernanke, "The Gold Standard, Deflation, and the Financial Crisis in the Great Depression," in his *Essays*, pp. 70–07.
14. Ben Bernanke, "The Global Savings Glut and the U.S. Current Account Deficit," Sandridge Lecture, Federal Reserve Board, March 10, 2005.
15. Roach, "The Case Against Ben Bernanke."
16. *Financial Times*, December 11, 2007.
17. For a running account of the CCMR's report, Paulson's speeches, and follow-up, see *Wall Street Journal*, November 29 and 30, 2006; *New York Times*, November 30, 2006. For a summary of the report's provisions, see *Wall Street Journal*, December 1, 2006.
18. *Financial Times*, December 4, 2007.
19. David Wessel, *In Fed We Trust*, Crown Publishing, 2009, p. 167.
20. *Financial Times*, March 27, 2008.
21. *Wall Street Journal*, March 31, 2008.
22. *Financial Times*, May 5, 2008.
23. *New York Times*, July 11, 2008, C6.
24. *Wall Street Journal*, September 13, 2008, p. B1.
25. *Bloomberg News*, October 10, 2008.
26. It was not until September 17 that any limits on short selling were finally restored by the SEC, albeit in limited fashion once again, and that calls arose from multiple quarters to do something about regulating CDSs which, as of October 2009, had yet to even remotely occur.
27. The estimates range from $3.6 trillion, according to New York University professor Nouriel Roubini, who has been accurately predicting the crisis for more than a year now, to $4 trillion by *Fortune* magazine, to $6 trillion by Treasury Secretary Geithner in a talk he gave in June 2008 before becoming Secretary.
28. *RGE Monitor*, January 6, 2009.

29. *Financial Times*, January 5, 2009, p. 3.
30. This data from *RGE Monitor*, February 11, 2009.
31. *Financial Times*, June 11, 2009, p. 2.
32. *Bloomberg News*, November 24, 2008.
33. *Wall Street Journal*, July 14, 2009, p. 4.
34. Notes on testimony before the House Budget Committee, *C-SPAN* video recording, June 3, 2009.
35. *New York Times*, June 4, 2009, p. B3. See also *RGE Monitor*, June 8, 2009.
36. *Financial Times*, June 8, 2009, p. 1.
37. *New York Times*, July 9, 2009, p. B1. See also commentary and analysis in *Financial Times*, June 5, 2009, p. 12, and June 4, 2009, p. 6.
38. *RGE Monitor*, April 10, 2009. Since the stress tests the banks have raised an estimated $87 billion. So total losses by summer 2009 were likely to be around $1 trillion.
39. *Financial Times*, September 20, 2009, p. 14.
40. *Financial Times*, October 1, 2009, p. 10.
41. Federal Reserve Board, *The July 2009 Senior Loan Officer Opinion Survey on Bank Lending Practices*, August 17, 2009.
42. Press Release, "U.S. Treasury June Monthly Bank Lending Survey," updated August 17, 2009.
43. *Financial Times*, July 8, 2009, and *RGE Monitor*, August 12, 2009.
44. Based on an analysis of FDIC data by the *Wall Street Journal*, July 20, 2009, p. C1.

Index